Global Perspectives on
Teaching Literature

College Section Committee

Cynthia Selfe, Chair
Michigan Technological University

Lil Brannon
SUNY at Albany

Doris O. Ginn, CCCC Representative
Jackson State University

Miriam T. Chaplin
Rutgers University

Brenda M. Greene
Medgar Evers College, CUNY

Jeanette Harris
University of Southern Mississippi

Tom Waldrep
University of South Carolina

Tilly Warnock
University of Arizona, Tucson

James Raymond, ex officio
University of Alabama

H. Thomas McCracken, CEE Representative
Youngstown State University

Louise Smith, ex officio
University of Massachusetts at Boston

James C. Davis, Executive Committee Liaison
Ohio University

Miles Myers, NCTE Staff Liaison

Global Perspectives on Teaching Literature

Shared Visions and Distinctive Visions

Edited by

Sandra Ward Lott, Maureen S. G. Hawkins, and Norman McMillan

University of Montevallo

National Council of Teachers of English
1111 W. Kenyon Road, Urbana, Illinois 61801-1096

NCTE Editorial Board: Rafael Castillo, Gail Hawisher, Joyce Kinkead, Charles Moran, Louise W. Phelps, Charles Suhor, chair *ex officio;* Michael Spooner, *ex officio*

Project Editor: William Tucker

Interior Design: Tom Kovacs for TGK Design

Cover Design: Doug Burnett

NCTE Stock Number 18542–3050

Library of Congress Cataloging-in-Publication Data

Global perspectives on teaching literature : shared visions and
    distinctive visions / edited by Sandra Ward Lott, Maureen S.G.
    Hawkins, Norman McMillan.
        p.   cm.
    Includes bibliographical references and index.
    ISBN 0-8141-1854-2
    1. Literature—Study and teaching (Higher)—United States.
I. Lott, Sandra Ward. II. Hawkins, Maureen S. G.   III. McMillan,
Norman.
PN70.G57   1993
809—dc20   93-4917
                                                                      CIP

Contents

Preface

This book is a collection of essays designed for high school and college teachers who seek to introduce non-Western and other non-canonical texts into their traditional literature courses. The essays explore the kinds of shared visions and distinctive visions encountered when teachers cluster Western texts with those outside the dominant Western tradition. In addition, they suggest literary works appropriate for students in high school and college as well as approaches to teaching these works.

Most of the essays in this book are comparatist, but within this model there are a variety of approaches. Some essayists emphasize issues related to cross-cultural readings; some explore interrelationships between cultural and historical contexts, biography, and literary texts; some explore themes in works from diverse times and places. All of the essayists assume that to teach well we must, as J. Paul Hunter says, change our sense of what is appropriately read in the contemporary classroom.

The essays are by no means exhaustive in covering any one theory or approach to the revision of literature courses, nor are they intended to be rigidly prescriptive. As Sarah Lawall writes, "Only the instructor, *in situ*, can make appropriate choices: the number and kind of texts, the best translations, the amount and nature of contextual material, the most thought-provoking sequences and juxtapositions, the selection of issues most important to the audience, and the best method for engaging the students' own worldviews in discussion of the material." Our essayists make suggestions about each of these areas of choice, but interested teachers will want to go much further in exploring the possibilities offered by such choices.

Our work on this book has been aided by numerous persons and groups to whom we wish to express appreciation. The editors first wish to acknowledge the help of our colleague Milton Foley, who served as an editorial consultant at the beginning of this project. His ideas were instrumental in bringing this project into being. We further acknowledge the support of our other colleagues in the English department.

We wish to thank the University of Montevallo for the sabbatical grant which supported some of the very first research on this project and to acknowledge the role of a series of seminars supported by the National Endowment for the Humanities and the role of the NEH Summer 1987 Institute on the Theory and Teaching of World Literature, both of which helped to guide our research in the early stages. We are also grateful to the University for a research grant which provided needed support during one year of the project. In addition, we wish to express our appreciation to the entire library staff of Carmichael Library at the University of Montevallo, and especially to reference librarians Patsy Sears and Diann Scales and to public services librarian Pauline Williams.

We also especially thank Beth Oedamer, whose work as editorial assistant on this book has been invaluable. Our thanks go as well to Nicki Walker, whose clerical skills and knowledge of the computer have made the work on the book go much more smoothly. Sandra Ray, director of the Word Processing Center, Robert Lightfoot, director of College of Education Micro Computer Lab, and Sean Arrington, Deborah Berthelot, Laura Caldwell, and Tara Manson, departmental student assistants, have also provided valuable help.

We acknowledge, finally, the guidance and assistance of Michael Spooner and his staff at the Department of Editorial Services at National Council of Teachers of English.

Montevallo, Alabama
July 31, 1992.

Introductory Essays:
Toward a New Definition of World Literature

The essays in this section explore the need for the expansion of literature programs to include a wider range of cultures and nationalities. Sarah Lawall discusses the history of world literature instruction and some of the theoretical and pedagogical issues facing today's teachers. J. Paul Hunter considers the implications of changing literature programs for English departments and their curricula. Sandra Lott describes one way of restructuring literature courses through thematic groupings of Western texts with texts which are outside the traditional Western canon. Her essay explores the difficulties and challenges as well as the opportunities for enrichment which accompany the process of bringing together works from diverse cultures.

1 World Literature in Context

Sarah Lawall
University of Massachusetts at Amherst

Formal instruction in world literature is a peculiarly American institution. Other educational systems have international booklists, recommended for classes or as part of general examinations. Only in the United States, however, has there been a systematic attempt to use a set of international literary texts as formal academic strategy—an effort to educate citizens with mature minds able to compete "in the world." The widespread acceptance of the world literature course in the United States since the early decades of the twentieth century is all the more remarkable in the absence of a centralized national educational system.[1]

The course as usually conceived combines two educational goals: the development of individual minds (the "world of the mind"), for which one needs the best ethical, intellectual, and aesthetic models, and a knowledge of other cultures (the world as geopolitical globe) which, by comparison, clarifies American national identity. The familiar course title, "Masterpieces of World Literature," correspondingly links both qualitative and quantitative criteria. The 1990 Report from the National Endowment for the Humanities preserves the traditional dual focus, calling for a return to "significant events and books" in "broad-based courses—Western Civilization, for example, or Masterpieces of World Literature" (Cheney 1990, 32, 39). Critics have pointed out that the title "Masterpieces of World Literature" generally implies selected works from a Western, male-oriented, ethnocentric, and bourgeois canon (T. S. Eliot's "ideal order") that is far from representing world civilization. Indeed, the quantities of new information about peoples and cultures around the globe, as well as inside the United States, have made it impossible to teach the "old" masterpieces course without putting it into perspective. Much of the controversy of the last three decades has come from a fertile clash between the concept of "mas-

terpieces" and the requirement of global representation: whose world
is being represented? to whom? According to what models and standards
of measurement?

Clearly these are more than literary considerations. In educational
policy alone, they overlap broader general education debates recurring
throughout the century.[2] Beyond academia, they engage questions of
national goals, self-image, and values. Such questions were not foreign
to the originator of the term "world literature." When Goethe proposed
Weltliteratur in 1827 as a way to enhance international understanding,
he had in mind a play of refracted identities. Those who read the
literature of different nations would be conducting a tacit conversation
with their counterparts in other cultures. Through the literary image,
they would become aware of different national characters (and of their
own) as so many separate personalities capable of neighborly understanding. Here is transactional analysis on a grand scale, with individuals
from different cultures comprehending each other—and themselves—
by reciprocal reading. Despite the differences of historical context,
Goethe's emphasis on the exchange of cultural images still dominates
the academic practice of world literature. Such courses are not just
"literature"; they are distinguished from introductions to literature
precisely by their international reading lists and cross-cultural comparisons.

The specifically American academic tradition of world literature
stems also from another and older curriculum: instruction in ancient
texts (not yet "great books") and in moral philosophy. Colonial education adapted European classical training (something Samuel Eliot
Morison likened to "a course on the works of Aristotle, in Latin
translation") together with moral and religious instruction to prepare
first a ministerial class and later the lawyers and businessmen who
would be the leaders of society. This governing elite was to be guided
by a shared philosophy based on a common course of studies emphasizing grammar, logic, rhetoric, and natural and moral philosophy.
Literature was not *in itself* a serious subject, and in fact a professor of
Greek language at Princeton was forced to resign in 1846 for introducing
commentary on Greek literature into his language courses (Rudolph
1977, 89–90). During the latter half of the century, however, theology
and the classical languages gradually lost their hold on American
education and only the missionary spirit remained. In the radical
revision of the curriculum, scientific subjects became part of general
education, electives replaced required courses, and the way opened for
humanists to insist on the role of aesthetics and imaginative literature
in shaping the mind.

The new humanistic curriculum recognized diverse categories of knowledge, with the result that no one sphere—whether biblical study or classical texts—could lay claim to a comprehensive perspective. Instead, this perspective was to be gained from a series of more specialized views, offered in a list of books that represented a new scholastic canon of civilized thought. Charles Eliot's fifty-volume *Harvard Classics* (1910) and the Hundred Great Books that later formed the basis of the degree program at St. John's University at Annapolis included, as the latter put it, "the great books of literature, history, mathematics, science, philosophy and religion" through which "the student . . . learns to be a free and responsible person" (Rosenberg 1954, 24). Charles Gayley began teaching a course in Great Books at Berkeley in 1901 (Graff 1987, 134), and John Erskine developed an enormously influential model at Columbia in 1919 as a general honors course beginning with Homer. The same social and moral purpose pervaded both early classical education and the humanistic model provided by Great Books. This mission was part of the accepted responsibility of education towards society at large,[3] and it continued to influence the way much world literature was taught, including the frequent equation of literary masterpieces with Great Books.

A good example of the mixing of strands comes in *World Literature and Its Place in General Culture* (1911), written by Richard Green Moulton, professor of literature at the University of Chicago from 1892 to 1919. Moulton had been part of the Cambridge University movement which saw literature as a crucial part in the education of the working and middle class, and he concluded his volume with "The Place of World Literature in Education." For him, world literature was "nothing less than the Autobiography of Civilization" (Moulton 1911, 56), while literature itself was a unity, a "literary field" that should be studied for itself and especially through the "exposition of masterpieces" (Moulton 1911, *v*). He criticized popular reliance on booklists and the "right compendium," and was keenly aware of the inevitability of perspectives in literary study: "World Literature will be a different thing to the Englishman and to the Japanese: the Shakespeare who looms so large to the Englishman will be a small detail to the Japanese, while the Chinese literature which makes the foreground in the one literary landscape may be hardly discernible in the other" (Moulton 1911, 7). Given the impossibility of an unbiased list, Moulton chose to define the scope of world literature as simply the range of universal (global) literature that was significant from a given (national) perspective. He situated himself therefore firmly inside the English-language tradition and discussed "World Literature from the English Point of View."

Moulton's world literature clearly represents a highly selective and Westernized perspective, first in its emphasis on the Western-European tradition and second in its organizing principle of "Literary Bibles." His bibles are not exclusively individual texts but are also clusters of significant works: for world literature, he names "The Holy Bible"; "Classical Epic and Tragedy"; "Shakespeare"; "Dante and Milton: The Epics of Medieval Catholicism and Renaissance Protestantism"; and "Versions of the Story of Faust."

Few readers today would accept the homogeneity of Moulton's "Literary Pedigree of the English-speaking Peoples," the categories he finds suitable for "Collateral Studies in World Literature," or his dismissal of global representation. His recognition of different vantage points for the study of world literature is a refreshing change, however, from approaches that pretended such differences did not exist or did not matter. Ford Madox Ford's *The March of Literature from Confucius to Modern Times* (1938), in contrast, implied global scope while actually selecting a range of ancient Egyptian, Hebrew, and Chinese texts to discuss insofar as they prefigured modern European and American literature. Moulton's more thoughtful example survives in broader world literature courses that thematize the concept of Western heritage, comparing and contrasting canonical texts with those from other countries or finding new dimensions inside the "Western" tradition.

The division of knowledge inside the humanistic curriculum ensured a separate niche for literature, but it also initiated a split between literary studies and the study of civilization (or history) which had hitherto been linked inside Great Books. The first academic courses devoted specifically to world literature seem to have been Philo Buck's "Masterpieces of Western Literature" and "World Literature in Translation" at the University of Wisconsin in the late twenties.[4] Great Books courses were now often paired with classes in history or civilization. John Erskine's general honors course at Columbia (which inspired many similar courses, including those by Mortimer Adler and Robert Hutchins at the University of Chicago) was offered in tandem with a contemporary civilization course, both sharing in the representation of Western culture.[5] Each was a required course, and, as such, part of a pattern that would soon be solidified in the sudden expansion of higher education after World War II. In 1945, an influential Harvard report, *General Education in a Free Society,* popularized the term "core curriculum" and proposed separate "core" categories of humanities, social sciences, and natural sciences. Responsibility for introducing the Western heritage was to be shaped by humanities and social sciences in a pair of required courses: "Great Texts of Literature" and "Western

Thought and Institutions" (Levin 1981, 358; Graff 1987, 133–35, 162–73). For two decades, Harvard's general education curriculum was a model for other institutions which moved to establish series of courses inside each category.

World literature courses grew apace in the period after World War II. More students were entering college, many of them veterans who had been abroad, and there was a general feeling that the United States should be better acquainted with the global society in which it had begun to play a major role. Literature courses provided a link with the traditional past as well as an attractive introduction to other cultures, but the wealth of new courses also brought problems. What should be covered in a world literature course? T. S. Eliot's order of Western masterpieces, or non-Western works, or a combination? Would the texts be chosen on the broader Great Books model, including philosophy and history as well as imaginative fiction and poetry, or would they be more strictly "literary"? If the latter, what genres were most feasible? What time span was appropriate? What connections could be made? Were translations available, and contextual material? In fact, most of these courses were taught by members of English departments who adapted their own training to present works from other traditions in whatever translations were available. The lack of suitable texts made a reliance on familiar authors inevitable. Existing anthologies offered what René Wellek called "snippets from famous authors and great books ranging from the *Rig-Veda* to Oscar Wilde [that] encourage an indiscriminate smattering, a vague, sentimental cosmopolitanism" (Wellek and Warren [1949] 1956, 41).[6] It was not easy or, apparently, desirable to learn about other cultural traditions in order to teach unfamiliar texts. The exemplary Harvard model effectively domesticated the teaching of foreign works by recommending that the "Great Texts of Literature" be presented without added information, and that the instructor be merely "a means by which the authors teach the course" (Graff 1987, 169). In these circumstances, world literature courses proliferated along with Great Books and humanities courses with which they were often fused or confused. Criticism soon arose of the way in which they were taught—or *could be* taught, given the enormous number of classes and the limited number of faculty members trained in comparative literature.

Different critiques of world literature teaching emerged in the fifties and sixties. Discussion in the fifties centered on academic preparation (or lack of it), and on ways to represent a subject that still seemed largely a literary continuation of the Western heritage course. In 1953, the comparatist Calvin Brown complained about "Debased Standards in World Literature Courses," noting that current courses emphasized modern English-language texts to the virtual exclusion of others, and predicting that such courses would only "confirm the student's linguistic, geographical, and chronological provincialism" (Brown 1953, 13). Brown used responses to a questionnaire issued that year to estimate the prevailing academic practice of world literature. Course content, it appeared, was veering increasingly towards English-language texts, which were more accessible to the majority of teachers, and towards modern works, which were more palatable to contemporary students. Out of the questionnaire's proffered sample list of thirty-five works, twenty-six were originally written in English and twenty-seven were modern—that is, written in the last hundred years. Brown was shocked at the substitution of minor pieces for recognized major works (Rostand's *Cyrano* was the only French text listed) and at the elimination of authors who had always been included in the masterpiece tradition: the sample listing omitted Vergil, Montaigne, Cervantes, Goethe, and Voltaire—Dante was "voted out" by respondents. A student would necessarily conclude, he remarks, that "the literature written in English since 1850 outweighs all other literature put together; that there is nothing of great value in German, Spanish, or Italian" (or French). The modernist and English-oriented bias simultaneously undervalued linguistic difference and the task of translation, for the chief criterion was not faithfulness to the original but ease of reading in modern English: Homer reproduced in the style of Hemingway.

Six years later, in 1959, Haskell Block hosted a conference on the Teaching of World Literature at the University of Wisconsin. Bringing together a group of world literature teachers to discuss principles and practice, he hoped to achieve a consensus that would provide guidelines for future courses. Although the conference did not produce a summary statement of principles, its collected papers provide an excellent overview of the pedagogic issues then current. They also represent a shared reaffirmation of humanistic education in the face of what many saw as the major educational dangers of the day: a tendency towards narrow academic specialization and an emphasis on vocationalism at the expense of broader liberal arts. The Western heritage remained the core of this world literature experience, for, in Block's words, the common task of world literature, humanities, and Great Books courses was to convey "the literary and intellectual heritage that has entered in a vital and compelling way into our present civilization" (Block 1960, 1). Essays such as "The Teaching of European Literature from St. Augustine to Dante," "Teaching the Classics in Translation," "The Role of Philosophical Texts in a Humanities Program" focused on questions of coverage, chronological depth, and the transmission of cultural values inside the Western tradition. Others, like "The Evaluation and Use of Translations," "Correlating the Teaching of Literature in Translation," and "Intensive and Extensive Approaches in the Teaching of World Literature," stressed problems of pedagogy peculiar to world literature. Any broader definition of "world" was left in the background with the exception of an essay on "Non-Western Literature in the World Literature Program." Block's initial remarks do take up the paradoxical image of a "world" literature course restricted to the Western heritage, and he cites Lionel Trilling's criticism of the Columbia humanities course as representing not the world but the "literary and intellectual tradition of the West, what is called the Judaic-Hellenic-Christian tradition" (Block 1960, 3). The conference papers as a whole, however, demonstrate that the geography of "world literature" in the fifties was to be that of the Western heritage and the T. S. Eliot tradition of masterworks.[7]

It was precisely this concept of "world" that came under attack in the sixties. Although most attacks were directed against the teaching of English and American literature, "world literature" clearly had a credibility problem as soon as the term "world" was taken literally. The globe could hardly be reduced to the Western hemisphere, no matter how impressive its literature. Eliot's ideal order of literary monuments had a suspiciously unworldly air (Eliot [1920] 1966, 50). With a student body growing more and more diverse, world literature's claim to introduce readers to a variety of cultural experiences seemed more and more shakily based on claims of universality which were, in practice, exemplified by a single tradition. Even inside the Western heritage, critics objected, there were more dimensions than appeared in standard booklists and pedagogical strategies. A meaningful canon of Western experience would include literature written by women, by people of color, and by working-class authors.[8] Meaningful teaching would eschew the New Critical practice of relegating contextual information to the background; it would explicate the cultural dimensions of a work as an integral part of its expression. The term "masterpieces," moreover, stemming from the Great Books tradition but by now closely allied with world literature, recalled to many a hierarchy of values allied with patriarchal "masters" and the slavery of colonial empire. Much later, the Modern Language Association would rename its *Approaches to Teaching World Masterpieces* series, *Approaches to Teaching World Literature.* By now, world literature courses were almost indelibly marked with the image of the Eliotic canon. Many were simply abandoned or lost their status as a requirement. Some resurfaced as token courses in interdisciplinary humanities or area studies courses, or inside revised versions of a "Western Culture" core.

Paradoxically, it was a newly precise image of the world that was used to attack courses in world literature. Revised editions of standard encyclopedias reflected the demand for broader and more particularized coverage. The 1971 revised edition of *Cassell's Encyclopedia of World Literature,* in response to "the changed attitudes of the last twenty years," added to its existing articles on Afrikaans and South African writing in English "new articles covering the major indigenous literatures, Ethiopian, Hausa, Yoruba, Southern Bantu and Swahili (with a separate section on oral literature) and the literatures of both Anglophone and Francophone Africans" (*Cassell* 1973, 1: vii). New area studies programs and interdisciplinary humanities courses reflected current desires to obtain a more detailed and specific understanding of global culture. The "African and New World Studies" program at Tufts, for example, coordinated courses in (among others) anthropology, art history, economics, history, modern languages, music, and political science. Books of literary criticism, and culturally oriented discussions of literary pedagogy, linked the demographic world of the classroom with the implied worlds of literary texts: e.g., *Gendered Subjects: The Dynamics of Feminist Teaching; The Resisting Reader; The Black Presence in English Literature; Gender and Reading: Essays on Readers, Texts, and Contexts; Textual Power; Theory in the Classroom;* and *Critical Teaching and Everyday Life* (see references for this chapter). The broad world civilization courses that had been paired with world literature or humanities courses underwent similar transformations, most notably in the Stanford revision of its "Western Culture" sequence into a pluralist "Cultures, Ideas, and Values" program that was promptly attacked by a Secretary of Education committed to a traditionalist model.[9] Throughout, reformers hoped to achieve a truer perception of the world—the context in which world literature promised to situate its readers.

In the last decade of the century, we have come to a transitional period where the "world literature" course cannot relapse back into parochialism, but where it must also find a way to fulfill the function assigned it by American higher education. That is, the same course is expected both to introduce future citizens to an international span of cultural experience and also to provide—by comparison and contrast— a workable sense of *home* in the "Western heritage." The task is made more difficult by the breakdown of monolithic images of the Western heritage. Scholars have repeatedly demonstrated the many connections between Western civilization and other cultures: the influence of Asia

Minor and Africa on ancient Greece, the contribution of Arabic scholarship to medieval Western letters, and most obviously the multicultural heritage of the United States. Yet "more difficult" may be the wrong way to look at it, for there is another way of interpreting such complexity: as an opportunity to use the diverse pattern of "Western" or American society in order to establish bridges, comparisons, and contrasts with other cultures which are also not monolithic entities.

Certainly there is great public anxiety over the disintegration of earlier models; after the revisionary polemics of the sixties and seventies, a reaction set in that disclosed a real fear of losing any sense of cultural identity. Titles of national reports tell part of the story. In 1983, the National Commission on Excellence in Education warned that the United States was *A Nation at Risk,* and the National Endowment for the Humanities subsequently planned *To Reclaim a Legacy* (1984). The 1987 NEH report on humanities in the nation's public school system warned of the loss of *American Memory,* the 1989 Report recommended a standard fifty-hour core curriculum modeled on the traditional Western Great Books (minimizing literature), and the 1990 NEH report, *Tyrannical Machines,* indicted "Educational Practices Gone Wrong," while outlining "Our Best Hopes for Setting Them Right."[10] Literature teachers, in turn, hesitated over how to handle the breadth of material that should be touched on in any course that implies offering the world, or even a small portion of it. An NEH Institute on "The Theory and Teaching of World Literature," held at the University of Massachusetts at Amherst in 1987, came up with a summary statement of principles which individuals could adapt to their own teaching situations, but the group did not choose to prescribe a universal course outline any more than did the earlier conference in Wisconsin.

One cannot move back, however, either by ignoring the "rest" of the world outside the West (and how artificial that boundary is) or by pretending that world literature does not fill a specific function in United States education. The course is traditionally dependent on its dual role as mediator between national and global culture, or between a "world" of experience beyond local norms and a newly-clarified sense of national (and "Western") identity. The notion of Western culture is not irrelevant, as an egalitarian conscience might have it. The Western heritage does exist as a peculiar geographic and social continuity, a set of dominant cultural habits, even though it is also a complicated heritage and must be understood as such.[11]

Whatever the political underside of this tradition as privilege for a particular class of individuals, it is the *idealized version* that its defenders claim to preserve. That version is locatable and debatable in textual history. The idealized image of the Western core—seen as an impulse to open inquiry and debate, and to publicly accessible knowledge; as the valuing of individual experience and therefore of different personal and cultural beliefs; as openness to change; as an ideal of participatory government, of scientific method as a procedure; and also as a means of democratizing understanding—represents a series of enormously important anchor issues that can be examined in themselves and as part of tradition. While there can be no one way of teaching world literature (as the many national histories of world literature show),[12] it is perfectly possible to sketch a global representation in which Western texts play their part, or openly to examine the concept of a Western heritage while making references to other cultural traditions.

Whatever the approach, our measurements have become more specialized and more precise; in addition, the map has changed. The separate categorical identities that once gave familiar substance to world literature have lost their authority. As nation, culture, language, art, or race, they merge into one another, duplicate or defy definition, fragment into numerous wayward subsets, and generally transgress administrative boundaries. Political frontiers shift, creating, dividing, and merging "national" states around the world; cultures evolve and sometimes disappear under the pressures of economic or social change.

Languages travel and adapt to different contexts, so that former "national-language" traditions imbued with a presumed national essence have been metamorphosed into a variety of Anglophone, Francophone, Germanophone, Lusophone, African, Chinese, or Indian literatures that display, frequently, several linguistic or ethnic identities inside the same work. One cannot even identify one language or culture in these texts as the "dominant" one, and others as foils or contributing elements, without ignoring the new identity of the mix (the significance of creole, gender-oriented, and class-specific languages), and without overlooking the aesthetic and social implications when, for example, one language in a work is used to comment on another, or is given tacit approval over its less "civilized" twin. Works by Nigerian authors Wole Soyinka and Chinua Achebe, for example, play differently with the linguistic and cultural competition between two orders. Soyinka's comment that the African image in European eyes is generally "a universal-humanoid abstraction defined and conducted by individuals whose theories and prescriptions are derived from the apprehension of *their* world and *their* history, *their* social neuroses and *their* values systems" (Soyinka 1976, x) is a good reminder of the need, in teaching world literature, to beware of abstract images—unless they can be studied for themselves. As George Lakoff reminds us in his examination of reality-structures in language and culture, "The fact is that people around the world categorize things in ways that both boggle the Western mind and stump Western linguists and anthropologists" (Lakoff 1987, 92).

What, then, are some of the practical concerns that face the world literature teacher today? Institutions which choose a "full world" literature course, with global examples, will be cautious about privileging any geographic location—whether European, American, African, or Asian. Since there must always be a selection, however, the real problem lies in choosing and organizing material to provide the liveliest possible interaction and the most illuminating reading experience. Only the instructor, *in situ,* can make appropriate choices: the number and kind of texts, the best translations, the amount and nature of contextual material, the most thought-provoking sequences and juxtapositions, the selection of issues most important to the audience, and the best method for engaging the students' own worldviews in discussion of the material. This freedom is not as easy or unconditionally subjective as it sounds: its corollary requires that the teacher be open from the beginning about these same principles of selection, describing the range of opportunities they create, and the limitations that had to be accepted. It is important to convey—without apologizing—that any presentation of the world is also an arrangement and, thus, a further subject of inquiry.

In some institutions, the preliminary organization of material is already established—as it is, for example, in schools where world literature is actually "Western world literature" and is charged with clarifying for its students the Western heritage. The concept of the Western heritage itself is already a profitable starting point. World literature teachers will want to point out how rich and mixed that heritage is, how Western history and ideas have drawn from and contributed to other cultures, and how the Western heritage is refracted today (as both ideal and reality) in other parts of the globe. In instances where a traditional Western curriculum remains central, new dimensions can be suggested by clustering familiar texts or topics with non-traditional texts that help articulate the complexity of the local heritage, and with non-Western works.

The world literature syllabus, like any syllabus, is never neutral. If it is to fulfill its charge of enlarging horizons and clarifying values, then more than the content must be considered. Some procedures are already recognized to provoke thought processes, such as thematic comparisons—this book provides a series of rich and imaginative examples. Clustering material around a particular issue (whether theme, image, event, or current controversy) helps readers situate themselves in relation to different value systems. Many teachers of world literature try to avoid—or defamiliarize—frameworks that clearly reflect Western models, such as the genre of the novel, the nuclear family, or heroic individualism (especially the coming-of-age of the adolescent male). The present volume's suggested cluster of personalized expression (diaries, autobiographies, letters, etc.) is an example of such an attempt to find a common reference point that has not been canonized inside a single tradition. Similarly, the influence of priority in setting up expectations is often overlooked. The first work in a syllabus establishes, for better or worse, a model of aesthetic form and cultural perspective against which succeeding texts are tacitly compared. If the anchor point is to be an epic (a choice with its own implications), should the initial paradigm be the *Iliad, Gilgamesh,* the *Sundiata,* the *Tale of the Heike,* or one of the suppressed national narratives of medieval Central Asia? Might the epic itself be introduced by a philosophic parable, a newspaper report of military invasions, or a work of cross-cultural theory? Thoughts will develop along different lines in each case.

Much of what one can do depends on available resources. Locating good translations—sometimes *any* translation—has always been a problem. Luckily, publishers have been issuing new or revised translations at a rapid pace, and most modern translators try increasingly to reproduce the cultural overtones of a term, image, gesture, or pattern of speech. Translations must be handled with care: each age and each society stamps a translated text with the style of its own worldview, as is evident in the many versions of Homer from Chapman (1598) to modern times. The standard multivolume translations of Greek drama in the fifties (some of them printed simply because copyright had run out) have long been superseded. It is always worth comparing translations when more than one is available, and worth remembering that sometimes the most "accessible" translation is also the most domesticated: the one least useful in class because it fails to register the points at which a different experience is being conveyed. Texts, edited works, and commentaries are becoming progressively more available, nonetheless, and reference works provide broader and more detailed information.[13] When working with material from unfamiliar linguistic, religious, and social traditions, there is no substitute for knowing the basic cultural and linguistic allusions. Essays in disciplinary journals give important pointers on what a work means to specialists in the field; critical editions of original texts can be surprisingly helpful even if one is without knowledge of the particular foreign language. In one or another form, consultation is indispensable. Team-teaching is a strategy at some institutions, and ongoing discussion groups at others; electronic networks offer an opportunity to exchange information and views nationwide. At some point in teaching world literature, everyone needs to look outside. Only a small proportion of faculty members are trained in more than one literary tradition or in cross-cultural comparison, and no one is an authority in all areas. We all explore the world to some degree.

Exploration characterizes, in fact, the world literature course, reflecting both its roots in Goethe's international vision and its traditional academic mission to educate broadly aware mature minds. The study of representative texts from around the world quickly demonstrates the enormous variety of human experience. More importantly, it initiates a developmental "othering" process that clarifies values because it obliges readers to match their own frameworks against different systems of reality. The complex educational mission of world literature is fulfilled when teachers and students position themselves inside the changing, multiple world views that constitute, according to the philosopher, our experience of "truth" (Gadamer 1989, 442).

Notes

1. Compare Joan DeJean's discussion of the French use of literary texts to teach a particular image of French identity (DeJean 1988).
2. In studying United States educational history, Ernest Boyer and Arthur Levine discovered fifty different purposes for general education (Ernest L. Boyer and Arthur Levine, n.d., 53).
3. Frederick Rudolph notes that a committee of the Massachusetts General Court proposed in 1850 that Harvard professors be paid according to the number of students they taught: "Those only would succeed who taught . . . in a manner acceptable to the public. That which was desired would be purchased and that which was not, would be neglected" (Rudolph 1977, 102).
4. Rosenberg also quotes a description (taken from a 1953–54 Wisconsin catalogue) of a subsequent "graduate course in 'Great Books of World Literature,' in which the ideas and philosophies of ten masterpieces are studied each semester" (Rosenberg 1954, 27).
5. John Erskine's course was based on an adult education course he had devised for American soldiers in France, and the "Contemporary Civilization" course was similarly based on a 1917 "War Issues" course that introduced newly conscripted soldiers into the European heritage for which they were about to fight (Pratt 1990, 8; Graff 1987, 135).

6. It was a revolution in anthology traditions when Norton introduced, in 1956, the first world literature anthology offering complete works (Lawall 1986, 26).

7. Frederic Will, "The Evaluation and Use of Translations" (23–30); Walter R. Agard, "Teaching the Classics in Translation" (31–34); John C. McGalliard, "The Teaching of European Literature from St. Augustine to Dante" (35–44); Hazel S. Alberson, "Non-Western Literature in the World Literature Program" (45–52); H. V. S. Ogden, "On Defining the Humanities" (53–64); M. Isenberg, "The Role of Philosophical Texts in a Humanities Program" (65–72); Weldon M. Williams, "Intensive and Extensive Approaches in the Teaching of World Literature" (73–82); and Ralph Freedman, "Correlating the Teaching of Literature in Translation" (109–19).

8. See, in terms of American literature, the revisionary *Reconstructing American Literature: Courses, Syllabi, Issues* (Lauter 1983).

9. Secretary of Education William Bennett's attack on the new program at Stanford was reported in the editorial section of *The New York Times* on April 19, 1988. See also Pratt 1990.

10. Individual proposals, from Allan Bloom's description of how higher education had "Failed Democracy and Impoverished the Souls of Today's Students" to E. D. Hirsch's various attempts to impart *Cultural Literacy* to every American, also asserted the need for American education to help formulate a sense of national identity. The issue was summed up in a plaintive question asked by the editors of *Challenges to the Humanities* (1985): "Is there no common heritage that belongs to us all?" (Finn, Ravitch, and Roberts 1985, 8).

11. René Wellek sketches its customary boundaries as follows: it is "the continuity between Greek and Roman literatures, the Western medieval world, and the main modern literatures; and, without minimizing the importance of Oriental influences, especially that of the Bible, one must recognize a close unity which includes all Europe, Russia, the United States, and the South American literatures" (Wellek and Warren [1949] 1956, 41).

12. Jan Brandt Corstius, "Writing Histories of World Literature," *Yearbook of Comparative and General Literature* 12 (1963): 5–14. Etiemble, "Faut-il réviser la notion de *Weltliteratur?*" *Proceedings of the International Comparative Literature Association* (1966): 5–16.

13. It is still wise to be alert to hierarchies of value in the most apparently neutral sources when, for example, a major electronic encyclopedia contains pictures in twenty-seven categories including frontiersmen and Indians, fruit and nuts, invertebrates, military leaders, presidents of the United States, reptiles, ships, and writers and dramatists, but not a single work of art or architecture.

References

Bennett, William. 1984. *To Reclaim a Legacy: A Report on the Humanities in Higher Education.* Washington, D.C.: National Endowment for the Humanities.

Block, Haskell M., ed. *The Teaching of World Literature (Proceedings of the Conference on the Teaching of World Literature at the University of Wisconsin, April 24-25, 1959).* Chapel Hill: University of North Carolina Press, 1960.

Bloom, Allan. *The Closing of the American Mind: How Higher Education Has Failed Democracy and Impoverished the Souls of Today's Students.* New York: Simon and Schuster, 1987.

Boyer, Ernest L. and Arthur Levine. *A Quest for Common Learning: The Aims of General Education.* Washington, D.C.: The Carnegie Foundation for the Advancement of Teaching, n.d.

Brown, Calvin S. "Debased Standards in World Literature Courses." *Yearbook of Comparative and General Literature II* (1953): 13.

Cassell's Encyclopedia of World Literature, 2 vols. edited by S. H. Steinberg; rev. and enl. 3 vols., general editor: J. Buchanan-Brown. London: Cassell & Co., 1973.

Cheney, Lynne V. *Tyrannical Machines: A Report on Educational Practices Gone Wrong and Our Best Hopes for Setting Them Right.* Washington, D.C.: National Endowment for the Humanities, 1990.

———. *50 Hours: A Core Curriculum for College Students.* Washington, D.C.: National Endowment for the Humanities, 1989.

———. *American Memory: A Report on the Humanities in the Nation's Public Schools.* Washington, D.C.: National Endowment for the Humanities, 1987.

Corstius, Jan Brandt. "Writing Histories of World Literature." *Yearbook of Comparative and General Literature* 12 (1963): 5-14.

Culley, Margo and Catherine Portuges. *Gendered Subjects: The Dynamics of Feminist Teaching.* Boston, London: Routledge and Kegan Paul, 1985.

DeJean, Joan. "Teaching Frenchness." *French Review* 61, no. 3 (1988): 398-404.

DiPietro, Robert J. and Edward Ifkovic, eds. *Ethnic Perspectives in American Literature.* New York: Modern Language Association of America, 1983.

Eliot, T. S. "Tradition and the Individual Talent." In *The Sacred Wood: Essays on Poetry and Criticism.* 1920. Reprint. London: Methuen, 1966.

Etiemble. "Faut-il réviser la notion de *Weltliteratur?*" *Proceedings of the International Comparative Literature Association* (1966): 5-16.

Fetterley, Judith. *The Resisting Reader: A Feminist Approach to American Fiction.* Bloomington, IN: Indiana University Press, 1978.

Finn, Chester E., Jr., Diane Ravitch, P. Holley Roberts, eds. *Challenges to the Humanities.* New York: Holmes and Meier, 1985.

Flynn, Elizabeth A. and Patrocinio P. Schweickart, eds. *Gender and Reading: Essays on Readers, Texts, and Contexts.* Baltimore: Johns Hopkins, 1986.

Gadamer, Hans-Georg. *Truth and Method.* Translated by Joel Weinsheimer and Donald Marshall. New York: Crossroad Publishing Corporation, 1989.

Graff, Gerald. *Professing Literature: An Institutional History.* Chicago: University of Chicago Press, 1987.

Grimm, Reinhold. "Identity and Difference: On Comparative Studies Within a Single Language." *Profession 86* (1986): 28-29.

Hirsch, E. D., Jr. *Cultural Literacy: What Every American Needs to Know.* New York: Houghton Mifflin, 1987.

Lakoff, George. *Women, Fire, and Dangerous Things: What Categories Reveal About the Mind.* Chicago: Chicago University Press, 1987.

Lauter, Paul, ed. *Reconstructing American Literature: Courses, Syllabi, Issues.* Old Westbury: Feminist Press, 1983.

Lawall, Sarah N. "The Canon's Mouth: Comparative Literature and the World Masterpieces Anthology." *Profession 86* (1986): 25–27.

Levin, Harry. "Core, Canon, Curriculum." *College English* 43, no. 4 (April 1981): 352–62.

Miller, Christopher L. "Theories of Africans: The Question of Literary Anthropology." In *"Race," Writing, and Difference,* edited by Henry Louis Gates, Jr., 281–300. Chicago: Chicago University Press, 1986.

Moulton, Richard. *World Literature and Its Place in General Culture.* Norwood, MA: Macmillan, 1911.

Nelson, Cary. *Theory in the Classroom.* Urbana: University of Illinois Press, 1986.

Parker, Kenneth. "The Revelation of Caliban: 'The Black Presence' in the Classroom." In *The Black Presence in English Literature,* edited by David Dabydeen, 186–206. Manchester, Eng.: Manchester University Press, 1985.

Pratt, Mary Louise, "Humanities for the Future: Reflections on the Western Culture Debate at Stanford." *The Politics of Liberal Education,* edited by Darryl J. Gless and Barbara Herrnstein Smith. Special issue of *South Atlantic Quarterly* 89, no. 1 (1990): 7–25.

Rosenberg, Ralph P. "The 'Great Books' in General Education," *Yearbook of Comparative and General Literature III* (1954): 20–35.

Rudolph, Frederick. *Curriculum: A History of the American Undergraduate Course of Study Since 1636.* Prepared for the Carnegie Foundation for the Advancement of Teaching. San Francisco: Jossey-Bass Publishers, 1977.

Scholes, Robert. *Textual Power: Literary Theory and the Teaching of English.* New Haven: Yale University Press, 1985.

Shor, Ira. *Critical Teaching and Everyday Life.* Boston: South End Press, 1980.

Soyinka, Wole. *Myth, Literature and the African World.* Cambridge: Cambridge University Press, 1976.

Strich, Fritz. *Goethe and World Literature,* translated by C. A. M. Sym. Westport, CT: Greenwood Press, 1971.

The National Commission on Excellence in Education. *A Nation at Risk: The Imperative for Educational Reform: A Report to the Nation and the Secretary of Education, United States Department of Education.* Washington, D.C.: The National Commission on Excellence in Education, 1983.

Wellek, René and Austin Warren. *Theory of Literature.* 1949. Reprint. New York: Harcourt Brace, 1956.

2 Facing Others, Facing Ourselves

J. Paul Hunter
University of Chicago

What does it mean to be a Department of English? The question of what belongs in the department—one of the most hotly debated issues in the academy today—crucially depends on a fundamental choice of definition. What is "English" in the sense that we have "departments" of it? Ultimately the question is more historical than analytical; the borders of "English" in colleges and universities involve pragmatics, politics, and territoriality more than precise categorical distinctions and clear logic. The conceptual problem here reminds me of Will Rogers's response when someone asked his political affiliation. "I don't belong to an organized political party," Rogers said. "I'm a Democrat." English as a department does not belong to any recognizable organized structure either. It is not a discipline but a series of disciplines—philological, linguistic, critical, historical, cultural—loosely confederated to deal with texts written or spoken in the English language. English is inclusive by habit and by historical tradition. And the question of exclusion, either indirectly through an accepted canon that damns by omission or directly by defining out certain texts and methods, is a serious matter because of the sheer magnitude of inclusivity. Yet, in practice even more than in theory, exclusion remains a pressing issue.

On the basis of precedent it would be difficult to argue the exclusion of practically anything from an English department, even if it were not a lettered text and did not use English as its native language, for whenever the going has been tough in the academy, English departments have regularly crossed the most opportune border and claimed more land for themselves, usually offering "humane" justifications even as they balkanized their friendly neighbors—in history, philosophy, film, communications, or other languages. But my purpose here is not to

This essay is a revised version of the annual address to the South Atlantic Association of Departments of English in Washington, D.C., on November 12, 1988.

rehearse the fascinating history of "English" as a university subject;[1] rather I want to apply some of the implications of that history to definitional questions now gathering gale force.

Toward a New Definition

The "field" of English has recently come to include many texts not originally written in English (by Foucault and Kristeva, for example, or Marx and Freud), many texts in English whose primary intellectual force is not "literary" in the traditional narrow sense (by Defoe and Parkman, for example, or Law, Hume, and Wollstonecraft), and many cultural "texts" that do not conform to the usual expectations of being verbal and written (films, work from oral traditions, advertising slogans, cartoons, stamps, costumes, and pin cushions, for example). But this process is not new; the old canon, after all, included Aristotle, Horace, Burton, Clarendon, Addison, Franklin, Chesterfield, Boswell, Burke, Gibbon, Macauley, Ruskin, Mencken, Hogarth, Blake, and "Boz"— not to mention miscellaneous autobiographies, personal letters, private papers, sermons, ballads, epitaphs, book illustrations, designs for gardens, engravings, and inscribed or signed materials of many other kinds. It is hard to see why—if these texts belong—Longinus or Locke, Darwin or Derrida, Job or Genet, Kristeva or Kierkegaard should be excluded from "our" courses or be considered an inappropriate focus of our scholarly and interpretive efforts. What English is now and what it was then turn out to be very much the same.

But I want to ask whether our *working* definition of English in departments is yet comprehensive enough to do the job we set ourselves. Even though "English" is, in its operative sense, already too much to specialize in, it still may not cast a wide enough net to do the teaching job we need to do in modern university classrooms, and it may not provide a clear and solid enough intellectual base to operate from. I wonder whether, in thinking of ourselves as specialists in English, we do not too severely limit ourselves, cutting ourselves off from some of the most powerful forces in the writings we teach. My perspective on this issue is not that of a comparatist who finds definition only in sorting out the details of difference, a structuralist who considers all varieties of language to be somehow alike, or a formalist who lives within the text. Rather it is that of a dyed-in-the-wool contextualist, a dedicated historicist, a traditional scholar, someone who believes in cultural history, who regards literature as a manifestation of cultural consciousness, and who thinks that all works are firmly grounded in particulars of time and place. And that is why I think that we, as teachers not only of language and texts—writing and reading—but of a cultural tradition embodied in texts, have a major dilemma today in the courses we teach and, even more importantly, in how we design a curriculum and communicate to our students a sense of how texts relate to contexts.

My concern here is with a new frontier of this issue that centers not on a definition of textuality but on questions of the borders of language and culture. Traditionally, we have gone with borders of language rather than of culture—that is why we have departments of English rather than departments of British and U.S. studies or programs divided by nations, regions, and tribes—on Australia, for example, or the Commonwealth, or New England, or Scotland, or California, or the Piedmont. But recent developments—genuine advances, I think—in the way writing now (both "creative" and critical) is being done mean that the problem has new faces that affect departments of English in a profound way. The issues are complex and reach in a variety of directions, but let me try to get hold of them by speaking of their implications in two ways—for undergraduate teaching and for graduate programs. The undergraduate side first, not because it is simpler, but because it has a more obvious (if incomplete) practical solution.

The Implications for Undergraduate Education

Let me try synecdoche, a list of names. The list I offer is a list of authors, contemporary authors who write in the English language, most of them from an address in the United States. This particular list is from the table of contents of an anthology I recently coedited with Jerome Beaty, *New Worlds of Literature* (Norton, 1989). The anthology was conceived—for first-year courses in writing and in literature—as a less traditional, alternative text, and it includes only works written in English, mostly about contemporary life in the United States. Here is the list:

Jamaica Kincaid
Li-Young Lee
Luis Cabalquinto
Ray A. Young Bear
Pat Mora
Cathy Song
Jimmy Santiago de Baca
Agha Shahid Ali

Leslie Marmon Silko
Ishmael Reed
Maxine Hong Kingston
Mitsuye Yamada
Bharati Mukherjee
Yvonne Sapia
Carter Revard
Neil Bisoondath
Rita Dove
Toshio Mori
Amy Tan
Lorna Dee Cervantes
Mary TallMountain
Wakako Yamauchi

This is a mere sample, but it is indicative. I can imagine a traditional, experienced teacher of first-year English responding to such a list with total bewilderment. Where are the familiar writers—Shakespeare, Faulkner, Keats, Donne, Dickinson, Eliot, Hemingway, Roethke, Marvell, Yeats, Milton, Swift? More troubling, perhaps, to many is another question: where are the familiar names, ones we can recognize and pronounce with confidence even if we do not know anything about what they have written? What is a professor of *English* supposed to do with such a list?

In the book itself, the list of authors is not there for its shock value, and neither are the selections, which collectively and individually justify themselves by their own excellence. They are not for a historical course in obscure or representative books. They are stories, poems, plays, and essays of extremely high quality, fully as good as traditional English selections and (I think) far more immediately useful to students in the nineties. On their own merits, they belong in the English tradition as vital expressions of American life and letters, and they provide, in the classroom, an appropriate and effective introduction to good writing, illustrating questions of theme, structure, craft, language, and context that enhance the reading and writing skills of students and make them want to learn more, read more, and take more courses in literature. Whether we, as editors, have chosen the right individual selections remains to be seen, but I am confident of the two larger premises involved in the book: that contemporary writings of high quality offer the best way to get the attention of many students who are encountering serious literature for the first time at the college level, and that in the kind of materials selected—written in English by writers with a variety of national, linguistic, ethnic, and racial backgrounds—lies the future (and present) treasures of our cultural tradition.

The literature of the United States has long offered especially complicated issues of context to readers, for our culture is a mixed and mixing one, bringing together writers of diverse personal and cultural backgrounds and melting them into, or at least comprehending them as, a single tradition. The United States is a large country and a diverse one, and its history has moved faster than most. It has always had a culture which, for better and worse, has brought new cultures into contact and conflict with our dominant one, continually changing the definitions of dominance and ultimately of our culture itself. The literature of the United States has long been something beyond English literature displaced to a new continent. It is imperialistic (and not altogether in a bad sense), absorbing into its mainstream writers from eastern and central Europe, those from unfamiliar places and unfamiliar faiths. This literature is almost by definition hyphenated or cross-cultured literature, for example, Anglo-American, African-American, Jewish-American, and (because of our peculiar presentist sense of history) Native-American literature. Each of these infusions of tradition involves far more than absorption or modification; each has come to be an important central aspect of the national tradition itself, just as crucial to understanding the culture as Southern literature or New England literature, or Western literature, for we are all of us all of these things in our identity, not just one strand of them. And what was true about Ireland and Italy and Poland and Germany and Armenia earlier in this century is now true of Japan, China, Mexico, India, Korea, Vietnam, and the Caribbean. Or rather it is true about literature written by people who have the cultures of those places deeply imbedded in themselves from their past, but who now (appropriately) define themselves both in terms of the United States where they live and the varied traditions of families, tribes, peoples, and nations in their personal and collective ancestry. My point here in bringing up these matters— and the list of names—is to suggest how radically the world of writing has been changing in the past few years, not only adding many unfamiliar names to the tradition but modifying the familiar subjects and themes to encompass the cultural clashes that a melting pot produces. People who have not been paying attention to the best new writing may be peacefully unaware of just how different the landscape of writing in English—especially in the United States—now looks. And the implications of this change, first for teaching writing and reading to beginning college students and soon for reflecting on literature with upper-level students, is enormous.

When teaching undergraduates, it is no longer enough to know about the Anglo-American tradition and the Greek, Roman, and Judeo-Christian traditions that lie behind it—not enough even to know Western thought and writing in its full tradition. Teaching works by David Hwang or Louise Erdrich makes different demands on us as teachers—even as teachers of first-year students—than does teaching works by Flannery O'Connor or John Steinbeck. It may help if we study oral narrative, know United States history, read widely in gender studies, are sensitive to East/West symbolism, or see a lot of operas, but the interpretive demands of *M. Butterfly* or a poem or story by Erdrich are far greater than the particulars of our rather narrow educational backgrounds are likely to meet. The training most of us received in graduate school—training which emphasized one particular literary history, habits peculiar to a particular culture, and traditions in thought and language rather like those most of us grew up with every day—is not the best possible preparation for many of the texts we will find ourselves teaching over the next few years. But we must teach these texts, ready or not. If we do not choose to, our changing student bodies—which in ten years will have one in four students whose first language is not English—will demand it, not because the language will be more familiar to them but because it reflects the confrontation of cultures they know first hand.

We may take some comfort in the training we do have, which has given us abilities of analysis, rhetorical and critical terminology, research skills which will at least get us to the right sections of the library, an understanding of how historical and cultural contexts work, knowledge of questions to ask about texts, and perhaps adaptability and common sense. But we are likely to feel increasingly inadequate in the face of texts we will not feel altogether comfortable about, and it will not every day be a comfort to think that we once learned, somehow, to adapt our skills from the study of Shakespeare or Milton or Chaucer to the teaching of Sylvia Plath, Katherine Anne Porter, Adrienne Rich, and Tennessee Williams. At the very least, our sense of what we must read in order to teach appropriately is bound to change; at the worst, we might turn into hopeless reactionaries, waiting for the world to return to texts and days more familiar to us. Somewhere in the middle, the old, worn notes will disappear and with them a lot of shopworn assumptions about literature, culture, and ourselves. The primary immediate implication of the new range of writers who work in English but come from a variety of cultural pasts involves attitudes more than expertise, and that we can change right away, with an act of will. It is our willingness to work with new—and new kinds of—texts that seems crucial; openness to the unfamiliar, to alien customs, strange habits, strategies that derive from other traditions, other lands, other languages, will go a long way to opening worlds of writing and reading to beginning students. But for advanced students, and particularly for graduate students who will be the next generation of teachers, the demands of knowledge and expertise will finally and in painful detail have to be addressed too. These are the longer-range implications, and they may involve serious structural changes that make English a misnomer for what we profess.

Implications for Graduate Education

The graduate challenges ultimately derive from the same internationalized, intercultural context I have been describing as characteristic of writing now, but there are also intertextual, interlanguage, and historical factors that complicate the issues. Just as no single linguistic and cultural tradition is adequate for the serious study of most present-day texts, so most contextual questions about *older* texts turn out to have dimensions that take us as well beyond a particular national tradition.

It has, I suppose, long been obvious to those who specialize in literature since the mid-nineteenth century that national distinctions tend to oversimplify texts and that to speak of, say, a novel of the 1960s as American or English is, except in unusual cases such as fiction about Vietnam, to slice things a little too fine contextually. And what was true across the English-speaking world was only slightly less true across the Continent and throughout the European linguistic systems, whatever language or national tradition was immediately imbedded in the text. Writers read each other, poets as well as novelists, across all language barriers one way or another, and—more important—they increasingly tend to operate from some sort of global perspective, whatever their own local bias. Even in cases in which a particular national consciousness and a specific cultural moment seems crucial, like the novels about Vietnam, it would be a mistake to think strictly in terms of the American or even the Anglo-American tradition—not only because the issue is informed by French perspectives and a variety of Asian ones but also because the writers see themselves participating in a discourse that transcends Melville and Faulkner and the "Great Tradition" from Fielding to Joyce, feel themselves to be part of something more powerful culturally. It is hard to say how this shared consciousness among writers originated—or exactly what loyalties writers feel when they define themselves—but regardless of the definition of community, the authorial discourse had already changed by the late nineteenth century when English departments were invented.

But even in older ages apparently more insular, the complexities of context are likely to make students of a single national and linguistic tradition rather nervous. The emergence of the novel is a case in point. The English novel develops as a distinct phenomenon with features that reflect characteristic aspects of the English national culture in the early eighteenth century, and many traditional contextualists, including myself, are interested in linking the origins of the species with particular features of the culture, finding the modern novel's formal features related to things deeply imbedded in the cultural consciousness. The classic statement of this view, from a sociological perspective, is Ian Watt's *Rise of the Novel* (1957), and Michael McKeon, working from Marxist assumptions, has supported it in a powerful way.[2] My own work, summarized most fully in *Before Novels: The Cultural Contexts of Eighteenth-Century English Fiction* (1990), strongly supports the cultural thesis by examining reading habits and patterns of social history. But there is another side to the story, as critics of Watt, reviewers of McKeon, and doubters of Hunter quickly point out. For what is one to make of the fact that similar moves occur in the national traditions of novels elsewhere, in France and Germany, for example, and how is one to explain the influencing relationships between different national traditions, or account for the apparently uncontextual emergence of a figure like Cervantes? These are not trivial questions. One cannot do—at least not yet—textual work that is intensely cultural and purely structural at once. Ultimately, we choose between doing serious contextual work that makes connections between the consciousness of a culture and its artistic manifestations or work that points to bridges that cross cultural, often national and linguistic, gaps. No one, at present anyway, can adequately do both. But both are legitimate, and for a contextualist or cultural analyst—old and new historicists face a similar problem—the dilemma is serious.

Because sophisticated scholarship has developed now in a variety of national literatures, in comparative studies themselves, and in critical theory that has suddenly, through the several cultural historicisms now competing for dominance, discovered time and culture, the question of how to do serious study has become very complicated for serious students of all stripes. The difficulties are particularly important for anyone who takes the temporal dimensions of literature seriously. Those who regard the essential dimensions of texts as existing within language or who view individual texts as the center of any issue can ultimately adapt to comparatist studies more simply, for the forms and structures that concern them can be seen to move among languages, and texts loosened from their cultural context can intertextuate freely, regardless of space or time. The rest of us face a serious intellectual problem, one that will not readily or quickly go away.

Conclusion

I offer no easy solution, but I do end with some practical advice. Obviously, the answer is not to draw our wagons into a circle and teach only the narrowest of English texts at the undergraduate level or draw up graduate programs in English in ever-narrower terms. There is no possibility of returning to earlier and simpler times, either in the writing of poems, plays, and fiction, or in criticism and theory—coping with a more complex set of intellectual intercultural issues seems necessary even for those of us whose virtues lie in the deep, intense, close analysis of issues within a particular culture and its consciousness and who need history to illuminate our texts. We are going to have to be interested in what people who know other traditions better than we do have to say to us; increasingly, we are going to have to include experts in other languages and cultures in our graduate programs. Their expertise is necessary if we are ultimately to train teachers of undergraduates to do the thorough job envisioned in my analysis of the current U.S. literary scene—a mirror by the way, though an enlarged one, of what is going on in late twentieth-century writing all over the world as borders change, emigration speeds up, and cultures clash and interact. And graduate students need such expertise for their future and we ourselves for our present.

Departments of *English?* Perhaps they literally make less sense today than they once did (as I suggested at the start) departments of English never depended on a pure or even clear idea, despite the claim to definitional rigor. I doubt that we will disappear, though I think we will learn to be more inclusive—to provide in our tents shelter for those who specialize in cultures where the English language is not spoken and in the literatures of other languages. Already a goodly portion of what we teach, because we want to claim it, is written by Sophocles, Sartre, Dostoevsky, Molière, Ibsen, Cervantes, Borges, Calvino, Homer, and the Jewish and Christian Bibles. And our critical maternity and paternity now comes not only from Sidney, Dryden, Johnson, Coleridge, Arnold, and Empson, but also from Woolf, de Beauvoir, Lacan, Altusser, Benjamin, Bakhtin, Starobinski, and Foucault.

Five recommendations can be derived from such considerations:

1. Develop tolerance in our teaching and research ranks for comparatist studies, which are on the rise and which tend to find homes in departments of languages or departments of history or history of art because English departments act insularly or talk hostilely, often like a bunch of village bullies.

2. Scrap the coverage model as a way of building departments. No one, no matter how big, can do everything anymore, and if we try to do serious contextual study, as a way of training graduate students and of fulfilling intellectual commitments to any text, we are going to have to do it selectively—maybe by having one contextual specialist who does deep cultural studies in seventeenth-century England, another who does similar studies on the Chicano culture in California, along with those who doubt the value of that model altogether as resident Doubting Antagonists.

3. Develop—consciously, carefully, and intelligently—new areas of expertise in individual departments that border on areas of English expertise now in the department. Some of these "contiguous areas" could be surprises; a department strong in Restoration and early eighteenth-century public poetry, for example, might wish to build an expertise in African American, Hispanic, and Native American poetry that draws on oral tradition and speaks to public issues out of deep tribal and cultural loyalties.

4. Develop cultural studies units that address specific interrelationships between some aspect of an English-speaking culture and the same structural aspect of a non-English speaking one.

5. Court, and I do mean actively court, language departments so that cooperative—beyond comparative—programs can be set up. We are so used to thinking of the departments that house other languages as Montenegro or Bulgaria—hapless little duchies not worthy of our exalted attention, that we may not be sufficiently aware of just how much energy has shifted to their work. It is no accident that in many fine universities, language departments have seized comparative programs or the more general "literature" programs that deemphasize the nationality of literatures, leaving English holding its inflated view of itself while standing on more limited turf. The old isolationist view of English departments toward fellow literature departments is now as dangerous as it is outmoded.

I end with a quotation. It is not from Shakespeare or Pope or Churchill, but from Sam Patch, a local hero in Rochester, New York. Sam Patch had an unusual speciality; he jumped into waterfalls, such as Niagara Falls, carrying a live bear cub, and after several successful and spectacular leaps he died boldly in his trade in a late autumn jump in Rochester; they found his body during spring thaw; the bear was his only survivor. Patch was a man of few words but he was rich in ambiguity, rather like Yogi Berra, making of his language often more than its literal syntax seemed to offer. When asked about his unusual occupation, he said simply, "Some things can be done as well as others." So can English.

Notes

1. On the history of departments of English, see Jo McMurtry, *English Language, English Literature: The Creation of an Academic Discipline* (Hamden, CT: Archon Books, 1985); Richard Ohmann, *English in America: A Radical View of the Profession* (New York: Oxford Univ. Press, 1976); and (especially) Gerald Graff, *Professing Literature: An Institutional History* (Chicago: Univ. of Chicago Press, 1987).

2. In *The Origins of the English Novel, 1600–1740* (Baltimore: Johns Hopkins Press, 1987).

3 Global Perspectives: A Thematic Approach

Sandra Lott
University of Montevallo

The expansion of courses in world literature to include works outside the traditional Western canon and the addition of those works to the literature curriculum now seems to many to be necessary and inevitable. As Harry Levin writes in "Core, Canon, Curriculum," "It is the nature of literature and of knowledge, as it has been of human experience itself, to keep moving on, for better or for worse" (Levin 1981, 354).

Describing ways in which Harvard University's initial curriculum differed from the medieval European model, Levin writes, "For the changing light of vistas opened up by the age of Humanism, the old prescriptive syllabus would have to be revised, absorbing new inclusions of recognized importance while dropping out extraneous remnants of obsolete lore" (Levin 1981, 354). At a conference on "The Teaching of World Literature" held at the University of Wisconsin in 1959, Hazel Alberson noted that another such vista was opened up a century and a half ago with Goethe's definition of world literature as a bridge between peoples, which must include works from the Orient and from other non-Western cultures. Professor Alberson went on to note that "today the pressures upon all of us to become acquainted with non-Western countries are more urgent and more vital than in Goethe's time. Today we are faced with *one world*. No longer can we hide behind the facade of our ignorance and our provincialism; no longer can we be indifferent to those parts of the world we do not know" (Alberson 1960, 45). Participants in the Summer 1987 Institute on the Theory and Teaching of World Literature, held at the University of Massachusetts in Amherst and sponsored by the National Endowment for the Humanities, reported that "readers of world literature need to encounter an image of human experience that corresponds to global reality. Any narrower view will only hinder their understanding of their own and others' cultures, and render them less able to act in a world whose diversity they do not expect" ("Report on World Literature" 1). This need is even more urgent in 1993.

However, even for those who have come to accept the importance of non-Western cultures, planning world literature courses which preserve what many have come to regard as essential works, while adding texts from the growing body of nontraditional works, still presents serious difficulties. These problems are exacerbated by the conflicts between those who defend the traditional canon as the best that has been thought and said and those who strongly object to what they perceive as the patriarchal and elitist values in many canonical works. In an attempt to resolve this conflict, J. Paul Hunter writes in his introduction to *New Worlds of Literature,*

> Although an hour spent reading recent Native American poetry cannot at the same time be spent reading Montaigne, there is no conflict of interest between the classical and new. . . . The time you spend reading is not fixed: an hour of Maya Angelou does not mean you have no time for Aristophanes. If you read Angelou with pleasure and excitement, you are likely to find time to read more—and sometime . . . read Aristophanes. (xi, xii)

Moreover, many teachers who are challenged to explore innovative ways of designing courses to meet these new demands will want to find ways of teaching both Maya Angelou and Aristophanes, quite possibly in the same course.

For such teachers, one useful approach is to employ a thematic pattern of organization rather than a strictly chronological one. This pattern can be applied within rough chronological parameters or by deliberately juxtaposing ancient and modern texts. The thematic paradigm is one which has been recommended by noted scholars and teachers of world literature of both the past and the present. For example, Hazel Alberson described a cumulative method of presenting world literature, "drawing together books of similar genres, or similar subject matter, or those illustrating some theme or some literary movement, or any of the other problems related to literature" (Alberson 1960, 47–48).

According to Alberson, such an approach involves "cutting across national lines, language barriers, time boundaries, or epochs. As each new book is added and comparisons and contrasts explored, there emerges in fuller perspective an understanding of that genre of epic, or that subject matter of heroism, or that theme of self-revelation, or that view of romanticism." She further notes that non-Western books "increase this total cumulative discovery," though she cautions that these books must be carefully studied, not to erase or minimize differences, but to understand their cultural slant and their distinctive qualities (Alberson 1960, 47–48).

More recently, in his address to participants in the National Endowment for the Humanities Institute on the Teaching and Theory of World Literature, held at the University of Massachusetts at Amherst in the summer of 1987, Thomas Greene also supported the notion of thematic groupings which "illustrate differences while still revealing the underlying common obsessions."

In this book, we assume that suggestions such as these by Alberson and Greene may provide the basis for an exciting program in world literature in which the old and the new are allowed to interact with each other in such a way as to illuminate the past and the present, the familiar and the "other." Such an approach may allow us to shake off the old accustomed tiredness with which we sometimes come to regard familiar texts and to read them freshly as works which newly engage our minds and imaginations. Such juxtapositions may also enhance our understanding of historical and geographical distinctions if we are careful to follow Greene's warning that we must explore the differences, the "otherness," of works at the same time that we stress their common concerns.

Curricular changes such as those called for in this book have been accompanied in every age by debate and controversy. In the eighteenth century, Jonathan Swift satirized such literary debates in *The Battle of the Books,* depicting the controversy in his day over whether modern literature should be studied along with the classical works of Greece and Rome. That such literary debates are sometimes so fierce may, in fact, be a tribute to the power of the storyteller to shape and interpret life. This literary power has been a focal point in works from a variety of cultures and times. In ancient Greece, Homer pays tribute in *The Odyssey* to poets who "are dearest to the Muse / Who puts upon their lips the ways of life" (IX, 498–99), and the modern American poet, Archibald MacLeish, warns the politicians and journalists of his day not to disregard the poet's interpretation of contemporary events. In "A Poet Speaks from the Visitor's Gallery" of Congress, MacLeish writes of the enduring power of the poet, "whose songs are marble / and whose marble sings" (lines 31–32), and he expresses disregard for reporters who "write the tittle in the papers" and "tell the tattle on the air" (lines 9–10).

Today's journalists also recognize the power of storytellers whose interpretations give a preferred "spin" to their experiences. In an article on the controversy over the movie *JFK,* columnist Ellen Goodman comments on "what it must be like to have a storyteller in the family. A novelist, a memoirist, who takes the central events of a shared life and makes them his own" (Goodman 1992, C 2).

Similarly, Puerto-Rican American author Judith Ortiz Cofer comments on the conflict she experiences with her mother over whose stories will prevail. She writes,

> I want my mother to tell me that what I remember is true. But... her memories are precious to her.... She wants certain things she believes are true to remain sacred, untouched by my fictions. (*Silent Dancing* 1990, 163)

Unlike the mother of Judith Ortiz Cofer, who realizes that well-told stories can take on such power and truth that others begin to readjust their memories to fit the storytellers' accounts, many listeners or readers, even when uncomfortable with or irritated by the "spin" given by their storytellers, are often too impressed by the force of a well-written story to ask the kinds of questions posed by Ortiz Cofer's mother—questions such as "Whose story is this, and what values and attitudes are privileged by this story?" Under the spell of a compelling piece of literature, we do not always stop to ask, "What persons or groups are empowered by this story? What other persons or groups who have a place in this story are silenced or marginalized?" In the antebellum South, for example, does "truth" lie with the slave narratives, with the writing of Northern abolitionists, or with the narratives of white Southerners about an idyllic agrarian society in which slaves and masters lived in harmony?

Such questions make us keenly aware of the need to hear the stories of many persons and many groups. Furthermore, multicultural or cross-cultural reading clusters such as those described here may help us to understand the need to examine the authors' underlying assumptions and to enter imaginatively into the experiences of people with diverse and often conflicting perspectives.

Breaking "Mind-Forg'd Manacles"

Some years ago Robert Penn Warren, a critic who is now somewhat out of favor but whose voice may well be heard and respected once more, wrote that the process of identification with fictional characters helps us to understand ourselves and others (553–59). If Warren is correct, it is especially important that we continue our efforts to include in our curriculum literary styles, cultures, and genres which have not previously been a fully recognized part of our heritage. Many of us who were educated in an earlier era were never told in our schools about Langston Hughes, Paul Lawrence Dunbar, or Zora Neale Hurston. As far as our textbooks and teachers were concerned, they did not exist. Similarly, in her autobiography *I Know Why the Caged Bird Sings,* African American writer Maya Angelou tells of being afraid to memorize Shakespeare for a school presentation for fear her grandmother would find out Shakespeare was white.

Such silences, which restrict rather than expand our understandings of ourselves and others, have long cut us off from a rich literature which is rightfully a part of our heritage. At the turn of the century, Virginia Woolf wrote in "A Room of One's Own" about Shakespeare's hypothetical sister who in that culture would not have been able to voice her poetic genius (46–51). In our time, another kind of silencing occurs when certain expressions are voiced but are not heard or valued. In our schools and colleges, such has frequently been the fate not only of the voices of women, but also of America's ethnic writers and of non-Western, Third World writers as well. Such persons are sometimes seen as colonized subjects, regarded as possibly charming, but certainly untutored children, who should listen quietly and respectfully to their superiors. But William Blake would remind us that in rejecting the voices of the oppressed of our world, we may "drive an angel from [our] door," and thus expose ourselves to grave danger ("Holy Thursday" I, line 12).

Other writers who share Blake's concern about such dangers include Alice Walker, Stephen Spender, and Gwendolyn Brooks, all of whom advocate removing literary, social, and educational restrictions. Alice Walker, for example, opposes the concept of a segregated literature, commenting that "black and white writers seem to be writing one immense story . . . with different parts . . . coming from a multitude of different perspectives." Walker suggests that only through these multiple perspectives can we begin to know "the whole story" instead of just fragmented parts of our human adventure (*In Search* 5, 43). Walker also comments on the power of literature to save us from ourselves by showing us a wider vision, by expanding our perspectives on the past and the present (*In Search* 5). In her visionary work *The Temple of My Familiar,* Walker gives us a black woman's panoramic perspective on the history of the human race. In "Saving the Life that Is Your Own," Walker suggests that much of her own writing is intended to save us from "the narrowed and narrowing view of life" (*In Search* 5) which preserves what Blake called "mind-forg'd manacles" ("London" line 8).

According to Blake, such narrowed perspectives have produced the "marks of weakness, marks of woe" (line 4) which he encounters "in every voice, in every ban" (line 7) throughout the chartered streets of London. In our time as well, poets have traced the sad effects for us and for our students of such mental restrictions. In "Boy Breaking Glass," Gwendolyn Brooks's speaker says, "I shall create! If not a note, a hole. / If not an overture, a desecration" (lines 7–8). Accusing a system which denies his very humanity, Brooks's delinquent boy exclaims, "It was you, it was you who threw away my name!" (line 20). The tragic loss of potential and the ensuing danger to society posed by such youthful estrangement is suggested in Brooks's final description of the boy as "A mistake. / A cliff. / A hymn, a snare, and an exceeding sun" (lines 25–27).

Such expressions make us keenly aware of our need to engage in the kind of mental fight which Blake advocated to overcome the misery which pervaded his city: "I will not cease from Mental Fight, / Nor shall my Sword sleep in my hand, / Till we have built Jerusalem / In England's green & pleasant land" (lines 13–16). Similarly, in the first part of our century, Stephen Spender wrote in his poem "An Elementary Classroom in a Slum" of the need for educational change. Urging reforms which would make schools expansive and liberating rather than restrictive, Spender concludes his poem with a plea to those responsible—"governor, teacher, inspector, visitor" (line 26) to break through the stultifying educational and social system in which clouded classroom windows "open on . . . lives like crouching tombs" (line 28). Spender challenges educators of his day to "show the children to the fields and all their world / Azure on their sands, to let their tongues / Run naked into books, the white and green leaves open / The history theirs whose language is the sun" (lines 31–33).

This battle for psychological liberation urged by writers such as Walker, Blake, Brooks, and Spender is also being waged in the so-called canon wars and the literary battles about political correctness. In the final analysis, however, it seems clear that the desire to limit access to ideas and experiences must give way to a genuine openness to the voices of those who historically have been silenced or marginalized and to the voices of those who may yet be silenced by the current debate. Otherwise, all of us are deprived of vital sources of power and of identity.

Hearing such varied voices can help us to understand more fully different forms and uses of human power, to explore the relationships between ruler and ruled, and thus to free ourselves and others from Blake's "mind-forg'd manacles." As suggested by the thematic model which Alberson provided many years ago, this process can be enhanced by designing courses which bring together works from diverse cultures which reflect shared human needs and concerns.

"The Individual and the World"

One such course might employ an umbrella theme such as "The Individual and the World: The Quest for Values and Self-Definition." As suggested in Section I of this book, a good place to begin in this quest would be with a grouping of personal writings—journals, letters, autobiographies, testimonials—by men and women of various times and places. Possible assignments include Sei Shonagon's *The Pillow Book,* Camara Laye's *The Dark Child,* Wole Soyinka's *Aké,* Maya Angelou's *I Know Why the Caged Bird Sings,* and Maxine Hong Kingston's *The Woman Warrior.* Through such reading, students would explore, in a personal and immediate way, the feelings, experiences, and lives of these writers in the context of the cultures and social structures of each writer's particular time and place. Students might also come to understand the power of language to capture the distinctive quality of a period in an individual life.

For example, *The Pillow Book,* Shonagon's journal of court culture in tenth-century Japan, includes lively listings of likes and dislikes, of elegant things (duck eggs, a white coat worn over a violet waistcoat, wisteria blossoms), hateful things (the sound of dogs when they bark a long time in chorus, a lover who leaves without proper ceremony); perceptive comments on personalities; and advice on the correct behavior of lovers and servants. She also provides delightful vignettes of court diversions (an outing to hear the cuckoo sing or a wager with the empress over how long a snow mountain will take to melt). Students may be intrigued by the otherness of Shonagon's world, in which blackened teeth are a sign of beauty and also struck by the strange familiarity of her accounts of embarrassing things or of things which make one's heart beat faster. Readers familiar with J.D. Salinger's *The Catcher in the Rye* might see parallels between Shonagon's commentaries on the manners and customs of tenth-century Japan and Holden Caulfield's pronouncements on American culture in the middle of our century.

Like *The Catcher in the Rye,* the other works in this grouping give personal accounts of the process of coming of age in diverse cultures.

Camara Laye's *The Dark Child* and Wole Soyinka's *Aké* are autobiographies by contemporary African authors, both of which recount their growing up amid conflicting influences of traditional African and Western cultures. Readers can readily relate these accounts to those of Maya Angelou, who narrates her early days in Stamps, Arkansas, where she learns from her black teachers to love literature but is expected by white school administrators to pursue a career in home economics. Readers can also connect these works with the painful experiences of Maxine Hong Kingston, who struggles to correlate her Chinese American identity and traditions with those of the "white ghosts" who are her school teachers and social workers. These readings could be accompanied by journal assignments in which students are asked to record some of their own feelings, experiences, and ideas, and to write occasional autobiographical sketches in something of the manner of Angelou or of Kingston. Such assignments, which can make world literature seem less remote and impersonal, may also serve the goals of value clarification and of increased self-awareness. In addition, they may prepare students for the more formally structured and less personally accessible assignments which might follow. (The bibliographic essay at the end of Section I of this book explores more fully such possibilities for the classroom use of personal writing from diverse cultures.)

"The Heroic Quest"

Another group of readings, such as those discussed in Section II of this book, could include ancient and modern treatments of the heroic quest. To traditional texts such as *Gilgamesh* and *The Odyssey,* one might add the West African tale, *Sundiata.* Originating in the thirteenth century, the work relates the miraculous conception and birth of a legendary ruler, Sundiata, to the hunchbacked Buffalo Woman and the Lion King. It recounts his youthful trials as a despised and crippled stepchild and his eventual defeat of those who have usurped his rightful place as king of Mali. The heroic pattern of separation from homeland, initiation through trials and hardships, and eventual triumphant return to homeland are clearly evident in *Sundiata* as well as in the other works mentioned above. In later periods, this same quest can also be examined in works such as Cervantes' *Don Quixote* and Voltaire's *Candide,* and, still later, in modern variants of the hero's journey of achievement and self-definition. Here one might include Toni Morrison's *Song of Solomon,* Ralph Ellison's *Invisible Man,* and Mexican novelist Juan Rulfo's *Pedro Paramo*. A final choice might be *The Memoirs of a Survivor* by Doris Lessing, a book which relates the quest of a middle-aged woman in a deteriorating futuristic society to discover her essential self by revisiting scenes from her early life in a kind of dream world beyond or within the walls of her London apartment. Each of these modern works depicts a quest for identity through an exploration of personal history and of the history of family, race, or gender. (The bibliographic essay in Section II of this book gives further suggestions for ways of bringing together heroic works from many cultures.)

"The Ruler and the Ruled"

In such a thematic course, one might then turn to works which explore various forms of power relationships, of ruler and ruled. These readings could begin with selected works such as Euripides's *Hippolytus* and Ibsen's *Hedda Gabler,* then progress to works such as Toni Morrison's *Sula,* Japanese novelist Yasunari Kawabata's *Snow Country* and *Thousand Cranes,* Doris Lessing's "To Room 19," Margaret Atwood's *A Handmaid's Tale,* and Alice Walker's *Possessing the Secret of Joy.* Each of these works explores questions of gender roles, of inner and outer identities, of reason and emotion, emphasizing the tragic waste of human potential which results from the denial or the "silencing" of such "feminine" traits as emotion and intuition when these conflict with predetermined social roles. (For a fuller consideration of such issues, see Sections II and V of this book.)

"Colonialism"

As suggested in Section IV of this book, another sequence could be works such as Shakespeare's *The Tempest* and Wole Soyinka's *Death and the King's Horseman,* which provide contrasting but complementary studies of colonialism, while on another level they explore the possibilities for growth and renewal through the process of death and regeneration or, as Soyinka puts it, "transition" (Author's Note, *Death and the King's Horseman*). Readers can relate the transformation suggested in Ariel's song:

> Full fathom five thy father lies,
>   Of his bones are coral made;

> Those are pearls that were his eyes:
> Nothing about him that doth fade
> But doth suffer a sea-change
> Into something rich and strange.
>
> (I. ii. 396–401)

to the transformation which Soyinka's hero anticipates through the death of his father, who, as the king's horseman, is expected to sacrifice his own life when the old king dies. To this grouping one might add Mexican author Carlos Fuentes's *The Death of Artemio Cruz,* a work which powerfully and intricately examines the dangers of exploitation and cruelty and the possibilities for renewal and liberation which the post-colonial experience holds for an individual and for an entire culture. These dangers are also explored in the *Dance of the Forests* and *Kongi's Harvest* by Soyinka as well as in *Going Down River Road* by Mwangi. Such writers are strongly aware that these dangers can be avoided and renewal achieved only if the protagonists and other members of their societies can cease blindly to emulate their conquerors and can find the courage to rediscover their own best selves. (A wide range of works dealing with colonialism and post-colonialism is suggested in the bibliographic essay in Section IV of this book.)

"Culture and the 'Other' "

In such a thematically organized course one might also address the theme of cultural conflicts and of our human tendency to dehumanize the "other," the aliens of any society, as variously presented in Shakespeare's *The Merchant of Venice,* Flannery O'Connor's "The Displaced Person," Chinua Achebe's *Things Fall Apart,* and Alice Walker's *The Color Purple.* Each of these works includes a religious conflict in which missionaries of one sort or another try, by force or persuasion, to convert the "heathen or barbarians" of another faith. In Shakespeare's *The Merchant of Venice,* the despised Shylock seeks revenge on his oppressors. In Flannery O'Connor's "The Displaced Person," a group of farm workers are psychologically threatened by and in turn conspire to destroy a Polish refugee whose Catholicism is suspect because, as one worker puts it, "none of the foolishness had been reformed out of it" (O'Connor [1953] 1981, 198). The Christians of Achebe's *Things Fall Apart* and of Alice Walker's *The Color Purple* are also guilty of the worst sort of religious chauvinism in attacking the religions of traditional African tribal belief. Ultimately, each of these works calls upon its readers in some manner to envision another plane of being in which oppressed and oppressor alike are freed of their "mind-forg'd manacles" and can realize more fully their own humanity through acknowledging that of others, a world in which, as Gonzalo says at the end of *The Tempest,* each man has himself again "when no man was his own" (5.1.213). Portia in *The Merchant of Venice* pleads eloquently for "the quality of mercy" (4.1.184). When O'Connor's farm owner complains of the outcast Polish immigrant, "He didn't have to come here," the visiting priest, speaking at cross purposes, not of the immigrant, but of a beautiful peacock which to him symbolizes Christ, replies, "He came to redeem us" (O'Connor [1953] 1981, 226). Thus readers realize that this redemption has been a possibility all along if the characters could achieve the larger vision and empathy for the Polish outcast which would free them from the paranoia which displaces them. Celie, in Alice Walker's *The Color Purple,* perhaps most clearly attains this larger vision which allows for growth and renewal. Freed of her oppressive views of religion in which God is an old white man, and of her rigid notions of sex and race, she can address her final letter to "Dear God. Dear stars, dear trees, dear sky, dear peoples. Dear everything. Dear God" (Walker 1983, 249).

Despite this emphasis on a wider vision, however, each of these works also reflects some of the limited perspectives of its author's time and place. Modern readers will rightly note Gonzalo's use of generic masculine references as evidence of a phallocentric world, and they will debate the degree to which Shakespeare allows a "space" for the colonized Caliban. Students will certainly acknowledge that Shakespeare's "Christians" in *The Merchant of Venice* are guilty of the worst sort of anti-semitism, that Flannery O'Connor's white characters refer repeatedly to the black farm workers as lazy, childlike "niggers," and that Alice Walker's black characters regard whites as stereotypical rednecks or pampered southern belles. Nor is it clear that these authors entirely repudiate such prejudices and stereotypes. However, the thematic grouping of works from diverse times and cultures relieves us somewhat from the impossible quest for "pure" works. Despite their immense capacity for humane sympathies, our greatest authors are not independent of their own cultural framework.

A Caution for Course Designers

Critics will undoubtedly warn that in bringing together works from such diverse cultures we too are culture bound and thus are in danger of essentializing or of homogenizing other cultures into our own vision of the world. Concerns about the dangers of too quickly assuming an understanding of persons of different cultures without adequate background in historical and cultural contexts are certainly valid. In teaching the West African epic, *The Sundiata,* for example, teachers and students can readily identify the basic elements of the familiar heroic pattern in which the hero confronts and eventually overcomes evil forces. However, to understand the particular ways in which good and evil are conceived in this society, they will also need to understand the importance of Islamic influences, as well as the importance of traditional African beliefs concerning kinship with nature, the unity of the spiritual and the temporal realms, and strong fatalism. In responding to Sundiata's polygamous family structure, readers will also need to understand both African and Islamic concepts of polygamy. Without such concepts, readers might not realize that the hostile acts of the stepmother Sassouma Berete are a distortion of expected behavior in a polygamous society in which the oldest wife should support and nurture the children of her co-wives and that, according to the moral beliefs of her culture, she is wrong to contest what the universe has already decreed (Sarr).

Similarly, students of Murasaki's novel *The Tale of Genji* or of Sei Shonagon's *The Pillow Book* will want to consult works such as *The World of the Shining Prince* in which Ivan Morris gives an excellent discussion of the relationship of these texts to the history and culture of the Japanese Heian Age. By providing such needed resources, teachers can enhance their students' discovery of new worlds and new concepts reflected in heroic adventures such as those in *The Sundiata.*

Moreover, it is likely that many contemporary students need as much help with contextualizing Shakespeare as with contextualizing Soyinka, and, in fact, studying the two together will help to make students more aware of the impact of historical and cultural frameworks on both authors. In studying *The Tempest,* readers need to understand the voyage literature which influenced Shakespeare's play; in studying *Death and the King's Horseman,* readers will be helped by a knowledge of the recurring African narratives about the native "been to" who returns to his community transformed by travels in Europe or America. Students of Shakespeare need information about the Elizabethan theater, just as readers of Soyinka will be enlightened by knowledge of the total-theater traditions from the Yoruba tribe in Southwest Nigeria. However, with proper attention to contextualizing, bringing works from diverse cultures into traditional literary courses can help us to understand more clearly and fully the underlying human obsessions which are reflected in all literature.

Especially helpful in making readers conscious of the interplay of particular cultural contexts with these underlying human concerns are works in which the authors are themselves grounded in both the pains and the rewards of multicultural experience. The value of reading personal accounts given by Maxine Hong Kingston and Maya Angelou in conjunction with works by Wole Soyinka and Camara Laye has already been touched on. Clustering such works by Chinese American, Hispanic American, or African American writers with works by writers from colonized areas of Africa or India will help to dramatize the importance of understanding cultural differences, especially in the context of various forms of oppression. Such clusters should also help to underscore the rich life to be gained from multicultural experiences.

Judith Ortiz Cofer writes of the pain and also the rewards of living alternately in the embrace of a lively extended family in a rural Puerto Rican village and in an isolated nuclear family in an immigrant tenement house in New Jersey. In an impressive *tour de force,* she depicts some of the same situations and characters in three different genres. Her volume of poems, *Terms of Survival,* deals with many of the experiences reflected in her autobiographical sketches in *Silent Dancing.* Her novel, *The Line of the Sun,* is the life story of the wild and mysterious Guzman, a kind of mythical figure, who in his youth defies society's small-minded pressures to conform, but who in maturity returns to his family seeking renewal and reconciliation. Readers of *Silent Dancing* will recognize in this work, narrated by Guzman's niece, many of the events from Ortiz Cofer's own life, reshaped and embroidered into fiction. All three books deal with the pain and trauma of multicultural identity, but together the books also testify to the richness of Ortiz Cofer's experiences and especially to the vital role of storytelling in providing, as her title suggests, the "terms of survival" for herself and others.

These books might well be taught in conjunction with Doris Lessing's *Children of Violence* series, in which Lessing draws heavily on her own life to depict the personal development of the heroine Martha Quest in the context of her early life in Colonial Rhodesia and of her later experiences in England. Lessing concludes her heroine's personal odyssey in the visionary work, *The Four-Gated City,* also with an international, intercultural setting.

Both Maxine Hong Kingston and Maya Angelou have also written a series of books based on personal experience in which they depict the challenges faced by individuals growing up in the context of cultural contrasts and conflicts. Like the authors mentioned above, these writers stress the power of storytelling as a cultural bridge and as a means of survival. At the end of *The Woman Warrior,* in a chapter entitled "A Song for a Barbarian Reed Pipe," Kingston writes of a legendary poetess who in years of exile among the barbarians learned to express her sadness and her anger in high clear songs suited for the "barbarian" flutes. When she was ransomed and brought back to her Chinese homeland, she brought her music with her. Kingston writes, "One of the three [songs] that has been passed down to us is 'Eighteen Stanzas for a Barbarian Reed Pipe,' a song that Chinese sing to their own instruments." She adds, "It translated well" (242–43).

Maya Angelou also writes of the importance of poetry for African Americans, who "survive in direct relationship to the dedication of our poets (include preachers, musicians and blues singers)" (156). In addition, Angelou praises the triumphs of black women in mastering a multicultural environment. Marvelling at her Arkansas-bred grandmother's adjustment to life in Los Angeles, she writes:

> An old Southern Negro woman who had lived her life under the left breast of her community learned to deal with white landlords, Mexican neighbors and Negro strangers. . . . She, who had never been more than fifty miles from her birthplace, learned to traverse the maze of Spanish-named streets in that enigma that is Los Angeles. (*Caged Bird* 1971, 171)

In *I Know Why the Caged Bird Sings* (1971), Angelou writes wistfully of the grandmother's "solid air packed around her like cotton" (172), and comments that the strength of such formidable black women "is an inevitable outcome of the struggle won by survivors and deserves respect if not enthusiastic acceptance" (231).

Angelou suggests that her own association with a motley group of "homeless children, the silt of war frenzy," who survived together in a used car lot in L. A., served to initiate her "into the brotherhood of man" (216). She writes, "After hunting down unbroken bottles and selling them with a white girl from Missouri, a Mexican girl from Los Angeles and a Black girl from Oklahoma, I was never again to sense myself so solidly outside the pale of the human race" and adds, "our ad hoc community influenced me, and set a tone of tolerance for life" (216).

Other works which might be added to such a grouping include *How the Garcia Girls Lost Their Accents* by Julia Alvarez, who came to America from the Dominican Republic, and *The Mambo Kings Play Songs of Love* by Cuban American Oscar Hijuelos. Grounded in personal experience, these books depict the multicultural experiences of young Hispanic Americans, and together they provide readers with the complementary perspectives of Alvarez's female and Hijuelos's male protagonists. To these selections we might add *The Shadowlines* by Amitav Ghosh, a book which moves back and forth between London and Calcutta, giving the family history of a narrator born in India and educated in London.

In reading these works, we realize that, despite the pain the authors have faced in struggling for multicultural identity, they have been enriched by the process. We realize also that, as Reed Way Dasenbrock suggests, the process of reaching for multicultural awareness enriches us as well, enlarging and changing our frame of reference (13). As Robert Penn Warren would be quick to note, in addition to extending our understandings of others, such works ultimately bring us back to ourselves with heightened and deepened understanding of our own problems and possibilities. Thus readers will be able to acknowledge the power of literary texts, admittedly culture-bound in many ways, to aid us in our quest for human dignity and enlargement, not only through appreciation of the individual worlds men and women have created at particular times and places, but also through ever-renewed concern with what Thomas Greene has called the "underlying obsessions" of men and women—to show, in Arthur Miller's phrase, that "attention must be finally paid" (328).

Thematic groupings such as those proposed in this book may be especially effective in demonstrating this power. Certainly, there are pitfalls in such thematic clusters: teachers must be careful to avoid the trivializing which could reduce Oedipus Rex or King Lear to characters who need family counseling, and we must be careful not to ignore the historical and cultural contexts of such works. If judiciously handled, however, thematic groups can free us of the trap of prescribed canons and coverage and can allow the imaginative teacher endless possibilities for variation and discovery.

References

Achebe, Chinua. *Things Fall Apart.* New York: Fawcett, 1985.

Alberson, Hazel S. "Non-Western Literature in the World Literature Program." In *The Teaching of World Literature: Proceedings of the Conference at the University of Wisconsin, April 24–25, 1959,* edited by Haskell M. Block, 45–52. Chapel Hill: University of North Carolina Press, 1960.

Alvarez, Julia. *How the Garcia Girls Lost Their Accents.* Chapel Hill, NC: Algonquin Books of Chapel Hill, 1991.

Angelou, Maya. *Gather Together in My Name.* New York: Random House, 1974.

———. *The Heart of a Woman.* New York: Random House, 1981.

————. *I Know Why the Caged Bird Sings.* New York: Bantam, 1971.

————. *Singin', Swingin' and Gettin' Merry Like Christmas.* New York: Bantam, 1985.

Atwood, Margaret. *The Handmaid's Tale.* New York: Fawcett, 1986.

Blake, William. "London," "And Did Those Feet," "Holy Thursday I." In *The Norton Anthology of World Masterpieces,* 5th ed., edited by Maynard Mack et al., 571–76. New York: W. W. Norton, 1985.

Brooks, Gwendolyn. "Boy Breaking Glass." In *The Norton Anthology of Modern Poetry.* Edited by Richard Ellman and Robert O'Clair. 978–79. New York: Norton, 1988.

Cervantes Saavedra, Miguel de. *Don Quixote.* New York: New American Library, 1965.

Cofer, Judith Ortiz. *The Line of the Sun.* Athens: University of Georgia Press, 1989.

————. *Silent Dancing: A Partial Remembrance of a Puerto Rican Childhood.* Houston, TX: Arte Publico Press, 1990.

————. *Terms of Survival.* Houston: Arte Publico Press, 1987.

Dasenbrock, Reed Way. "Understanding Others: Teaching Multicultural Literature." *Multicultural Readings.* Urbana, IL: NCTE, n.d.

Ellison, Ralph. *Invisible Man.* New York: Random House, 1989.

Euripides. *Hippolytus.* Translated by David Greene. In *Euripides: Four Tragedies,* vol. I. Edited by David Greene and Richmond Lattimore. Chicago: University of Chicago Press, 1955.

Fuentes, Carlos. *The Death of Artemio Cruz.* Translated by Sam Hileman. New York: Farrar, Straus, & Giroux, 1964.

Ghosh, Amitav. *The Shadow Lines.* New York: Penguin, 1990.

Goodman, Ellen. "Fuss Over JFK Is Generational." In Birmingham *News/Post Herald.* 4 Jan. 1992: C-2.

Greene, Thomas. Address to the Participants in NEH Institute: The Theory and Teaching of World Literature. Amherst, MA, June 15–July 24, 1987.

Hunter, J. Paul. *New Worlds of Literature.* New York: W. W. Norton, 1989.

Hijuelos, Oscar. *The Mambo Kings Play Songs of Love.* New York: Harper and Row, 1990.

Homer. *The Odyssey.* Translated by Robert Fitzgerald. New York: Doubleday, 1963.

Ibsen, Henrik. *Hedda Gabler* and *A Doll's House.* Translated by Christopher Hampton. London: Faber and Faber, 1990.

Kawabata Yasunari. *Snow Country.* Translated by Edward G. Seidensticker. New York: Putnam Publishing Group, 1981.

————. *Thousand Cranes.* Translated by Edward G. Seidensticker. New York: Putnam Publishing Group, 1981.

Kingston, Maxine Hong. *The Woman Warrior: Memoirs of a Girlhood Among Ghosts.* New York: Random House, 1977.

————. *China Men.* New York: Knopf, 1980.

————. *Tripmaster Monkey, His Fake Book.* New York: Knopf, 1989.

Laye, Camara. *The Dark Child.* Translated by James Kirkup and Ernest Jones. New York: Farrar, Straus, & Giroux, 1954.

Lessing, Doris. *Children of Violence* series. *Martha Quest.* New York: M. Joseph, 1952. *A Proper Marriage.* New York: M. Joseph, 1954. *A Ripple from the Storm.* New York: M. Joseph, 1958. *Landlocked.* New York: Simon and Shuster, 1966. *The Four-Gated City.* New York: Knopf, 1969.

————. *Memoirs of a Survivor.* New York: Random House, 1988.

————. "To Room 19." In *The Norton Anthology of World Masterpieces,* vol. II, 5th ed., edited by Maynard Mack et al., 2026–57. New York: Norton, 1985.

Levin, Harry. "Core, Canon, Curriculum." *College English* 43, no. 4 (April 1981): 352–62.

MacLeish, Archibald. "A Poet Speaks from the Visitors' Gallery." In *Sound and Sense,* edited by Laurence Perrine. (131). New York: Harcourt Brace and Company, 1952.

Morris, Ivan. *The World of the Shining Prince.* New York: Penguin, 1985.

Morrison, Toni. *Song of Solomon.* New York: New American Library, 1989.

————. *Sula.* New York: New American Library, 1987.

Murasaki, Shikibu. *The Tale of Genji.* Translated by Edward G. Seidensticker. New York: Vintage Books, 1985.

Mwangi, Meja. *Going Down River Road.* Portsmouth, NH: Heinemann, 1976.

Niane, D. T. *The Sundiata.* Translated by G. D. Pickett. Chicago: Longman Trade, 1965.

O'Connor, Flannery. "The Displaced Person" and "The Enduring Chill." In *Flannery O'Connor: The Complete Stories.* New York: Farrar, Straus, & Giroux, 1981.

"Report on World Literature." In *Collected Papers of Participants in the Summer 1987 NEH Institute "Theory and Teaching of World Literature."* Edited by Sarah Lawall. Amherst: University of Massachusetts, 1988.

Rulfo, Juan. *Pedro Paramo.* New York: Grove-Weidenfeld, 1983.

Shakespeare, William. *The Merchant of Venice.* In *The Complete Works.* Rev. ed., edited by Hardin Craig and David Bevington. 256–92. Glenview, IL: Scott Foresman, 1980.

————. *The Tempest.* In *The Complete Works.* Rev. ed., edited by Hardin Craig and David Bevington. 1497–1527. Glenview, IL: Scott Foresman, 1980.

Sarr, Ndiawar. Classroom Lecture. University of Montevallo, 1988.

Shonagon, Sei. *The Pillow Book.* Translated by Ivan Morris. New York: Penguin, 1971.

Spender, Stephen. "An Elementary Classroom in a Slum." In *An Approach to Literature.* Edited by Cleanth Brooks, John Purser, and Robert Penn Warren. 386–87. New York: Meredith Publishing Company.

Soyinka, Wole. *Aké, The Years of Childhood.* New York: Random House, 1989.

————. "Author's Note." In *Death and the King's Horseman.* New York: Hill and Wang, 1975.

———. *Dance of the Forests.* Oxford: Oxford University Press, 1963.

———. *Death and the King's Horseman.* New York: Hill and Wang, 1987.

———. *Kongi's Harvest.* Oxford: Oxford University Press, 1967.

Swift, Jonathan. *A Tale of a Tub and The Battle of the Books.* Edited by Robert Folkenflik. In *The Mind of Man* series. Malibu, CA: J. Simon, 1979.

Voltaire. *Candide.* Translated by John Butt. New York: Penguin, 1950.

Walker, Alice. *The Color Purple.* New York: Washington Square Press, 1983.

———. *In Search of Our Mothers' Gardens: Womanist Prose.* New York: Harcourt Brace Jovanovich, 1984.

———. *Possessing the Secret of Joy.* New York: Harcourt Brace Jovanovich, 1992.

———. *The Temple of My Familiar.* New York: Harcourt Brace Jovanovich, 1989.

Warren, Robert Penn. "Why Do We Read Fiction?" In *An Approach to Literature,* 4th ed. Edited by Cleanth Brooks et al., 553–58. New York: Meredith Publishing Company, 1964.

Woolf, Virginia. *A Room of One's Own.* New York: Harcourt Brace Jovanovich, 1981.

I Private Worlds: The Value of Teaching Diaries, Autobiographies, Letters, and Other Forms of Personal Expression

The essays in this section discuss the value of personal writing as a means of self-discovery and self-definition. Ronald Ayling suggests that for those who have been marginalized by various forms of authority, personal writing becomes a way of asserting a self in contrast with that prescribed by the dominant culture, ideology, or power structure. Dorothy Grimes considers personal writing as a tool for the "womanist" articulation of self. The contributors suggest that readers, as well as authors, experience the personal empowerment and saving potential of life narratives. According to Grimes, "Books allow individual choices: a way of developing the inner voice." The bibliographic essay explores some of the many choices available to teachers and students, giving special attention to personal accounts of childhood, to the voices of those who contend with personal and social oppression and abuse, and to the voices of women.

4 Colonial Encounters of an Autobiographical Kind: Bringing the Personal Voices of Sean O'Casey and Wole Soyinka to the Literature Classroom

Ronald Ayling
University of Alberta

There has never been more interest in life-writings (that is, narratives of autobiographical or biographical intent) than there is at the present moment, both by the general public and the learned community alike. Indeed, it could be argued that life-writings are now more popular than fiction in general in many English-speaking countries, and if we pause to consider that many of the most popular novels are those with an autobiographical or biographical flavour, then this orientation is even more obviously manifest.

Given the wide scope and diverse nature of life-writings, it is hardly surprising that there can be a great number of productive critical approaches to their better understanding and appreciation—of which the present exercise is but one—and that they can provide excellent and varied material for teaching purposes for pupils of all levels, from a very young age up to advanced graduate seminars. A useful monograph detailing many of the more obvious advantages in using lives, whether actual or fictional, in secondary school teaching, is that produced by Margaret Fleming and Jo McGinnis for the National Council of Teachers of English (Fleming and McGinnis 1985).

Students of all ages can appreciate and even identify with the real-life or fictional adventures of children or young people growing up in a world often difficult to apprehend, let alone fully comprehend. Pedagogically, the field of colonial childhood writings affords a rich and relatively easily accessible topic for students. One cannot think of a single worthwhile childhood autobiography, from however remote a region or linguistic group, that does not strike a responsive chord in readers of both sexes. Imaginative accounts of actual childhood experience can convey the same deep-rooted capacity for self-identification and empathy for the reader that their better-known fictional counterparts embody. The enduring popularity of *David Copperfield, The Adventures of Huckleberry Finn,* and (despite various censorship campaigns by over-zealous educational authorities) *The Catcher in the Rye* are clearly relevant in this context. In nonfictional as well as fictional narratives, we also find a rich field of experience in non-canonical writings from the newer literatures in English, whether African, Asian, Caribbean, Australian, New Zealander, or Canadian. Because these countries have experienced somewhat similar patterns of colonial dependency followed by revolt or reaction (not always as violent or warlike as that undertaken by the United States or, early in this century, Ireland), we can observe a great number of thematic similarities in what appear to be vastly different or disparate cultures. And the eventual outcome of achieved independence—or apparent independence in the case of countries still undergoing neocolonial dependency, whether they are consciously aware of that status or not—is as various and unpredictable as that accomplished by individuals once they have cut themselves loose from parental authority and support.

Childhood and Colonialism

Colonial childhood autobiography may perhaps usefully be approached as something of a subgenre in its own right. As a child's situation is, in certain respects, comparable to that of a colonized subject in a state with little or no autonomy for its indigenous people(s), so one can see the analogy to be meaningful for political dissection in the creation of narratives exploring the evolution of a young man or woman's mind and sensibility. Indeed, the parallels with patriarchal oppression for a young woman can also be explored in this context. Certainly, the subject matter of many colonial autobiographies, whether or not they are consciously critical of the powers-that-be in their community, allows negative and constrictive features of colonialism to be personally apprehended and understood by all readers, irrespective of gender, nationality, race, or social environment. Who is there among us who has not at some stage of infancy, youth, or adolescence, harboured a grudge or resentment—if not open rebellion—against authority?

If memoirs of childhood frequently evoke a sense of wonder and are characterized by lyrical intensity, just as often they evince a sense of alienation and questioning of the status quo. However conservative the narrator may be, and however favourably disposed he may be to the norms of the community in which he lives, it is impossible to conceive of anyone worthy of appearing in fiction or autobiography who will not have rebelled (or reacted) against the values and judgments of those responsible for his upbringing. Often, this has nothing to do with politics or morality, save in the sense that all human relationships are political and invoke moral valuation. Because adult values are vastly different from those of a child and frequently seem unfair or even nonsensical in that child's eyes, there are bound to be considerable disagreements with, and dissent from, the judgments of one's elders; not infrequently, such conflict leads to a comic resolution, but heartbreak can also be occasioned by similar strains inevitable in the growing-up process.

Consider, for example, the way in which the six-year-old Sean O'Casey (Johnny Casside in the early sections of *I Knock at the Door*) is forced to commune with himself after an argument with his older brothers and sister that is to his mind conducted unfairly against him. The family, returning home after attending the father's funeral, unite to criticize Johnny, whose mind has been running on death—on the question of "Who killed cock robin?":

> Johnny fell silent. He hated, hated all these people, all, except his mother, with their big heads, big faces, big hands, and big feet. He was angry with them; but they were too big to fight, for one of them could easily stamp him under his big feet. He wanted to spit at them, to answer them back, but he shut his little mouth tight, and answered them never a word. But in his mind he sang, and sang loudly: And the birds of the air went a-sighing and a-sobbing when they heard of the death of poor cock robin, when they heard of the death of poor cock robin. If his dad was as happy as they were eager to make out, getting warmed up again in Abraham's bosom, and sure of everything going where he was gone, why did they all sit so still and stiff and stony? How they all loved to cheat a kid out of anything he had a thought to do. And anyhow, if they only knew. Who killed cock robin was a funeral song, wasn't it? Of course it was, of course it was. (O'Casey 1970, 58)

Similarly, in Wole Soyinka's *Aké: The Years of Childhood* an even younger narrator feels compelled to blurt out: "I was overwhelmed by only one fact—there was neither justice nor logic in the world of grown-ups" (104). *Aké*, in realizing subjectively the child's viewpoint and his undoubted sense of logic and justice (according to his own lights), graphically demonstrates the incompatibility of the values of the two worlds; more than this, it concretely realizes that vast and seemingly unbridgeable gulf that yawns between the two scales of evaluation.

In the circumstances, the child rebels—in words or deeds or, more often than either, just in his thoughts. Both Wole and his younger brother Fermi decide on various occasions to leave home, to walk away from a household whose grown-up inhabitants (and arbiters) do not appear to understand or appreciate them for the individuals that they are.

Such rebellion is in opposition to an all-powerful law enforcer (or enforcers) against whose edicts the child has little or no recourse or defense, save the occasional support of another adult family member whose pleas for forgiveness on the child's behalf by their very nature assume the guilt of the "offender" and thus show the adult defender's allegiance to the oppressor's worldviews. In some cases, moreover, the connection between being a child and being a colony is more than mere analogy, and it is no accident that a good deal of African literature, following (though not necessarily consciously so) many Anglo-Irish precedents, should be of this type. Many of these writings, while primarily concerned with the growth in self-awareness and knowledge of the world of one or more individuals, reflect even larger evolutionary patterns. The heroes' or protagonists' progress through life and their education, formal and informal alike, mirror somewhat similar patterns discernible in the development of emergent nations too—before, during, and after independence—so that the theme, in some writings, may well attain political, social, and even ideological dimensions that transcend the individual's personal story. Readers can apprehend the experience on both the private and the public levels, and those who have never lived through anything remotely approaching the conditions and travails of a colonized subject can yet identify with those aspects that correspond to a powerless child subjected to limitless and unanswerable, as well as often seemingly irrational, authority. In this way, although autobiographies of childhood may constitute a distinct genre (Coe 1984), they nevertheless have much to say to adults.

A number of fictionalized autobiographies created in recent years have shown the colonized individual and his society victimized by the system and the various agencies that it uses or which naturally operate—as in the case of various religious bodies and missionary organizations—to further the value systems of the "imperialistic powers." *A Portrait of the Artist as a Young Man* is the classic archetype, of course. Though, as a student, Joyce's protagonist eschews any kind of political commitment, even signing nationalist petitions at the university, the book of his life—like his life itself—shows itself to be shaped by forces such as church, state, and family commitment, against which he feels compelled to react. He eventually comes to the realization that, in his art, he can (and, indeed, he *must*) fly beyond the nets set by the established authorities to confine and restrict his free spirit. Stephen

Daedalus (who himself uses the word "revolt" to characterize his reaction) knows that, beginning with his parents and closely followed by his clerical teachers, almost all his education has sought to control every aspect of his personal and social being (Joyce [1916] 1967, 247). Joyce's novel, in its attempts to understand and come to terms with the forces of nationality, language, and religion, and in its highly subjective method of realizing the conflicts arising from such "imperialistic" pressures and seeking to resolve them, offers one extreme of rebellion in the realm of "colonial" childhood autobiography.

Various spiritual confessions such as those by Saint Augustine and Cardinal Newman can be seen, with variations, as the other extreme— that of ideological acceptance or acquiescence—and no doubt certain Marxist parallels to them could be found, though here the emphasis on the necessity for individual submission to authority would probably be less individuated in the final analysis, less subjectively focused.

The Child's Questions

If it is granted that there are significant similarities in the inherent contradictions and internal tensions consonant with childhood and colonial experience, will the inevitable limitations to a child's political vision raise insurmountable difficulties in the way of using childhood autobiography for critical or exploratory purposes? (Questions stemming from this apparent dilemma can make for interesting seminar debate in advanced classes.) Unless the recollections are consciously presented from the hindsight of later understanding, it would seem that the child's ignorance must forestall any serious revaluation of the past. Yet quite the opposite can be observed from the finest examples of colonial childhood autobiography, whether the opening segment of *Tell Freedom* by Peter Abrahams (much of the first two sections of the three-part self-portrait by the South African novelist), *Aké* by Wole Soyinka, or *I Knock at the Door* by Sean O'Casey (and much of *Pictures in the Hallway,* the second of O'Casey's six autobiographical books). Indeed, in these examples that very lack of knowledge, allied to the natural curiosity of childhood, gives rise to a compelling interrogation of everything that surrounds and affects the youthful protagonist (this is another pedagogical device, akin to Socratic practice, that allows for rapport between student and teacher); nothing is sacrosanct or beyond fundamental examination starting from first principles.

The cumulative questions of a youngster, ultimately exasperating even to the most patient of parents, is a device used brilliantly by both

O'Casey and Soyinka to realize most graphically that infuriating nagging insistence of youth to find out things despite the sustained resistance of the older and supposedly wiser world. It is precisely the ignorance of the grown-ups—often about the most fundamental of questions regarding the origins of life and the universe, the existence of God, and the future for humankind and, naturally, for the questioner and his or her family—that make them most annoyed. Eventually, they are forced to acknowledge—if only to themselves—that they really have no reliable answers to such questions nor have any absolute authority to which they may turn, though various scientific hypotheses and religious beliefs attempt to provide some framework of reference. That science and religion do not in any completely satisfying manner answer many of our most insistent questions—for when one answer is provided almost always another one or two unanswerable questions arise in company with it—affords a worrying reality about which the younger generation often reminds its elders, usually without itself realizing just how fundamentally disconcerting the experience can be for them.

Certainly, O'Casey's manner of presenting the young Johnny's persistent queries about all manner of trivial and significant questions, accompanied as they are by his practical habits of enquiry (he will never rely on book learning as the sole means of acquiring knowledge), enables us to see that such innocent self-education is what will make him as both a man and an artist unafraid to question and to criticize all forms of human activity and all manner of authority. What is more, as realized in the scene of the family party returning from the father's funeral in the seventh chapter of *I Knock at the Door* ("We All Go the Same Way Home"), the reaction of family members to the boy's questioning affords considerable insight into their individual characters and his subsequent relationships with them. The surface irritability and the underlying family tensions—between mother and the older children as well as between the latter themselves—are subtly evoked as the following extract illustrates, though the full effect is dependent upon the lengthy buildup that precedes it. Young Johnny's naive interest is not really in the aesthetic discrimination of God, of course, but in the colour and beauty that may be found in even the most appalling of urban environments. Despite his weak eyesight (or perhaps because of it) he appreciates the primary colours of nature and will grow up to make symbolic use of them in his mature dramatic work:

> —But I don't think He cares a lot for blue, Mother, for there's only the violets and the bluebells—but I forgot about the sky, the blue of the sky that's everywhere on a fine day. He must be specially fond of blue, mustn't He, Mother?

—What about a cup of tea, or something, said Archie, and never mind the colour choice of God?

—Lay the table, Ella, said the mother, and we'll have some tea, an egg each, and some cold meat that's left over.

—He seems to cotton on a good deal, too, to white, went on Johnny; for look at the daisies, the hawthorn, and the clouds. Curious that God likes white. Why does He like white—it's not much of a colour, is it Mother? And black, too, for look at the dark night; but then He always softens that a little with a golden moon or the silver stars.

—Oh, chuck it, Johnny, chuck it, boy, broke in Michael, who felt uncomfortable, as they all did, with the name of God dangling around; half an hour's enough with God for one day. . . .

His mother went over to Johnny, and, bending down, whispered to him, Keep quiet, Johnny, and some other time when no one but ourselves is here, we'll talk of all those things.

Johnny turned away from her, full up of a feeling to cry, but he shut his teeth together tight, and looked out of the window at the redness of the sun in the sky over the house opposite, making the roofs of the houses look like polished bronze. Big heads, big hands, big feet, big voices, bitter snap and bitter snarl. If he was only up to their size, or they down to his, he'd give them snarl for snap and snap for snarl. (O'Casey [1939] 1970, 60–61)

Soyinka's autobiography somewhat similarly depicts a household of parents, adult relatives, brother and sister driven almost demented by the young lad's continual "interrogations" and his almost legalistic querying of statements made by others. His belief in his own cleverness ("Yes, they had missed the point; I was confident, as usual, that I had discovered the loophole in their argument" [53]) is one which we are meant to laugh at and enjoy—yet to understand that, on a more ambitious (and dangerous) stage in the future, such an attitude of self-righteous egotism blended with genius would contribute to make him both a daring experimental artist and a courageous satirist of brutal tyranny. At the same time, we can wholeheartedly sympathize with the boy's mother, who at one point snaps at her tolerant schoolmaster husband, known familiarly as "Essay" because his initials are "S. A.":

"I'll leave him to plague you with his arguments. In any case he only embarrasses me at the shop with all his foolish questions. Why is your stomach bigger than my father's? Are you pregnant like the organist? Yes, that's the sort of thing he asks, in case no one has told you."

"Really." His mouth opened wide with laughter. "When was this?"

"Ask him. He's your son. Omo, let's go. My customers are waiting." She gave the maid a shove and was gone from the house.

> I stayed on the spot. Essay's laughter did not mean that there
> was definitely no reprimand to come. (Soyinka 1983, 56)

It is inevitable that there should be much in common—socially, psychologically, and aesthetically—as well as much that is wildly different in the autobiographical writings about childhood by Sean O'Casey and Wole Soyinka. *I Knock at the Door*, an account of the first twelve, largely grim, years of O'Casey's life, is set in the Dublin slums; the period covered is from 1880 to 1891 or thereabouts. The full title of Wole Soyinka's autobiography—*Aké: The Years of Childhood*—accurately sums up the book's locale and compass, that is, memories associated with life in a Christian parsonage in the market town of Aké, in Western Nigeria over the first decade of his existence from 1934 to 1944 or so. There are swift glances forward—to the late 1950s and 1960s—and, to start with, occasional backward glances too, to a period before the boy's birth, but the primary focus is upon the often idyllic pastoral world of Aké and its surrounding Yoruba countryside in Egbaland immediately before and during the Second World War.

Conflict in Parallel Cases

Each of these works is projected, first and foremost, as a work of art in its own right; each has a clear but not unambiguous colonial context. Both considerations provide fascinating similarities in writings that, to all outward appearances, appear to be radically dissimilar works. At first sight, indeed, the only elements in common would seem to be that the two authors grew up to become well-known (and equally controversial) dramatists, though both also assayed a variety of other literary genres; that the chronological scope of each book should be the first decade or so of its author's life; and that the language of communication in each case is English though both authors belonged (during the periods covered by the narratives) to colonized peoples whose native language is not English. Artistically, however, there are many further illuminating parallels in these autobiographies. Both give memorable portraits of parents, relatives, and a number of neighbourhood characters (including several eccentric figures); they evoke public ritual and ceremonial tribal events, as well as private fantasies and humiliations familiar to most children, and they realize in various striking ways the sights, sounds, tastes, and smells of childhood.

Both *I Knock* and *Aké* recapture graphically yet with compassion examples of what Soyinka calls the "strange cruelties" to be encountered in their childhoods, whether it be the stoning of the pregnant mad-woman, Sorowanke, who lived by the mango tree in the village square at Aké or the tormenting of the itinerant Jewish glazier by Johnny Casside and a group of Dublin slum children in the seventeenth chapter of *I Knock at the Door.* The brief but arresting episode concerning Soyinka's father's brush with death (section eleven) is also reminiscent of the illness of O'Casey's favourite brother Tom in "Death on the Doorstep" (chapter 14 of *Autobiography,* Volume 2). Both incidents are remarkable for the direct and straightforward style on the surface (accompanied by a half-suppressed feeling of mental dread) that builds to a climax swiftly reached and almost casually transformed into an anticlimax by the patient turning the corner in his fight for survival, to be followed by a slow movement of relief: in each case, the narrative pattern clearly reflects a process that is to be found in many a life story.

O'Casey, deprived of a formal education by ill health and extremely bad eyesight, had to battle to acquire a first-rate reading knowledge of English and Gaelic literature (and much besides); Soyinka, though brought up in a relatively privileged and scholarly atmosphere, similarly had to balance the demands of life and of literature. Both authors became enormously well-read and even bookish individuals, admired as such by some friends and acquaintances, and just as heartily detested by others for the same accomplishments. Yet both stress—implicitly, as much as explicitly, in the very texture of their autobiographical writings—the importance of tactile experience, of sensory perceptions, in the education of a writer-to-be. Sights, sounds, tastes, and smells are deliberately emphasized as a significant part of the changing texture of Aké's rich and multifaceted life; brief glances forward to events sub-sequent to the narrator's boyhood reveal a decline in many of the traditional customs and tribal ways of life that, for Soyinka, are symbolized in changing culinary tastes from piquant and varied Yoruba dishes to the homogenized fast foods of McDonald's and Colonel Sanders that have more recently invaded his homeland.

In neither childhood autobiography is the protagonist-narrator, sen-sitive though he may be to physical as well as intellectual matters, projected as an artist, let alone as an author-to-be. Yet readers cannot help but become implicitly conscious of this factor—particularly in the casual yet recurrent emphasis on the importance of words to both protagonists. At the same time, reading both books, we gradually become aware that the autobiographers are also growing up as colonized subjects in the last years of a colonial system against which their writings will eventually but inevitably be pitted—largely in retrospective terms in Soyinka's case, but in active anticolonial struggle as well as postcolonial reassessment for O'Casey. In each case the lads grew up in countries that were colonies of the British Empire and, though both shared some part of the privileged existence of that colonial world (an aspect which has led to some critics of O'Casey as well as Soyinka approaching them—wrongly, I think—as elitist writers), both were even more assuredly part of the exploited mass of colonial peoples within that empire.

It took both writers some years before either of them became fully aware of the magnitude of this exploitation and of their own places within it. Much of the burden of their childhood autobiographies, subterranean at first but increasingly overt as the narratives proceed, is taken up with their growing realization of the theme. O'Casey's family being Protestant, it was ideologically aligned with the ruling class in Dublin, and there are a number of occasions when such an allegiance stands them in good stead in finding a job or in obtaining admission to hospital; when the family declines economically, however, the adolescent boy becomes aware that they have far more in common with the largely destitute Catholic proletariat than with anyone else; it was a revelation that was to stay with him for the rest of his life.

The Dublin of O'Casey's childhood is seen in *I Knock* as a city rent by class consciousness and snobbery at all levels of society. His own family participates in this as naturally as they breathe. A representative instance is the pride Johnny takes in possessing a black fee-paying card for admission for treatment in a medical dispensary, once he has been told that paupers are given documents of a different colour. Although he can be no more than five years of age and, heavily bandaged to protect badly ulcerated eyes, quite unable to see the document himself, "he held the card of admission out so that all could see it was printed in black" (O'Casey [1939] 1970, 30). The irony is extended, by implication, when we realize that the eye specialist's recommendations regarding the boy's diet and his prescription for Parrish's Food suggests that the doctor believes that malnutrition has contributed towards the lad's eye disease. After the father's death, the O'Casey family could not long enjoy even the privilege of paying sixpence per month for Johnny's treatment. Increasingly, his childish questionings—seen initially as comic in effect—quite naturally reveal the, by this time, blatant contradictions in his family's social and religious prejudices. Such exposure is especially apparent in "The Street Sings" and in "The Red Above the Green," where we have his mother admitting in one instance that "his father had said that Parnell was a great Protestant, a great Irishman, and a grand man; and it was a good thing there was someone, anyway, fit to hinder the English from walking over the Irish people" (87) and where, under excited interrogation by him later, she can confess that even Catholic Fenians can, morally, be "quite good" (175). The dialogue continues:

> —Besides, some of the Fenians were Protestants too.
> —But we're not really Irish, Ma; not really, you know, are we?
> —Not Irish? echoed his mother. Of course, we're Irish. What on earth put it into your head that we weren't Irish?
> —One day, an' us playin', Kelly told me that only Catholics were really Irish; an' as we were Protestants, we couldn't be anyway near to the Irish.
> His mother's face reddened and her breath came in little pants.
> —Th' ignorant, cheeky, little Roman Catholic scut! she ejaculated venomously. I could tell the whole seed, breed, and generation of the Kellys that the O'Casside Clan couldn't be more Irish than they are; and that when the Irish ruled in Ireland, the Clan Casside was just as important an' princely as the Clan Kelly.... And Protestants are Catholics, too; not Roman Catholics, but Catholics, pure an' simple; real Irish, without a foreign title like Roman stuck on to it. If your poor father was alive, he'd show you in books solid arguments, never to be gainsaid, that St. Patrick was really as Protestant as a Protestant could be; and that the early Irish didn't hold with many things Roman Catholics now make a part of their creed.... (175–76)

Though Johnny's mother can thus be brought to acknowledge her nationality and, spontaneously though temporarily, to recognize where her true allegiance lies, she will nonetheless die thirty-three years (and three autobiographical volumes) later with a picture of Queen Victoria and another of King William crossing the Boyne still loyally adorning the walls of her wretchedly poor dwelling. That deep and mostly unconscious division within her psyche (and her family's psyche) lies well embedded within her argument in the conversation just quoted, for, while stressing her own deep sense of nationality, she can at the same time denigrate that of her neighbours and fellow-sufferers. Meanwhile, the division within herself is reflected in her sons, two of whom serve for periods in the British Army while the youngest, before finding his vocation as a writer, grows up to become a jobbing labourer on the Irish Railway and a member of the most militant of nationalist and labour organizations; by the time he came to write *I Knock at the Door*, a large part of Ireland—formally independent for eighteen years— was in neocolonial relationship to Britain, and he himself was living in disillusioned exile there.

A somewhat similar pattern may be discerned in Wole Soyinka's case. Black subjects within British Nigeria, his family nonetheless lives

a doubly privileged existence. On the one hand, Wole's grandfather is
a Yoruba chief at Isara, and the family is made much of in that district.
His father, on the other hand, is the much respected headmaster of
Aké's junior high school (part of the district's chain of educational
establishments run by the Anglican church through the medium of
English) and one of the officials responsible for the large Christian
educational community that exists almost like a medieval monastery
in the town. There, Wole is brought up from infancy in English and
Yoruba. As a very small boy he gets lost when he first ventures beyond
this school compound to follow a marching band of black policemen.
There follows an amusing and warmhearted encounter with the first
white man he has seen; the official is amazed not only that such a
small black child can speak English, but that, seeing an English journal
on the man's desk, he can actually claim his own father as a fellow-
subscriber. While there is some condescension on the officer's part, he
is good-natured and kind to the boy, and there is a genuine acknowledgment of a community of shared interest.

The whole incident is lighthearted, and here, as elsewhere to start
with, the white man's rule appears beneficent or invisible. The significance of the final part of *Aké,* however, lies in its seemingly inadvertent
unmasking of indirect colonial rule, when the tribal authorities through
which British rule is administered come into conflict with a genuinely
spontaneous revolt from the rank and file. The white officials immediately—and unquestioningly—line up with a show of force behind
the most reactionary positions of the local black chieftains. We can
then see what political attitudes really exist behind the tolerant exterior
of the white man with his journal and the friendly strains of the local
police band that had earlier acted like those of the pied piper of Hamelin
upon the ears (and feet) of the entranced Wole.

Such revelations justify the substantial scale and compass of the last
part of *Aké.* The final three sections of Soyinka's book, comprising a
sustained narrative of at least sixty-three pages, are primarily concerned
with the formation of the Women's Union in Aké (and then Egbaland
and, we must assume, throughout Nigeria eventually), and its radical
transformation into a movement for social reform that leads to a
militant rebellion by the women of the region. Soyinka, by then ten
years of age, observes the transformation at close quarters—the only
male to do so quite so fully—because he is used by his mother as a
messenger, scout, and courier to the movement. The boy's formal
education is continued during this period, the narrative recording two

visits by him to Ibadan in search of a state scholarship to the colonial administration's Government College in the regional capital. But the primal impulse that drives this culminating section is the lad's informal and indeed inadvertent education in practical politics and in the power of the working people (here, mostly women market vendors and shopkeepers to start with), once their fierce resolution and sense of social injustice is armed by the moral support and practical knowledge provided by sympathetic members of the educated middle class. Soyinka's story is direct and forceful in its narrative thrust, and there is a perceptible sense of social momentum that, once attained, seems to propel events along on a strange and bizarre current—which is even more interesting in that the clash between the women and the tribal elders (supported by the colonial administration) is not resolved one way or the other by the close of the book.

During this final segment of *Aké* the narrator becomes more of an observer on an upstairs balcony than (as in the rest of the narrative) a full-fledged dramatic participant. It is true that he joins in the movement as a very youthful tutor when a drive is made to teach the working women to read and write—O'Casey was to do the same, only later in his life (in his thirties), teaching the Irish language to English-speaking members in the nationalist Gaelic League. The strongest impulse in *Aké,* however, as it is in *I Knock at the Door,* is towards what is perhaps the most significant kind of education: not the knowledge that is gleaned from books (important though they are in both men's lives), but that knowledge which comes from closely and intelligently observing what goes on around one, from grasping a sense of life as it is felt in the pulses and by one's whole being, to be subsequently reflected upon in one's mind and in discussion with others involved in the same or similar experiences. In each case, rebellion is a natural result of one's practical acquaintance with colonial politics, and, indeed, such rebellion is shown as an instinctive as well as intellectual part of that education. It is, surely, a process that all students can relate to in a number of relevant if infinitely diverse particulars in their own apprenticeship to life.

Biographically, for both O'Casey and Soyinka, a potent (but dissimilar) admixture of privilege and deprivation led to dramatic conflict and tension that, while it may have occasioned many personal and familial problems associated with identity and allegiance, also afforded much essential and otherwise unobtainable material for their art, both in dramatic and in autobiographical expression.

References

Coe, Richard E. *When the Grass Was Taller: Autobiography and the Experience of Childhood.* New Haven: Yale University Press, 1984.

Fleming, Margaret, and Jo McGinnis. *Portraits: Biography and Autobiography in the Secondary School.* Urbana, IL: National Council of Teachers of English, 1985.

Joyce, James. *A Portrait of the Artist as a Young Man.* 1916. Reprint. New York: Viking Press, 1967.

O'Casey, Sean. *Autobiography Volume 1: I Knock at the Door.* 1939. Reprint. London: Pan Books, 1970.

———. *Autobiography Volume 2: Pictures in the Hallway.* 1942. Reprint. London: Pan Books, 1971.

Soyinka, Wole. *Aké: The Years of Childhood.* New York: Aventura Books, 1983.

5 Mariama Bâ's *So Long a Letter* and Alice Walker's *In Search of Our Mothers' Gardens:* A Senegalese and an African American Perspective on "Womanism"

Dorothy Grimes
University of Montevallo

Although Alice Walker received a writing fellowship in 1966 to go to Senegal, she went instead to Mississippi, realizing that she "could never live happily in Africa—or anywhere else—until [she] could live freely in Mississippi" (Walker 1983, 163).[1] Walker's recognition that she had to face the obstacles to freedom for her people in her own country—even in her own region of her country—seems an apt metaphor for the message one finds in many of the essays she calls her "womanist prose." Had she gone to Senegal in 1966, however, she might have found a kindred spirit in Senegalese novelist Mariama Bâ (1929–1981).

In fact, critic Abena P. B. Busia has used Walker's term *womanist* to describe what she calls the "novel of the African diaspora." Busia says that within the feminist movement, "our plight as *black* women is symbolically dramatized by Alice Walker's insistence on employing for us the word *womanist,* as distinct from *feminist*" (Busia 1988, 5). Busia singles out the title essay of *In Search of Our Mothers' Gardens,* with its emphasis on "the central place of art . . . as a means of self-expression and survival." She says Walker's "defiant blurring of distinctions" between artist, critic, and subject is "very important" for African women writers, for "in the traditional African context . . . , the artist is an integral part of the community and is expected to be social historian, critic, and commentator" (13). Busia compares Mariama Bâ's *So Long a Letter* with Walker's *The Color Purple,* emphasizing "the reclamation of voice, in particular the stress on *spoken* voice" (14).

Defining Womanism

Reclamation of voice is an important theme in womanist prose, but the term *womanist* itself also suggests much more. In the epigraph to her 1983 collection of essays, *In Search of Our Mothers' Gardens*, Walker gives four related definitions of the term, all of which are playful and richly connotative. The first emphasizes knowledge and responsibility:

> From *womanish*. (Opp. of "girlish," i.e., frivolous, irresponsible, nor serious.). . . Wanting to know more and in greater depth than is considered "good" for one. . . . Responsible. In charge. *Serious.* (xi)

The second emphasizes relationships with others, wholeness, and strength:

> *Also:* A woman who loves other women, sexually and/or nonsexually. Appreciates and prefers women's culture, women's emotional flexibility. . . , and women's strength. Sometimes loves individual men, sexually and/or nonsexually. Committed to survival and wholeness of entire people, male *and* female. . . . Traditionally universalist. . . . Traditionally capable. (xi)

The third not only enumerates the objects of womanist love but notes its unconditional nature: "*Loves* the Spirit. . . . Loves struggle. *Loves* the Folk. Loves herself. *Regardless*" (xii). And the fourth is an analogy apparently intended to capture the texture and intensity of *womanist* as opposed to *feminist:* "Womanist is to feminist as purple to lavender" (xii).

Busia is right in emphasizing the reclamation of voice as a kind of precondition of womanism. Certainly the black woman must reclaim her voice if she is to be "responsible" or "in charge." Throughout the essay collection, Walker calls for voices that both define personal identity and inspire others. In her 1988 review of *Gifts of Power: The Writings of Rebecca Cox Jackson,* Walker describes how Jackson's inner voice led her to break with custom. Her "inner voice" instructed her that "though she might live with her husband and serve him in every other way, she could not indulge in what she termed the 'sin of the fall'" (75). Jackson eventually left her husband and, with her friend Rebecca Perot, ministered to blacks in Philadelphia in the 1870s. The last part of Walker's review is a rebuttal to a "nonblack scholar's attempt to label something lesbian that the black woman in question has not." Walker says that her "own guess is that . . . the two Rebeccas became spiritual sisters *because* they cared little for sex. . . ." Whatever the case, she says that the term *womanist* allows the "naming [of] our own experience after our own fashion . . . [which] in this society may well be our only tangible sign of personal freedom" (80–82). At the same time, Walker calls for voices to inspire reclamation. She speaks of being "called to life" (122) by Martin Luther King, Jr., whose "voice you would recognize sooner than any other voice you heard in this century" (144). In "The Black Writer and the Southern Experience," Walker speaks of the black writer's responsibility to "give voice to centuries not only of silent bitterness and hate but also of neighborly kindness and sustaining love" (21). In her 1971 review of Florence Engel Randall's *The Almost Year,* Walker says, "The artist then is the voice of the people, but she is also The People" (138).

So Long a Letter: Reclaiming a Voice

Mariama Bâ's short epistolary novel, *So Long a Letter,* embodies the reclamation of such a voice. The novel is a letter from Ramatoulaye Fall, a widow still in mourning, to her lifelong friend Aissatou Bâ. Busia appropriately calls the novel "a confessional, self-discovering text" (34). The reader "overhears" a written conversation and thus becomes both participant and confidante. The reader knows from the outset that Ramatoulaye views her composition as no ordinary letter. She begins by acknowledging Aissatou's letter and saying, "By way of reply, I am beginning this diary, my prop in my distress" (Bâ 1981, 1). Although the reader is always aware that Aissatou is the intended audience for the letter, parts of the letter are not addressed directly to her. In Chapter 6, for example, Aissatou herself seems to be among those who overhear: all of the chapter except the first and last paragraphs are addressed to Ramatoulaye's dead husband, Modou Fall. The entire chapter seems a kind of reverie on their courtship and life together. Furthermore, the novel's use of letters within the longer letter creates a kind of interiorized drama. For example, in the part of Chapter 6 addressed to Modou Fall, Ramatoulaye quotes from the letters he wrote her from France while he was attending law school there (14). In Chapter 12, she quotes Aissatou's own letter to her husband, Mawdo Bâ, declaring her intention to divorce him (31–32). As Ramatoulaye tells her story to a friend who never hears it, the reader overhears it, and the text becomes Ramatoulaye's reclaimed voice.

Ramatoulaye's account of events in the novel often shows that she herself is conscious of the importance of breaking the silence that had become her habit. She is clearly aware of the significance of speaking as she describes the event that is probably the turning point of the novel, her rejection of the proposal of Tamsir, Modou's brother, after Modou's death: "My voice has known thirty years of silence, thirty years of harassment. It bursts out, violent, sometimes sarcastic, some-times contemptuous" (57–58). Her rage is vented on Tamsir at least partly because Tamsir had been one of the three men who five years earlier had come to tell her of Modou's plans to marry Binetou on the very day when the marriage was to occur (58).

At the same time, Ramatoulaye sometimes distinguishes voice from words, suggesting a distinction between emotion and reason. When Daouda, Ramatoulaye's mother's choice for her in her youth, offers to marry Ramatoulaye in her widowhood, the two of them have a lengthy discussion about women's rights and progressive government. She concludes that "more than my ideas, it was my voice that captivated him" (61). She suggests that one must be wary of the seductive powers of voice, something that Ramatoulaye associates with tribal education. Ramatoulaye's awareness of the dangers of the purely oral is apparent in her comments about Nabou and Binetou. Nabou, the woman whom Mawdo Bâ (Aissatou's husband) takes as a co-wife, is tribally educated. Binetou, Ramatoulaye's co-wife, is not; she is a classmate and friend of Daba, the daughter of Ramatoulaye and Modou. Ramatoulaye treats both Binetou and young Nabou with some sympathy, recognizing both as victims of religious and social custom, but she is more sympathetic toward Nabou. Mawdo's mother, Aunty Nabou, wanted Mawdo to marry his cousin Nabou because his mother believed that Aissatou would "tarnish [Aunty Nabou's] noble descent" (28). Although young Nabou is formally educated as a midwife, most of her education has been "oral education," and Aunty Nabou's voice wields power over young Nabou:

> It was especially while telling folk tales, late at night under the starlit sky, that Aunty Nabou wielded her power over young Nabou's soul: her expressive voice glorified the retributive violence of the warrior; her expressive voice lamented the anxiety of the Loved One, all submissive. . . . And slowly but surely, through the sheer force of repetition, the virtues and greatness of a race took root in this child. (47)

Ramatoulaye attributes young Nabou's acceptance of Aunty Nabou's plan for her to marry Mawdo to her tribal education; except for this, Ramatoulaye writes to Aissatou, young Nabou is "like you, like me" (48).

Ramatoulaye also values the written voice, yet books are not the medium in which she seeks refuge. Ramatoulaye says that "books saved" Aissatou after her divorce. Her rather lengthy digression on the peculiar power of books suggests that she sees them as representing the world of progress, the world of the white missionaries who taught both Aissatou and Ramatoulaye:

> The power of books, this marvelous invention of astute human intelligence. Various signs associated with sound: different sounds that form the word. Juxtaposition of words from which springs the idea, Thought, History, Science, Life. Sole instrument of interrelationships and of culture, unparalleled means of giving and receiving. Books knit generations together in the same continuing effort that leads to progress. (32)

Yet Ramatoulaye herself seems to prefer films and radio over books. After Modou marries Binetou, Ramatoulaye seeks distraction in films and says that she "learned from them lessons of greatness, courage and perseverance." But she "gave the radio the role of comforter" (52). Film and radio have an immediacy that books do not. Ramatoulaye's choice of them seems consistent with her views about tradition and progress: the culture must not turn its back on the oral and the traditional, despite their dangers; at the same time, it must not refuse the written and the progressive. Clearly, the voice Ramatoulaye reclaims in the novel seeks such a balance.

Reclaiming Custom

The novel, then, is an example of what Alice Walker would call "saving the life that is your own" (3–14). Yet it does more than embody the reclamation of a voice. It seems that Mariama Bâ, in the persona of Ramatoulaye, would have women also seek to reclaim traditional custom and thus to redefine it. To do so is to show one's commitment "to survival and wholeness of entire people, male *and* female" (Walker 1983, xi). An epigraph at the beginning of Part I of Walker's *In Search of Our Mothers' Gardens* comes from Bernice Reagon: "I refuse to be judged by the values of another culture. I am a black woman, and I will stand as best I can in that imagery." Walker's essay collection emphasizes her sense that black women must change the culture rather than take refuge in individual fulfillment. Walker's refusal to flee from the South is a refusal to give up her region and culture for individual opportunity. For example, in the same essay in which she vows that she cannot go to Senegal until she can live freely in Mississippi, Walker speaks of the need for blacks to reclaim the South:

> To the Southern black person brought up expecting to be run away from home—because of lack of jobs, money, power, and

respect—[the idea of staying in the South] was a notion that took
root in willing soil. We would fight to stay where we were born
and raised and destroy the forces that sought to disinherit us. We
would proceed with the revolution from our own homes. (161)

In her 1972 convocation address at Sarah Lawrence College, Walker
emphasizes this same need: she says that for the young black woman
"there is not simply a new world to be gained, there is an old world
that must be reclaimed" (36).

The old world to be reclaimed in *So Long a Letter* is marriage and
the home. If Ramatoulaye is Mariama Bâ's persona in the novel, then
the novel seems to question divorce as the stereotypical feminist
response to hopelessly patriarchal marriage customs.

Some critics argue, however, that Ramatoulaye does not represent
Mariama Bâ's point of view. Indeed Aissatou's presence is invoked so
strongly throughout the novel that some critics see the novel more as
Aissatou's story than Ramatoulaye's. Such critics see the novel as a
story of choice between initiating divorce, the route that Ramatoulaye's
friend Aissatou takes, and suffering abandonment, the route that
Ramatoulaye takes. In an excellent study of archetypes in female
experience, Florence Stratton builds her interpretation of *So Long a
Letter* on the principle of psychological doubles. She argues that Aissatou
is simply Ramatoulaye's alter ego, that "Ramatoulaye writes to herself
in an attempt to locate the source of her disequilibrium." Thus the
novel becomes "a psychological case study of a contemporary, middle-
aged and middle-class Senegalese woman," one who "is unable to face
the . . . dreadful prospect of being a single woman" (Stratton 1988,
160). In a note, Stratton uses biographical evidence to support her
interpretation: "Bâ did not specify the character [Ramatoulaye or
Aissatou] with whose stance she identified: in addition to making
Aissatou a divorced woman, as she herself was, she gave Aissatou her
own last name." Stratton sees Ramatoulaye as having "sprung full-
blown from the pages of studies such as Betty Friedan's *The Feminine
Mystique.*" For Ramatoulaye, Stratton argues, her own house becomes
a prison. Aunty Nabou, Aissatou's mother-in-law, "is a grim parody
of Ramatoulaye. Nurturing mother metamorphosed into destructive
demon, she is an image of what not only Ramatoulaye but every
woman is in danger of becoming if she does not seek the power to
liberate herself." Nevertheless, Stratton concludes that "Bâ, though she
treats her creation with a gentle irony, neither trivializes nor mocks
her anguish and bewilderment. . . . In effect, Ramatoulaye mourns her
own demise" (Stratton 1988, 160–68).

Although Stratton's analysis of the novel is convincing, other critics have seen Ramatoulaye as "an embodiment of all that is noble and dignified in a woman" (Taiwo 1984, 19). A more balanced interpretation would grant the narrator/protagonist the power of her story and recognize her change in the process of the telling. Ramatoulaye may have made the more difficult choice, one that may make things better for her daughters but probably not for herself. Ramatoulaye's choice to remain Modou's wife even though he abandons her in his marriage to Binetou may be viewed as a statement that to reclaim her home, the home that she and Modou shared, is a nobler choice than to escape.

The events of the story revolve around marriages, at least seven of them. The central marriage of the novel is that of Ramatoulaye, now the middle-aged widow who tells the story, to Modou Fall, a lawyer and a technical adviser in the Ministry of Public Works. Both Ramatoulaye, a teacher in Dakar, and her friend Aissatou have been educated by Western missionaries. Aissatou and Mawdo Bâ, the doctor whom Aissatou marries, are friends of Ramatoulaye and Modou. Both Ramatoulaye and Aissatou marry for love, viewing marriage as personal choice. Mawdo Bâ takes a co-wife first, one that is thrust upon him by his mother, Aunty Nabou, because she has always felt that Aissatou, a goldsmith's daughter, does not fit the family's noble lineage. Modou Fall, after twenty-five years of marriage to Ramatoulaye, succumbs to Binetou, the friend of his daughter Daba. Other marriages which invite comparison to these four include the marriages of two of Ramatoulaye's daughters—Daba and Aissatou—and the marriage of Ramatoulaye's friend from the Ivory Coast, Jacqueline, to a young Senegalese.

It seems noteworthy that while marriage is central to the novel, Ramatoulaye does not describe her husband's abandonment of her until Chapter 13, almost the center of the novel. The demise of Aissatou's marriage, an obvious parallel to Ramatoulaye's experience, is described in the preceding chapter. Ramatoulaye's husband marries her daughter's friend, but Ramatoulaye chooses not to divorce him. Ramatoulaye's explanation of her choice is preceded by a rather long account of Jacqueline, a Protestant girl from the Ivory Coast who married a Senegalese doctor but was not accepted in Senegal. Jacqueline's marriage is eventually saved, but only after she has a nervous breakdown and visits many doctors and hospitals. Finally one doctor tells her, "You must react, go out, give yourself a reason for living" (45). Ramatoulaye then connects Jacqueline's story to her own:

> Why did I recall this friend's ordeal? Was it because of its
> happy ending? Or merely to delay the formulation of the choice

I had made, a choice that my reason rejected but that accorded
with the immense tenderness I felt towards Modou Fall?
    Yes, I was well aware of where the right solution lay, the
dignified solution. And, to my family's great surprise, unanimously
disapproved of by my children . . . I chose to remain. (45)

Two chapters later, in a chapter that begins with "I am surviving," and
in which three other paragraphs begin, "I survived," she says, "I had
the solution my children wanted—the break without having taken the
initiative" (52). She has forced Modou to desert her. It is at the end
of this chapter that she learns to drive the car that her friend Aissatou
has bought for her. Her doing so may indicate that she has gained
control of her own house and can now move out from it. It is in the
following chapter that she speaks of the voice in which she rejects
Tamsir's proposal.

    In view of Ramatoulaye's reference to "a choice that my reason
rejected," one may also look at Ramatoulaye's decision to stay in her
marriage as a choice of the heart, and Aissatou's decision to seek
divorce as a choice of the head. Many critics quote Ramatoulaye's
explanation of her choice as reflecting her weakness:

> I am one of those who can realize themselves fully and bloom
> only when they form part of a couple. Even though I understand
> your stand, even though I respect the choice of liberated women,
> I have never conceived of happiness outside marriage. (56)

It is this chapter, however, in which she begins to change, to clearly
take charge. The chapter begins, "I take a deep breath" (55). When
she refuses Daouda Dieng's proposal, she says, "My heart does not
love Daouda Dieng. My mind appreciates the man. But heart and
mind often disagree" (66). Ramatoulaye speaks of refusing "the easy
way because of my ideal" (70), her belief in monogamous marriage
based on the choice of two equal partners. Ramatoulaye is thinking of
Daouda's wife and children, as well as herself, as part of her ideal.
Ramatoulaye's responses to marriage proposals from both Tamsir and
Daouda are consistent with what critic Edris Makward says about
Mariama Bâ's view of marriage: "Mariama Bâ was the first African
writer to stress unequivocally the strong desire of the new generation
of Africans to break away from the age-old marriage customs and
adopt a decidedly more modern approach based on free mutual choice
and the equality of the two partners" (Makward 1986, 278).

    It is in Ramatoulaye's relationship with her daughter Aissatou (named
for her friend) that one may see the possibility for the ideal woman—
one that can reconcile head and heart. Aissatou is not like Ramatoulaye's
older daughter Daba, who "reasons everything out" (74). Ramatoulaye

discovers that Aissatou is three months pregnant. Although Iba Sall, Aissatou's boyfriend, is a struggling law student, he asks to marry Aissatou. Ramatoulaye comments that Aissatou, not Iba, will risk being expelled from school because her condition will become apparent. But after her initial rage, Ramatoulaye accepts Aissatou's and Iba's decision, and the recurrent sentence of the following chapter, the next to the last of the book, is "reassuring habits regain ascendancy" (86–87). Critics have pointed to the sexism in Ramatoulaye's remark in this chapter that she envies her friend "for having had only boys" (87), but her remark precedes her explanation of her attempt to help her daughters deal with a changing world, a world in which "modern mothers . . . help to limit the damage, and better still prevent it" (87).

Irène Assiba d'Almeida, in her essay "The Concept of Choice in Mariama Bâ's Fiction," argues that Ramatoulaye and Aissatou "have made different choices in similar situations. However, what is important is that the choices have been made." Clearly, the novel emphasizes the vital importance of choice, but D'Almeida sees the conclusion of the novel as less than satisfactory. She says that if Ramatoulaye's point of view is that of Mariama Bâ, "then Mariama Bâ belongs to a generation of African female novelists whose writing is characterized by a certain malaise," the result of "the dilemma women face in wanting to keep traditions while at the same time, wanting to reject what, in society, ties women down." It seems, however, that choice is important not only because it is "the ultimate affirmation of self" but also because the individual (and the culture) continue to grow through such choices (D'Almeida 1986, 165–71).

Promise of Ramatoulaye's continued growth and promise of the constructive change it will bring to society are evident at the end of the novel. As Ramatoulaye looks forward to a visit from Aissatou in the final chapter, she speaks directly of her feelings about women's liberation. Her statement that "my new turn of mind is hardly surprising to you" suggests that she has learned that one must take into account that "all women have almost the same fate, which religions or unjust legislation have sealed." Ramatoulaye insists that "love, imperfect as it may be in its content and expression, remains the natural link between [man and woman]" and that "the success of a nation . . . depends inevitably on the family" (88–89). Her final paragraphs indicate that she will greet Aissatou in traditional custom and will seek her help in reclaiming tradition rather than escaping it:

> Beneath the shell that has hardened you over the years, beneath your sceptical pout, your easy carriage, perhaps I will feel you vibrate. I would so much like to hear you check or encourage my

> eagerness, just as before, and, as before, to see you take part in
> the search for a new way.....
> The word "happiness" does indeed have meaning, doesn't it?
> I shall go out in search of it. Too bad for me if once again I have
> to write you so long a letter. (89)

Ramatoulaye suggests that neither she nor Aissatou has found the way,
but together they will search for it.

Reclaiming Connection

In her essay, "Looking to the Side, and Back," Alice Walker tells of
attending a symposium at Radcliffe where a panelist said that because
she spoke so often of her mother, "her problem was that [she] was
'trying to "carry" her mother, and the weight was too heavy.'" The
friend sitting next to her comforted her by saying, "But why shouldn't
you carry your mother; she carried *you,* didn't she?" (318–19). Alice
Walker's anecdote explains the necessity of personal connection for the
womanist, the importance of recognizing one's connection both to
foremothers and friends. Without a friend named Aissatou, Ramatoulaye would not have written so long a letter "in the search for a new
way." The occasion of the letter is the death of Ramatoulaye's husband
of thirty years, but the letter is also a celebration of friendship.
Ramatoulaye begins her letter by recalling details of their "long association" and then reciting a traditional invocation that indicates a
serious discussion is to follow: "My friend, my friend, my friend. I call
on you three times" (1). The novel is the story of a healing relationship,
one that Alice Walker describes as part of a womanist's appreciation
of "women's emotional flexibility . . . and women's strength" (xi). Over
half of the novel is a flashback in which Ramatoulaye recreates for
Aissatou the happiness of their childhood and their respective courtships
and marriages in contrast to the agony of their middle years when
their husbands chose younger wives. It is after describing her own
ability to survive her abandonment that Ramatoulaye speaks of friendship directly:

> Friendship has splendours that love knows not. It grows
> stronger when crossed, whereas obstacles kill love. Friendship
> resists time, which wearies and severs couples. It has heights
> unknown to love. (54)

As womanist prose, Ramatoulaye's story seems an example of
Walker's belief that "the real revolution is always concerned with the
least glamorous stuff" (135). Reclaiming traditional places and insti-

tutions is difficult. Reclaiming religion is probably the most difficult, and marriage customs are part of religious tradition—Islamic and Christian. Walker says that her parents transformed a religion "into something at once simple and noble" (18). Certainly Walker is far from the religion of her parents. In a 1973 interview she speaks of being "intrigued by the religion of the Black Muslims" as well as by "our *changing* of Christianity to fit our needs" (265). But her search for wholeness clearly has broad parallels with that of Mariama Bâ's protagonist, a search perhaps best described in "Saving the Life That Is Your Own":

> What is always needed in the appreciation of art, or life, is the larger perspective. Connections made, or at least attempted, where none existed before, the straining to encompass in one's glance at the varied world the common thread, the unifying theme through immense diversity, a fearlessness of growth, of search, of looking, that enlarges the private and the public world. And yet, in our particular society, it is the narrowed and narrowing view of life that often wins. (5)

Mariama Bâ's novel is a powerful voice for reclamation and change, the larger perspective provoked by what Alice Walker calls womanist prose.

Notes

1. Unless otherwise stated, the prose of Alice Walker is quoted from *In Search of Our Mothers' Gardens* (New York: Harcourt Brace Jovanovich, 1983).
2. Unless otherwise stated, quotations from Mariama Bâ are from *So Long a Letter,* translated by Modupé Bodé-Thomas (London: Heinemann, 1981).

References

Bâ, Mariama. *So Long a Letter.* Translated by Modupé Bodé-Thomas. London: Heinemann, 1981.

Busia, Abena P. B. "Words Whispered over Voids: A Context for Black Women's Rebellious Voices in the Novel of the African Diaspora." In *Black Feminist Criticism and Critical Theory.* Volume 3, *Studies in Black American Literature,* edited by Joe Weixlmann and Houston A. Baker, Jr., 1–41. Greenwood, FL: Penkevill, 1988.

d'Almeida, Irène Assiba. "The Concept of Choice in Mariama Bâ's Fiction." In *Ngambika: Studies of Women in African Literature,* edited by Carole

Boyce Davies and Anne Adams Graves, 161–71. Trenton, NJ: Africa World Press, 1986.

Makward, Edris. "Marriage, Tradition and Woman's Pursuit of Happiness in the Novels of Mariama Bâ." In *Ngambika: Studies of Women in African Literature,* edited by Carole Boyce Davies and Anne Adams Graves, 271–81. Trenton, NJ: Africa World Press, 1986.

Stratton, Florence. "The Shallow Grave: Archetypes of Female Experience in American Fiction." *Research in African Literatures* 19 (Summer 1988): 143–69.

Taiwo, Oladele. *Female Novelists in Modern Africa.* New York: St. Martin's Press, 1984.

Walker, Alice. *In Search of Our Mothers' Gardens: Womanist Prose by Alice Walker.* New York: Harcourt Brace Jovanovich, 1983.

6 Private Worlds: A Bibliographic Essay

Sarah Palmer
University of Montevallo

Ronald Ayling's essay, "Colonial Encounters of an Autobiographical Kind," provides us with an excellent start in exploring ways of clustering works of personal expression within the curriculum, for not only does his essay give us the example of two nontraditional texts with engaging personal voices; he prompts us to consider related texts, including established works in English and American literature, for inclusion in a unit on the response of various writers to the colonial experience. Ayling's definition of colonialism refers not only to political control of a country by outsiders but also to any authority/obedience system which, especially when involving children in oppressive situations, is destructive of self and invites rebellion. Personal writing becomes both a way of facing the limiting conditions of one's life and a means of forging one's own identity.

Like Ayling, Dorothy Grimes recognizes the value of personal writing to explore the experiences of the outsiders of society who have been subjected to some form of colonialism. As she notes, both Mariama Bâ and Alice Walker employ personal writing as a vehicle for womanist prose—not only to express their concern for the oppression of women but also to distinguish their voices from those of the mainstream of the feminist movement rooted in white Eurocentric traditions. According to Ogunyemi (1985), black women writers prefer "integrative images of the male and female worlds" which also "empower the black man" (68). These authors aim "to knit the world's black family together to achieve . . . the unity of blacks everywhere" (71). Thus "black womanism is a philosophy that celebrates black roots, the ideals of black life, while giving a balanced presentation of black womandom"

(72). Ogunyemi goes on to say, "Most Afro-American womanist novels, culture oriented as they are, abound in hope." In these novels there is an affirmative spirit; womanism is a "gospel of hope" (79).

This affirmative spirit, which, in fact, may be found in much personal writing, is one of its great values for a classroom setting. Other values of studying works such as *In Search of Our Mothers' Gardens* and *So Long a Letter* are abundantly clear. For example, reading *So Long a Letter* can introduce students to another culture, thereby enabling them to learn of the customs, the religion, the experiences of women in a polygamous society. The intimate nature of this personal writing also allows students to relate to Bâ's protagonist—to her problems, her grief, her valor—and to the close friend to whom she is writing. Particularly, young women students can identify with the narrator and the friend/confidante to whom the letter is addressed, since according to surveys, adolescent readers value most their friends.

Likewise, the personal nature of the essays in *In Search of Our Mothers' Gardens* should appeal to women who will be able to relate in particular to the womanist essays dealing with such figures as Zora Neale Hurston and Coretta King. They should easily identify with Walker, with the self she presents as she tells of her search for identity, of her struggles against poverty, injustice.

For the teacher, another prime value in assigning the reading of personal writing is that such works provide students incentives for their own writing. In personal writing, such as the works discussed in the essays by Ayling and Grimes, the protagonists reclaim a place through their discovery of the power of the spoken and the written voice: Alice Walker herself was "called to life" by Martin Luther King, Jr., particularly by the power of his voice. In the introductory essay to *In Search of Our Mothers' Gardens,* she says, "It is, in the end, the saving of lives we writers are about. Whether we are 'minority' writers or 'majority.' It is simply our power to do this" (Walker 1983, 14).

Our students too can experience the saving power of writing. Reading works such as those discussed here can inspire them to express their own aspirations, dreams, disappointments—prompting them to share their own experiences, their own lives. Indeed, after reading diaries, journals, letters, and other personal writing and discussing these in a classroom setting, students may begin to write with a real purpose—writing for the very motives of the original authors: to be sincere, to satisfy a need to express themselves—their doubts, their fears, their sense of isolation, their traumas—to break the bonds of loneliness, to attempt to find an identity, to assert a self, to establish a significance, and simply "to create out of the materials of the human spirit something which did not exist before" (Faulkner, 743).

Below are further suggestions for additional clusterings of personal writing from authors of the traditional canon as well as from those whose voices are just beginning to be heard. Again, the clustered works are centered around some of the topics and themes which should have strong appeal to high school and college-aged readers.

For example, to the works by O'Casey, Soyinka, and Abrahams which Ayling discusses, we might add Janet Frame's biography of a New Zealand colonial childhood, *To the Is-land;* South African writer Es'kia Mphahlele's *Down Second Avenue;* the contemporary Korean novel *Lost Names* by Richard E. Kim, which treats the survival of a family under the oppressive period of Japanese annexation; Jose Rizal's Filipino novel, *The Lost Eden,* which recounts the story of the revolution which ended Spain's 500-year domination of the Philippines; *Obasan,* by the contemporary Japanese Canadian author Joy Kogawa, a work recounting the forced relocation of Japanese Canadians during World War II; and the nineteenth-century Urdu poetry of Mirza Asadullah Khan, published in a volume entitled *Ghazals of Ghalib,* a work which celebrates the endurance of a people experiencing extremely painful circumstances. To this list may also be added the works of three Latin American authors who deal with remembrances of childhood: *Sweet Diamond Dust* by Rosario Ferre, "Black Woman" by Nancy Morejon, and "Song to a New Day" by Giaconda Belli.

With these nontraditional works, the teacher might juxtapose such British standards as Dickens's *David Copperfield* and Brontë's *Jane Eyre,* works which fit Ayling's broader definition of colonialism. In American literature, standard works like Twain's *The Adventures of Huckleberry Finn* and Salinger's *The Catcher in the Rye* fit nicely, as does Styron's *The Confessions of Nat Turner.* The instructor might also look at *The Road from Home* by Armenian American David Kherdian and *The Joy Luck Club* by Chinese American Amy Tan. Kherdian recounts his mother's escape from Turkish persecution at the turn of the century and her journey to establish a new home in America. Amy Tan's novel explores the mysterious bond, the shared secrets and sorrows of four Chinese American women and their daughters whose interrelationships span a period of forty years.

Other clusterings of works that deal with the theme of oppression— the search for identity during a time of oppression and the triumph over adversity, discrimination and injustice—follow. *The Diary of a Young Girl* by Anne Frank—a well-known coming-of-age account of a young girl living in hiding during World War II in Nazi-occupied

Holland—is a testimony to the indomitable spirit of humankind, all the more poignant because of her death in a concentration camp soon after the last entry. This work can be studied with Masuji Ibuse's *Black Rain,* an account of the bombing of Hiroshima based on authentic diaries and interviews with victims of this holocaust and of the effect of the disaster on those who survived. *The Diary of a Young Girl* may also be compared with *The Narrative of the Life of Frederick Douglass,* an account of grim injustice written by a former American slave. Wole Soyinka's *Aké,* the autobiography of the contemporary Nigerian poet, dramatist, essayist, and novelist can also be paired with the Douglass autobiography. With these accounts of oppression and yet of triumph over adversity might be studied the following Latin American works: *Of Love and Shadows* and *The House of the Spirits* by Isabel Allende and *The Back Room* by Carmen Martin Gaite. Since it deals with the horrors following the partition of India, *Cracking India* by Bapsi Sidhwa, the contemporary novelist from Pakistan, can also be read with either of these two works.

Camara Laye's *The Dark Child* is another rich personal record of childhood experiences in a traditional Islamic community in Guinea, recounting as well the influence of European culture from the time the author first ventures into the European world as a small lost boy until the time when he leaves to go to college in France. Laye's work might be compared with *Sound-Shadows of the New World* by Ved Mehtah, an account of the experiences of the author, then a blind adolescent in India, who must come to the United States to attend a school for the blind. (In another volume of his autobiography, Ved Mehtah relates the loss of his closest friend, a Japanese American who did not make it at the school: he killed himself. The author attributes his own salvation to his *writing*—his first piece of autobiography—another testimonial to the power of personal writing to preserve a life. Other autobiographical works by Ved Mehtah—equally valuable, equally inspiring—are *Vedi, The Ledge Between the Streams,* and *The Stolen Light: Continents of Exile.*)

Li Mirol's *The Yalu Flows,* an autobiography and coming-of-age account of a Korean boy, a narrative of warm family relationships during a troubled time when his land was threatened by powerful industrial nations, can be read with Rahn Adjeng Kartini's *Letters from a Javanese Princess.* Either of these works might be paired with one of the two following Hispanic American autobiographies: *Enplumada* by Lorna Dee Cervantes, and *Bloodroot* by Alma Villanueva. Or they might be read with *Silent Dancing: A Partial Remembrance of a Puerto Rican Childhood,* by Judith Ortiz Cofer, whose childhood was divided between the little Puerto Rican town of her birth and New Jersey. This small book, a collection of stories with occasional poems by the author, can also serve as an introduction to works written in the oral tradition— or even to women's literature. Booker T. Washington's *Up from Slavery,* a famous black educator's account of his struggles to overcome poverty and discrimination in the South, can be paired with Jacqueline Cochran's *The Stars at Noon,* the autobiography of a deprived, abused child growing up in the South during the twenties and thirties.

Another account of one who was grossly mistreated as a child is Richard Rhodes's *A Hole in the World,* a moving narrative by the prominent author who was subjected to the cruelest of treatment and yet was able to triumph over this injustice. This work can be compared with Virginia Woolf's *Moments of Being* (for mature readers), the posthumously published account of—among other things—the time of her abuse. To great advantage, these works dealing with gross mistreatment may also be read with Alice Portnoy's *The Little School* and Jose Donoso's "Ana Maria," another account of triumph over upbringing by immature, abrasive parents.

Some additional clusters follow: *Six Records of a Floating Life* (Shen Fu)—a love story by the eighteenth-century Chinese writer, a sensitive, talented, but impractical man, who was regarded as the "black sheep" of his family—can be compared with *The Duke of Deception* (Geoffrey Wolff), a son's moving account of his life with his father, the "black sheep" of his family.

Two other books which can be very effectively paired are autobiographies by two American brothers separated by a divorce. *The Duke of Deception* by Geoffrey Wolff (mentioned above) and *This Boy's Life* by Tobias Wolff can be read together: both present moving accounts of growing up with an immature and abusive parent. Because both authors triumphed over their upbringing, their personal writing should appeal to a vast audience of troubled American youth today. Young history buffs may find very appealing some of the personal writing of the Civil War—letters and diaries and memoirs written from both the Southern and Northern viewpoints. In this category, *All for the Union: The Civil War Diary and Letters of Elisha Hunt Rhodes* may be read with *Memoirs of a Confederate Soldier* by John S. Jackman of the Orphan Brigade. The eyewitness reports of the former served as commentary for the PBS series *The Civil War.* The account of the latter well depicts the excitement—and the horror and tediousness— of the Confederate soldier's everyday life.

To turn to the feminist/womanist theme: a work that can perhaps serve as an introduction to feminist personal writing is *Revelations:*

Diaries of Women, (edited by Mary Jane Moffatt and Charlotte Painter), a collection of diary excerpts from a wide range of women writers. To the works by Alice Walker and Mariama Bâ already discussed may be added Virginia Woolf's *A Room of One's Own,* a collection of essays in which the author, writing for the intellectual freedom of women, stresses the necessity of their having an income and a room of their own in order to write. This book may be paired with Maxine Hong Kingston's *The Woman Warrior,* a memoir of a Chinese girl growing up in twentieth-century America who is haunted by the ghosts of China's past, one being the "female avenger." This work may also be paired with Maya Angelou's *I Know Why the Caged Bird Sings,* an autobiography in which the author recounts her growing up in the segregated South—a moving study in strong family relationships, and in courage.

To continue this theme: Sei Shonagon's *The Pillow Book*—partly diary, partly reminiscences (a book to be hidden under her pillow), an amazing work by a court lady of tenth-century Japan in which the author notes what pleases or displeases her, including her highly competitive attitude toward men—may be read with *The Diary of Anaïs Nin,* a thorough documentation of the twentieth-century French author's life about which Nin has said: "It is the woman who has to speak. And it is not only the woman Anaïs who has to speak, but I have to speak for many women" (Moffat and Painter 1975, 86). Either of these works may be studied with *My Prison,* a Latin American woman's view of society by Isabel Alvarez de Toledo, Duchess of Medina Sidonia. Or they may be read with *Rituals of Survival: A Woman's Portfolio* by Nicholasa Mohr, a New York Puerto Rican woman, who here writes from her background of indomitable women who endure urban poverty and the restrictive roles that have been created for them.

Mary Boykin Chesnut's *A Diary from Dixie*—an account of the American Civil War by an aristocratic Southern woman whose vision extended to a broad view of the war in which both North and South were guilty—may be studied with *I Know Why the Caged Bird Sings,* noted above. The *Kagero Nikki*—by the author known only as the "Mother of Michitsuna," a Japanese noblewoman of the tenth century— is concerned with the author's unhappy marriage, her loneliness, her abandonment. It can be read along with *The Intimate Journal,* by George Sand, a work in which the author records the unhappiness that results from her marriage of convenience and from her relationships with Alfred Musset and other well-known men of the time.

Some poets using feminist/womanist themes are as follows: Sappho (*The Poems of Sappho*), the ancient Greek poet, the first writing from the feminist imagination—works distinguished by their personal quality, their intensity, their handling of family, friends, religious feeling. Her work may be studied with that of Adrienne Rich (*The Dream of a Common Language*), a leading contemporary American poet who also writes very personally, using several of the same themes that are Sappho's. Either of these two poets may be read along with the Hispanic American poet Kyra Galvan ("Ideological Contradictions in Washing a Dish").

Gabriela Mistral (*Desolacion* [*Desolation* or *Destruction*])—the Chilean Nobel Prize winner who wrote with great intensity about nature and love, particularly with great tenderness of the mother/child relationship—can be paired with Sharon Olds (*The Gold Cell*), whose poems so warmly present the love of mother for child, the ambivalent love of an older child for the mother. (Prose works dealing with the mother/child relationship are *My Mother's Hands* by Nellie Campobello, *The Same Sea as Every Summer* by Esther Tusquets, "The Two Elenas" by Carlos Fuentes, and *Mrs. Caldwell Speaks to Her Son* by Camilo Jose Cela. Any one of these authors may be studied with Sharon Olds.)

Another poet using feminine themes is Sor Juana Ines de la Cruz (*Complete Works*)—a brilliant seventeenth-century Mexican lady-in-waiting who became a nun—who wrote intensely of the conflict between religious holiness and her passion for learning. (One of her poems, "Reply to Sor Filotea," is in the readily available *Norton Anthology of World Masterpieces*.) Her work can be paired with that of Emily Dickinson (*The Poems of Emily Dickinson*), the nineteenth-century American poet who also handled conflict in an intense lyrical style. Audre Lord (*Chosen Poems, Old and New*), the contemporary African-American poet, author of powerful womanist verse, may be studied with Margaret Atwood (*Selected Poems II*), the contemporary Canadian poet/novelist/essayist whose poems, to a considerable extent, deal with oppression and injustice—gender injustice—but also with fellowship. The poems of Puerto Rican-born Judith Ortiz Cofer (*Terms of Survival*) may be read along with the poetry of Lord and Atwood.

Students will find in much personal writing, then, the affirmative spirit which Ogunyemi finds in womanist prose. They will discover in personal writing by the authors such as those discussed in the essays by Ayling and Grimes—and by the authors given in the clusters—a vehicle for definition of self, for exploration and expression of their own worldviews as well as those of other people, and for affirmation of the possibilities of individual and communal empowerment and unity.

References

Allende, Isabel. *The House of the Spirits*. Translated by Magda Bogin. New York: Knopf, 1983.

———. *Of Love and Shadows*. Translated by Margaret S. Peden. New York: Knopf, 1987.

Alvarez de Toledo, Isabel. *My Prison*. Translated by Herma Briffault. New York: Harper and Row, 1972.

Angelou, Maya. *I Know Why the Caged Bird Sings*. New York: Bantam, 1971.

Atwood, Margaret. *Selected Poems II: Poems Selected and New, 1976-1986*. Boston: Houghton Mifflin, 1987.

Bâ, Mariama. *So Long a Letter*. Portsmouth, NH: Heinemann, 1989.

Belli, Giaconda. "Song to a New Day." In *The Defiant Muse: Hispanic Feminist Poems from the Middle Ages to the Present,* edited by Angel and Kate Flores. New York: Feminist Press, 1986.

Brontë, Charlotte. *Jane Eyre*. New York: Bantam, 1983.

Campobello, Nellie. *My Mother's Hands* (with *Cartucho*). Translated by Doris Meyer and Irene Matthews. Austin: University of Texas Press, 1988.

Cela, Camilo Jose. *Mrs. Caldwell Speaks to Her Son*. Translated by J. S. Bernstein. Ithaca: Cornell University Press, 1968.

Cervantes, Lorna Dee. *Enplumada*. Pittsburgh: Pittsburgh University Press, 1981.

Chesnut, Mary Boykin. *A Diary from Dixie*. Edited by Ben Ames Williams. Cambridge: Harvard University Press, 1980.

Cochran, Jacqueline. *The Stars at Noon*. New York: Knopf, 1986.

Cofer, Judith Ortiz. *Silent Dancing: A Partial Remembrance of a Puerto Rican Childhood*. Houston: Arte Publico Press, 1990.

———. *Terms of Survival*. Houston: Arte Publico Press, 1987.

Cruz, Sor Juana Ines de la. *Complete Works*. Mexico City: Fondo de Cultura Economica, 1962.

———. "Reply to Sor Filotea." In *Norton Anthology of World Masterpieces*. 5th Continental edition. Edited by Maynard Mack et al. New York: Norton, 1987.

Dickens, Charles. *David Copperfield*. New York: Bantam, 1981.

Dickinson, Emily. *The Poems of Emily Dickinson*. Cambridge: Harvard University Press, 1955.

Donoso, Jose. "Ana Maria." In *Latin American Writing Today,* edited by J.M. Cohen. Baltimore: Penguin Books, 1967.

Douglass, Frederick. *Narrative of the Life of Frederick Douglass, an American Slave*. Cambridge: Harvard University Press, 1960.

Faulkner, William. "Nobel Prize Award Speech." In *The Conscious Reader,* 3d. ed., edited by Caroline Shrodes, Harry Finestone, and Michael Shugrue. New York: Macmillan, 1988.

Ferre, Rosario. *Sweet Diamond Dust.* New York: Ballantine Books, 1988.

Frame, Janet. *To the Is-land: An Autobiography.* New York: Braziller, 1982.

Frank, Anne. *The Diary of a Young Girl.* New York: Random House, 1978.

Fuentes, Carlos. "The Two Elenas." Translated by Jose Luis Cuevas. In *The Eye of the Heart: Short Stories from Latin America,* edited by Barbara Howes. New York: Avon Books, 1990.

Gaite, Carmen Martin. *The Back Room.* Translated by Helen R. Lane. New York: Columbia University Press, 1983.

Galvan, Kyra. "Ideological Contradictions in Washing a Dish." In *The Defiant Muse: Hispanic Feminist Poems from the Middle Ages to the Present,* edited by Angel and Kate Flores. New York: Feminist Press, 1986.

Ibuse, Masuji. *Black Rain.* New York: Bantam, 1985.

Jackman, John J. *Memoir of a Confederate Soldier: Soldiering with the Orphan Brigade.* Columbia, SC: University of South Carolina Press, 1990.

Kartini, Raden Adjeng. *Letters from a Javanese Princess.* New York: Asia Society, 1985.

Khan, Mirza Asadullah. *Ghazels of Ghalib.* Translated and with an introduction by Basho Swanner. Santa Barbara, CA: Bandanna Books, 1990.

Kherdian, David. *The Road from Home: The Story of an Armenian Girl.* New York: Penguin, 1988.

Kim, Richard E. *Last Names: Scenes from a Boyhood in Japanese-Occupied Korea.* New York: Universe, 1988.

Kingston, Maxine Hong. *The Woman Warrior.* New York: Random House, 1976.

Kogawa, Joy. *Obasan.* Boston: Godine, 1982.

Laye, Camara. *The Dark Child.* New York: Farrar, Straus & Giroux, 1954.

Li Mirok. *The Yalu Flows.* Elizabeth, NJ: Nollym International, 1987.

Lord, Audre. *Chosen Poems, Old and New.* New York: Norton, 1982.

Mehtah, Ved. *The Ledge between the Streams.* New York: Norton, 1984.

———. *Sound-Shadows of the New World.* New York: Norton, 1985.

———. *The Stolen Light: Continents of Exile.* New York: Norton, 1989.

———. *Vedi.* New York: Norton, 1983.

Mistral, Gabriela. *Desolacion.* New York: Institute de las Espanas on los Estados Unidos, 1989.

Moffatt, Mary Jane and Charlotte Painter, eds. *Revelations: Diaries of Women.* New York: Random, 1975.

Mohr, Nicholasa. *Rituals of Survival: A Woman's Portfolio.* Houston: Arte Publico Press, 1985.

Morejon, Nancy. "Black Woman." In *The Defiant Muse: Hispanic Feminist Poems from the Middle Ages to the Present,* edited by Angel and Kate Flores. New York: Feminist Press, 1986.

The Mother of Michitsuna. Excerpts from *Kagero Nikki*. In *Anthology of Japanese Literature,* edited by Donald Keene. New York: Grove Press, 1960.

Mphahlele, Es'kia. *Down Second Avenue: Growing Up in a South African Ghetto.* London: Faber and Faber, 1985.

Nin, Anaïs. *The Diary of Anaïs Nin.* 3 vols. New York: Harcourt Brace Jovanovich, 1981.

Ogunyemi, Chikwenge Okonjo. "Womanism: The Dynamics of the Contemporary Black Female Novel in English." *Signs* II, no. 1 (1985): 63–80.

Olds, Sharon. *The Gold Cell.* New York: Knopf, 1987.

Ornelas, Berta. *Come Down from the Mound.* Phoenix, AZ: Miter, 1975.

Portnoy, Alice. *The Little School: Tales of Disappearance and Survival in Argentina.* Translated by Lois Athey et al. Pittsburgh: Cleis Press, 1987.

Rhodes, Elisha Hunt. *All for the Union: The Civil War Diary and Letters of Elisha Hunt Rhodes.* Edited by Robert H. Rhodes. New York: Crown, 1991.

Rhodes, Richard. *A Hole in the World: An American Boyhood.* New York: Simon and Schuster, 1990.

Rich, Adrienne. *The Dream of a Common Language.* New York: Norton, 1978.

Rizal, Jose. *The Lost Eden.* Bloomington: Indiana University Press, 1961.

Salinger, J.D. *The Catcher in the Rye.* New York: Bantam, 1984.

Sand, George. *The Intimate Journal.* New York: John Day, 1929.

Sappho. *The Poems of Sappho.* New York: Macmillan, 1966.

Shen Fu. *Six Records of a Floating Life.* Translated by Leonard Pratt. New York: Penguin, 1983.

Shonagon, Sei. *The Pillow Book.* Translated by Ivan Morris. New York: Penguin, 1971.

Sidhwa, Bapsi. *Cracking India.* Minneapolis: Milkweed Editions, 1991.

Soyinka, Wole. *Akè: The Years of Childhood.* New York: Random, 1983.

Styron, William. *The Confessions of Nat Turner.* New York: Bantam, 1981.

Tan, Amy. *The Joy Luck Club.* New York: Putnam, 1989.

Tusquets, Esther. *The Same Sea as Every Summer.* Translated by Margaret E. W. Jones. Lincoln: Nebraska University Press, 1990.

Twain, Mark. *The Adventures of Huckleberry Finn.* New York: Macmillan, 1967.

Villanueva, Alma. *Bloodroot.* Austin: Place of Herons Press, 1977.

Walker, Alice. *In Search of Our Mothers' Gardens.* New York: Harcourt Brace Jovanovich, 1983.

Washington, Booker T. *Up from Slavery.* Williamstown, MA: Penguin, 1988.

Wolff, Geoffrey. *The Duke of Deception: Memoirs of My Father.* New York: Random, 1990.

Wolff, Tobias. *This Boy's Life: A Memoir.* New York: Harper and Row, 1989.

Woolf, Virginia. *Moments of Being: Unpublished Autobiographical Writings.* New York: Harcourt Brace Jovanovich, 1985.

———. *A Room of One's Own.* New York: Harcourt Brace Jovanovich, 1989.

II The Hero's Quest

The essays in this section explore some of the ways in which heroes of various cultures define themselves through heroic action or through the equally heroic journey within. In discussing heroes from a variety of cultures, the essayists lead us to consider how concepts of heroism relate to social and historical realities as well as to consider the implications of heroic patterns which recur in many cultures. Essays in other sections of our text which also explore concepts of heroism include the consideration by Sandra Lott and Steven Latham of the adolescent hero in Salinger's *The Catcher in the Rye* and Ngũgĩ's *Weep Not, Child;* the discussion by Norman McMillan of heroism in *The Aeneid* and *Things Fall Apart,* and the discussion by Ndiawar Sarr of feminine and masculine perspectives on heroism in *Things Fall Apart.* The bibliographic essay points to ways of clustering works from diverse cultures, works which represent some of the many variants of the hero's quest.

7 Heroic Visions in *The Bhagavad Gita* and the Western Epic

Milton J. Foley
University of Montevallo

There are several approaches which can make *The Bhagavad Gita* more understandable and acceptable to the Western mind, most particularly, for our purposes, to the minds of American students in our literature courses. One approach is to discuss its influence on several Western writers of note: for example, Henry Thoreau. In *Walden,* Thoreau speaks of bathing his "intellect in the stupendous . . . philosophy of the Bhagvat Geeta, since whose composition years of the gods have elapsed, and in comparison with which our modern world and its literature seem puny and trivial . . ." ([1889] 1961, 230). One might also point out the influence of *The Gita* on the poetry of William Blake, although much remains to be done to trace Blake's indebtedness to *The Gita*. Or one might discuss *The Gita* in relation to the Sermon on the Mount, which it resembles in its essential meaning. Jesus' reference, for example, to the need to "pluck out" the offending eye and to "cut off" the offending hand in order to find the "light" of the soul within oneself parallels Krishna's advice to Arjuna in *The Gita* to be like the tortoise, which pulls in its feet and head (the senses) to find safety under the shell (the soul). A book could be written on the similarities between *The Gita* and the Sermon on the Mount.

My approach here, however, is to draw an analogy between *The Gita* and several Western epics—*The Iliad, The Odyssey, The Aeneid,* and *The Prelude*—and to show that the increasing interiorization of the heroic struggle in the Western epic, as the genre evolves, makes that genre compatible with a work, *The Gita,* whose main focus is the struggle of the individual to find and to become anchored in the soul. *The Gita,* like many Western epics, does deal with literal prowess in battle, but its main (and deeper) meaning involves the heroic efforts of the spiritual warrior to overcome temptations of the flesh in order to know the soul.

Some evidence of this evolution from external to internal struggle in the Western epic can be seen in the movement from *The Iliad* to *The Odyssey.* It can be argued, as George de F. Lord has done, that *The Odyssey* presents a significant shift away from the heroic code of *The Iliad,* with its emphasis on the hero's desire for glory through great feats of arms. Certainly, *The Odyssey* is full of the physical heroics of its protagonist—for example, in his battle with the suitors near the end of the poem—and the poem depicts the hubris of Odysseus after the defeat of Polyphemos when Odysseus arrogantly shouts out his name so that Polyphemos, the vanquished, will know his identity. In his " 'glorying spirit,' " Odysseus fails to heed the advice of his men that he not " 'bait the beast' " (1963, X, 159–60). Lord has stated, "*The Odyssey* mediates between . . . two concepts of the hero—the old and the new" (1954, 407). He points out that "Odysseus grows in the course of his experiences from the shrewd 'sacker of cities' to the wise restorer of Ithaca" (407). Even the gods of *The Odyssey,* unlike their counterparts in *The Iliad,* "are just and responsible" (407). Lord agrees with Denton J. Snider, who, in Lord's words, points out "the spiritual evolution of Odysseus, the moral character of his universe, and the pre-eminence of freedom and moral responsibility throughout the poem. . . ." (408–409). Lord quotes Snider as follows:

> "The theme . . . deals with the wise man, who, through his intelligence, was able to take Troy, but who has now another and greater problem—the return out of the grand estrangement caused by the Trojan expedition. Spiritual restoration is the key-note of the *Odyssey,* as it is with all great Books of Literature." (409)

Lord shows us that "Odysseus's last encounter with the wrath of Poseidon literally beats him to his knees and drives him once and for all out of the attitude of cocky self-sufficiency which characterized him earlier" (413). Odysseus humbly prays to the "lord of the stream" (V: 94) on the shores of the Phaiakian nation:

> "How sorely I depend on your mercy!
> derelict as I am by the sea's anger.
> Is he not sacred, even to the gods,
> the wandering man who comes,
> as I have come, in weariness before your knees,
> your waters? Here is your servant; lord, have
> mercy on me." (V, 94)

Odysseus has arrived in Phaiakia, a very different world from that of *The Iliad.* As Lord states, "the Trojan war was dominated by the heroic code of men" (414), but *The Odyssey* shifts the focus to "family and community life whose values are centered in several extraordinary women—Arete, Nausicaa, Penelope" (414–15). *The Odyssey* also depicts Odysseus, after his spiritual awakening, returning home, ridding his nation of the parasitic suitors, and resuming his benevolent rule over Ithaca.

Although T. S. Eliot would largely disagree with Lord's interpretation of *The Odyssey,* Lord agrees with Eliot's views on *The Aeneid.* Lord states that Eliot "has redefined for us the Christian-like qualities of *The Aeneid* and its hero" (406). Thus the interiorization of the epic struggle continues in the sense that the epic figure Aeneas, like Odysseus, is introspective and more interested in creating a civilization than in destroying one. As Eliot says, Aeneas "is . . . the prototype of a Christian hero. For he is, humbly, a man with a mission; and the mission is everything" (10). His mission was the creation of a Roman Empire, a more ideal one than, in Eliot's words, "the Roman Empire of the legionnaires, the proconsuls and governors, the business-men and speculators, the demagogues and generals" (12). It was an ideal "which Vergil passed on to Christianity to develop and to cherish" (13).

William Wordsworth's epic poem *The Prelude* is a major progression in the trend in the Western epic toward the internalization of the heroic struggle. Although Wordsworth was not responsible for the title of the poem, including the subtitle, *Growth of a Poet's Mind,* the subtitle reflects the theme of his work. More apt, however, as a subtitle, would be the words "Growth of a Poet's *Soul."*

Karl Kroeber, among others, has discussed the epic characteristics of *The Prelude* (1960, 78–112). The most obvious one is that the poem begins, as do all Western epics, *in medias res,* and there is an echo of Milton's epic *Paradise Lost* (a poem which will not be discussed here but which is obviously rich in associations with the subject at hand) in Wordsworth's line, "The earth is all before me" ([1850] 1964, I: 14). This reminds one of the ending of *Paradise Lost,* when the narrator says, concerning Adam and Eve, "The world was all before them, where to choose / Their place of rest . . ." ([1674] 1962, XII: 646–47).

The only affinity *The Prelude* has with epics which involve physical heroics is found in the sections dealing with the French Revolution. Wordsworth had cut himself off from his spiritual roots, Nature and the contemplation of Nature, not just physical nature but "spirit" or God in nature, as well. In his excessive preoccupation with the French Revolution and political questions in general, Wordsworth had lost his ties to Nature. This loss was particularly significant for Wordsworth, who was primarily a poet of Nature, a poet who excelled most when he was preoccupied with spiritual truth.

At the beginning of Book First, however, Wordsworth is seeking mental and spiritual regeneration in Nature. And he is desirous of a creative awakening:

> Dear Liberty! Yet what would it avail
> But for a gift that consecrates the joy?
> For I, methought, while the sweet breath of heaven
> Was blowing on my body, felt within
> A correspondent breeze, that gently moved
> With quickening virtue, but is now become
> A tempest, a redundant energy,
> Vexing its own creation. (I, 31–38)

In this first book, Wordsworth uses numerous words which are associated with religion and spirituality: "holy services" (54), "Pilgrim" (91), and "priestly robe" (52).

The poet contemplates various subjects for his next creative endeavor, some of which resemble the heroic subjects of earlier epics: a subject which lies "Within the groves of Chivalry" (I, 171) and the story of "How Wallace fought for Scotland" (I, 214). He eschews such subject matter and decides, instead, to tell the story of his life.

In typical epic style, he flashes back to his childhood, the "Fair seed-time" of his "soul" (I, 301) when he was "fostered alike by beauty and fear" (302) as he interacted with Nature. He tells of "One summer evening" (I, 357) when, in "an act of stealth" (361), he took "A little boat tied to a willow tree" (358) and began to row across a lake. He then begins a description of how Nature seemed to correct him, to reprove him for the theft of the boat:

> With an unswerving line, I fixed my view
> Upon the summit of a craggy ridge,
> The horizon's utmost boundary; for above
> Was nothing but the stars and the grey sky.
> She was an elfin pinnace; lustily
> I dipped my oars into the silent lake,
> And, as I rose upon the stroke, my boat
> Went heaving through the water like a swan.
>
> (I, 369–76)

Behind the craggy ridge, he sees "a huge peak, black and huge, / As if with voluntary power instinct / Upreared its head" (378–80). Afraid and guilt-ridden, "With trembling oars" he turns, "And through the silent water" steals his way "Back to the covert of the willow tree" (385, 386, 387). Wordsworth attributes to experiences such as this one the stimuli for "The passions that build up our human soul" (I, 407). In an apostrophe to the "Wisdom and spirit of the universe" (I, 401), he states this belief:

> Thou Soul that art the eternity of thought,
> That givest to forms and images a breath
> And everlasting motion, not in vain
> By day or star-light thus from my first dawn
> Of childhood didst thou intertwine for me
> The passions that build up our human soul.
>
> (I, 402–07)

The Prelude contains many examples of the positive influences of Nature on Wordsworth's upbringing, some of them involving, as in the case of the one just discussed, fear and guilt, others being much more pleasant. The latter, of course, deal with the ministry of beauty, experiences which obviously uplift Wordsworth spiritually.

It is necessary now, however, to leave this subject temporarily in order to understand the severity of Wordsworth's epic struggle to free himself from the deep depression which resulted from his crushed hopes for a new political order which he, and others, foresaw rising out of the violence of the French Revolution, a hope that "a people from the depth / Of shameful imbecility" had, indeed, "uprisen, / Fresh as the morning star" (IX, 383–84, 384–85). Wordsworth "saw, in rudest men, / Self-sacrifice the firmest; generous love, / And continence of mind, and sense of right / Uppermost in the midst of fiercest strife" (IX, 386–89). However, the "September massacres" (X, 73) and the denunciations of Robespierre lead Wordsworth ultimately to turn away from his optimism and to despair of political revolutions as a quick solution to mankind's needs. As he puts it,

> Long time have human ignorance and guilt
> Detained us, on what spectacles of woe
> Compelled to look, and inwardly oppressed
> With sorrow, disappointment, vexing thoughts,
> Confusion of the judgment, zeal decayed,
> And, lastly, utter loss of hope itself
> And things to hope for! (XII, 1–7)

However, as Wordsworth next states, "Not with these began / Our song, and not with these our song must end" (XII, 7–8). Indeed, by returning to the root of his inspiration and spiritual peace, to Nature, Wordsworth is regenerated:

> From Nature doth emotion come, and moods
> Of calmness equally are Nature's gift:
> This is her glory; these two attributes
> Are sister horns that constitute her strength.
> Hence Genius, born to thrive by interchange
> Of peace and excitation finds in her
> His best and purest friend; from her receives
> That energy by which he seeks the truth,
> From her that stillness of the mind
> Which fits him to receive it when unsought.
>
> (XIII, 1–10)

In Book Fourteenth, Wordsworth describes the victory of the soul over the fallen, dualistic world. Reaching the heights of Mt. Snowden in Wales, he sees, at his feet, "a silent sea of hoary mist" (42). Just before this, he had seen "The Moon hung naked in a firmament / Of azure without cloud (40–41), and, "through a rift" (56) in the cloud of mist, he experiences what, to him in this vision, represents the world of dualism. Having transcended this dualism for the moment, he experiences something of even greater importance: a realization of the relationship of the transcendent perfection to the imperfect world. In other words, Wordsworth experiences the whole, the extension of the perfect out into the apparent imperfection. Heretofore, the mist of ignorance had somewhat obscured this realization. The rift in the mist, however, unites the transcendent (i.e., the moon) with the dualistic world. Wordsworth has reached his highest spiritual state, and, in reaching it, has attained, at least momentarily, the state that Krishna desires for Arjuna permanently.

The Bhagavad Gita, which seems to have been written as a separate poem, is now a part of that great Hindu epic *The Mahabharata,* a poem that has for its subject the people who descended from the ancient Indian king, King Bharata.

The Gita mediates between the two extremes found in the Western epic, those being *The Iliad,* largely concerned with physical, egotistically motivated heroism, and *The Prelude,* which, as we have seen, deals almost exclusively with the struggle to develop the mind and spiritual consciousness. *The Gita* opens as a war between the forces of Duryodhana and the army of Yudhisthira, Arjuna's eldest brother, is about to begin. This is an internecine war, for Duryodhana is a first cousin of Yudhisthira and Arjuna. The battle will take place at Kurukshetra, traditionally a holy site, a place of pilgrimage.

This site is very important to our subject because the dialogue between Krishna and Arjuna, which is the essence of *The Gita,* involves an attempt by Krishna to convince Arjuna that doing his duty as a member of the Kshatriya class (i.e., the warrior class) will fulfill him spiritually if his sole purpose is to serve his people (the nonaggressors in this war) and God. Going into war with the right motivation, experiencing the horrors of war without losing sight of God, whom Arjuna has experienced through deep meditation—this will be a test of Arjuna's spiritual realization. This will be a test which is far more exacting than the one which Wordsworth faced and passed on the top of Mt. Snowden. If Arjuna can see God (perfection) even in the heat of literal warfare, he will have reached the highest spiritual state, for he will have kept sight of God in the midst of His apparently imperfect creation. Thus, the site of the battle is of utmost importance to an understanding of this great poem and, of course, to an understanding of *The Gita*'s place in a literature course involving the Western epic. In other words, the "exterior" epic *The Iliad* and, to a lesser degree, *The Odyssey* and the almost entirely internalized struggle of *The Prelude* come together in *The Gita,* for Kurukshetra is the location of both a literal battle, without any of the egotism and desire for spoils (at least in the case of Arjuna) associated with *The Iliad,* and the spiritual struggle to transcend God's maya, or apparently dualistic "dream" or play. The meaning of "Kshatriya" itself is two-fold, since one can be a spiritual warrior without being a literal one or, as in the case of Arjuna, can be both a literal warrior and a spiritual one. Indeed, in the strict sense, *The Gita* tells us—all of us who seek God through meditation and through testing and bringing our God-realization into the trials of whatever work we are called to fulfill—we can be Kshatriyas.

As the dialogue between Arjuna and Krishna begins, Arjuna shows the purity of his mind and soul, his lack of any selfish motives in regard to the war, when he says to Krishna, "Lo, I hate / Triumph and domination, wealth and ease, / Thus sadly won!" (8). He asks Krishna, rhetorically, "Shall I deal death on these / Even though they seek to slay us? Not one blow, / . . . will I strike" (8). This is followed by Arjuna's statement concerning his personal guilt should he kill someone in the ensuing battle: "If they be / Guilty, we shall grow guilty by their deaths" (9). To all of this, Krishna replies,

> Nay Arjun!
> Forbid thyself to feebleness! It mars
> Thy warrior-name! cast off the coward-fit!
> Awake! Be thyself! Arise, Scourge of thy Foes!
> (II, 11)

Arjuna, however, persists in his abhorrence of this war:

> Ah! were it worse—who knows?—to be
> Victor or vanquished here,

When those confront us angrily
Whose death leaves living drear? (II, 12)

To set Arjuna's conscience at ease, Krishna begins a long speech on the immortality of the soul in order to show Arjuna that the one who is killed in battle is not killed in the soul, that the person will live again in a future incarnation. Of course, this is no justification of wanton killing. Killing an innocent (i.e., when self-defense is not involved) cuts off that person's opportunity to evolve spiritually in that person's present incarnation and involves sin for the one doing the killing. If we are to understand Krishna's meaning, we must understand the Hindu concept of the perfect soul and the need to experience that soul through deep meditation. A person who is killed in battle, or otherwise, and the person doing the killing out of self-defense—both of them will have to reincarnate if they have not experienced their perfect souls at the deepest level. Reincarnation is the result of attachment to God's maya (or play or dream), but knowledge of one's soul and union of the soul with God leave one with attachment to only the soul (and God) and thus release from subsequent incarnations. Since Arjuna is not the aggressor, and because he is without any desire for spoils or glory (and, in fact, is devoid of any desire to harm anyone for whatever reason), he is justified in taking part in the war. Indeed, it is his duty as a warrior to defend his people and to prevent a defeat which might cause his people to degenerate morally, spiritually, and economically. Since evil must be punished (or else people will not cease to find evil attractive), if Arjuna resists aggression, with love in his heart, even for the aggressor (the same love which God feels for the sinner, even as God allows the sinner to suffer as a result of the sin), no sin will accrue to Arjuna. In fact, Arjuna will have an opportunity to progress to the highest state of spirituality. He will have found God, as I previously suggested, in perhaps the most difficult place to find Him: in warfare. Arjuna thus will have won his internal battle, even as he wins the outer battle, which, of course, is exactly what takes place. The aggressor who is killed will die to his body but later reincarnate in another to continue his spiritual progress.

In his lengthy speech, Krishna discusses reincarnation when he speaks of "raisings-up and layings-down / Of other life-abodes, / Which the wise know and fear not" (II, 13). He tells of how sense-attachments anchor our consciousness to maya and points out that the soul is immortal and that freedom lies in awareness of the soul's perfection:

> This that irks—
> Thy sense-life, thrilling to the elements—
> Bringing thee heat and cold, sorrows and
> joys,
> 'Tis brief and mutable! Bear with it, Prince!
> As the wise bear. The soul which is not
> moved,
> The soul that with a strong and constant
> calm
> Takes sorrow and takes joy indifferently
> Lives in the life undying! that which is
> Can never cease to be. (II, 13–14)

Then he tells Arjuna to do his duty: "Do thy part! / Be mindful of thy name, and tremble not!" (II, 17). Arjuna must realize that "Naught better can betide a martial soul / Than lawful war..." (II, 17). He must understand that "happy [is] the warrior / To whom comes joy of battle—comes, as now, / Glorious and fair, unsought; opening for him / A gateway unto heav'n" (II, 17). Indeed, it would be a sin for Arjuna to shun this war:

> But if thou shunn'st
> This honorable field—a Kshatriya—
> If, Knowing thy duty and thy task, thou bidd'st
> Duty and task go by—that shall be a sin! (II, 17)

It is "with perfect meditation" that "perfect act" comes (II, 20). Arjuna must realize that if "right deeds" are his "motive, not the fruit which comes from them," and if he casts "all self aside, / Contemning gain and merit" (II, 20), all of which derives from meditation (i.e., calming the senses and the mind and thus experiencing the soul), then his actions in the war will further ennoble him:

> with perfect meditation
> Comes perfect act, and the right-hearted rise—
> More certainly because they seek no gain—
> Forth from the bands of body, step by step,
> To highest seats of bliss. (II, 20)

Arjuna is not to shun action but to become "the true Recluse" (II, 21), who, like "the wise tortoise[,]draws its four feet safe / Under its shield [the soul], his five frail senses back / Under the spirit's buckler from the world / Which else assails them" (II, 22).

Much later in *The Gita,* Arjuna asks Krishna for a vision of God's (or Krishna's, since Krishna is an incarnation of God) "glory of . . . Form / Wholly revealed" (XI, 91). Krishna consents, and Arjuna beholds

"All this universe enfold / All its huge diversity / Into one vast shape . . ." (XI, 94). Arjuna beholds everything as a part of God, as apparent diversity within "the Undivided" (XI, 96). In essence, there are "no Earth and Heaven" but, rather, "Thee [God] only—only Thee!" (XI, 100). Arjuna thus learns that, when one is attuned to God and sees God in everything, and, therefore, loves everything, it is God Himself who is the only doer and the only one who punishes the wrongdoer, in this case Arjuna's enemies in the opposing army. Thus, Krishna says to Arjuna,

> Arise! obtain renown!
> destroy thy foes!
> Fight for the kingdom waiting thee when
>   thou hast vanquished those.
> By Me they fall—not thee! the stroke of
>   death is dealt them now,
> Even as they show thus gallantly; My
>   instrument art thou! (XI, 102–03)

The "renown" which Krishna wants Arjuna to attain is not, of course, worldly fame but, rather, a heavenly reward, in the ultimate sense. Even on earth, however, there is the bliss of seeing God and loving God in all things. This is the way Krishna puts it:

> He sees indeed who sees in all alike
> The living, lordly Soul; the Soul Supreme,
> Imperishable amid the Perishing:
> For, whoso thus beholds, in every place,
> In every form, the same, one, Living Lord,
> Doth no more wrongfulness unto himself,
> But goes the highest road which brings to
> bliss.   (XIII, 120)

The date of composition of *The Gita* is unknown, but it was written in ancient India, possibly after *The Odyssey* was written, although some think it was composed before that great Western epic. In any event, it far surpasses all of the epic poems heretofore discussed, including even *The Prelude,* in regard to spiritualizing the epic struggle. And, at the same time, it incorporates, and finds no contradiction in doing so, the idea of the validity of doing courageous deeds in a literal war. Nevertheless, this magnificent work symbolizes, through the warrior, all right activity performed for the sake of mankind and with God as one's source of inspiration.

Thus, *The Bhagavad Gita* can very easily be incorporated into a course which deals with any or all of the epic poems mentioned in this essay. Others which have not been mentioned, such as Blake's

Milton, could be discussed in the context of the trend toward internalizing the heroic struggle in the Western epic and thus in the context of *The Gita.* One should not be put off, either, by the fact that reincarnation is not a doctrine which has wide acceptance in the "religions of the West," as Judaism and Christianity are often thought to be, even though they, like all the great religions, had their genesis in the East. At a time when there is much confusion in Christianity concerning what is in store for Christians in afterlife, the theory of reincarnation is receiving increasing attention. In any event, as I have shown, especially with *The Prelude,* and in my brief discussion of the similarities between *The Gita* and The Sermon on the Mount, there is much to be found in *The Gita* which has relevance to Western literature, including, of course, those early epics of Homer and Vergil. Arjuna, like Hector and Achilles, possesses great physical courage, but, beyond that, he possesses, to a greater degree perhaps than did Wordsworth, the courage to struggle, to go within himself in the hopes of finding perfection of the soul and bringing that perfection to bear on maya in the form of literal warfare.

Note

The Mahabharata itself has been dramatized by Peter Brook, whose version is based on the Jean-Claude Carriere adaptation of the poem. Brook's production is available from the Parabola Video Library, and this film version was shown on the Public Broadcasting System's stations in March 1991. Part II of this film has the greatest relevance to *The Gita,* and it has been used in classrooms very effectively to enhance the students' understanding and enjoyment of *The Gita. The Gita* itself is available in inexpensive paperback translations.

References

Eliot, T. S. "Vergil and The Christian World." *The Sewanee Review* 61 (1953): 1–14.

Homer. *The Odyssey.* Translated by Robert Fitzgerald. Garden City, NY: Doubleday, 1963.

Kroeber, Karl. *Romantic Narrative Art.* Madison: The University of Wisconsin Press, 1960.

Lord, George de F. "*The Odyssey* and the Western World." *The Sewanee Review* 62 (1954): 406–27.

Milton, John. *Paradise Lost: A Poem in Twelve Books.* 1674. Reprint. Edited by Merritt Y. Hughes. Indianapolis: The Odyssey Press, 1962.

The Song Celestial or Bhagavad-Gita. Translated by Sir Edwin Arnold. Los Angeles: Self-Realization Fellowship, 1975.

Thoreau, Henry David. *Walden.* 1889. Reprint. New York: Holt, Rinehart and Winston, 1961.

Wordsworth, William. *The Prelude or Growth of a Poet's Mind.* 1850. Reprint. Edited by Thomas Hutchison and Ernest De Salincourt. London: Oxford University Press, 1964.

8 Contending with the Masculinist Traditions: *Sundiata*'s Sogolon and the Wife of Bath

Sidney Vance
University of Montevallo

The *Sundiata: An Epic of Old Mali* (1965) is G. D. Pickett's English version of D. T. Niane's French version of *Soundjata, ou l'Epopee Mandingue* (1960), a transcription of the "story of the ancestor of great Mali" (Niane 1986, 1), as told by Djeli Mamadou Kouyate, a modern Mandingo griot. The historical events which underlie the epic occurred in the early thirteenth century, and the story has been passed from griot to griot in the Kouyate family for about seven hundred years. Some scholars maintain that a responsible American reading of the story cannot take place in "the vacuum of a direct and unmediated relationship with the text" (Miller 1990, 4). However, the typical American English professor need not be daunted at the prospect of leading a typical class of American undergraduates across the chasms which seem to thwart a reading of *Sundiata.* Although finding and using texts on language, anthropology, religion, and critical theory that mediate between non-African readers and the text is something an Africanist in an advanced class could be expected to do, there are texts accessible to the canonically trained generalist which can be used to foster just readings of *Sundiata,* readings which have some grounding in sociological intelligence and literary theory.

Sundiata, read as the epic account of the return of a warrior-prince from exile to claim his rightful throne and to restore order and justice, obviously suggests comparisons with such canonical texts as *The Odyssey* and *Beowulf.* The professor of literature knows of the ways of the Greeks and the Anglo-Saxons, and of the texts produced by their oral traditions. Obviously these texts, even in their modern English versions, can mediate our relationship with *Sundiata,* revealing much about griots and heroes, politics and poetics.

Sundiata, however, contains a unique subtext which establishes its central difference from comparable Western epics. The early parts of the story focus on the marvelous mother of the hero, including the fantastic events that lead to her conceiving of Sundiata. The story of Sogolon the matriarch presents her struggle with the masculinist Muslim society of western Africa in her time. Sundiata, both as text and protagonist, germinates from Sogolon, mother and namesake of Sogolon Diata.

This subtext, the Sogoloniad, includes a distinctive set of structural increments which suggest comparison with other texts in addition to Western epics. In the Sogoloniad the quest of two young males is resolved by an old hag, a shape-shifter, the wraith or alter ego of the heroine. A marriage between the heroine, described as ugly and misshapen, and a handsome high-born man results in a reluctant consummation—a rape, in fact. *The Canterbury Tales* includes a comparable female character whose narrative asserts her independence from the patriarchy. The Wife of Bath co-opts a masculinist narrative form, the romance, for feminist ends, using a set of narrational increments with striking parallels to and interesting obversions of similar increments in Sogolon's story. The tale of Alice of Bath *begins* with a rape and contains a quest, an old hag who knows what the young male questor needs, a marriage between an ugly old woman and a handsome high-born man, shape-shifting, and a momentous consummation.

The features shared by the two texts offer different, but complementary, perspectives on woman as "other" functioning within an oppressive society. These two views are not strictly analogous or congruent, but they both employ some of the principal sources of gender oppression as identified by feminine theorists. Both subtexts foreground the feminist concerns of voice, agency, and the commodification of women (Dinshaw 1989, 96–99; Rubin 1975, 160–64). Both subtexts resonate with insistent, if unacknowledged, feminism throughout the larger texts of which they are a part.

The most obvious and most telling difference in the two texts is in the narratorial voices. Sogolon's story is presented as if told by a male griot, but narratorial layers objectify and distance her from the reader. Intermediaries—translators, transcribers, oral narratives by griots of the words of characters in the story—lie between the contemporary reader and Sogolon's story. For example, the first portion of her story, the narrative of the buffalo hunt, is written in English from the French from the transcription of the griot's Malinke account of what the hunters of Do told King Nare Maghan kon Fatta. Even the powerful Buffalo Woman who starts it all is ultimately an object rather than a subject. The text conveys her clear but elaborate directions to the hunters, but she remains passive. Her story is retold by male agents of the patriarchy for their profit or reward. The hunter, for instance, pointedly, perhaps self-servingly, reports that the Buffalo Woman explicitly acknowledged his generosity. He also enhances Sogolon's status by saying that the Buffalo Woman referred to her as "my wraith" (7).[1] The griot presents the hunters as having appropriated the words of the Buffalo Woman for their own advancement.

In contrast, Chaucer's Wife of Bath is presented as being her own griot. She is given personal and artistic voice as virtually no fictional woman was up to that time. She creates herself through her voice, first in her autobiographical prologue, second in her tale—a romance about sexual politics. The wife, as agent in her prologue, creates herself, functioning as agent in her own career as wife. Her creation of woman as subject or agent in her tale uses a typically masculine genre as a narrative method to present her own brand of feminism.

Even though the Buffalo Woman is objectified in the narrative of the hunt, she is not rendered powerless. Sogolon's wraith exerts power because man commodifies woman. The hunters are rewarded for killing the Buffalo with their choice of the eligible women of Do, but the Buffalo Woman has directed that they choose Sogolon, the ugliest of all. Their obedience enhances the comedy of the hunters' description of the display of the daughters of Do competing like beauty queens to be chosen as the bride of the mighty hunter:

> All the daughters of Do wore their festive dress; gold shone in their hair and fragile wrists bent under the weight of heavy silver bracelets. Never did so much beauty come together in one place. Full of pride, my quiver on my back, I swaggered before the beautiful girls of Do who were smiling at me, with their teeth as white as the rice of Mali. (9)

Their happy complicity with the marketing of women and his proud but empty swagger convert the misogyny of the scene into pointed comedy. Their attractive packaging does not entice the hunter, who chooses the ugly hunchback, Sogolon, as directed by the Buffalo Woman. Her directions alter, but do not cancel, the position of the male, the selective chooser of the female. The criteria are modified from superficial beauty—presumably sexual attractiveness—to some deeper, less visible qualities somehow associated with Sogolon's capabilities as breeder and nurturer of a messianic male child.

The Buffalo Woman has earlier associated Sogolon's worth with her virginity. Sogolon, she says, "will be an extraordinary woman if you manage to possess her" (11). Niane's version does not detail the hunters' attempts to "possess" Sogolon as does Camara Laye's *The Guardian of the Word*. Her extreme means to frustrate the lusty hunters suggests that she is more valuable as a virgin, even worthy of being "possessed" by a king in order to get a prince.

The Wife of Bath convinces her readers that she is no reluctant virgin. She has had experience with men and with their system that trades women and justifies it with texts. She knows she is merchandise and "uses that knowledge of woman's commodification to her own advantage" (Dinshaw 1989, 112). As we know from her prologue, she can also regard men as merchandise; variously she reduces her husbands to sides of bacon (418), barrels "ful of lyes" (308), or "nether purses" (45) who are equipped with "sely instruments" (132).[2] She has profited in one way or another from at least four of her five marriages. But it is her tale that offers a broader feminism that "adjusts the crucial workings of the patriarchal exchange of women" (Dinshaw 1989, 127). Her text suggests that her principal aim is not to overthrow the patriarchy, but rather to instruct the wielder of patriarchal power, here the rapist, as to "what thyng it is that women most desiren" (l. 905). Her tale aims to assert the ways of woman to man that he might "acknowledge the integrity of the feminine body and act in reference to feminine desire" (Dinshaw 1989, 127).

The emphatically positioned rapes in the narratives clarify and weaken the validity of patriarchal power. Even though Sogolon's "romance" culminates with rape and Alice's begins with rape, both instances of violent male possession empower women by exposing the contempt for the integrity of the female body and female desire latent in the patriarchy. As the final act of Sogolon's honeymoon, her rape represents a result of the trade in women. As the initial act toward a honeymoon consummation, the rape in "The Wife of Bath's Tale" represents a cause of or impetus for the lessons that the text can deliver to the masculine world.

When Maghan kon Fatta seizes Sogolon "by the hair with an iron grip," threatening her with death, frightening her into unconsciousness, penetrating and impregnating her (12), he graphically reveals some of the powers traditionally granted to husbands and potentates. He has been "given" Sogolon as if she were a fine brood mare: "She will be an extraordinary woman if you manage to possess her." Sogolon's week-long resistance renders Maghan's frustration comical at first, but, in a rich manifestation of patriarchal powers, the handsome king enlists text, religion, deceit, threat of death, and physical violence to consummate his marriage to his ugly alien bride seven nights after the wedding ceremony.

One consequence of the rape, Sogolon's pregnancy, gives her temporary privilege and status, but sows discord in the royal house. While she flaunts "her pregnancy about the palace," a rival wife, Sassouma Berete, mother of another male child, plots to displace Sogolon and the son she carries. Because the male is valorized, females associated with males are valorized. Shortly Sogolon and Maghan will be wounded by the failure of their precious male child to live up to expectations. The rivalry between males will be the source of discord in the family and in the kingdom until Sundiata regains the scepter.

In "The Wife of Bath's Tale," when the "lusty bachelor" of Arthur's court "by verray force" rapes a virgin, he exposes himself first to an iron retributive patriarchal law that demands his decapitation. However, he is saved by a rehabilitative lesson on the blessings of respecting feminine desire. The wife acknowledges that this is a capital "oppression," but suggests that under patriarchal law it is such because the knight has damaged the woman as merchandise by rupturing her hymen—at least the wife's narration suggests that. Her sentence describing the deed valorizes virginity by repetition. "He saugh a mayde . . . which mayde anon . . . by verray force he raft hire maydenhed" (886–88). She immediately ties the offense to Arthur's punishment: "For which oppressioun . . . dampned was this knight for to be ded" (889–91). The rehabilitative probation that Guinevere imposes instead suggests that, while the knight "may not do al as hym liketh" (914), the masculine order values virginity more than the feminine order does.

The Wife of Bath has already demonstrated in her prologue that she knows well how men use texts, religious teachings, and physical violence to try to have their way with women. She has armed herself with such patriarchal powers so that her "wraith," her alter identity, the ugly old peasant hag, gains power over her young knight of a husband. The hag-bride creates her text, the "gentilesse" sermon in which she teaches the advantages of base lineage, poverty, old age, and ugliness out of texts by Cicero, Boethius, Dante, and others. She demonstrates that she knows something of the textual claims of the masculinist system for moral and doctrinal validity, but she also knows that the commodification of sexual woman is probably a more potent force among men in the world. As Carolyn Dinshaw points out, "after she undoes all patriarchal ideas of lineage . . . possession . . . and feminine beauty . . . she concedes, 'But natheless, syn I know your delit, / I shal fulfille your worldly appetit' " (1217–18). Offered the option of a foul old true wife, or a fair young wife who might be untrue, he says she can choose, "for as you liketh, it suffisith me" (1235). He says he grants her "maistre" to govern as she chooses. In return she grants her concession which includes obeying "hym in everything / That myghte doon hym plesance or likyng" (1255–58). She has used some powers of the masculinist system to get control over a representative male and to present him with a model of female desire and power. She grants him a sexually satisfying reciprocity as she unveils her femininity. The husband-knight is made vulnerable to her instruction because of his masculine desires.

Gender codes have usually kept lay women at home. Men went on quests, crusades, and pilgrimages, and they were sometimes forced into exile. But women, once acquired, stayed home, not because they wanted to but because, as valuable property, they were in danger of being rustled or hustled when "wandrynge by the way." To travel is to act as an agent. Both Sogolon and Alice undertake major journeys, Sogolon's a voluntary exile of several years to protect herself and her family, Alice's a pilgrimage of a few days for some spiritual and social revitalizing. While their trips differ in motive and meaning, they do clarify their individual struggles as females in male-dominated societies.

That Alice is the only lay woman on the pilgrimage to Canterbury validates the rarity of women travelers. This trip and the others that we know about—to Rome, thrice to Jerusalem, and to other major shrines—indicate extraordinary independence and prosperity. She has earned her freedom and her money from her activities in the female commodity exchange. There is some evidence that she has earned a measure of safety, becoming through age and use a less valuable commodity. There is even evidence that she may be pilgrimaging in order to get back in the market: "Welcome the sixte, whan that evere he shal" (45). We can certainly say that she is a vigorous pilgrim, partially because of her successful manipulation of some of the major games of the patriarchy.

Sogolon, as "wise mother," leaves Niani to become the stabilizing matriarch to balance the disorder spawned by the patriarchy. Maghan's polygamy makes for a disorderly succession to the throne as Sassouma Berete threatens Sogolon and Sundiata, who has been designated for the throne now occupied by Sassouma's son, Dankaran Touman. Politics force Sogolon to Djedeba, to Tabon, to Wagadon in Ghana, and to Mema, where she dies just before Sundiata starts his victorious campaign. Sogolon's stability as matriarch contrasts with the monarchical disorder of the courts she and her family visit. Simultaneous with Sogolon's nurturing exile is the rise of Soumaoro, Sundiata's ultimate adversary.

Soumaoro's unrestrained acquisition of women is finally the source of his defeat. Subjects and rivals alike rally to oppose the man who "defiled every family ... everywhere in his vast empire there were villages populated by girls whom he had forcibly abducted from their families without marrying them" (41). Later Nana Triban, Sundiata's half-sister, tells him that she was one of Soumaoro's "numerous wives" (57). In Camara Laye's *The Guardian of the Word,* Nana Triban is unimpressed when Soumaoro tells her just before she seduces him that she is "better built and certainly more seductive than any of the three hundred wives in [his] harem" (168).

Soumaoro's failure to regard women as anything but objects finally destroys him. The incestuous rape of Keleya, wife of his nephew, Fakoli Koroma, excites "all those long-repressed hates and rancours . . . and everywhere men answered the call of Fakoli" (42). Deluded by vanity and lust, he indiscreetly tells Nana Triban of his Tana, the spur of a white cock, which Sundiata uses to destroy him.

It is significant that Sundiata in Niane's version avoids contact with women outside of his family. There is no hint of any sexual interest in this version, which seems more nearly to capture the qualities of the oral tradition. In Camara Laye's *The Guardian of the Word,* a more novelistic treatment, "adorable" Aisha Aminu shares the hero's bed (182). When he leaves Mema to confront Soumaoro, Sundiata tells her, "When the war is over I shall have you brought to Niani" (184), but there is no textual evidence that he did. Niane's version suggests that the hero avoids any activity which might present him as a user of women.

The Wife of Bath has trafficked in men, but she is spouseless and apparently childless when she makes her texts. Like the Sogoloniad, her narrative resonates throughout the larger story of which she is an essential part. The brilliant stories of the center of *The Canterbury Tales* that explore gendered relationships, such as the Nun's Priest's, the Clerk's, the Merchant's, and the Franklin's tales are in some sense generated by the Wife of Bath's performance. The male narrators attempt to reply to the wife's feminism, to engage her in dialogue. Her own text also helps English-speaking readers to engage in a dialogue with an African text that narrates another woman's heroic confrontation with a system that would use her and other women. Such dialogue may not carry us back to the oral tale before transcription and translation, but it can help us to see how a traditional West African epic struggle has some of its causes and effects in issues of gender.

Notes

1. Unless otherwise stated, all references to the *Sundiata* are from G. D. Pickett's English translation of D. T. Niane's French version of *Soundjata, ou l'Epopee Mandingue.*

2. All references to *The Canterbury Tales* are in *The Riverside Chaucer,* 3d ed., edited by Larry D. Benson, Boston: Houghton Mifflin, 1987. Citations are by line numbers.

References

Chaucer, Geoffrey. *The Riverside Chaucer,* 3d ed. Edited by Larry Benson. Boston: Houghton Mifflin, 1987.

Dinshaw, Carolyn. *Chaucer's Sexual Poetics.* Madison: University of Wisconsin Press, 1989.

Laye, Camara. *The Guardian of the World.* Translated by James Kirkup. New York: Vintage Books, 1984.

Lee, Sonia. *Camara Laye.* Boston: Twayne Publishers, 1984.

Leicester, H. Marshall. *The Disenchanted Self: Representing the Subject in the Canterbury Tales.* Berkeley: University of California Press, 1990.

Miller, Christopher. *Theories of Africans.* Chicago: University of Chicago Press, 1990.

Niane, D. T. *Sundiata: An Epic of Old Mali.* Translated by G. D. Pickett. Essex, England: Longman, 1986.

Olney, James. *Tell Me Africa: An Approach to African Literature.* Princeton: Princeton University Press, 1973.

Rubin, Gayle. "The Traffic in Women: Notes on the 'Retired Economy' of Sex." In *Toward an Anthology of Women,* edited by R. R. Reiter, 157–210. New York: Monthly Review Press, 1975.

Schipper, Mineke. "Mother Africa on a Pedestal: The Male Heritage in African Literature and Criticism." In *Woman in African Literature Today,* edited by Eldred D. Jones, 35–54. London: James Curry, 1987.

9 Soseki's *Kokoro:* The Voice of the Exile in Quest of a Modern Self

Paul Anderer
Columbia University

[*Editor's Note: Professor Anderer's introduction to Soseki's* Kokoro *brings to our attention several significant issues related to the hero. Drawing on the long tradition in Japanese literature of personal expression in journals, diaries, and letters, Soseki uses his own personal experiences and the personal narrative voice of his characters to depict the hero's quest for identity within the context of cultural change. Professor Anderer shows that Soseki himself was regarded both as a hero of the Meiji period and as one of the first Japanese intellectuals to master Western culture and to reflect the modern temper. Both Soseki and his fictional characters confront the anxieties created by this cultural change and by a modern sense of isolation, alienation, and loss. Professor Anderer's discussion suggests to us that Soseki himself may be regarded as a courageous literary hero who creates experimental forms out of Japanese and Western traditions and who refuses, despite his personal suffering, to abdicate moral responsibility to follow decadent literary fashion. According to Professor Anderer, Soseki and his characters are equally courageous in confronting the loneliness and guilt which so often plague the modern hero. Determined to employ literature, language, and the personal voice to break out of silence and secrecy, Soseki clings heroically to the belief "that literature is language shared, and that such language could heal hearts and re-order the world" (Anderer, 116).*

Professor Anderer suggests parallels with the work of Joseph Conrad, and his remarks evoke other literary connections with works such as Dostoevsky's Crime and Punishment, *Kafka's* The Metamorphoses, *James Joyce's* Ulysses, *Virginia Woolf's* To The Lighthouse, *and Doris Lessing's* "To Room 19." *Parallels with African writers who have also created new forms out of traditional African and Western sources are especially strong. Among the African works which also depict isolated and disillusioned heroes courageously confronting the frustrations and disappointments of modern life are Ayi Kwei Armah's* The Beautiful Ones Are Not Yet Born, *Sembene Ousmane's* The Money Order, *Chinua Achebe's* No Longer at Ease, *Buchi Emecheta's* The Bride Price, *and Bessie Head's* A Question of Power.]

When Natsume Soseki (1867–1916) completed *Kokoro,* he was seriously ill and near the end of his life. Illness, to be sure, figures as a metaphor in much of his writing. He is often perceived as a novelist of victims, especially the self-victim, those Japanese intellectuals who had serious, prolonged exposure to the West, and were showing pathological signs. His life spanned the Meiji period (1868–1912), and is wholly identified with it. If any modern writer can be said to speak for his time, it is Soseki. Though he did not begin writing in earnest until his middle years, in little more than a decade he produced more than a dozen books on a very few themes—betrayal, loss, a Kierkegaardian "sickness unto death" are chief among them. His work reveals a scrutiny and an intelligence, lacerating enough to expose not just inner turmoil but the dislocations of this transformative age.

Like the shadows which fall over the characters in *Kokoro,* Soseki has cast his shadow over much Japanese writing of his own and later generations. When critics say he has no rightful successor, they signal respect for the integrity and force of Soseki's fiction, which has not diminished over time. Tanizaki, for example, took him to task for a priggish portrayal of love, and a brooding moralism which left no room for sensuality. In his late writing (i.e., from the trilogy of *Sanshiro, And Then,* and *The Gate,* begun in 1908, through *Light and Darkness,* his last uncompleted work, in 1916) Soseki does seem to have severed connections with the richly comic, parodical fictional style of the Tokugawa period (1600–1868), which his early work had put to good use. Yet in grappling with his own increasingly depressive self, Soseki found a method to inscribe a cultural crisis. Nowhere does this method show forth with greater simplicity and dramatic power than in *Kokoro.*

It was not conceived as a long novel, but as a story, then a set of stories, on a related theme. This is characteristic not only of most post-Restoration fiction and the exigencies of serial publication in newspapers and magazines but of much fine or influential Japanese prose of preceding eras. There are generic affinities as well with the traditional diary and memoir since *Kokoro,* in all its parts, is told by a personal narrator. Indeed, terms already used, like "novel" or "fiction," based on different narrative or epistemological premises, may seem inadequate to describe the type of story even Soseki—an avowedly modern, experimental writer—has produced.

In *Kokoro,* as in *Grass on the Wayside* (1915), the work which followed it and is cited by critics as his only "autobiographical novel," Soseki seems to be writing confessional prose, revealing traces of the older diary and epistolary styles, yet charging it with a heightened awareness; that a personal story might be dramatically revealing, both of individual consciousness and a wider, social world. Too dense and circumstantial to be allegory, *Kokoro* might be called a tale of moral disorder. If the tone and quality of the writing seem reminiscent of Conrad, so too is the critique of cultural adventurism, the crisscrossing ambitions of modern individuals, driven by a historical imperative to overreach old boundaries and definitions. Soseki pushed Japanese prose toward new, if isolating, limits. With skill and exercise of will, he traced in his fiction the shape of ideas and beliefs, old and new, even as the characters who held them were about to vanish.

Soseki's Background

Natsume Kinnosuke ("Soseki" is a pen name) was born in Tokyo in 1867, the eighth child of elderly parents. By general account, he was unwanted. He was left out for care to one couple who neglected the infant, then for adoption to another couple who would divorce. At the age of nine, Soseki was shunted back to his parents. Later he would claim, credibly, that his childhood memories were cast over by "a cold and sad shadow."

Of his schooling, Soseki's early immersion in the Chinese classics is conspicuous. Throughout his life, even at the end when he was feverishly turning out his modern novels, Soseki wrote *kanshi,* or Chinese poetry, which specialists judge among the finest composed by a Japanese of any period, much less one as distracting as was Meiji Japan. In his Chinese studies, too, Soseki would have gleaned a neo-Confucian sense of an ordered universe, subject to violation by selfish excess. The moral urgency of his fiction, the fear it generates in the face of transgression, derives, no doubt, from this classical, ethical background.

Yet to enter college in the mid-1880s, Soseki proposed to study English, either by choice or in acquiescence to the powerful current of the time (many advanced textbooks, in a variety of disciplines, were still in the English language). Soseki complained incessantly about the dull instruction, yet acquired a stunning fluency in the written language, attested to both by his superb English translation (ca. 1891) of Chomei's twelfth-century parable, "The Account of My Hut," and later by his trenchant criticism, based on wide and careful reading, ranging from Arthurian legend to Swift, *Tristram Shandy* to George Meredith.

In college he expressed a career wish to become a writer—in the 1890s still a suspect, if not a demeaning, profession for someone with a degree—or to become an architect, for which he was wholly untrained. Instead, on graduation, he accepted a middle school teaching post on the island of Shikoku, then moved even further west to Kumamoto in Kyushu, where he taught at the Fifth National College. It was a bizarre path for a brilliant graduate of Tokyo Imperial University to follow. There is evidence he wished to inflict a certain austerity on himself, that he left Tokyo for the provinces "in the spirit of renouncing everything." The experience shows up in the fiction, from the early comic *Botchan,* actually set in a remote provincial town, to the late *Kokoro,* set between Tokyo and the provinces. Throughout his career, Soseki proved himself to be a keen observer of the multiple tensions, misrecognitions, and hostilities which separated the country and the city.

Then, in 1900, at the age of thirty-three, already married and a father, Soseki accepted a government grant to study in England for two years. Alone, he set sail from Yokohama in what has often been described as the most fateful move of his life.

His London sojourn, personally harrowing for Soseki, has assumed over the course of this century in Japan, a paradigmatic significance. The misery and humiliation Soseki encountered—skimping along on a meager stipend in a shabby flat, passing up meals to purchase books, spending days on end in isolation, handing over an extortionary fee to a diffident tutor (W. J. Craig, an editor of the Arden Shakespeare), being eyed in a crowd like some exotic, helpless prey ("a lost dog in a pack of wolves"), imagining in his despair detectives at his heels—all this has been passed on as a cautionary tale about deception and betrayal on the outside, by the Western "other." Soseki did arrive in England with great expectations, believing he would leave his mark on English letters, and returned a profoundly disillusioned man. He had studied the West, to the point of adulation, and the West ignored him. In this way Soseki in London has come to symbolize not only Meiji Japan, struggling against unequal treaties and the full force of nineteenth-century colonialist prejudice to "arrive" in the modern world, but also twentieth-century Japan which, by so many technological and economic indices, has indeed "arrived," yet with a schizophrenic cultural identity, and a morbid concern about its image in the "world outside."

It is remarkable that upon his return in 1903, Soseki should have been such an outspoken critic of that Japanese nationalism which was prevalent between the Sino-Japanese and Russo-Japanese wars. Cries of "yamato damashi"—Japanese spirit—were a cover, he claimed, to hide a real fear that no such thing, no cultural confidence, still existed. In eloquent essays and public lectures, Soseki sought to reach and warn an often youthful audience that civilization meant more than a materialistic accumulation of laborsaving devices, or that rote and random copying of Western ways would lead eventually to superficiality or mental collapse. Yet he was no reactionary, and was equally stoic in saying there was no turning back. Soseki's many physical ailments, the gastric ulcers of which he was to die, have been well documented, as have signs of mental disorder during and following his stay abroad. It is fair to suggest that Soseki had himself become a casualty of that unbridled competition he would warn others against. That he was in no sense superficial is clear from all he wrote.

Back in Japan, Soseki took up residence in Tokyo and a position of prestige at the Imperial University. He succeeded Lafcadio Hearn as lecturer in English, an act he ruefully felt would be hard to follow. It was while teaching that he began to write fiction, beginning with *I Am a Cat* (1905), a ranging and exuberant social satire, skewing both Meiji commercialism and academic pomposity. But by 1907, exhausted in his attempt to be a teacher in what was, after all, a government bureaucracy, Soseki accepted an offer from the Asahi Shimbun, a mass circulation daily, to join its editorial staff. By the existing standards of social respectability, Soseki again had taken a puzzling downward step. Yet it also gave him more time to devote to his fiction, and a more visible, public presence. Over the years he conscientiously used his position at the newspaper to discover and advance promising young writers, even those from literary "schools" he might have despised.

Trained as a classical scholar, prodigious too in his knowledge of Western literatures, Soseki, when he came to write his own fiction, was acutely aware of the relativity of narrative forms. He approached literature, if not quite scientifically, at least with an experimental bias and seemed eager to generate hybrid stories, mixing, for example, a "fictive" Western strain of allegory or romance with Japanese prose, grounded, as it often was, in the lyric, as well as in the certainties, shared by Japanese writers and readers alike, that literary art was a concrete and imitable activity. No modern author, except perhaps Mishima, tried to write prose in so many different styles. For all his acknowledged greatness as a Meiji culture-hero, Soseki has thus appeared, to some Japanese readers, to be unpredictable and, in a strict sense, inimitable.

A line which seems crucial to *Kokoro*—"You see I am lost. I have become a puzzle even to himself"—is a declaration identical to St. Augustine's, and we might conclude that this book is a species of literary confession. Yet it should be noticed that Soseki was a fierce critic of the prevailing literary school of his day, the Japanese naturalists, writers who advertised their goal as a plain, unvarnished depiction of objective reality, yet in practice wrote grim or salacious self-confessions, whose details were regularly traced back to the author's real life. However unpalatable, this writing claimed the virtue of being sincere, "true to the self." Soseki reviled much of this "confessional" work as a self-serving sham. He had no faith that the modern self even existed, much less had a capacity to be sincere (his doubts were more intricately laid out in *The Miner*, where, under the pretext of exploring life "underground" in a copper mine, he really explores the various narrative tricks behind the construction of a fictional "character"). By this light, the confessional naturalists appeared to Soseki both ethically misconceived and stylistically narrow. To the end, Soseki believed that as a writer he bore a moral responsibility which transcended devotion either to his own suffering self or to an aloof and decadent art.

We can trace in Soseki's fiction, then, a wide range of "influence," from Edo raconteur to William James, Zen koan to Jane Austen, but what identifies his various fictional experiments as a corpus is a will to illuminate, but not glorify, the conditions of outsiders, even exiles. In this way, Soseki has emerged not just as a spokesman for Meiji culture, but as the dominant presence in modern fiction down to our own day. This is because in book after book he engaged the various ways Japanese have become—or been made—strangers in their own land. This represents a crisis of spirit, a sickness of sorts, and though other writers have styled themselves "doctors of the soul," Soseki only traced the affliction, offering no quick cures.

Kokoro

"I should never have noticed him had he not been accompanied by a Westerner," the youthful narrator of *Kokoro* tells us, explaining how on a crowded beach he discovered the stranger who would change his life. The youth gravitates toward this stranger, whom he calls Sensei, or teacher. Sensei lives in the city, an intellectual who holds no position and is unrecognized by the world. Yet he will grow in stature in the youth's eyes, until by the end of the first section, he has become a presence to rival the youth's real father, who lies ill and dying of a kidney disease in the provinces. Finally, prior to his suicide, Sensei will write a long letter to the youth, confiding in him the secret of his past, heretofore revealed to no one, not even his wife.

Few other characters appear in *Kokoro*, and none of the major characters have personal names. The prose is spare, stark. For a Japanese book of reminiscence (the "events" have all occurred, we know, before the story begins), there is scant lyrical detail. More to the point, such details do not float free, unhinged from the drive of the narrative. "Sensei's hat, which had hung on top of a slender cedar sapling, was blown off by the breeze," we read, at the close of one episode, then read, at the opening of the next: "I picked up the hat immediately." Edwin McClellan, who translated the book, has remarked on a beauty within *Kokoro*'s simplicity, especially in the last section. This has less to do with the influence of classical poetry on the prose (as we find regularly, for example, in Kawabata's fiction) than with the austere beauty of medieval prose, as in Chomei's "The Account of My Hut" or the exile chapters in the *Tale of the Heike,* writings which, like Soseki's, trace hesitant, ambivalent movements across a barren, monochromatic terrain.

The three-part structure of *Kokoro* seems endlessly replicated internally by an array of triangular relationships. It is as though no character, no element of the world, reacts directly with any other. Between the youth and his father stands Sensei; between Sensei and his wife, the shadow of K; between even flowers and their natural appreciation, the grave at Zoshigaya. Finally, shuttling between country and city, belonging nowhere, the youth reads Sensei's "testament" in isolation, on a train.

It is a still, impotent, deadlocked world in which no one goes anywhere, or wants anything, unless someone else has already been there (recall the Westerner at the beach) or wanted the same thing too. Sensei, we come to know, feels love for Ojosan, but does not profess love and marry her until after his friend has made his own feeling known. After betraying oneself by not expressing one's deepest desires, any other betrayal seems not only possible but likely. "Can a man change so because of the death of one friend?" Sensei's wife asks the youth early in the book. "That is what I want you to tell me." But he will never tell her, even after he learns the answer, because by then he has himself become a betrayer, a modern self, baptized, as it were, in the blood of his Sensei, and so incapable of having direct, human contact.

As the narrative unfolds, the heroes disappear as if processionally, each one smaller, more diminished, than the one gone by—the Meiji Emperor, General Nogi, K, and the last Sensei, putatively, the truest hero of the book, who could not in life say to those who loved him what he will confess, on paper, at his death. And even this "truth" he leaves as a legacy to the youth and no other.

"I would rather be truly ill than suffering from a trifling cold like this," Sensei once tells the youth. "If I must be ill, then I should like to be mortally ill." This "higher illness," a mental suffering, becomes a token of value, for Sensei and for the youth, just as K's highmindedness—a rectitude which had him live according to the Koran, the Bible, and Buddhist doctrine simultaneously, and which killed him as surely as any shock at being betrayed by a friend—comes to appear in retrospect, a positive spiritual ideal. But it is an ideal, like Sensei's and the youth's, which is bound up in secrecy and, ultimately, silence.

On one hand, then, we encounter the language of the "hero," the isolated modern self, that monster which Soseki relentlessly tracked throughout his career, and captured most fully in this book. It is language veering toward silence. But there are other languages in *Kokoro*. We hear, for example, the wife speak plainly of her concern and fear for her husband, and the voice of the youth's father, dying of an ordinary illness, expressing a simple joy in his son's accomplishments. And there is this:

> I believe that words uttered in passion contain a greater living truth than do those words which express thoughts rationally conceived. It is blood that moves the body. Words are not meant to stir the air only; they are capable of moving greater things. (142)

Here surely is Soseki's own voice, condemning every secrecy and silence of his heroes or of any merely self-referring art. It is the voice of a writer who, almost in defiance of actual experience, clung to a belief that literature is language shared, and that such language could heal hearts and reorder the world.

References

Soseki, Natsume. *And Then*. Translated by Norma M. Field. New York: Perigee Books, 1982.

———. *Botchan*. Rutland, VT: Charles E. Tuttle, 1968.

———. *Grass on the Wayside*. Translated by Edwin McClellan. Chicago: University of Chicago Press, 1969.

———. *I Am a Cat*. 3 vols. Rutland, VT: Charles E. Tuttle, 1972, 1979, and 1986.

———. *Kokoro*. Translated by Edwin McClellan. Washington, D. C.: Regnery Gateway, 1957.

———. *Light and Darkness*. Translated by V. H. Viglielmo. New York: Perigee Books, 1982.

———. *The Miner*. Translated by Jay Rubin. Stanford, CA: Stanford University Press, 1988.

———. *Mon* ("The Gate"). Translated by Francis Mathy. New York: Putnam, 1982.

———. *Sanshiro*. Translated by Rubin Jay. New York: Perigee Books, 1982.

10 The Hero's Quest: A Bibliographic Essay

Cynthia Gravlee
University of Montevallo

Elaine Hughes
University of Montevallo

As our essayists note, narratives of the hero's quest abound in literature throughout the centuries. These many expressions are effective in engaging students in the study of literature and in helping them to realize its value in coming to know one's self and to understand others as well. Such works offer excellent possibilities for expanding and enriching our concepts of heroism by bringing together narratives from diverse cultures.

As Milton Foley observes, this quest may be both internal and external. Although many ancient epics such as *The Iliad, The Odyssey,* and *The Aeneid* from Greece and Rome and *The Sundiata* from West Africa emphasize external action, most also involve strong elements of inner growth. Furthermore, according to Foley, in works such as *The Bhagavad Gita* the more significant quest is that of the hero to overcome the temptations of the world and to find his soul. This internal journey has become a quest for self-understanding not only in William Wordsworth's *The Prelude,* but also in Natsume Soseki's *Kokoro* and Fyodor Dostoevsky's *Crime and Punishment.*

In *The Power of Myth,* Joseph Campbell describes the physical quest as one in which the heroes set out to conquer foes, either dragon or enemy, and free their countries from fear and bondage; in contrast, the spiritual quest is one in which heroes seek to restore that which has been lost to their world or to set right the wrongs of their societies (123). For example, in the Hebrew Bible, as well as in the Koran's account of "this fairest of stories" (Surah XII), Joseph is able, after betrayal by his brothers, to restore the structures of his world, overcoming pride, sibling rivalry, and false accusations to achieve, through wisdom and love, reunion with his family.

In works from many cultures, aspects of the physical and the spiritual quest are interwoven in endlessly complex variations. In Chinua Achebe's *Things Fall Apart,* set in West Africa around the turn of the century, Okonkwo seeks to restore stability and unity to the communal life of his Ibo village as his culture falls apart in the wake of European colonialism. Tragically, Okonkwo seems to resist the spiritual and moral growth which might have made him a more effective advocate for his people. In many works however, such as *Gilgamesh* from ancient Sumeria, the physical quest leads inadvertently to a spiritual quest which ultimately benefits both the hero and his society. The numerous facets of the quest include a search for social, economic, or political status; a quest for power, control, or spirituality; and a search for personal or communal identity.

According to scholars such as Carl Jung, Sir James Frazer, Northrop Frye, and Joseph Campbell, the structural elements often found in the quest narrative include (1) a journey, usually through forest or across seas; (2) an extended passage of time; and (3) a series of adventures linked by the quest motivation and divided by a moment of recognition when heroes realize that they have not achieved their goal, perhaps because their efforts have been thwarted or misdirected. After confronting these obstacles, they continue their quests, often after redefining their goals, with renewed commitment. Heroic figures frequently journey to the far corners of the known world, and sometimes even to the deep reaches of the unknown world, in search of knowledge, conquest, power, or spiritual fulfillment.

Examples can be readily drawn from sources ranging from ancient folktales to twentieth-century films. The heroic pattern is reflected in "Aladdin and His Lamp" in the young hero's successful attempts to overcome his poverty and gain status in life. The pattern is also represented in *The Thief of Baghdad* (directed by Michael Powell). In this film, set in medieval Persia, a young adventurer and an outcast king struggle to regain a lost kingdom, learning, in the process, to reject pride and selfishness and to develop loyalty and love.

The variations of this pattern are endless. The youthful search for identity that Gilgamesh embarks upon when he sets out to restore life to his lost friend but finds, instead, his own, echoes throughout the patterns of Telemachus's search and that of Juan Rulfo's twentieth-century portrayal in *Pedro Paramo.* It is seen in the journeys of James Joyce's Stephen Daedalus, and J. D. Salinger's Holden Caulfield, as well as in the escapades of Henry James's Daisy Miller, of Henrik Ibsen's Nora from *A Doll's House,* and of J. M. Synge's Nora from

The Shadow of the Glen. Such variations are also present in Maxine Hong Kingston's *The Woman Warrior* and Alex Haley's *Roots.*

For Westerners, Homer's portrayal represents perhaps the archetypal pattern of the hero's quest: Odysseus's journey home to Ithaca after the ten-year battle for Troy carries him through many ordeals and obstacles—earthly and supernatural—as he seeks to regain his home and finally set things right in his kingdom. The basic pattern is also found in the medieval West African epic, *Sundiata: An Epic of Old Mali,* which deals with the struggles of a young man, aided by his strong and supportive mother, to claim his birthright while learning the qualities of kingship.

Through examination of hero tales, with careful attention to contexts so as to avoid essentializing works from different cultures, students will find opportunities for personal development and growth. As Joseph Campbell says, each of us is a hero if we recognize that our journey through life's obstacles is a journey toward fulfillment, in which we confront some of the major issues and concerns experienced by human beings in different times and places (*The Hero with a Thousand Faces,* 1956).

The heroic pattern frequently takes the form of a search for values as a youthful hero is initiated into the world of adulthood. Sophocles' Antigone and William Faulkner's Sarty Snopes from "Barn Burning" must venture into the darkness of the unknown as they grope to find their own sense of integrity, rebelling against authority as their conscience dictates. Samuel Clemens's Huckleberry Finn seeks to overthrow the legacy of his father as he gropes for adulthood during his "odyssey" on the river to escape his father's tyranny and to find independent values and personal freedom. In Mexican author Juan Rulfo's *Pedro Paramo,* Juan Preciado's journey takes him on a search for his father, Pedro Paramo, and for the knowledge that would help him understand the corruption and deterioration of his society.

Similarly, Shakespeare's hesitant young Hamlet and Sophocles' impetuous King Oedipus must face the dilemmas caused by their heritage; Ola Rotimi portrays a similar situation in *The Gods Are Not to Blame,* an African drama based on *Oedipus Rex,* which also functions as an allegorical analysis of the causes of the Nigerian Civil War. Homer's Telemachus shares the uncertainties of the young son who struggles with the daunting shadow of a hero father figure, much as do the youthful heroes of today's cinematic epics *Star Wars* and *Field of Dreams. The Makioka Sisters,* by Japanese author Junichiro Tanizaki, portrays the efforts of four young Japanese women to come to terms with the influence of parents and of decaying Japanese traditions which dictate a woman's choice of lifestyle and of marital partner. Similarly, Irish author J. M. Synge's *Playboy of the Western World* portrays a young man's attempt to overcome the authority of his father and to start a new life.

Many readers will relate positively to the quest for the ideal, manifested in works from many ages and cultures. In Sir Thomas Malory's *Le Morte D'Arthur,* set in Celtic Britain, King Arthur and his Knights of the Round Table strive to establish an ideal kingdom, which is brought down by power struggles and vendettas among the knights, as well as by adultery between Guinevere and Lancelot. In Spanish literature, a prime example is seen in Cervantes's Don Quixote, whose quest for knightly ideals is at odds with the realities of ordinary life. The ridicule, physical punishment, and mental anguish that Quixote suffers underscore the dangers sometimes inherent in the search for the ideal.

Much modern-day literature, such as Synge's *Playboy of the Western World* and Carlos Fuentes's *The Old Gringo,* reflects the continued influence of Cervantes's work. Colombian author Gabriel García Márquez's *One Hundred Years of Solitude,* set in his imaginary world of Macondo, depicts a series of idealists whose passions and obsessions frequently defy the realities of their everyday lives.

Márquez's "The Handsomest Drowned Man in the World" recounts the manner in which villagers create a heroic myth to romanticize the corpse of an unknown drowned sailor which is washed by chance to their shore. In *The Temple of the Golden Pavilion,* by Yukio Mishima, a young Zen Buddhist acolyte, Mizoguchi, dares to risk his life to achieve the ideal, seeking "self-enlightenment" through traditional Buddhist techniques and rituals. His inward journey leads to a psychopathic obsession with the beauty of the Golden Pavilion, a revered historic and religious shrine, as he seeks his deliverance by destroying his revered object—the temple.

The quest for the ideal often highlights not only the possibilities for greatness, but also the dangers of seeking to assert an ideal vision of life within a temporal framework. Distortion of the spiritual quest into a quest for personal power and advancement can stunt the hero's growth and can cause painful conflicts with family and society. Many ancient stories such as that of Cain and Abel reflect this pattern. The Cain/Abel story is retold in Miguel de Unamuno's *Abel Sanchez,* in which the ostensibly saintly Abel Sanchez is envied and hated by his close "friend," Joaquin (Cain) Monegro, whose dark visions cloud the two men's "brotherly" relationship.

The hero's quest often pits his or her idealism against social pressures to conform to external standards of success based on materialism and power. This theme appears in nineteenth-century European literature such as Ibsen's *The Enemy of the People* as well as in contemporary works such as Alexander Solzhenitsyn's "Matryona's House" and *The First Circle.* Lorraine Hansberry's Younger family, in *Raisin in the Sun,* must confront and choose what is truly important to them in a society driven by socioeconomic factors, instead of fidelity and honor. Young Gordie LaChance, in *Stand by Me,* Rob Reiner's 1986 film version of Stephen King's novella "The Body," must assert his own values in the face of peer pressure and the allure of fame. Similarly, in works such as Mario Vargas Llosa's "Sunday, Sunday" and Yukio Mishima's *The Sound of the Waves,* the young heroes successfully defy peer pressure, survive physical tests of endurance, and defeat formidable rivals for the favor of a beautiful and pure young woman. Both successfully prove themselves by resisting the corrupting influences which threaten their youthful idealism. However, in other works, such as Friedrich Durrenmatt's *The Visit,* Carlos Fuentes's *The Death of Artemio Cruz,* and Juan Rulfo's *Pedro Paramo,* initial idealism gives way to the corrupting pursuits of power and wealth.

In works whose diversity includes the French medieval allegory, *The Romance of the Rose* by Guillaume de Lorris and Jean de Meun, as well as nineteenth-century novels such as Charlotte Brontë's *Jane Eyre* and Jane Austen's *Pride and Prejudice,* the youthful quest frequently involves love pursuits. In such works, the quest for love may lead the young to a new definition of self and a renewal of life, often shared by family and society.

In colonial settings, this pattern is complicated by conflicting social values as seen in Ama Ata Aidoo's *Dilemma of a Ghost,* a work which depicts a young African American woman's search for love and self-knowledge in Africa. Another variant is Wole Soyinka's *The Lion and the Jewel,* which examines conflicts between the sexes, between generations, and between modernism and tradition.

Tragic manifestations of the quest for love also frequently depict youthful idealism in conflict with familial and social forces which would diminish the dreams of young lovers. Examples of such tragic expressions of the quest for love found in the stories of many cultures range from Shakespeare's *Romeo and Juliet* to Japanese playwright Chikamatsu's *The Love Suicides at Sonezaki.* Through death the lovers in these works transcend the limits imposed by their societies; and in the case of Romeo and Juliet there is hope as well that their deaths may help to transform their society. A modern-day variant is found in the Swedish film, *Elvira Madigan,* directed by Bo Widerberg, in which a noble, young military officer and a beautiful tightrope dancer flee from society and share a romantic idyll in the countryside of nineteenth-century Sweden. Because social attitudes preclude their marrying, the romance ends in tragedy. Another tragic variant is found in Elechi Amadi's novel *The Concubine,* a work which highlights the Ibo belief in the interaction of the spirit world with the temporal realm. This work, depicting the village life of precolonial Nigeria, shows how the faithful Ihuoma seeks love and security, but mysteriously brings doom to all of the men who love her.

In some cases, the quests of mature characters for love end more positively than those of their youthful counterparts. A modern example is dramatized in the film version of Horton Foote's *Tender Mercies* (directed by Bruce Beresford), in which a fading country musician, who refuses to commercialize his music, learns to face his problems and to cope with loss through his new relationship with a young widow in rural Texas. Gabriel García Márquez' *Love in the Time of Cholera* depicts a man's life-long quest for an idealized love. The quest is finally realized when in advanced old age he and his loved one finally venture forth together in an endless voyage from port to port, avoiding societal and familial control by announcing at each port that their ship is infected with cholera.

As many of these examples indicate, the quest, particularly for female protagonists, often involves an "escape from" rather than a "coming to": Scheherazade's quest is to avoid literal death by telling tales to her new husband for *The Thousand and One Nights;* Gustave Flaubert's *Madame Bovary* and Ibsen's *Hedda Gabler* seek escape from a restrictive society that represses their attempts at independence, and denies their desire for love and for the freedom to express their sensuality. Along with these works, Kate Chopin's *The Awakening* also illustrates that risking all for romantic love can end in tragedy. The contemporary Indian filmmaker Satyajit Ray's film of Rabindranath Tagore's *The Home and the World* depicts the confusion and tragedy experienced by a traditional wife who ventures out of the secure enclosures of home into political and romantic involvement. Doris Lessing's *The Summer Before the Dark* portrays the similar quest of a middle-aged wife and mother who leaves the traditional home setting to seek fulfillment of her inner desires.

Other female questers who refuse to conform to society's mold include Becky Sharp in William Thackeray's *Vanity Fair,* "Maggie the Cat" in Tennessee Williams's *Cat on a Hot Tin Roof,* Scarlett O'Hara in Margaret Mitchell's *Gone with the Wind,* and Regina Hubbard in Lillian Hellman's *The Little Foxes.* Each of these ambitious women pursues wealth and status without regard to conventional scruples. The film *Thelma and Louise* (directed by Ridley Scott) is a picaresque "female buddy" film in which two women's daring attempts at self-assertion end in tragedy. Another work depicting defiance of social expectations and close female bonding is Toni Morrison's *Sula.*

In Euripides' *Medea* and in Toni Morrison's *Beloved,* the heroines commit heinous acts rather than submit themselves or their offspring to a life of humiliation or servitude. Medea unleashes her destructive power to kill their two sons in her quest for revenge upon her husband. Morrison's Sethe rebels against the tyranny of a slave master who would commit her children to a life of servitude, ultimately choosing to kill her young daughter rather than to return her to slavery. Sethe subsequently struggles to escape the psychological and emotional bondage of her guilt and the suppressed horrors of her past. In *Foundation Stone,* a novel first published in 1940 and reissued in 1986, Alabama author Lella Warren depicts the struggle of her female protagonists to find their identity in a frontier, antebellum society dominated by male values of power and greed. Refusing, like Medea, to relinquish their spirit and will to their husbands or children, the mother and daughter take on a superhuman strength in their frightening power to destroy as well as to create.

The tragic fates experienced by many of these women point up the ambivalence with which female power and sexuality are regarded, especially when contrasted with the positive treatment of more traditionally nurturing and stabilizing females. For example, the traditionally feminine Thea Elvsted in Ibsen's *Hedda Gabler* remains to reconstruct the manuscript of Eilert Lovberg after both Hedda and Eilert are dead.

Although in earlier literature female characters who break out of their prescribed roles are punished with rejection and death, much contemporary literature presents the woman's quest for a new voice and identity in a more positive light. In *Two Women in One* by Egyptian writer Nawal el-Saadawi, Bahiah Shaheen is outwardly a dutiful daughter and compliant medical student, but she is able, through her encounter with a dynamic and intriguing fellow-student and through her subsequent involvement in the struggle for political and social justice, to release the assertive woman who lies beneath her conventional surface.

Nadine Gordimer's *A Sport of Nature* depicts the remarkable exploits of a white African woman who defies her conventional upbringing to marry a black political leader and, after her husband's death, becomes the savior figure who effects change in her troubled nation. In *The Temple of My Familiar* Alice Walker uses literary traditions in a highly innovative way to depict the quest for wholeness of four young characters who learn expanded notions of gender and race through their encounters with ancestral female figures.

Zora Neale Hurston's *Their Eyes Were Watching God,* Maya Angelou's *I Know Why the Caged Bird Sings,* and Alice Walker's *The Color Purple* all portray the often painful struggles of determined African American females to attain their potential, despite the racism and sexism they encounter. (Filmed versions of the works by Angelou and Walker are available.)

As these examples indicate, there has been an explosion in recent years of works expressing various forms of the female quest. To cite only a few additional examples, the female quester has found her voice in the writings of American authors Amy Tan (*The Joy Luck Club*), Annie Dillard (*An American Childhood, Pilgrim at Tinker Creek*), and Adrienne Rich (*Diving into the Wreck, A Wild Patience Has Taken Me This Far*); in the writings of African authors Buchi Emecheta (*The Bride Price, Double Yoke*), Bessie Head (*A Question of Power, Serowe, Village of the Rain-Wind*), and Mariama Bâ (*Scarlet Song, So Long a Letter*); in works by Latin American authors Isabel Allende (*House of Spirits, Eva Luna*) and Maria Luisa Bombal (*New Island and Other Stories*); and in the writings of Indian author Kamala Markandaya (*Nectar in a Sieve*), Pakistani author Bapsi Sidhwa (*Cracking India*), and Japanese authors Oba Minako ("The Pale Fox") and Kono Taeko ("Iron Fish").

In much modern literature, both the male and the female quests for personal identity are put in the context of a quest for a just society. Such works explore individual identity quests in relation to issues of gender, race, poverty, and class. Such works give us a clear picture of the social and economic conflicts with which the individual heroes must contend. In *The Anthills of the Savannah,* Achebe's male and female protagonists oppose the corruption and abuse of power of their postcolonial rulers. Gabriel García Márquez's *One Hundred Years of Solitude* depicts the quest of several generations of the Buendia family for fulfillment, achievement, and love, within the context of colonial corruption and oppression. A similar quest for love and personal fulfillment is presented in *The Unbearable Lightness of Being* by Czech writer Milan Kundera. Much postcolonial literature depicts the disillusionment experienced by individual heroes when they find that the officials of newly independent governments often turn out to be as oppressive as their colonialist forerunners. One such example is found in *No Longer at Ease,* Chinua Achebe's continuation of the saga of African families in an Ibo village from precolonial times to the present. Achebe's *A Man of the People* deals with similar themes. Other such examples are found in Soyinka's *A Dance in the Forest* and *Kongi's Harvest.*

Frequently, as seen in these examples, many heroes engage in a critical examination of their society's ruling classes or cultural groups as they undertake a quest for personal and ethnic identity. The works of Alexander Solzhenitsyn depicting his opposition to various forms of governmental and bureaucratic mismanagement and/or oppression are prime examples. (These include the prison experiences recounted in *One Day in the Life of Ivan Denisovich, The First Circle,* and *Cancer Ward* and his view of prerevolutionary history in *August 1914.*) This theme is evident as well in the work of Czech writer Vaclav Havel. In Maxine Hong Kingston's *The Woman Warrior,* a modern Chinese American woman confronts her "roots" in an attempt to understand her role in contemporary American society. Alex Haley's *Roots* depicts an African American family's quest for family and cultural beginnings and its struggle for equality in modern America.

Barry Levinson's contemporary film, *Avalon,* is the story four generations of a Jewish American family from the arrival of the patriarch Sam Krichinsky in America to his final days in a nursing home where he is visited by his grandson and great grandson. The family, which begins as a loyal and loving unit, is gradually fragmented by materialism and modernism, although the special relationship between Sam and his grandson endures.

In *Middle Passage,* Charles Johnson attempts, through his protagonist Rutherford Calhoun, to chronicle the search of a newly freed slave for his identity. Rutherford flees the choices of his New Orleans world and journeys to Africa aboard a slave ship to find himself. Another journey into the past is described in *Obasan* by Japanese Canadian author Joy Kogawa, who gives a poignant portrayal of the quest of Naomi Nakane, a third-generation Japanese Canadian, to understand the anguish of her family members as they experienced the racism and ostracism of a culture that denied their basic rights as citizens and rejected them and their suffering as less than human.

Much modern literature has changed the traditional heroic pattern to that of the anti-hero seen in twentieth-century works such as John Updike's *Rabbit, Run,* Ken Kesey's *One Flew Over the Cuckoo's Nest,* and Kurt Vonnegut's *Slaughterhouse Five.* This development also is clearly evident in Soseki's *Kokoro* and in his *Grass on the Wayside.* Other variants in world literature include Senegalese author Sembene

Ousmane's *The Money Order* and *Xala*, which depict the destructive effects on individuals of governmental corruption and bureaucracy and of the loss of traditional family and community values. (Film versions of these two works, adapted by Sembene himself, are available for classroom use.)

Nkem Nwankwo's *Danda* and Mario Vargas Llosa's *Aunt Julia and the Script Writer* depict lively heroes whose humorous escapades are in contrast with traditional concepts of heroism. As is demonstrated in the delightful escapades of the irrepressible hero in Amos Tutuola's *The Palm-Wine Drinkard,* such comical anti-heroes may well have their roots in the trickster tales found in the folklore of many cultures, exemplified in the Native American coyote tales, the African Anansi spider tales, and in European variants such as "Puss in Boots." Other works in this vein include the amusing stories in *When Schlemiel Went to Moscow* and *Zlateh the Goat,* in which I. B. Singer retells the Yiddish tales from his childhood village in Poland.

The movement of modern literature toward parody and black humor has been countered by American cinematic portrayals, many of which have demonstrated a concerted effort by filmmakers such as Steven Spielberg, George Lucas, and Rob Reiner to reinstill the traditional heroic values in their protagonists, sometimes to the extent of tracing *per se* the mythic pattern of the hero's journey. For example, *Indiana Jones and the Last Crusade* (directed by Steven Spielberg) depicts an archetypal struggle between good and evil through a modern search for the Holy Grail. The Holy Grail remains elusive, but Jones and his scientist father learn that the quest can be more important than its object, as it brings them to enhanced understanding of themselves and one another.

Another strong example is seen in the *Star Wars* cycle directed by George Lucas. Northrop Frye, in his essay "Historical Criticism: Theory of Modes," observes the popularity of science fiction in contemporary literature and notes that science fiction is a "mode of romance with a strong inherent tendency to myth" (*Anatomy of Criticism* 1971, 49). George Lucas employs the monomythic pattern for his *Star Wars,* in which the hero, Luke Skywalker, in his quest to become a Jedi knight, must overcome evil in order to save the Federation and to rescue Princess Leia. His victory is not only physical, but also psychological, as he realizes the strength of his inner resources in combatting the evils of the world.

Rob Reiner's film *Stand by Me* provides another view of this development. When Gordie LaChance sets out on a youthful expedition with his adolescent friends, he does not realize that he will be a changed person when he returns. His spiritual growth results from the ordeals he endures and the realization he comes to upon finding the body of a missing youth killed by a train; with that realization, he crosses the threshold from childhood to adulthood. Still another recent example is the film *The Karate Kid* (directed by John G. Avildsen) in which a wise older man helps a young boy achieve confidence and maturity while learning the martial arts.

The traditional heroic pattern has also been strongly present in the work of international filmmakers. Films such as Satyajit Ray's Apu trilogy (*Pather Panchali*, 1955; *Aparajito*, 1956; and *Apu Sansar*, 1959), Ingmar Bergman's *Wild Strawberries*, and Kurosawa's *Ran* and *Dreams* all depict the individual's quest for identity, maturity, and values at stages of life ranging from early childhood to old age. Though these works depict positive growth and development, they are also more closely allied with the realities of daily life than are the adventurous epic-style chronicles of Lucas and Spielberg. More realistic and more sobering aspects of the hero's quest are also given in the work of American filmmakers such as Spike Lee and Horton Foote. Despite some comic elements, Lee's *Do the Right Thing* raises serious questions about whether even well-meaning and courageous persons can hope to overcome the racial barriers which divide our nation. Foote's *Convicts,* from his series of nine plays called *The Orphans' Home Cycle,* dramatizes the initiation experiences of young Horace Robedaux. Horace's loss of his father and rejection by his stepfather lead him to a thankless job at a plantation store, where he is confronted with the injustice of life through the suffering of the convict laborers and his ambivalent relationship with the dying overseer of the plantation.

This essay cites only a few representative examples that illustrate the quest theme across genres, across cultures, and across time. Students can become engaged in the hero's quest by debating critical questions in small-group sessions and/or by writing assignments that call for a creative response that personally involves them in the quest narratives. They can apply the traditional hero's quest pattern to their own lives by describing their personal quests and the reasons for them. As an alternative, they can write as a character evaluating him- or herself and the other characters and concluding what was learned from the success or failure of the textual quests. In accord with the ethnic concerns of the literary questers, students can explore their own ethnic heritage and its importance in shaping their personalities, their values, and their goals. Moreover, they can learn that the hero's quest is a universal pursuit which fosters global perspectives on literature and life.

The possibilities for exploration of the hero's quest—of what Joseph Campbell describes as the "everlasting recurrent themes of the wonderful song of the soul's high adventure" (22)—are limitless. Examples range from folk tales to learned literary epics, from comedy to tragedy, from the most ancient to the most contemporary voices. These works vary in tone from high seriousness to the irreverence of black comedy. Through bringing together some of these rich and diverse works, students and teachers may engage in their own quests for heightened understanding of their cultural values and of those of other people, thus seeking, and perhaps finding, increased understanding of themselves and of the worlds which they inhabit.

References

Achebe, Chinua. *The Anthills of the Savannah*. Garden City, NY: Doubleday, 1988.

————. *No Longer at Ease*. New York: Astor-Honor, 1961.

Aidoo, Ama Ata. *Dilemma of a Ghost*. New York: Collier Books, 1971.

Allende, Isabel. *The House of Spirits*. Translated by Magda Bogin. New York: Bantam, 1986.

————. *The Stories of Eva Luna*. Translated by Margaret Peden. New York: Macmillan, 1991.

Amadi, Elechi. *The Concubine*. Portsmouth, NH: Heinemann, 1966.

Angelou, Maya. *I Know Why the Caged Bird Sings*. New York: Bantam, 1983.

Austen, Jane. *Pride and Prejudice*. Edited by James Kinsley and F. W. Bradbrook. New York: Oxford University Press, 1980.

Bâ, Mariama. *Scarlet Song*. Chicago: Longman Trade, 1991.

————. *So Long a Letter*. Translated by Modupë Bodé-Thomas. London: Heinemann, 1981.

Bhagavad Gita. Edited by Juan Mascaro. New York: Penguin, 1962.

Bombal, Maria Luisa. *New Islands and Other Stories*. Translated by Lucia Cunningham and Richard Cunningham. Ithaca: Cornell University Press, 1988.

Brontë, Charlotte. *Jane Eyre*. Edited by Margaret Smith. New York: Oxford University Press, 1980.

Campbell, Joseph. *The Hero with a Thousand Faces*. Cleveland, OH: World Publishing, 1956.

Campbell, Joseph and Bill Moyers. *The Power of Myth*. New York: Doubleday, 1988.

Chikamatsu, Monzaemon. "The Love Suicides at Sonezaki." In *Stories from a Tearoom Window*. Edited by Tashiko Mori. Translated by Kozaburo Mori. Rutland, VT: C. E. Tuttle, 1982.

Chopin, Kate. *The Awakening*. New York: Avon, 1982.

de Lorris, Guillaume and Jean de Meun. *The Romance of the Rose.* Translated by Charles Dahlberg, 1971. Hanover and London: University Press of New England, 1983.

De Unamuno, Miguel. *Abel Sanchez and Other Stories.* Translated by Anthony Kerrigan. Washington, D. C.: Regnery Gateway, 1956.

Dillard, Annie. *An American Childhood.* New York: Harper and Row, 1987.

———. *Pilgrim at Tinker Creek.* New York: Harper and Row, 1988.

Dostoevsky, Fyodor. *Crime and Punishment.* Translated by Constance Garnett. New York: Random, 1978.

Durrenmatt, Friedrich. *The Visit.* Translated by Patrick Bowles. New York: Grove-Weidenfield, 1987.

El-Saawadi, Nawal. *Two Women in One.* Translated by Osman Nusairi and Jana Gough. Seattle: Seal Pr. Feminist, 1986.

Emecheta, Buchi. *The Bride Price.* New York: Braziller, 1976.

———. *Double Yoke.* New York: Braziller, 1983.

Euripides. *Medea.* Edited by Allen Elliot. New York: Oxford University Press, 1969.

Faulkner, William. *The Sound and the Fury.* Edited by Noel Polk. New York: Random, 1954.

Flaubert, Gustave. *Madame Bovary.* Translated by Francis Steegmuller. New York: Random, 1982.

Foote, Horton. *Four Plays from the Orphans' Home Cycle: Convicts, Roots in a Parched Ground, Lily Dale,* and *The Widow Claire.* New York: Grove Press, 1988.

———. *Three Plays from the Orphans' Home Cycle: Courtship, Valentine's Day, 1918.* New York: Grove Press, 1987.

———. *Two Plays from the Orphans' Home Cycle: Cousins and The Death of Papa.* New York: Grove Press, 1989.

Frazer, James G. *The Golden Bough.* New York: Macmillan, 1985.

Frye, Northrop. *Anatomy of Criticism: Four Essays.* Princeton, NJ: Princeton University Press, 1971.

Fuentes, Carlos. *The Death of Artemio Cruz.* Translated by Sam Hileman. New York: Farrar, Straus, & Giroux, 1964.

———. *The Old Gringo.* Translated by Margaret S. Peden. New York: Farrar, Straus, & Giroux, 1985.

Gilgamesh: A Verse Narrative. Translated by Herbert Mason. New York: New American Library, 1972.

Gordimer, Nadine. *A Sport of Nature.* New York: Knopf, 1987.

Haley, Alex. *Roots.* New York: Doubleday, 1976.

Hansberry, Lorraine. *Raisin in the Sun.* New York: New American Library, 1989.

Havel, Vaclav. *Disturbing the Peace.* New York: Knopf, 1990.

———. *Long Distance Interrogation.* New York: Knopf, 1990.

Head, Bessie. *A Question of Power.* Portsmouth, NH: Heinemann, 1974.

———. *Serowe: Village of the Rain-Wind.* Portsmouth, NH: Heinemann, 1981.

Hellman, Lillian. *Little Foxes.* In *Six Modern American Plays,* edited by Allan G. Halline. New York: McGraw-Hill, 1966.

Homer. *The Iliad.* Translated by Robert Fitzgerald. New York: Doubleday, 1989.

———. *The Odyssey.* Translated by Robert Fitzgerald. New York: Doubleday, 1963.

Hurston, Zora Neale. *Their Eyes Were Watching God.* New York: Harper and Row, 1990.

Ibsen, Henrik. *An Enemy of the People.* New York: Penguin, 1977.

———. *Hedda Gabler* and *A Doll's House.* Translated by Christopher Hampton. London: Faber and Faber, 1990.

Johnson, Charles. *Middle Passage.* Edited by Lee Goerner. New York: Macmillan, 1990.

Jung, Carl. *Modern Man in Search of a Soul.* New York: Harcourt, Brace, 1933.

Kesey, Ken. *One Flew Over the Cuckoo's Nest.* Edited by John C. Pratt. New York: Penguin, 1977.

Kingston, Maxine Hong. *The Woman Warrior.* New York: Knopf, 1976.

Kogawa, Joy. *Obasan.* Boston: Godine, 1982.

Kono Taeko. "Iron Fish." Translated by Yukiko Tanaka. In *The Showa Anthology.* Edited by Van C. Gessel and Tomone Matsumoto. New York: Kodansha, 1989.

Koran Interpreted. Translated by A. J. Arberry. New York: Macmillan, 1986.

Kundera, Milan. *The Unbearable Lightness of Being.* Translated by Michael Heim. New York: Harper and Row, 1987.

Malory, Sir Thomas. *Le Morte D'Arthur.* Edited by Janet Cowen. Introduction by John Lawlor. 2 vols. 1969. London: Penguin, 1988.

Markandaya, Kamala. *Nectar in a Sieve.* New York: New American Library, 1956.

Márquez, Gabriel García. "The Handsomest Drowned Man in the World." Translated by Gregory Rabassa. In *The Eye of the Heart,* edited by Barbara Howes. New York: Avon Books, 1990. 489–96.

———. *Love in the Time of Cholera.* Translated by Edith Grossman. New York: Knopf, 1988.

———. *One Hundred Years of Solitude.* Translated by Gregory Rabassa. New York: Harper and Row, 1970.

Mishima, Yukio. *The Temple of the Golden Pavilion.* Translated by Ivan Morris. New York: Putnam, 1981.

———. *The Sound of Waves.* New York: Putnam, 1981.

Mitchell, Margaret. *Gone with the Wind.* New York: Avon, 1976.

Morrison, Toni. *Beloved.* New York: Knopf, 1987.

———. *Sula.* New York: New American Library, 1989.

The New English Bible with the Apocrypha. Edited by Samuel Sandmel. Oxford Study Edition. New York: Oxford University Press, 1976.

Nwankwo, Nkem. *Danda.* New York: Heinemann, 1970.

Oba Minako. "The Pale Fox." In *The Showa Anthology.* Edited by Van C. Gessel and Tomone Matsumoto. New York: Kodansha, 1989.

Sembene, Ousmane. *The Money Order with White Genesis.* Translated by Clive Wake. Portsmouth, NH: Heinemann, 1987.

———. *Xala.* Translated by Clive Wake. Chicago, IL: Laurence Hill Books, 1983.

Rich, Adrienne. *Diving into the Wreck: Poems, 1971–2.* New York: Norton, 1973.

———. *A Wild Patience Has Taken Me This Far.* New York: Norton, 1981.

Rotimi, Ola. *The Gods Are Not to Blame.* London: Oxford University Press, 1971.

Rulfo, Juan. *Pedro Paramo.* New York: Grove-Weidenfeld, 1983.

Shakespeare, William. *Romeo and Juliet.* Edited by Maynard Mack and Robert W. Boynton. New York: McGraw, 1984.

Sidhwa, Bapsi. *Cracking India.* Minneapolis, MN: Milkweed Editions, 1991.

Singer, I. B. *When Schlemiel Went to Warsaw and Other Stories.* Translated by Elizabeth Shub. New York: Farrar, Straus, & Giroux, 1968.

———. *Zlateh, the Goat and Other Stories.* Translated by Elizabeth Shub. New York: Harper and Row, 1984.

Solzhenitsyn, Alexander. *August 1914.* Translated by Harry T. Willetts. New York: Farrar, Straus, & Giroux, 1989.

———. *Cancer Ward.* Translated by Nicholas Bethell and David Burg. New York: Random, 1984.

———. *The First Circle.* New York: Harper and Row, 1990.

———. "Matryona's House." Translated by H. T. Willetts. In *The Norton Anthology of World Masterpieces,* Sixth Edition, Volume II. Edited by Maynard Mack, et al. 2018–45. New York: Norton, 1992.

———. *One Day in the Life of Ivan Denisovich.* New York: Bantam, 1984.

———. *Grass on the Wayside.* Translated by Edwin McClellan. Ann Arbor, MI: UMI Japan.

———. *Kokoro.* Translated by Edwin McClellan. Washington, D. C.: Regnery Gateway, 1957.

Soyinka. *A Dance in the Forest.* London: Oxford University Press, 1963.

———. *Kongi's Harvest.* London: Oxford University Press, 1967.

———. *The Lion and the Jewel.* London: Oxford University Press, 1963.

Sundiata. Retold by D. T. Niane. Translated by G. D. Pickett. Chicago: Longman, 1986.

Synge, J. M. "In the Shadow of the Glen." *Complete Plays of John M. Synge.* New York: Random, 1960.

———. "Playboy of the Western World." *Complete Plays of John M. Synge.* New York: Random, 1960.

Tagore, Rabindranath. *Home and the World.* New York: Asia Book Corp., 1985.

Tales from the Thousand and One Nights. Translated by N. J. Dawood. New York: Penguin, 1973.

Tan, Amy. *The Joy Luck Club.* New York: Putnam Publishing Group, 1989.

Tanizaki, Junichiro. *The Makioka Sisters.* Translated by Edward G. Seidensticker. New York: Putnam, 1981.

Thackeray, William Makepeace. *Vanity Fair.* Edited by J. M. Stewart. New York: Penguin, 1969.

Tolstoy, Leo. *Death of Ivan Ilych.* Translated by Lynn Solotaroff. New York: Bantam, 1981.

Tutuola, Amos. *The Palm-Wine Drinkard.* New York: Grove-Weidenfeld, 1954.

Vargas Llosa, Mario. *Aunt Julia and the Script Writer.* Translated by Helen Lane. New York: Farrar, Straus, & Giroux, 1982.

———. "Sunday, Sunday." Translated by Alastair Reid. In *The Eye of the Heart,* edited by Barbara Howes. 535–56. New York: Avon Books, 1973.

Updike, John. *Rabbit, Run.* New York: Knopf, 1960.

Virgil. *The Aeneid.* Translated by Robert Fitzgerald. New York: Random, 1984.

Vonnegut, Kurt. *Slaughterhouse Five.* Chicago: Barron, 1985.

Walker, Alice. *The Color Purple.* New York: Washington Square Press, 1982.

———. *The Temple of My Familiar.* New York: Harbrace Jovanovich, 1989.

Warren, Lella. *Foundation Stone.* Tuscaloosa: University of Alabama Press, 1986.

Williams, Tennessee. *Cat on a Hot Tin Roof.* New York: New American Library, 1958.

Wordsworth, William. *The Prelude.* New York: Oxford University Press, 1970.

Films

Alazraki, Benito. *Roots.* 1955.

Avildsen, John G. *Karate Kid.* 1984.

Beresford, Bruce. *Tender Mercies.* 1982.

Bergman, Ingmar. *Wild Strawberries.* 1957.

Kurosawa, Akira. *Ran.* 1985.

Lee, Spike. *Do the Right Thing.* 1989.

Levinson, Barry. *Avalon.* 1990.

Lucas, George. *Star Wars.* 1977.

Masterson, Peter. *Convicts.* 1991.

Powell, Michael. *The Thief of Baghdad.* 1940.

Ray, Satyajit. *The World of Apu.* 1958.

Reiner, Rob. *Stand by Me.* 1986.

Robinson, Phil Alden. *Field of Dreams.* 1989.

Scott, Ridley. *Thelma and Louise.* 1991.

Sembene, Ousmane. *The Money Order.* 1968.

———. *Xala.* 1974.

Spielberg, Steven. *Indiana Jones and the Last Crusade.* 1989.

III The Individual, the Family, and Society

The essays in this section bring together texts, from varying traditions, which explore the individual's need for independence and achievement and the sometimes competing need for integration and acceptance into family and social groups. Sandra Lott and Steven Latham examine the theme of coming of age from the perspective of an American and an African author. Mary McCay looks at questions about the individual and social identity of Native Americans from the perspective of both colonizer and colonized. The essays in Section I on personal writing and in Section V on various approaches to *Things Fall Apart* also deal with the roles of individuals in family and society. The bibliographic essay, which suggests texts from a variety of historical periods, genres, and cultures, is structured around the widening circles of adolescent initiation, courtship, marriage, family relationships, and social conflicts.

11 "The World Was All Before Them": Coming of Age In Ngũgĩ wa Thiong'o's *Weep Not, Child* and J. D. Salinger's *The Catcher in the Rye*

Sandra W. Lott
University of Montevallo

Steven Latham
Montevallo High School

According to Robert G. Carlsen, adolescents readily identify with works which relate to the quest for identity and which address problems of the social order (118–19). Their strong interest in these themes perhaps reflects the need of young readers in many cultures for increased understanding of themselves and of others, and for heightened awareness of their own individual identity in the context of family and society. In oral folk literature, this need has been met by tales in which the quest theme follows a familiar pattern which satisfies the needs of young readers for independence, competence, and self-worth and which often depicts the young person as a savior figure who rights the wrongs of his or her society. As Elaine Hughes and Cynthia Gravlee note in their bibliographic essay on the hero, characters such as Aladdin, Scheherazade, Robin Hood, Jack the Giant Killer, Sundiata, and Momotaro are among the many folk heroes whose stories demonstrate these characteristics. As Gravlee and Hughes suggest, the journey motif in such stories often depicts the young protagonists venturing out into unknown territory, going beyond their own safe and familiar worlds, and thus attaining increased knowledge and understanding. This knowledge can take the form of increased understanding of self (*The Uses of Enchantment,* Bruno Bettelheim, 1976), increased and often critical understanding of the society (*Breaking the Magic Spell: Radical Theories of Folk and Fairy Tales,* Jack Zipes, 1984), and even increased understanding of new perspectives beyond those known and approved of by their own cultures (*Old Tales and New Truths,* James Roy King, 1992). Kenneth Donelson and Aileen Pace Nilsen, in their *Literature for Today's Young Adults,* identify modern-day books with these char-

135

acteristics as belonging to a genre called the adventure/accomplishment romance, which they suggest "has elements applicable to the task of entering the adult world." The story pattern they describe includes "three stages of initiation as practiced in many cultures" in which "the young and innocent person is separated both physically and spiritually from the nurturing love of friends and family... undergoes a test of courage and stamina" which may be "either mental, psychological, or physical," and "in the final stage is reunited with former friends and family in a new role of increased status" (1989, 126–27).

As Donelson and Nilsen note, there is a strong element of wish fulfillment in such literature (1989, 126). However, many of the best realistic books written for young adults today follow this basic pattern, but overlay it with a sense of the complexity and difficulties of real life in which the young person must inevitably make compromises with his or her ideals and dreams in order to achieve a sense of identity in keeping with the often harsh realities of family and social life. It is a life in which the welfare of his or her immediate family and society is often threatened by the negative impact of other cultural groups. Such books present moving and complex accounts of the inner challenges of coming of age at the same time that they give a good sense of the social and cultural pressures brought to bear on young persons. Many of the most distinctive books which have recently been written for a young adult audience deal with such issues. Good examples are found in the books of noted African American writer Virginia Hamilton. Hamilton's best-known work, *M. C. Higgins, the Great,* tells the story of young Mayo Cornelius Higgins's quest to save his family from the strip miners' spoil heap which threatens to destroy their Appalachian home. M. C.'s world is enlarged through contact with two visitors from the city who help him to overcome his family's prejudice and hostility to the communal style of the life led by their "witchy" neighbors, the Killburns, and who also help him to develop independence and competence within the family setting. Hamilton's *Arilla Sundown* depicts a young girl's attempt to resolve the conflict between her Native American and her African American family heritage, and her *Sweet Whispers, Brother Rush* shows how a young black girl's encounters with the ghost of her dead uncle help her to understand her mother's neglectful and sometimes abusive treatment of her children. In Katherine Paterson's *Bridge To Terabithia,* country-bred Jess Aarons learns and grows through his friendship with a privileged girl from a sophisticated and artistic family, and later he learns self-reliance and maturity in facing his grief over his friend's death. All of these works, which show a young person confronting the problems of family and society, deal also with cultural contrasts and conflicts and thus help the young reader not only to develop self-understanding but also to develop increased understanding of others and of the problems of the social order.

Moving beyond such young adult novels, young readers may well turn to contemporary adult literature which focuses on the experiences of adolescents engaged in the process of coming of age. Books such as Harper Lee's *To Kill a Mockingbird* and John Knowles's *A Separate Peace* have become perennial favorites with the young because of their honest and immediate treatment of the struggles of coming of age. Such works challenge readers to come to terms with personal and cultural limits, but they also retain sympathy for youthful idealism and dreams. In Julio Cortazar's story "The End of the Game," three young girls whose lives are restricted by poverty and by the physical handicap of one of the group transform these painful realities by devising a game of statues in which they impersonate famous people and abstract attitudes for the benefit of passengers on the train which regularly passes near their home. Reality intrudes on their game when a young male student, who has watched their performance on his trips to and from his school, arranges one day to get off the train and meet the three girls. His note, thrown from the train window, indicates his special interest in the crippled child, but when he learns of her physical handicap, he loses interest in her and in the game, moving thereafter to the other side of the train where he will not see the girls as he passes their accustomed spot. Thus the end of the game is also the end of the innocent pleasures of childhood, as the girls must now cope with a world which is harsher and more restricted than that created in their fanciful play.

Another work which deals with the interplay of imagination and actuality is Maxine Hong Kingston's *The Woman Warrior.* The title of this work comes from a folktale about a Chinese girl who leaves her home and family and undergoes an extended apprenticeship in preparation for warfare against the wicked barons who oppress her people. Recounting this story as a young girl living in contemporary America, not ancient China, Kingston is painfully aware that her own experiences are quite different from those of the folk tale heroine, but she comforts herself that she couldn't have done as well since, unlike the legendary swordswoman, she has no magic beads and no old people to tutor her, and since, as a Chinese American, she is no longer even sure what her village is. At the end of the story, she concludes that she can emulate the woman warrior by becoming a word warrior: "The reporting is the vengeance—not the beheading, not the gutting, but the words" (1989, 53).

Such a struggle to reconcile dreams and reality is present in much contemporary literature about adolescence. Two works from divergent cultures which present this conflict in an exceptionally memorable and moving fashion are *Weep Not, Child* by Kenyan author Ngũgĩ wa Thiong'o and *The Catcher in the Rye* by J. D. Salinger. Both novels give a strongly realistic account of an adolescent hero's quest for identity in an imperfect adult world. Salinger's Holden Caulfield and Ngũgĩ's hero Njoroge both dream of saving the disadvantaged of their society from suffering and oppression. In pursuing these goals, the heroes follow many of the typical experiences of the adventure/accomplishment romance, including separating themselves from home and familiar surroundings, facing serious and dangerous trials and challenges, and eventually returning with a transformed identity to home and family. However, in these novels, the heroes also experience disillusionment with themselves and with the world around them as they move from the innocent idealism of the very young to a more realistic acceptance of personal limits and social imperfections.

The cultural contexts of these works are strikingly different. Holden's experiences begin in the urban prep school environment of the Atomic Age of the United States, whereas Njoroge's experiences reflect Kikuyu tribal culture during the Mau Mau uprisings in Kenya in the 1950s. In fact, many young readers in today's high schools and colleges may find these worlds almost equally foreign, and they will certainly need some help with contextualizing. For example, African practices of polygamy, the history of colonialism, and the role of Africans in the two world wars are relevant to an understanding of Ngũgĩ's book. However, many of today's readers may find Holden's slang of the forties and fifties and his privileged lifestyle almost as culturally distant from their lives as the Mau Mau revolt in Kenya. Quite possibly, however, young readers will be able to approach the typical challenges of growing up which are raised in both books more openly and objectively just because these challenges are presented in a context different from their own. Juxtaposing these works from such different cultures can lead to a better understanding of the crises of growing up in both worlds and of the place of the individual in the larger community. As Reed Way Dasenbrock notes in an article about teaching multicultural literature, the readers of such works will themselves be changed through the inevitable expansion of their experiences in encountering and interacting with texts which reflect a world which is different from their own (13).

Readers of these books may wish to consider whether or not the differences in the two treatments of coming of age are culturally determined and to explore the degree to which the similarities reflect universally shared challenges of growing up. As Sarah Lawall points out in her introductory essay to this text, some scholars believe that works about the coming of age of the adolescent male hero may privilege the Western, masculine tradition. However, Ngũgĩ's book presents this theme in the context of a traditional African setting, which is, if anything, more patriarchal in many ways than Western society. Thus students and teachers may find it profitable to compare and contrast the effects of male dominance on the experiences of these two adolescent heroes.

Some scholars maintain that the very concept of adolescence is itself the invention of Western societies, which artificially prolong childhood dependency through extended educational programs, thus unnaturally postponing marriage and career. Certainly Holden's dreams about marrying "Old Sally" and running away from school and home might seem to confirm this view, but Ngũgĩ's hero, Njoroge, also dreams of escaping his present problems by leaving his school to marry his girlfriend Mwihaki. Because his school offers a Western-style education, Njoroge's frustrations, which to Westerners typify adolescence, may lead readers to consider whether or not Western influence, particularly in the area of education, may have introduced the trials of adolescence into a non-Western setting or whether these trials are an inevitable part of adolescence. Comparing Ngũgĩ's and Salinger's books with accounts of coming of age from various cultures may also shed light on this question.

In her autobiographical work *Silent Dancing,* Judith Ortiz Cofer writes:

> To a child, life is a play directed by parents, teachers, and other adults who are forever giving directions: "Say this," "Don't say that," "Stand here,"... If we miss or ignore a cue, we are punished.... The world—our audience—likes the well-made play, with everyone in their places and not too many bursts of brilliance or surprises. (1990, 101)

In a similar vein, Ronald Ayling suggests in his essay in this text that childhood in every culture may be compared with the process of colonization. Such comparisons make adolescent rebellion against authority seem a natural stage in which the well-made play described by Ortiz Cofer will inevitably be disrupted by the youthful "brilliance or surprises" which she suggests adults dislike. Certainly many young readers will recognize in these descriptions problems and conflicts inherent in their own struggle for independent identity, as well as in the struggles of the fictional heroes of *The Catcher in the Rye* and *Weep Not, Child.*

For the fictional characters, Njoroge and Holden, the quest for adolescent identity is connected to family and peer relationships; both confront questions about courtship and marriage; both struggle with conflicting religious and ethical values; and both oppose various forms of social and political oppression. However, Njoroge's rebellion takes place in a clearly colonized setting, whereas the objects of Holden's rebellion are more diffuse and less clearly identifiable. In contrast with Njoroge, who has grown up in a communal society, Holden is at first more individualistic, more lonely, and more alienated. Eventually, however, perhaps as a result of the incursion of Western values and conflicts, Njoroge, too, undergoes a process of alienation which can be compared in some ways with that experienced by Holden. And in the final sequences of both books, the heroes begin tentatively to regain a sense of community, of renewed connections with family and peers and, perhaps, with their society at large.

Comparison of the opening sections of the two books clearly shows that Holden is initially much further along the road toward disillusionment than is Njoroge. In the opening pages of *Catcher,* we learn that Holden has experienced a series of academic failures and is about to be expelled from his current preparatory school. Disaffected with himself and the world around him, Holden decides to leave early before the Christmas holidays begin, and the major action of the book concerns his three-day odyssey in New York City.

Salinger underscores Holden's world-weary pseudo-sophistication, revealing Holden's disillusionment with establishment institutions and values through an engaging and intimate first-person narration. Recounting the events which have led to his hospitalization, Holden tells the story of his departure from school, his adventures in New York City, and his earlier family traumas and educational misadventures. Holden's language, liberally sprinkled with profanity, conveys his dissatisfaction with headmasters, ministers, Jesus' disciples, and all "big shots." Such rebellious and irreverent attitudes, reflect his fear of being vulnerable, gullible, or "square." Wayne Booth has noted, however, that despite such indications of immaturity, Salinger's hero quickly enlists the sympathy of most readers with his funny commentary on the manifold forms of phoniness which he finds everywhere around him (1964, 161–63). Holden's narration, blending earnest idealism and naivete with self-protective skepticism, establishes his essential innocence and appeals to readers to become allies against all that is false, mean-spirited, and unjust. Holden's academic hopscotch reflects his conviction that there is little of worth in an educational system in which the "grand" people with money and power lord it over the disadvantaged. Holden sympathizes with a wide range of educational misfits, including the boy with cheap luggage, the boy whose sincere, if disorganized, speech about his uncle is interrupted by jeers of "digression," and, perhaps most significantly, the boy named James Castle, who was hounded to his death because he would not acknowledge the hazing rights of older school bullies. Prior to his expulsion from Pencey Prep, Holden visits his history teacher, who expresses disappointment in Holden's academic failure and tells him, "Life *is* a game that one plays according to the rules" (12). Opposing this view, Holden cynically reflects, "Some game. If you get on the side where all the hot-shots are, then it's a game, all right. . . . But if you get on the *other* side, where there aren't any hot-shots, then what's a game about it?" (12). Holden, who has already taken his place "on the other side," wants no part of an educational system designed to ensure that the game continues to be weighted against the "poor in spirit."

The causes of Holden's disillusionment may in some ways seem insignificant in comparison with the colonial oppression and even torture to which Ngũgĩ's hero Njoroge is subjected with at least the tacit approval of his educators. But Holden, too, is deeply disturbed by his perception that his educators do nothing to protect their innocent charges. One exception, in Holden's view, has been the English teacher Mr. Antolini, who shared Holden's deep concern and sorrow over the death of James Castle. During Holden's sojourn to New York, he goes late at night to the home of Antolini, who unquestioningly takes him in. Antolini displays a sincere interest in Holden's development and advises Holden to resume his education, assuring the boy that he is "not the first person who was ever confused . . . and even sickened by human behavior" (246). Antolini tells Holden that education will enable him to learn from others who have come through similar periods of moral and spiritual anguish.

However, when Holden awakens to find Mr. Antolini patting his head, he interprets this quite possibly innocent gesture as a homosexual pass and leaves in a panicky and bitter frame of mind. Disillusioned about the purity of even the best of educators, Holden sees the educational process as one intended to support the established power structure, inculcating values and attitudes which serve mainly to protect the privileged classes.

This sense of alienation and disaffection is also seen in Holden's relationships with his family, in his view of love and marriage, and in his attitude toward organized religion. From the beginning, Holden is estranged from his family as well as from the larger community. As the son of wealthy New Yorkers, Holden has been given every material advantage, but, saddened and guilty over his academic failures, he seems distanced from all of his family except for his adored younger sister Phoebe. He thinks his older brother D. B. has sold out by going to Hollywood to write movie scripts, and he is at least implicitly critical of his parents for shuffling him around from one "phony" school to another.

For Holden, religious concerns and questions about love and marriage also present difficult ethical and moral issues and serve further to alienate him from those he considers to be phony. Like many young people, he centers dreams, hopes, and illusions around an idealized figure of the opposite sex and thinks of love and marriage as an escape from social pressures. Though evidently quite confused about this area of life, Holden idealizes a girl named Jane Gallagher and wants to protect her from the type of boys he knows at school who would prey upon her innocence. He feels ashamed that he has never "given . . . [a girl] the time" (56), but he cannot bring himself to use girls in the heartless manner of his roommate Stradlater. His sympathy for the outsiders of his society extends to many of the girls he encounters; he feels sorry for ugly girls, for girls who marry "dopey guys" (160), and even for a prostitute, with whom he talks at great length because he cannot bring himself to have sex with her. He exclaims: "Sex is something I just don't understand. I swear to God, I don't" (82). Holden thinks frequently of Jane, but does not contact her, perhaps because he wants to keep the dream of her perfection and innocence intact; however, during his sojourn in New York, he does contact an old girlfriend named Sally Hayes. Though it is clear that he does not care for Sally as he does for Jane, he proposes in desperation that they run away to New England to live on his bank account of $180 "in cabin camps and stuff" (171). He says, "We could live somewhere with a brook and all and, later on, we could get married or something. I could chop all of our own wood in the wintertime and all" (171). When Sally suggests that they wait until after college, Holden's response shows the escapist nature of his attachment to Sally: "I'd be working in some office, making a lot of dough, and riding to work in cabs and Madison Avenue buses, and reading newspapers, and playing bridge all the time. . . . Christ almighty" (173). Realizing that Sally represents the very establishment phoniness he wants to avoid, Holden relinquishes the dream of love and romance as an escape from the inevitable changes of growing up.

Holden is also confused about religion. Though Holden claims to be "sort of an atheist" (99), he admires Christ, and he wants to protect the two nuns he meets from the corrupting influence of *Romeo and Juliet.* However, he cannot stand the all-too-human disciples, and he has only disdain for organized religions and dogma. Holden's hatred of religious phoniness is evident in his reaction to the Christmas show at Radio City Music Hall: "Old Jesus probably would've puked if He could see it" (137). Holden can tolerate only those religious figures who seem totally innocent, pure, and childlike. But perhaps realizing how far he himself is from this standard of purity, he turns his destructive impulses inward against himself, invites his roommate Stradlater and the pimp Maurice to hit him, and even imagines his own funeral. Toward the end of the book he plans to run away and live a reclusive life in the wilderness, pretending to be a deaf-mute. Such fantasies are sadly amusing, but they highlight Holden's unwillingness to seek community with ordinary people or to adjust his ideals to the requirements of his society.

The contrast between Salinger's alienated protagonist and Ngũgĩ's trusting and hopeful hero are striking. Ngũgĩ's narrative provides a moving account of Njoroge's attempt to fulfill himself through serving his community. Depicting Njoroge's passage to adulthood amidst the turmoil of the Mau Mau independence movement, the events of the novel recount the impact on Njoroge and his family of years of this political and economic upheaval.

Commenting on the colonial context of Ngũgĩ's book, Ndiawar Sarr observes that in East Africa, as in Southern Africa, the colonial settlers wanted more than raw materials and trade. These settlers, who came to stay, captured the best land and pushed out the Africans born on that land. The Mau Mau were the Kikuyu militants, whose blood oaths symbolized the people's eternal unity with the land. Though many, like Njoroge's father Ngotho, did not join the movement, the colonial powers tended to regard all Kenyans as Mau Mau, whose main goal was to recapture the land. Although Njoroge's family is divided over whether to take the oath, all of the family suffer from the British attempts to suppress revolt. In 1952, the British rulers began four years of military operations against the rebels. The struggle was a bloody one in which thousands of rebels were killed, and thousands more, including their leader Jomo Kenyatta, were put in detention camps. Sarr points out, however, that Ngũgĩ's book is not a mere catalogue of political events, nor is it a propagandistic work. Everything is concentrated on the family level, on the impact of these historical events on individual human beings (Sarr, 1988).

Ngũgĩ's simple and direct style of narration reflects the serious-minded and hopeful attitude of the hero in the first part of the book, and it also serves toward the end of the novel to convey the depths of Njoroge's sorrow when his dreams are shattered. At the beginning of the novel, Njoroge, who is about to enter school for the first time, is excited about the opportunity to attain a European education, which he sees as the key to success. Sarr has pointed out that as the Mau Mau rebellion challenges Europeanization and control, the tangle of history overtakes Njoroge and his family, and he sees everything he believes in scrambled. These events, which affect the entire society, are filtered through the consciousness of Njoroge, who at first does not understand what is going on (Sarr, 1988).

Perhaps the heroes' contrasting relationships to the community may be seen most clearly by looking at the educational experiences of the two protagonists. Unlike Holden, Njoroge initially demonstrates an innocent faith that a Western education promises him a bright future, as evidenced in his enthusiastic and childlike response when his mother first asks if he would like to attend school. As the years pass, he excels academically, while his family, indeed the whole of Kenya, begins to experience civil unrest as the Kikuyu attempt to reclaim their sacred land from the European settlers. His youthful idealism creates within him a messianic vision of the purpose of his education: "He knew that for him education would be the fulfillment of a wider and more significant vision, a vision that embraced the demand made on him, not only by his father, but also by his mother, his brothers, and even the village" (39). Only after the emergency intensifies is Njoroge's dream lost. In the village school, the Mau Mau leave notes threatening students and teachers; and his teacher, Isaka, is later killed by white police who blame the murder on the Mau Mau. Shocked, Njoroge exclaims, "I thought Mau Mau was on the side of the black people" (83). He thinks of leaving school at this point but takes his brother Kamau's advice to remain in school. Kamau tells him he would be no safer at home than in school: "There's no hiding in this naked land" (83). Njoroge does continue his schooling and later leaves home to attend the Siriana Secondary School.

When Njoroge goes to live at the mission secondary school, his hopes are at first renewed by the white missionaries' earnest efforts to teach their African charges. At first, the school seems "like a paradise . . . where children from all walks of life and of different religious faiths could work together without any consciousness" of difference (115). Njoroge eventually realizes, however, that the paternalistic spirit of colonialism exists in the school as well. The headmaster, for example, "believed that the best, the really excellent, could only come from the white man. He brought up his boys to copy and cherish the white man's civilization as the only hope of mankind and especially of the black races" (115). The headmaster makes no protest when the colonial authorities come to take Njoroge from the school for "questioning" about his family's alleged connections with the Mau Mau uprising.

Police officers take Njoroge away to his village, where the boy discovers that his father Ngotho has been tortured and castrated during an interrogation about the murder of a black collaborator, Jacobo. Ngotho has falsely confessed to this crime in order to protect his older son, also a suspect. Njoroge is accused of having sworn the Mau Mau oath and is also threatened with emasculation. As the young man sees his father die, he realizes that his dream is also perishing. The difference between Holden's cynicism about his schooling and Njoroge's innocent and romantic expectations that education will solve all of his problems is initially strong. But Njoroge's faith in a Westernized education turns bitter when he begins to realize the effects of this colonial system on his people. If we accept Ayling's premise that all children are in some sense colonized by the power structures of family and society, Njoroge's and Holden's disillusionments are parallel in the sense that school, for both, is a colonial power which socializes children to accept the rule of the powerful—whether of their own race or another.

If both boys are viewed as struggling against the effects of colonization, a significant difference is that in an obviously colonized situation, as in Kenya, it is easier to develop and maintain a sense of community because there is an oppressive "other," against which to rebel; in Holden's situation, on the other hand, it is more difficult to find a clear enemy. As a result, Holden lashes out almost indiscriminately against pervasive forms of "phoniness."

Thus another initial contrast is seen in Njoroge's idealization of his family and in his dreams of playing an important role in his community. Unlike Holden, Njoroge has few material advantages, but his entire extended family—including, in this polygamous society, not only his biological parents and siblings but also his father's second wife and her sons—all work together to provide money and other support for Njoroge's schooling. Eventually, however, Njoroge, like Holden, is estranged from or disappointed with family members whom he nevertheless loves very much.

As a young boy, Njoroge surprises himself with the thought that parents may not always be right. Later, he begins to doubt his father's infallibility as a family leader and to see him instead as somewhat ineffectual in dealing with the economic and political crisis which threatens the family's well-being. Njoroge's older brother, Boro, wants the father, Ngotho, to take a more militant stance, swearing allegiance to the Mau Mau cause, but Ngotho is reluctant to do so, especially as he would have to take the oath from his son. As a result, Ngotho loses his traditional role as unquestioned head of the household. Njoroge tries to retain his faith in his father, but he cannot help acknowledging the change in his father's stature: "He was no longer the man whose ability to keep home together had resounded from ridge to ridge" (81). Unlike the American Holden, for whom irreverence for family authority is almost an expected norm, Njoroge laments the tragic effects of colonialism in undermining his culture's traditional family structure.

Njoroge's romantic attachment to the daughter of his father's enemy, Jacobo, undermines family authority from another direction. Like Holden, Njoroge seeks relief from his growing loneliness and isolation through fantasies of love. Njoroge's childhood affection for the daughter of his rich neighbor, Jacobo, turns to romance as he moves into adolescence, and Njoroge dreams of running away to marry Mwihaki. He knows their families, who have taken opposing sides in the political crisis, will not bless the match. Mwihaki's father, Jacobo, works for the white landowner, Mr. Howlands, a role which many of the Kikuyus regard as that of collaborator and spy. At a protest meeting where Jacobo appears to oppose a general strike, Njoroge's father, who is moved for once to stand up for the cause his sons espouse, attacks Jacobo. As a result, Ngotho loses his home and his job, and he and Jacobo are clear enemies: "Jacobo on the side of the white people and Ngotho on the side of the black people" (59).

Because of this family rift, the friendship of Njoroge and Mwihaki must thereafter be conducted in secret, and, as with Shakespeare's Romeo and Juliet, their love may hold out the possibility of reconciliation for a strife-torn community. Even after one of Njoroge's brothers kills Jacobo in retaliation for the death of Ngotho, Njoroge dreams of escaping with Mwihaki from the calamity which surrounds them. Njoroge's shocking experiences have shown him "a different world from that he had believed himself living in" (120). Disillusioned, he turns to Mwihaki as his last hope, proposing that they run away to Uganda. Mwihaki dispels this last dream, telling Njoroge, "We are no longer children" (133). She suggests to Njoroge that they will have to face the future, though it will be different from Njoroge's childhood visions: "We better wait. You told me that the sun will rise tomorrow. I think you were right" (133).

Ngũgĩ also traces the process by which his hero becomes confused about and disillusioned with religion. Njoroge's youthful vision consolidates his Christian faith and education with the traditional beliefs of the Kikuyu people: "His belief in a future for his family and the village rested then not only on a hope for sound education but also in a belief in a God of love and mercy, who long ago walked on this earth with Gikuyu and Mumbi, or Adam and Eve" (49). He thinks that the Kikuyu people, "whose land had been taken by white men, were no other than the children of Israel" and that the freedom leader, Jomo Kenyatta, is the Black Moses (49). He himself is to be the David who slays the Goliath of colonialism. Eventually, however, Njoroge's experiences teach him that the Christian religion is not a placebo for the ills that have befallen his people; the revivalist Isaka is slain by Europeans, the very people who brought the religion to his people, despite Isaka's vain attempts to assure the assassins that he is devoutly Christian and not a Mau Mau guerrilla. And Jomo Kenyatta, the Black Moses, is imprisoned by the colonial government.

The religious questions which trouble both Njoroge and Holden reflect their essentially idealistic natures, but their ideals about coming of age are quite different. Holden resists growing up; he wants to protect innocence even at the cost of stopping the passage of time; Njoroge, however, longs to grow up and become the savior of his people. Holden dreams of escaping to go out West and become a deaf-mute; Njoroge dreams of leading his society to a "better tomorrow."

Reminiscent of the typical folk tale or of the adventure/accomplishment romance described by Donelson and Nilsen, both do see themselves as savior figures for groups which they perceive to be disadvantaged and threatened by a corrupt social system. Holden wants to be "the catcher in the rye," to protect all innocent children from falling from the cliffs of life, and Njoroge wants to be the leader of his people who will save them from colonial oppression.

Both look back nostalgically to an earlier period when life was better. Deeply disturbed by present conditions, Njoroge dreams of a time when his people held their land in an innocent, Eden-like state without the corrupting and exploitative presence of white Europeans. Holden, the less communally oriented hero, looks back, not to the childhood of his race, but to his personal experiences in childhood. He thinks of childhood—his own, that of his dead brother Allie, and that of his sister Phoebe—as a time of innocence which he would like to recapture or to perpetuate.

At the end of both works, the two young adults must tentatively begin the process of coming of age by relinquishing some of their dreams about their own messianic roles and by beginning to accept the inevitable imperfections, even corruption and brutality, of the worlds they inhabit. Toward the end of Salinger's novel, Holden's sister Phoebe scolds him about his refusal to participate in life. When Phoebe challenges Holden to name something he likes, the only people he can list are nuns or dead people, and the only occupation he can think of which would really please him is that of "a catcher in the rye." Later, when Holden realizes his little sister Phoebe plans to go with him when he leaves to go out West, he gives up his plans and takes her back home. He also begins to wonder if he was too hard on Mr. Antolini, who after all had tried to help, and he admits he misses everybody he left behind at school. Holden experiences a kind of epiphany when he sees Phoebe riding the carousel in Central Park. He realizes he cannot protect her from the risks and dangers of life but must affirm life despite these dangers:

> All the kids kept trying to grab for the gold ring, and so was old Phoebe, and I was sort of afraid she'd fall off the goddam horse, but I didn't say anything or do anything. The thing with kids is, if they want to grab for the gold ring, you have to let them do it, and not say anything. (273–74)

This realization makes Holden euphorically happy, at least for the moment. Of this key moment in the text, Wayne C. Booth writes:

> Though he cannot protect her from knowledge of the world, though he cannot, as he would like, put her under a glass museum case and save her from the ravages of the sordid, time-bound world, he can at least offer her the love that comes naturally to him. He does so and he is saved. Which is of course why he is ecstatically happy. (Booth, 1964,163)

At the end of the book, Holden is in a mental institution, but is preparing to return to school. His recovery, however, is still quite tentative. To his psychiatrist's questions about whether or not he is ready to apply himself in school next fall, he replies, "I *think* I am, but how do I know?" (276). His final words reflect his awareness of the dangers and pains which inevitably accompany involvement in life, but he recognizes that the very act of telling his story has committed him to just such involvement: "About all I know is, I sort of miss everybody I told about. . . . It's funny. Don't ever tell anybody anything. If you do, you start missing everybody" (277).

Like Holden, Njoroge must relinquish his dreams of escape in order to face the harsh realities of life. After his father's death, he returns home to care for his father's two wives. His job as shop assistant for an Indian merchant is a far cry from his earlier dreams; and when he is fired even from this job he decides to end his life. His suicide attempt, however, is aborted when his mother Nyokabi and her co-wife Njeri find him. Though he feels himself to be a coward for not following through with his intentions, he also feels "a strange relief." The torch his mother carries appears as "a glowing piece of wood which she carried to light the way" (135). He knows he has tried to evade "the responsibility for which he has prepared himself since childhood," but he also accepts the indictment of the inner voice which tells him, "You are a coward. Why didn't you do it?" (136).

The last sentence of the story, however, suggests an acceptance of his responsibilities to the living and a gritty determination to live in the world as it is: "And he ran home and opened the door for his two mothers" (136). The hopefulness which is implicit in the last sentence will be accentuated for young readers when they learn that, although the book ends before Njoroge's people achieve independence, the movement spearheaded by the Mau Maus eventually culminated in majority rule for Kenya. Information which will be helpful includes the fact that in 1961, the Mau Mau leader, Jomo Kenyatta, was released from prison; in 1962, the terms of independence were negotiated; in 1963, the new nation celebrated its independence with Kenyatta as prime minister and one year later became a republic with Kenyatta as president. Thus the "tomorrow" for which Njoroge has longed does eventually come to his people. (Useful resources for providing such contexts are Elizabeth Gunner's *A Handbook for Teaching African Literature* and G. D. Killam's *An Introduction to the Writings of Ngũgĩ*.)

For Njoroge, however, as the individual within this political context, the process of coming of age may truly begin when he relinquishes his dreams of personal glory, but also when he recognizes his obligations to his family and community, despite their very human flaws. In this respect, the parallels with Holden Caulfield are significant. Both Njoroge and Holden are, in a sense, victims of social corruption: Holden is victimized by the commercialism, snobbery, and shallowness of a privileged but empty world in which he cannot find meaningful values or traditions. Njoroge is victimized by the effects of colonialization on the values and traditions of his people. However, in coming of age, each hero must move beyond the role of victim to work toward personal identity and a renewed sense of community in a world which will yield slowly, if at all, to the forces of change. Ultimately, however, both heroes must realize that the lines between enemy and self are not clearly drawn: family and friends may be "collaborators" or "rebels," and a part of Holden's problem may be that he at first perceives his parents solely as "collaborators."

Young readers will find here an honest account of the agonies and uncertainties of growing up in a troubled world. Both books end in a realistically indeterminate manner, as the heroes begin to accept their own flaws and limitations and to acknowledge their interdependence with other equally flawed human beings. The lesson in Mr. Antolini's words to Holden is one which both heroes are beginning to learn: "The mark of the immature man is that he wants to die nobly for a cause, while the mark of the mature man is that he wants to live humbly for one" (244). Both heroes have contemplated their own deaths as a possible escape from their painful realities, but, unlike tragic figures such as Romeo and Juliet, they draw back from the final step. They begin instead, reluctantly and uncertainly, to define their world and themselves in more realistic terms. Young readers who have encountered the vividly recreated worlds of Holden and Njoroge, so different from their own, and who have identified with the struggles of these fictional heroes may be led to repeat this process in their own lives.

Though neither Holden nor Njoroge yet has a comfortable spot in the literary canon, teachers can point to numerous literary parallels within the traditional canon. For example, both heroes experience the stages of innocence, experience, and higher innocence defined by English romantic poet William Blake and both are in need of the comforting lines of Walt Whitman's "On the Beach at Night" which Ngũgĩ uses as his epigraph: "Weep not, Child / . . . . The ravening clouds shall not be long victorious, / They shall not long possess the sky. . . ." One is reminded also of Milton's Adam and Eve, who must also relinquish their hold on an idealized realm and take up residence in the fallen world of human and natural imperfection:

> Some natural tears they dropped but wiped
> them soon;
> The world was all before them, where to
> choose
> Their place of rest. . . .
> They hand in hand with wandering steps and
> slow
> Through Eden took their solitary way.
> (*Paradise Lost,* Book XII, Lines 645–49)

References

Bettelheim, Bruno. *The Uses of Enchantment.* New York: Alfred A. Knopf, 1976.

Booth, Wayne C. "Censorship and the Values of Fiction." *The English Journal* (March 1964): 155–64.

Carlsen, Robert. "For Everything There Is a Season." In *Literature for Adolescents: Selection and Use,* edited by Richard A. Meade and Robert C. Small. Columbus, OH: Charles E. Merrill, 1973.

Cofer, Judith Ortiz. *Silent Dancing: A Partial Remembrance of a Puerto Rican Childhood.* Houston: Arte Publico Press, 1990.

Cortazar, Julio. "End of the Game." Translated by Paul Blackburn. In *The Eye of the Heart,* edited by Barbara Howes. New York: Avon Books, 1973.

Dasenbrock, Reed Way. "Understanding Others: Teaching Multicultural Literature." *Multicultural Readings.* Urbana, IL: NCTE, n.d.

Donelson, Kenneth and Alleen Pace Nilsen. *Literature for Today's Young Adults.* New York: Scott Foresman, 1989.

Gunner, Elizabeth. *A Handbook for Teaching African Literature.* London: Heinemann Educational Books, 1984.

Hamilton, Virginia. *Arilla Sun Down.* New York: Greenwillow, 1976.

———. *M. C. Higgins, the Great.* New York: Collier Books, 1987.

———. *Sweet Whispers, Brother Rush.* New York: Putnam Publishing Group, 1982.

Killam, G. D. *An Introduction to the Writings of Ngũgĩ.* London: Heinemann Educational Books, 1980.

King, James Roy. *Old Tales and New Truths.* Albany: State University of New York Press, 1992.

Kingston, Maxine Hong. *The Woman Warrior.* New York: Vintage International, 1989.

Knowles, John. *A Separate Peace.* New York: Bantam, 1985.

Lee, Harper. *To Kill a Mockingbird.* New York: Warner Books, 1988.

Milton, John. *Paradise Lost and Other Poems.* New York: New American Library, 1961.

Ngũgĩ, wa Thiong'o. *Weep Not, Child.* Portsmouth, NH: Heinemann, 1964.

Paterson, Katherine. *Bridge to Terabithia.* New York: Harper Trophy, 1977.

Salinger, J. D. *The Catcher in the Rye.* New York: Random House Modern Library, 1951.

Sarr, Ndiawar. Classroom Lecture. University of Montevallo, Spring, 1988.

Zipes, Jack. *Breaking the Magic Spell: Radical Theories of Folk and Fairy Tales.* New York: Methuen, 1984.

12 Cooper's Indians, Erdrich's Native Americans

Mary A. McCay
Loyola University

Vivian Twostar, professor of Native American Studies at Dartmouth College, upon being asked to write a piece for the Dartmouth alumni magazine, observed of Columbus's discovery of America: "European powers had not only the *will* to win but the belief that it was their *right*. One god, one family from which all their languages originated, one creation story, one agenda: to rule the world" (*Crown*, 81).[1] What is central to this observation about the beginning of Anglo-America is its monolithic structure. James Fenimore Cooper writes of an America three hundred years more populated by the Anglo settler than the world Columbus set foot on, and the monolithic idea of one country, one culture was central in his Leatherstocking tales. Cooper's novels of Natty Bumppo and the disappearing American wilderness focus on the creation of American myths, which by their very structure exclude multicultural dimensions. It was, however, impossible for Cooper and his fellow early American novelists to write within the conventions of the European novel, for the experience of being an American was, in many ways, unique. What good would a middle-class novel of manners serve an American writer who deemed himself an aristocrat of the spirit? Cooper, in his attempt to define America, depended heavily on myths that had their origins in the discovery of the continent and have remained prevalent almost to this day: the myth of the American Adam living in the New World Garden of Eden. These related myths have helped define a body of classical American literature from James Fenimore Cooper to J. D. Salinger and beyond. They depend upon a belief system constructed on the idea that not only the novel, but also America, was created by Anglo settlers, that all experiences of being American can be synthesized into the myth, that all cultural disharmonies are blended into one national narrative which tells the story of the innocent Adam in the New World. David W. Noble observes of this type of writing that it led many American writers to "begin with the question: Is it possible that Americans are exempt from the human condition? Is it possible that men in the New World have escaped from the need to live with community, within a framework of institutions and traditions?" (Noble 1968, 5). It is precisely this kind of question that generates the creation of myth. And Cooper's Leatherstocking tales, from *The Pioneers* through *The Last of the Mohicans* to the final story, *The Deerslayer,* are the embodiment of myth creation.[2]

In contrast to the traditional, hierarchical, and monolithic myths of Anglo-American origin are the myths of Native Americans. The novels of Louise Erdrich also answer essential questions about the relationship of humans to the world around them. Those questions are focused, however, on the people who did not dominate the continent but on those who lived and still to a large extent live in a very different relation to the world. While one could argue that modern Native American literature, such as that written by Erdrich, N. Scott Momaday, James Welch, Leslie Marmon Silko and others, deconstructs the synthesis of the Anglo-American myths, it is also important to note that this literature does not simply oppose dominant cultural traditions; rather, it makes a real attempt to revitalize the tolerant, accepting way of life that sustained the first Americans. While Cooper's novels emphasize a single culture, Erdrich's chronicle many cultures; while Cooper represents the American wilderness as myth, Erdrich reconstitutes her tribe's past as valuable reality. While Cooper's paradigms necessarily lead to the destruction of the Native American cultures that existed in America before the discovery, Erdrich's patterns look for the possibility of the acceptance of all cultures.

It is in the tension between the single culture and the multicultural myths and the conflict between single vision and the many voices that the two writers reveal the essential differences in the two Americas they experience. While Cooper must work backward in time to explain the reasons for the destruction of the Indian and so works back from reality to myth creation, Erdrich must work backward in time to recapture Native American myths that will help her people retrieve the America they have lost. As Professor Twostar says, "I wanted America back" (*Crown,* 193).

It is Fenimore Cooper's *The Pioneers* that introduces readers to the destruction of the Indian in America. Published in 1823, *The Pioneers* chronicles the old age of Hawk-eye and Indian John (Natty Bumppo and Chingachgook). The once noble hunter and the fearless Indian now live a marginal existence on the edge of white civilization. Reminiscing on the lost past of his tribe, Indian John also mourns the loss of the land. "The land was owned by my people," but now he and

Bumppo must share a hut on the edge of Templeton. The past of the noble savage is dead; no longer can the two men hunt freely in the wilderness. The new world has established laws that prohibit hunting except at certain times, but the old men long for the wilderness of the past which Natty Bumppo describes as "a second paradise." He continues: "I have travelled the woods for fifty-three years, and have made them my home for more than forty. . . . It was a comfortable hunting ground then." Both Natty Bumppo and Indian John feel they have no place in the society that surrounds them. Templeton has become a prosperous community bounded by laws and the vision of Marmaduke Temple. And it is Temple's money and the "twisty ways of the law" that Natty Bumppo accuses of destroying the wilderness. In the wilderness that Natty and Indian John remember, the wilderness that will become the myth, "the game was plenty as heart could wish" (*P,* 224–25).

In *The Pioneers,* Cooper is dealing with two worlds, the imagined world of the Garden of Eden and the world being created by the Marmaduke Temples of America. The important question, however, is where does the Indian fit in either world? Cooper's answer might well come from D. H. Lawrence who, in *Studies in Classic American Literature,* points out the dual relationship that white men had with red men: "The desire to extirpate the Indian. And the contradictory desire to glorify him" (Lawrence 1961, 36). Cooper, in the earliest Leatherstocking tales, reveals the first desire. Indian John is alone in the world; all his brothers are dead; the Delaware are no more. He has sunk into old age, and only the excitement of the hunt for the deer (despite the fact that it is out of season and he will suffer the consequences of the white law) can revive in him any sense of his glorious past: "The Indian had long been drooping with his years, and perhaps under the calamities of his race, but this invigorating and exciting sport causes a gleam of sunshine to cross his swarthy face that had long been absent from his features. It was evident the old man enjoyed the chase more as a memorial of his youthful sports and deeds, than with any expectation of profiting by the success" (*P,* 231). The past of Indian John, the glory of the hunt, the youthful deeds, stands in stark contrast to what he has become. When he meets Elizabeth Templeton in the forest, she reminds him: "You promised me a willow basket, and I have long had a shirt of calico in readiness for you" (*P,* 307). The Indian brave has become the servant of the white woman who, despite all her good intentions, treats him as one. When he tells her "John's hand can make baskets no more—he wants no shirt," he is rejecting the world that she and her community have fashioned for

him. Yet he cannot return to the past he remembers with longing—
the past when he was young, when Hawk-eye was strong, when he
could provide for his tribe. Cooper realizes that there is no place for
the Indian in America except under the soil, and, indeed, that is just
where Indian John, the once great Chingachgook, reposes at the end
of the novel. As he is dying, Chingachgook, no longer the Christianized
John, returns to the customs of his own people and speaks, not to the
Christian God, but to his own Great Spirit: "I will come! I will come!
to the land of the just I will come!" (*P,* 321). The Christian preacher,
not understanding the language of the Delaware, assumes the Indian
is calling out to the Christian God, but Natty Bumppo disabuses him
of that notion. In death, the old Indian has a right to speak his own
praises, not sing the praises of a Redeemer who has hardly redeemed
him.

The death of Indian John is the death of the Indian in America for
Cooper. The New World of Marmaduke Temple, the order of the law,
the world of owned land, farmed land, and burgeoning communities
is what Cooper's America has become. In fact, there is as little place
for Natty Bumppo in that world as there is for Chingachgook, but
Natty can at least reject the comfortable fireplace of Elizabeth Temple
and Oliver Effingham and head out to the new wilderness. Alone in
the world, he is heroic because the monologic nature of the Anglo
myth gives credence to the isolated hero. Alone in the world, Indian
John has no place because the Indian needs his tribe. Natty's isolation
sets up the possibility of the Adamic myth that Cooper develops in the
other Leatherstocking tales. Natty represents the first in a long line of
mythic heroes. Chingachgook represents the elegiac look at a world
that must be destroyed in order for America to exist. Once again, D.
H. Lawrence best expresses what Cooper's mythic hero, Natty Bumppo,
says to America: "I feel I'm superior to most men I meet. Not in birth,
because I never had a great-grandfather. Not in money, because I've
got none. Not in education, because I'm merely scrappy." Where, then,
does the superiority lie in such a person? Lawrence says the American
answers, "Just in myself" (Lawrence 1961, 44). That is what Cooper
says of Natty Bumppo in the first of the Leatherstocking tales. He has
not yet formulated the myth that will blossom in the later tales, but
he has set up the two most important aspects of it: first, Natty Bumppo
is superior to the Templetons and the Bill Kirbys of the world because
he lives by an idea of the wilderness, and that idea will become solidified
as the Garden myth in the American psyche. Secondly, Chingachgook,
once noble warrior of the Delaware, must die. There is no room in
the American Dream for live Indians. Chingachgook must be destroyed;

then he can be eulogized and glorified. And that is exactly what happens to him and his tribe as the Leatherstocking tales evolve.

The second stage of the creation of the myth of the new Adam in the Garden is played out in *The Last of the Mohicans.* Cooper is careful to say in his "Preface to the First Edition (1826)" that he is a student of Indian history and has tried to understand the different tribal names and to authenticate the actual history of the Delawares. The debate that this has generated among critics as to whether Cooper used authentic sources or whether his Indians are created out of whole cloth obfuscates the real problem in dealing with Cooper's rendering of the loss of the Delaware's land and nation. In fact, Cooper is not chronicling the demise of the Mohicans in the novel (that is a foregone conclusion). Rather he is justifying it through the politics of the myths he is in the process of creating. One might well ask, as a student of American literature, how writers such as Cooper could subscribe to the myth of the virgin land when there were Indians already there, or how the myth of the new Adam could be so potent when clearly the white man wasn't the first in the Garden. What Cooper does is work backward to recodify experience from the point of view of Anglo-myth rather than looking back at the Indian myths or history as anything other than a part of the great white migration. Since the white experience is central, the red experience disappears, and Uncas's death, as elegiacally as Cooper treats it, serves to solve the problem of the virgin land and the new Adam.

Early in *The Last of the Mohicans,* the question of the relationship between the white and the red races is discussed by Chingachgook and Hawk-eye. Both are mature men, and both have seen a great deal of life and of the changes that have taken place in the wilderness. Recounting the arrival of the first pale men who came into the forest, the Indian says: "We were one people, and we were happy. The salt lake gave us its fish, the wood its deer, and the air its birds. We took wives who bore us children; we worshipped the Great Spirit" (*LM,* 33). Then the white man introduced liquor and the ancestors of Chingachgook "parted with their land. Foot by foot, they were driven back from the shores, until I that am a chief and a Sagamore, have never seen the sun shine but through the trees, and have never visited the graves of my fathers" (*LM,* 33). Clearly it is the Indian who lived in paradise and who might justifiably lay claim to Adamic status; but the white man when he pushes the red man out of paradise changes the experience and becomes the first man there—the *new* Adam. This is possible precisely because of what Natty himself, while not even educated, recognizes. It is the custom of the white man "to write in books what they have done and seen, instead of telling them in their villages, where the lie can be given to the face of a cowardly boaster, and the brave soldier can call on his comrades to witness the truth of his words" (*LM,* 31). Leatherstocking speaks to the difference between the two cultures, and he illuminates the way the white myth became ascendant. Because it was written, it gained power. There was no community to give the lie to it. Thus the Indian was trapped in the white man's image of him. He might be the noble savage, like Chingachgook, or he might be the devil incarnate as Magua is, but he is no longer himself.

Another element central to the creation of the white hierarchical structure of mythic experience which Cooper must deal with in *The Last of the Mohicans* and later in *The Deerslayer* is the problem of race mixing. In *The Last of the Mohicans* both Magua and Uncas want to marry Cora, yet the politics of white identity forbids intermarriage. Cora is mulatto and thus, throughout the novel, she is seen as marginal in her own family. Her all-white half-sister, Alice Munroe, is the character whom Heyward and Hawk-eye feel they must protect. By the taint in her racial background, Cora becomes problematic for Hawk-eye who depends heavily on the idea of "gifts." Since each race has distinct gifts (and in this case they are hierarchically structured) each race has a distinct place in the world. The white race is in ascendancy in the New World; the red race, for all its primitive honesty and stoic suffering, is in decline. The black race has dubious claim to any place in the hierarchy, so Cora's gifts as a white woman are diminished by the mixing of races. Because Cora cannot be the object of a white man's desire, Cooper makes her the object of the red man's and thus sets the stage for the struggle between Uncas and Magua which will destroy the young Mohican. As D. H. Lawrence observes, "Cora loves Uncas, Uncas loves Cora. But Magua also desires Cora, violently desires her. A lurid little circle of sensual fire. So Fenimore kills them all off, Cora, Uncas, and Magua, and leaves the White Lily [Alice Munroe] to carry on the race" (Lawrence 1961, 58). Lawrence expresses the fear of racial mixture that was a part of myth-making. For whites to intermarry was to deny the very hegemony of their myths, the myths which gave them a right to the land.

While Donald Darnell argues that it is really Uncas who is the hero of *The Last of the Mohicans* because of "the bright destiny legend has predicted for him" (Darnell 1965, 263), it is clear that for Cooper he is doomed from the beginning. He is doomed precisely because he wishes to carry on his race, his name, and his tribe, and he wishes to enlarge it by mixing his seed with Cora's. For Uncas the wish does not in any way contradict the values by which he lives because those values are inclusive, but for Cooper, whose values and myths are exclusive, the marriage threatens to dilute each race's gifts, so Uncas must die to keep his gifts untainted.

Natty Bumppo, on the other hand, becomes as the five novels develop more and more heroic. A shrivelled old man in *The Pioneers,* he has become, by the time of *The Deerslayer* (published in 1841, almost twenty years after the first Leatherstocking Tale), "a man who keeps his moral integrity hard and intact. An isolated, almost selfless, stoic enduring man" (Lawrence 1961, 63). It is in *The Deerslayer* that readers see the type of behavior that most annoyed Mark Twain when he took Cooper to task for the ridiculous behavior of his Indians and for the lack of verisimilitude in his tales. Yet verisimilitude is not the stuff of myths, and, by the time Deerslayer is captured by the Hurons during a battle, his actions are not the actions of a man, but of a "saint with a gun" (Lawrence 1961, 50). Sometimes he is without a gun as when he returns to captivity from a furlough. Very few of the Hurons believe that he, a white man, will honor their code, but Bumppo enters the camp and announces: "Here I am, and there is the sun. One is not more true to the laws of natur' than the other has proved true to his word. . . . My business with man and 'arth is settled; nothing remains now but to meet the white man's God, accordin' to a white man's duties and gifts" (*D,* 479). Offered marriage to Sumach, the widow of the man he has killed in battle, Bumppo responds: "I'm white, and Christian-born' 'twould ill become me to take a wife under redskin form, from among heathen" (*D,* 484). After Deerslayer's rejection of the Huron offer, he escapes and is recaptured to undergo tribal torture and finally death, which (much to the dismay of Twain)[3] he is spared because none of the Indian's tomahawks find their mark, nor does the trial by rifles end Deerslayer's life. In fact, after what seems interminable torture and talk, Chingachgook boldly enters the camp and frees his friend. This episode climaxes *The Deerslayer.* Surely a man who has defied death, escaped marriage, and finally returned to the wilderness with his friend Chingachgook is more than a simple hunter. He is the embodiment of the virtues Cooper sees as "white gifts," and a caution against miscegenation. Lake Glimmerglass, the setting of the novel, is also preserved in myth: "accident or tradition had rendered it a spot sacred to nature" (*D,* 564).

The last episodes in the novel capture both character and setting in static highlight. Those are the scenes that readers remember of Natty Bumppo. The old man who struggled in vain against the onslaught of civilization becomes, through the telescopic lens of myth, forever young, and the wilderness forever beautiful.

While Cooper himself had much in common with Marmaduke Temple, the judge of *The Pioneers,* and while his own ancestors despoiled the very wilderness that became sacred in *The Deerslayer,* the author does, through the five novels, reject what commerce and democracy have made of America in its first two centuries. Cooper, in rejecting Templeton, Bill Kirby, Hurry Harry March, and Thomas Hutter, rejects the basis of American entrepreneurial democracy in favor of American myth. The single heroic vision of the Leatherstocking tales becomes the currency of American cultural imperialism. It is this vision of the American Adam and the New World Garden of Eden that conquered all other visions of the New World, and it is, as Gayatri Spivaks defines it, the politics of identity suppressing the politics of culture.[4] The politics of identity which deifies the individual, and rejects community, is defined by Cooper's own description of Natty Bumppo:

> The imagination has no great task in portraying to itself a being removed from the every-day inducements to err, which abound in civilized life, while he retains the best and simplest of his early impressions; who sees God in the forest; hears him in the winds; bows to him in the firmament that o'ercanopies all; submits to his sway in a humble belief of his justice and mercy; in a word, a being who finds the impress of the Deity in all the works of nature, without any of the blots produced by the expedients, and passion, and mistakes of man. (*D,* vii–viii)

It is that single mythic vision of the white man, which leaves no room for other cultures or other visions, that Louise Erdrich shatters. Through the prism of Native American cultures, she shows the multi-faceted dimensions of her people's experience and of American *culture.* It is not the inviolability of the single individual which informs Erdrich's novels, but the dialogic voices of the tribe. *Love Medicine* and *Tracks* and her collaborative novel, *The Crown of Columbus,* written with her husband, Michael Dorris, set themselves in a tension with the Leatherstocking tales and indeed almost parody Cooper's myth-making. Just as Cooper begins with a somewhat realistic picture of Natty Bumppo and the disappearing wilderness, so Erdrich begins with a starkly realistic vision of the tensions, trials, and destruction within the Native American community. But while Cooper retreats to myth to reject the way America has developed, Erdrich, in *Tracks,* recaptures, through Native American myths, the strength of her people, and finally, in *The Crown of Columbus,* repeoples the continent with a bright array of different cultures.

A member of the Chippewa Nation, Erdrich is a product of the very process Cooper feared—race mixing. The eldest child of a Chippewa mother and a German American father, Erdrich grew up near and spent a great deal of time at the Turtle Mountain Chippewa reservation learning the tales of her tribal ancestors from her maternal grandmother. These stories blend, merge, and grow in Erdrich's fiction, which attempts to reconstruct a world in which Native Americans are not always dominated by whites, and in which the world is not constructed of a single dominant voice or vision.

The most important technique that Erdrich employs to help diversify the vision is the multiple narrative. Unlike Cooper, whose voice and vision are single, Erdrich allows for many voices and for events to be seen through a prism rather than through the Cooperian telescope. All of her novels employ this technique through which Erdrich asserts the possibility of many points of view and by which she insists upon the value of multiple perspectives. There is no single truth or vision for the author, nor should there be for the national psyche.

The first novel, *Love Medicine,* seems at first to be a series of short stories, yet, as the reader gets deeper and deeper into the text, it becomes clear that Erdrich is using many points of view to deal with the death of the Native American in his own world. The central death is that of June Kashpaw, a Chippewa woman, who dies in a snowstorm while walking back to her reservation. Her death releases the voices of her extended family and reveals the tribal interconnections of all those whose lives touched hers.

Many of the voices of the book are of mixed blood, so they speak of the internal conflict of white and Native American. Albertine Johnson, the daughter of Zelda Kashpaw and a Swede who did not stay long enough to be a father, tries, when she goes home for June's memorial, to understand the relationships in her family. They are made up of mixed marriages (June's son, King, has taken up with a white girl who has borne him a son), and casual adoptions. June herself has been taken in by Grandma Kashpaw and her husband Nector, and now Lipsha Morrisey has been taken in by Eli Kashpaw. Family and racial lines are blurred, and while there is disparagement of whites because of the way the tribe has been treated and cheated by them, there is a general acceptance of all the family members, mixed and full blood.

Perhaps the best paradigm of the way the Native American makes his peace with the white world is the story of the twins, Nector and Eli Kashpaw. The youngest sons of Rushes Bear, who had married the first Kashpaw, Nector and Eli represent the divided psyche of the

Native American. Rushes Bear "had let the government put Nector in school, but [had] hidden Eli, the one she couldn't part with, in the root cellar dug beneath her floor. In that way she gained a son on either side of the line" (*Love*, 17).[5] As a result Nector becomes the go-between for his brother and the white world, but he loses something as well, and when we first see him he sits in a senile state, not knowing where he is or who his family is. The whites deny his heritage, but use him as their token Indian. When young, he has been asked by a rich white woman to model for her Indian portrait. He finds out that it is a portrait of the *Plunge of the Brave*, a parody no doubt on the Cooperian death of Uncas who falls to his death off a cliff. When Nector sees the picture, he observes: "There I was, jumping off a cliff, naked of course, down into a rocky river. Certain death." When he begins to understand that the whites were only "interested in [his] doom," he returns home to his mother and his brother because he knows that "Nector Kashpaw would fool the pitiful rich woman that painted him and survive the raging water" (*Love*, 91). He does survive, but his stance in two worlds makes him a very different man from his brother, Eli, "for Eli had wizened and toughened while Grandpa [Nector] was larger, softer, even paler than his brother" (*Love*, 25). In old age, the ravages of contact with the white world shows in Nector's pale, flabby body and in his mind, which has simply dribbled away.

In another episode, Albertine Johnson introduces another mixed couple, Gerry Nanapush, a Chippewa, and "Dot Adare of the has-been, of the never-was, of the what's-in-front-of-me people" (*Love*, 155). Albertine's dismissal of Dot Adare is ironic on two levels: first, the two women come to be close friends, and secondly, Dot Adare is, in Erdrich's second novel, *Beet Queen*, a central character whose will to have her own identity and not be forced into a small-town mold separates her from the "never was ... what's-in-front-of-me people" Albertine first stereotypes her with. A further irony becomes apparent in the *Beet Queen;* Dot Adare is unavoidably part Chippewa. Albertine, herself a mixed blood, is drawn to Dot by the unborn mixed-blood baby, and when Gerry is sent to prison, the two women and the baby form a sort of family. Albertine sees the child as a "powerful distillation of Dot and Gerry" (*Love*, 171), a way for the two worlds to meet.

Throughout *Love Medicine*, the informing symbols are those of multiplicity and fertility rather than Cooper's images of singularity and celibacy. "Lulu's Boys" best exemplifies Erdrich's sense of the richness of the tribe. Lulu has eight boys; "some of them even had her maiden name. The three oldest were Nanapushes. The next oldest were Mor-risseys who took the name Lamartine and then there were more assorted younger Lamartines who didn't look like one another, either" (*Love*, 76). All are accepted; all see themselves as brothers and are linked and connected by Lulu.

Lewis Owens has commented about Erdrich's *Love Medicine* that the narrative allows readers "into an Indian world sans guilt, a wonderfully textured, brilliantly rendered fiction where the non-Indian reader is not forced to feel his 'outsideness'" (Owens 1987, 54). While the style of the book does, as Owens asserts, mute the pain of the Native American's experience, there is also in the book a willingness to allow whites to enter the experience—the experience of being outsiders, as the Indian has been since he was marginalized by the Anglo myth of the frontier. Though, Owens continues, it "isn't always emotionally profitable to be an Indian in the world of Erdrich's first novel" (Owens 1987, 54), there is a sense in which whites who enter that experience see how the dominant single-vision culture has oppressed and supressed the culture of the Native American. Those who live in two worlds come to realize that the symbolic landscape of America is not monolithic and that there is no easy category for anyone on the margins.

Beet Queen, Erdrich's second novel, does continue the quest for a way to speak of Native American experience in the context of a world that requires emotional toughness and psychic strength to survive. But the novel that most clearly continues the ordering of Native American experience in a way that counters the classic American stereotypes of the Indian and truly expresses the strength of the Native American community is *Tracks*.

Once again, Erdrich structures her novel with the prismed perspective. There are two points of view and two conflicting voices, but there is also a clear portrayal of a central Native American myth that sharpens the novel's focus and clarifies the quest for a Native American story. Unlike *Love Medicine*, which distances the reader from the pain of dispossession and loss, *Tracks* chronicles and reveals the manner in which Fleur Pillager survives her dispossession. Through the myth of Misshepeshu, the water man, which informs the book, Erdrich gives Native Americans back their cultural heritage, and, even though they are dispossessed of the land, they regain their past.

The two narrators of *Tracks* tell two very different stories. Old Nanapush begins his tale in 1912 and tells it to help his spiritual granddaughter come to terms with her heritage. Fleur's daughter, Lulu, needs to accept her mother so that she won't reject her heritage. So Nanapush's tale of Fleur Pillager, who drowned three times and came to hold the spirit of the Chippewa in her soul, is told with love. It is that power that the other narrator, Pauline, has sold to become white so that she can become a nun in an order that does not accept the vocations of Indian girls. Pauline's displacement begins when she is a child. She demands that her father send her to the nuns to learn lace making. Her father cautions her:

> "You'll fade out there," he said, reminding me I was lighter than my sisters. "You won't be an Indian once you return."
> "Then maybe I won't come back," I told him. I wanted to be like my mother who showed her half-white. I wanted to be like my grandfather, pure Canadian. That was because even as a child I saw that to hang back was to perish. I saw through the eyes of the world outside of us. I would not speak our language. (*T,* 14)

Pauline's displacement focuses her narration on Fleur as danger, Fleur as killer. She is afraid of Fleur's power and attempts to find a power equally strong to balance the power Fleur has through her heritage. In fact by becoming a bride of Christ, by starving herself, by becoming a "saint," Pauline hopes to deny her dual past. Fleur becomes the objective correlative for Pauline's torment about her past. Fleur is the Indian she is denying in herself. While she calls Fleur a killer, it is ironic that it is Pauline who is the murderer. She locked the icehouse door from the outside, trapping inside and killing the three men who raped Fleur. She also murders Napoleon Morrisey after leading him to believe she is attracted to him, and it is she who, through her ignorance of the medicinal herbs of her tribe, murders Fleur's baby. She is death, not Fleur or the waterman. Her narrative codifies Native American experience in much the same way Cooper's does. It must be denied, marginalized, and forgotten in order that the white vision may become dominant. The Christ image becomes for Pauline what she accuses the water man of being for Fleur. While Pauline maintains white myths are more powerful, Erdrich counterbalances Pauline's feverish quest for the best myth with an understated but powerful natural myth of the waterman that sustains Nanapush, Fleur, and Eli Kashpaw and orders their briefly idyllic existence on the shores of his lake.

The central issue in *Tracks,* much like the issue in the Leatherstocking tales, is the land. Whose will it be? Michael Dorris points out that until 1492 "more than three hundred cultures, each differentiated to a greater or lesser degree by language, custom, history, and lifeway, were resident north of the Rio Grande at the time Columbus first accidentally bumped into the Bahamas. . . . Social diversity was accepted, tolerated, and assumed, and each group took pride in its own distinctive features" (Dorris 1979, 147–48). Fleur and Nanapush feel they hold natural title to the land and want to keep it without necessarily excluding whites.

However, whites, through a system of tricks and taxes, gain control of Fleur's holding, and she retreats into the forest. The irony is that it is the Indians themselves who give Fleur's land to the whites. Nector Kashpaw (who has been sent to white schools and has chosen white ways) is sent with the allotment money by his brother Eli to pay for his and Fleur's allotment. When Nector arrives at the agency, the agent adds a late fee to the allotments, so Nector pays only for his and his mother's, leaving Fleur and Eli's to the auction block. During the winter, the loggers move closer and closer to the allotment and finally, Fleur is driven into hiding. Old Nanapush tells Fleur's daughter, Lulu, "Perhaps if your mother had herself taken the money in to the agent, you would still be living on the shores of Matchimato, but she was newly cheerful, trusting, drained from work. Eli was trapping, my hip was lamed, and Nector was eager to take on responsibility" (*T,* 191). Erdrich shows how the land was lost, but old Nanapush wants to give Lulu her heritage, so, after her return to the reservation and the tribe, she can find a place in it.

An essential element of *Tracks* is the way it gives a history to the characters in *Love Medicine.* If they are blurred by their contact with the white world in Erdrich's first book, the focus on each is sharper in *Tracks.* Lulu, the mother of eight sons in *Love Medicine,* is given a context in *Tracks*—old Nanapush gives her back the heritage she passes on to her many sons. Eli and Nector Kashpaw show, in *Tracks,* the beginnings of the characteristics that set them so far apart in old age. And Pauline, the unreliable narrator of *Tracks,* is the sadistic nun, Leopolda, who dies hard, cold, and without love, in *Love Medicine.*

In the two novels, Erdrich is able to reconstruct a tribe using the history of the Kashpaw, Morrisey, and Lamartine struggle to endure. On one level, the vision is a painful one of men and women dispossessed of land, living at the will of a government that they cannot trust. Lulu puts it succinctly when she says, "I never let the United States census in my door, even though they say it's good for Indians. Well, quote me. I say that every time they counted us they knew the precise number to get rid of" (*Love,* 221). On the other hand, the group has a strength that was never lost despite the waves of disease and conquest.[6] Erdrich's Native Americans are still "quite familiar and at ease with the realities of cultural pluralism" (Dorris 1979, 148–49).

In an attempt to reclaim their own culture and heritage more fully, Michael Dorris and Louise Erdrich have collaborated on a book which seeks to reconstruct (rather than deconstruct) what actually happened in 1492 when Columbus first arrived. This reclamation is especially important for the 500th anniversary of the "discovery" because one might well ask the question, "How could Columbus have discovered America if there were millions of people already here?"

The Crown of Columbus, like Erdrich's and Dorris's previous novels, is focused by a dialogic narrative structure. Roger Williams and Vivian Twostar, polar opposites in the academic world of Dartmouth, are the two central narrators fighting over who Columbus actually was and what his discovery meant to each one's concept of history. Roger, contemplating his vision of the man, asserts, "I insisted on my heroic one" (*Crown*, 275). Roger's heroic Columbus is based on the monologic myths of discovery. There was one discovery, one tribe to be dispensed with and one goal: conquest. Vivian, on the other hand, sees Roger's Columbus as "a villain, a pillager, and obtuse spoiler." The quest for the crown which Columbus was supposed to have hidden on the island of Eleuthera, but did not give to the people he met because he considered them unworthy, constitutes the narrative of the novel, and indeed, the crown is found by Roger and Vivian after a series of near-disasters. The crown itself, once found, poses and focuses the important questions about the relationship of the Old and the New World: "the hope for a new Utopia, for equity and respect between worlds, if it had been meant to symbolize a new beginning, a kingdom free of past mistakes, then its hard organic casket was indeed a fitting storage" (*Crown*, 343). Roger's interpretation of what the crown means solidifies the paradox of the dominant culture myth. He sees in the crown the possibility of a world in which man lives in a new, untrammeled relation to nature, a relationship in which the new American is exempt from the human condition. Of course, in that relationship, there was never any hope for equity and respect for the Indian because he is not a part of the European tradition of salvation or regeneration.

For the Native Americans, the crown represents what they were supposed to get. "Europe got America, everything and everybody in it and on it, and in exchange we were supposed to take . . . this [the crown]," Vivian Twostar proclaims (*Crown*, 360). Her son, Nash, however, sees the whole process of searching for the crown, deciphering the runes on the clamshells, traveling to Eleuthera, almost losing his mother and his sister, and then finding the crown, in quite a different light. His one narrative recapitulates the process for the reader and focuses on a broader perspective: "The world has become a small place, all parts connected. . . . Whatever happened next at least was new, at least had never happened before" (*Crown*, 361). For the young man, there is still a world of possibility, a world which can be made new, not new in the way that Cooper made America new by destroying Nash's past, but a world in which he can live—have a future. Of himself he says, "There are different ways of feeling like an Indian for me. There are moments in Hanover when it sets me off from everybody around me, for better or worse, and times, like when we're back on Mom's or Grandma's reservations, when it makes me be at home. Mostly it's just confusing or irrelevant, one disguise among the many I put on. Except it's not a disguise, it's skin" (*Crown,* 355). He has come to accept both his marginality and his centrality, and the quest for the crown, which creates a family for him, gives him a world in which to look for a future.

Both Dorris and Erdrich recognize that the history of the Native American in North America has been irrevocably changed and marginalized by the myth that powered Anglo-America; however, their novels, and the novels of James Welch, Leslie Silko, and Simon Ortiz, among others, discourage a view that glorifies homogeneity, hierarchical myths, and single visions of experience. To recall the various and diverse cultures of those whom white America has chosen to consider vanished or no longer a part of the national experience is to insist on an America that is what it is: multicultural, diverse, heterogeneous, and tainted by its past. The modern reader finds in Erdrich, Dorris, and other Native American writers pathways to the past that broaden rather than limit experience. The new myths of America will be, with the inclusion of the hundreds of Native American myths, truly enriched.

Notes

1. Quotations from the Dorris and Erdrich novel are cited in the text as: *Crown: The Crown of Columbus* (New York: HarperCollins, 1991).

2. I have chosen to discuss only three of the Leatherstocking tales because *The Prairie* and *The Pathfinder* reiterate but do not substantially change or add new dimensions to the development of the myth. Quotations from Cooper's works are cited in the text using the following abbreviations:

P: *The Pioneers* (New York: Airmont Publishers, 1964).
LM: *The Last of the Mohicans* (New York: Viking Press, 1986).
D: *The Deerslayer* (New York: Washington Square Press, 1961).

3. Twain's popular criticism of Cooper's literary offenses hides his own use of the same myth that Cooper employed. In *The Adventures of Huckleberry Finn* the only substantial difference is that Twain substitutes a Black for Cooper's Indian.

4. Gayatri Spivak used the phrase at a talk at Loyola in March, 1991, and I think it expresses the difference between Cooper's and Erdrich's myths.

5. Quotations from Erdrich's novels are cited in the text using the following abbreviations:

Love: Love Medicine (New York: Bantam Books, 1984).
BQ: *The Beet Queen* (New York: Bantam Books, 1986).
T: *Tracks* (New York: Harper & Row, 1988).
6. Eighty-five percent of the Native Americans who had dealings with Europeans during the contact period were victims of European diseases.

References

Cooper, James Fenimore. *The Last of the Mohicans.* New York: Viking Press, 1986.

———. *The Pioneers.* New York: Airmont Publishers, 1964.

———. *The Deerslayer.* New York: Washington Square Press, 1961.

Darnell, Donald. "Uncas as Hero: The *Ubi Sunt* Formula in *The Last of the Mohicans.*" *American Literature* 37, no. 3 (November 1965): 259–66.

Dorris, Michael. "Native American Literature in an Ethnohistorical Context." *College English* 41, no. 2 (October 1979): 147–62.

Dorris, Michael and Louise Erdrich. *The Crown of Columbus.* New York: HarperCollins, 1991.

Erdrich, Louise. *Tracks.* New York: Harper & Row, 1988.

———. *Love Medicine.* New York: Bantam Books, 1984.

———. *The Beet Queen.* New York: Bantam Books, 1986.

Lawrence, D. H. *Studies in American Literature.* New York: New America Library, 1961.

Noble, David. *The Eternal Adam and the New World Garden.* New York: Grosset and Dunlap, 1968.

Owens, Lewis. "Acts of Recovery: The American Indian Novel in the 80's." *Western American Literature* 22, no. 1 (May 1987): 53–57.

13 The Individual, the Family, and Society: A Bibliographic Essay

Elizabeth H. Rodgers
University of Montevallo

In their essay on J. D. Salinger's *The Catcher in the Rye* and Ngũgĩ wa Thiong'o's *Weep Not, Child,* Sandra Lott and Steven Latham show that despite the vast differences in setting in the two works, both dramatize the initiation of the child into the adult world. In each novel, the growing boy is vulnerable to the hypocrisy and disorder of his society. The hopefulness and idealism of the two boys, one American and one Kenyan, turn to disappointment, then disillusionment, and finally despair as Holden Caulfield ends up in a mental hospital and Njoroge, now twenty years old, is broken in body and spirit after the destructive Mau Mau wars. The Kenyan civil war that sears Njoroge's world contrasts with the American social disharmony that troubles Holden, but both novels portray the initiation of an optimistic boy into a cynical world that assails his dreams.

Several American and African short stories also dramatize adolescent initiation, but without the devastation experienced by Njoroge or the despair experienced by Holden Caulfield. Sarah Orne Jewett's "A White Heron," a product of nineteenth-century New England, portrays a girl of nine forced to choose between protecting the life of a bird whose habits she understands and whose company she treasures or catering to the wishes of the handsome ornithologist who wants to "bag" her white heron for his collection. The bittersweet resolution involves a growth in awareness for the child; she trades the potential friendship with the young man for the continued companionship with the heron. In "Power," by African writer Jack Cope, set in the African veld modernized by powerlines, a boy struggles to bring about the rescue of a bird rather than accept society's indifference to its fate. In the stories by Jewett and Cope, the child is portrayed as a champion of the right of nature's creatures to survive and as a symbol of individual conscience standing firmly against forces that would rob nature of one of its own ("Heron") or would refuse to free one of nature's creatures

168

from entrapment in a human power structure. In each case the seemingly powerless child asserts his or her belief in the sanctity of life and triumphs for the moment, if only in a minor way, against the power structure of science or economics. In Doris Lessing's African story, "A Sunrise on the Veld," a fifteen-year-old boy's sense of the limitless possibilities of life—his life, all life—is suddenly challenged during an early morning hunt on the veld by his discovery of a dying buck being devoured by hungry black ants—and the possibility that his quick shots at fleeing deer on previous mornings might have been the cause of the deer's fate.

Students of *Catcher* and *Weep Not, Child* could benefit from reading about these three children who move from innocent expectations about the goodness of the world to the sobering discovery that life often involves choices, demands personal courage, and sometimes results in unwitting destruction to life even when life seems most promising. Other short stories with initiation themes include Nathaniel Hawthorne's "My Kinsman, Major Molineaux" and Sherwood Anderson's "I Want to Know Why." Of these works treating initiation, Ngũgĩ's *Weep Not, Child* is the most tragic. Other works that portray the innocent adolescent encountering confinement in life-threatening situations are Anne Frank's *Diary of a Young Girl,* Joy Kogawa's *Obasan,* and Frederick Douglass's *Narrative.*

While several of the works about adolescent initiation, including those by Ngũgĩ and Salinger, involve love relationships, a number of works focus more directly on courtship and marriage. Two contemporary works, *The Sound of Waves,* a Japanese novel by Yukio Mishima, and "Sunday," a contemporary Peruvian short story by Mario Vargas Llosa, recount a first love which triumphs over adversity. Chinese writer Tsao Hsueh-Chin's *Dream of the Red Chamber,* written in the eighteenth century, recounts the tempestuous love of two cousins in the context of the extended Chinese family. The Japanese dramatist Chikamatsu Monzaemon treats ill-fated love in eighteenth-century Japanese society in the timeless play *The Love Suicides at Sonezaki,* written for the puppet theatre. In Chikamatsu's work, the lovers experience a conflict between their duty to society ("giri") and their own wishes ("ninjo"). This couple can be compared with that in Shakespeare's *Antony and Cleopatra,* who, finding no way to live in this world as husband and wife, commit suicide, though not through a suicide pact as in Chikamatsu's play. These works can also be compared with *Weep Not, Child* and with such novels as Tolstoy's *Anna Karenina* and Nathaniel Hawthorne's *The Blithedale Romance,* in which the female protagonist kills herself when disappointed in love. These nineteenth-century treatments of the desperate woman, both written by men, contrast sharply with the late nineteenth-century novel *The Awakening* by Kate Chopin. The protagonist, Edna Pontellier—a mother, yet not a "mother-woman," a wife, yet not a happily married woman—has unmet emotional needs that she tries to satisfy outside of marriage. The failure of her male friends to meet her needs, and her own unwillingness to return home and "give up her life" for her husband and two children, lead Edna to take her own life by walking into the sensuous embrace of the ocean. An interesting contrast to *The Awakening* is Buchi Emecheta's novel *The Joys of Motherhood,* in which the Nigerian mother Nnu Ego devotes her life to her husband and nine children only to doubt her decision in later years when her family disappoints and mistreats her and she experiences a lonely old age and death.

Other works in which society's definition of the woman's role seems confining include George Bernard Shaw's *Candida,* Alice Walker's *Possessing the Secret of Joy,* Bobbie Ann Mason's "Shiloh," and "Paseo" by the Chilean writer José Donoso. In addition, three works by African writers on this theme are Nadine Gordimer's "Town and Country Lovers," set in South Africa; Isak Dinesen's autobiographical love story *Out of Africa,* set on a coffee plantation near Nairobi; and Doris Lessing's "To Room 19," the story of a woman's madness. Two stories about sheltered, restless wives who move toward personal freedom are Kate Chopin's "The Story of an Hour" and Chilean author Maria Luisa Bombal's "The Tree," in which the rubber tree is Brigida's substitute for children and her escape from an unfeeling husband and a tawdry world. Doll imagery in Henrik Ibsen's realistic *A Doll's House* contrasts with that in the contemporary short story "The Youngest Doll" by Puerto Rican writer Rosario Ferré in which a doll becomes a surreal symbol for the life-thwarting roles of women. Two contemporary Japanese works by Yasunari Kawabata reveal a man's futile longing for love. "The Izu Dancer" recounts the nameless protagonist's erotic fascination—at a distance—with the Izu dancer Kaoru. This story, with its emphasis on the futile longing for love, has much in common with Kawabata's novel *Thousand Cranes,* in which the yearning without fulfillment is complicated by the fact that Kikuyi falls in love with the mistress of his deceased father—and then with her daughter.

Fulfillment of desire complicates life in a number of literary works. Nadine Gordimer's "The Bridegroom" foreshadows life changes for a simple Afrikaner overseer of a road gang after his imminent marriage. In Bessie Head's "Snapshots of a Wedding," South African traditions of courtship and marriage compete with Westernized, modern customs.

The stories by Gordimer and Head end with the implicit question, "Happily ever after?" and thus invite comparison with Shakespeare's ironically titled *All's Well that Ends Well*, which leaves the reader with similar questions about the future of the characters' relationships. The theme of guilt plaguing romantic relationships pervades Kawabata's modern Japanese novel *Thousand Cranes*, which contrasts in mood with Sophocles' tragedy *Oedipus Rex* (dramatizing Oedipus's equivocal relationship to his parents). These works might also be read in conjunction with Aeschylus's *Agamemnon* (involving the burden of inherited guilt), and with Shakespeare's *Hamlet*, Ibsen's *Ghosts*, and Canadian author Michel Tremblay's *Bonjour, là, Bonjour*, where incest is central to the dramatic conflict.

The Ghanan writer Ama Ata Aidoo treats the difficulties of being female and African in her short story "Certain Winds from the South." In her play *Dilemma of a Ghost*, African women and African American women discover cultural tensions which they find difficult to resolve. Elechi Amadi's *The Concubine* reveals the struggles of a strong-willed Nigerian woman without reference to the Western world, while Zora Neale Hurston's *Their Eyes Were Watching God* dramatizes Janie's efforts to find love in Southern black society in which white culture plays a minor role.

Contemporary treatments of the difficulties of parenting include not only Buchi Emecheta's *The Joys of Motherhood* but also Doris Lessing's *The Fifth Child* and Anne Tyler's "Average Waves in Unprotected Waters," both of which portray a mother's effort to cope with an "exceptional child." John Updike's "Separating" pictures the confusion of a "good" upper middle-class father who no longer wants to be married to the mother of his children. In Joyce Carol Oates's "Where Are You Going, Where Have You Been?" a sassy teenaged girl is estranged from parental authority and therefore more vulnerable to society's vice and violence.

The difficulties for parent and child of living in acquisitive, competitive urban America are dramatized in Saul Bellow's novel *Seize the Day*. Useful to compare with *Seize the Day* is Tremblay's *Bonjour, la, Bonjour*, which dramatizes the disfunctional lower-class urban family in Quebec, complete with two bickering aunts, a "deaf" father, and manipulative daughters eager for incest with brother Serge. In both works, the protagonist looks for love and affirmation only to find, for the most part, misunderstanding or rejection. Ironically, the soundest emotional relationship in either of the two works is the incestuous love between Serge and his sister Nicole. Poisoned relationships and poor communication between family members also mark Edward Albee's

Who's Afraid of Virginia Woolf? Tremblay's play raises the question of how families deal with aging and death, especially of a parent. This question is addressed with biting humor in Herb Gardner's play *I'm Not Rappaport* and in a tragic manner in Arthur Miller's *Death of a Salesman.* South African playwright Athol Fugard portrays an eccentric female protagonist's struggles with aging in *The Road to Mecca.* In Eudora Welty's short story "The Death of the Traveling Salesman," Mr. Bowman discovers just before his death the inadequacy of a life without a family. Shakespeare's *King Lear* explores the relationships between an aging father-king and his daughters, Eudora Welty's novel *The Optimist's Daughter* humorously portrays a widowed father's efforts to remarry despite his daughter's objections, and Horton Foote's play *Trip to Bountiful* explores an elderly Southern woman's effort to recover something of her past before her death. Two works by Native Americans are particularly useful to compare as treatments of aging: Joseph Bruchac III's "Turtle Meat" and Leslie Marmon Silko's "Lullaby" both portray an elderly couple facing separation through illness or death.

In the works by Salinger and Ngugi discussed by Lott and Latham, and in the other works mentioned above which treat the themes of adolescent initiation, courtship, marriage, and family relationships, the individual or the family often holds values which conflict with those of a society which is found wanting. Three contemporary African works which address the difficulties of being a good person in a corrupt or amoral society include Ayi Kwei Armah's urban novel *The Beautiful Ones Are Not Yet Born,* Sembene Ousmane's satiric novella *The Money Order,* and Jomo Kenyatta's beast fable "The Gentlemen of the Jungle." Other works on this theme include Henrik Ibsen's *Enemy of the People,* George Bernard Shaw's *Major Barbara,* Henry David Thoreau's "Civil Disobedience" and *Walden,* Herman Melville's *Billy Budd,* and Martin Luther King's "Letter from Birmingham Jail."

The tensions between family and society are sometimes caused not by social corruption but by change. The clash between traditional and contemporary practices is evident not only in James Fenimore Cooper's Leatherstocking tales and in the novels by Louise Erdrich and Michael Dorris discussed in Mary McCay's essay, but also in the novels *House Made of Dawn* and *Ceremony* by Native Americans N. Scott Momaday and Leslie Marmon Silko, Chinua Achebe's Nigerian novel *Things Fall Apart,* the Japanese novel *Thousand Cranes* by Kawabata, Anton Chekhov's *The Cherry Orchard,* and Faulkner's *The Bear, The Sound and the Fury,* and *Absalom, Absalom.* William Trevor's short story "The Distant Past" dramatizes the loyalty of the Middleton family to the past and to their crumbling family home, Carraveagh, amidst dramatic changes in Southern Ireland. Two other short stories, "The Man to Send Rainclouds" by Native American Silko and "Witchcraft" by South African Bessie Head, treat humorously the collision between native belief and Christianity. The Native American/African American characters in Faulkner's *The Bear* and in Michael Dorris's *A Yellow Raft on Blue Water* struggle with their divided heritage as does Adam, the Native American/white protagonist in Momaday's *House Made of Dawn*. Young women try to negotiate a path between the old and the new in South African Nadine Gordimer's "Which New Era Would That Be?" and in African American Toni Cade Bambara's "The Lesson," both of which dramatize the difficulty of understanding racial or class conflicts, but the necessity of trying to reach this understanding. As different as they are in background, the white woman in Gordimer's story and the black woman in Bambara's tale both purport to empathize with those less fortunate than themselves, but their beneficence has ironic consequences.

In the works by Cooper, Erdrich, and Dorris discussed by McCay, conflicts of value are central and often not only involve the struggle of individuals (or family) with society but also involve tensions between cultural groups, tensions that are often caused by contrasting perceptions of groups like the Native Americans. James Fenimore Cooper's myopic treatment of the Native American, and Erdrich's and Dorris's more balanced picture of the "first Americans" provide the teacher with the opportunity to pose questions about who Native Americans were and are, and how the images that white authors create of Indians compare with the images they create of themselves. Useful in addressing these questions are *American Indian Literatures: An Introduction, Bibliographic Review, and Selected Bibliography,* by A. LaVonne Brown Ruoff, and *Literature By and About the American Indian: An Annotated Bibliography,* edited by Anna Lee Strensland. Legends of the American Indians are collected in several volumes in The American Folklore Series published by August House. Such sources can provide a counterbalance to the white myth of the American Adam in the New World Garden that, according to McCay, Cooper uses to justify the whites' treatment of the Indian. Two intellectual histories helpful in placing the New World Garden myth in a larger context are Roderick Nash's *Wilderness and the American Mind* and Roy Harvey Pearce's *Savagism and Civilization,* studies which address the significance of the wilderness and the Native American, respectively, for the white Americans. In addition, Paula Allen Gunn's *The Sacred Hoop* focuses on another neglected part of Native American culture and literature—the feminine.

For the teacher who wants students to recapture Native American myths and other elements of oral culture rather than dismiss them as Cooper did, several works might be especially useful. Modern Native American writers like Silko, Elizabeth Cook, and Momaday interweave the oral tradition into their narratives, especially in Silko's *Ceremony,* in Cook's *Then Badger Said,* and in Momaday's account of his heritage *The Way to Rainy Mountain,* his Pulitzer Prize-winning first novel *House Made of Dawn,* and his second novel *The Ancient Child,* which incorporates myths of American Indians along with heroes of the American frontier like Billy the Kid. These Native American novels are not marked by the monolithic cultural vision of Cooper, as noted in McCay's essay, but are characterized by a pluralistic cultural vision involving the interplay of multiple authentic, but competing, cultural values. They might well be taught in conjunction with works by Chinese American authors Maxine Hong Kingston and Amy Tan, by Hispanic American author Nicolassa Mohr, and by such African Americans as Toni Morrison, Alice Walker, and Ralph Ellison.

Teachers can thus provide perspective on American culture, past and present, by incorporating Native American myths and tales as well as works by Native American writers that embody elements of the oral tradition, and they can compare these works with literature throughout the world that dramatizes value systems in conflict.

The essays by Lott and Latham and by McCay dramatize the importance of themes such as adolescent initiation; courtship, marriage, and family relationships; and conflicts between the family and society or between cultural groups within society. These themes, which often involve issues of colonialism, race, gender, or class, recur in a wide variety of genres and settings. By bringing together such works from different cultures and historical periods, teachers and students can experience more fully their dramatic power and enduring relevance.

References

Achebe, Chinua. *Things Fall Apart.* London: Heinemann, 1987.

Aeschylus. *Agamemnon, Aeschylus One.* Chicago: University of Chicago Press, 1969.

Aidoo, Ama Ata. "Certain Winds from the South." In *African Short Stories: Twenty Short Stories From Across the Continent,* edited by Chinua Achebe and C. L. Innes. London: Heinemann, 1987.

———. *Dilemma of a Ghost.* New York: Collier Books, 1971.

Albee, Edward. *Who's Afraid of Virginia Woolf.* New York: Macmillan, 1962.

Allen, Paula Gunn. *The Sacred Hoop: Recovering the Feminine in American Indian Traditions.* Boston: Beacon Press, 1987.

Amadi, Elechi. *The Concubine.* London: Heinemann Educational Books, 1966.

Anderson, Sherwood. "I Want to Know Why." In *The American Tradition in Literature,* edited by George Perkins et al. Seventh edition, vol. 2. New York: McGraw Hill, 1990.

Armah, Ayi Kwei. *The Beautiful Ones Are Not Yet Born.* London: Heinemann, 1968.

Bambara, Toni Cade. "The Lesson." In *The Dolphin Reader,* edited by Douglas Hunt. Boston: Houghton Mifflin, 1990.

Bellow, Saul. *Seize the Day.* New York: Penguin, 1984.

Bombal, Maria Luisa. "The Tree." In *The Spanish American Short Story: A Critical Anthology.* Los Angeles: UCLA Latin American Center Publications, 1980.

Bruchac, Joseph, III. "Turtle Meat." In *The Dolphin Reader,* edited by Douglas Hunt. Boston: Houghton Mifflin, 1990.

Chekhov, Anton. *The Cherry Orchard, Anton Chekhov's Plays: A Norton Critical Edition.* New York: W. W. Norton, 1978.

Chikamatsu Monzaemon. *The Love Suicides at Sonezaki.* In *Four Plays by Chikamatsu,* translated by Donald Keene. New York: Columbia University Press, 1961.

Chopin, Kate. *The Awakening: A Norton Critical Edition.* Edited by Margaret Culley. New York: W. W. Norton, 1976.

———. "The Story of an Hour." In *Complete Works of Kate Chopin.* Baton Rouge: Louisiana State University Press, 1969.

Cook, Elizabeth. *Then Badger Said.* New York: Vantage, 1977.

Cooper, James Fenimore. *The Leatherstocking Tales.* Edited by Blake Nevius, 2 vols. New York: The Library of America, 1985.

Cope, Jack. "Power." In *Stories from Central and Southern Africa,* edited by Paul A. Scanlon. London: Heinemann, 1983.

Dinesen, Isak. *Out of Africa.* New York: Random, 1984.

Donoso, José. "Paseo." Translated by Lorraine O'Grady Freeman. In *The Dolphin Reader,* edited by Douglas Hunt. Boston: Houghton Mifflin, 1990.

Dorris, Michael. *A Yellow Raft on Blue Water.* New York: Henry Holt and Company, 1987.

Douglass, Frederick. *Narrative of the Life of Frederick Douglass, An American Slave, Written by Himself.* Cambridge, MA: Belknap Press, 1971.

Emecheta, Buchi. *The Joys of Motherhood.* New York: George Braziller, 1979.

Faulkner, William. *Absalom, Absalom.* New York: Random, 1987.

———. "The Bear." *Go Down, Moses.* New York: Random, 1973.

———. *The Sound and the Fury.* New York: Random, 1987.

Ferré, Rosario. *The Youngest Doll.* Lincoln: University of Nebraska Press, 1991.

Flaubert, Gustave. *Madame Bovary.* New York: Random, 1982.

176   *The Individual, the Family, and Society*

Foote, Horton. *To Kill a Mockingbird, Tender Mercies, and The Trip to Bountiful: Three Screenplays.* New York: Grove-Weidenfeld, 1989.

Frank, Anne. *Diary of a Young Girl.* New York: Random, 1978.

Fugard, Athol. *The Road to Mecca.* New York: Theatre Communications Group, 1988.

Gardner, Herb. *I'm Not Rappaport.* New York: Grove-Weidenfeld, 1988.

Gordimer, Nadine. "The Bridegroom." In *African Short Stories,* edited by Chinua Achebe and C. L. Innes. Portsmouth, NH: Heinemann, 1987.

———. "Town and Country Lovers." In *The Norton Anthology of Literature by Women: The Tradition in English,* edited by Sandra M. Gilbert and Susan Gubar. New York: W. W. Norton, 1985.

———. "Which New Era Would That Be?" In *The Dolphin Reader,* edited by Douglas Hunt. Boston: Houghton Mifflin Company, 1990.

Hawthorne, Nathaniel. *The Blithedale Romance: A Norton Critical Edition.* Edited by Seymour Gross and Rosalie Murphy. New York: W. W. Norton, 1978.

———. "My Kinsman, Major Molineaux." In *The Complete Novels and Selected Tales of Nathaniel Hawthorne.* New York: Random House, 1977.

Head, Bessie. "Snapshots of a Wedding." In *African Short Stories,* edited by Chinua Achebe and C. L. Innes. Portsmouth, NH: Heinemann, 1987.

———. "Witchcraft." In *Stories from Central and Southern Africa,* edited by Paul A. Scanlon. Portsmouth, NH: Heinemann, 1983.

Hurston, Zora Neale. *Their Eyes Were Watching God.* New York: Harper & Row, 1990.

Ibsen, Henrik. *A Doll's House, Ghosts,* and *Enemy of the People.* In *Eight Plays.* New York: Random House, 1981.

Jewett, Sarah Orne. "A White Heron." In *The American Tradition in Literature,* edited by George Perkins et al. Seventh edition, vol. 2. New York: McGraw Hill, 1990.

Kawabata, Yasunari. "The Izu Dancer." In *House of the Sleeping Beauties and Other Stories.* New York: Kodansha, 1982.

———. *Thousand Cranes.* New York: Perigee Books, 1959.

Kenyatta, Jomo. "The Gentlemen of the Jungle." In *African Short Stories,* edited by Chinua Achebe and C. L. Innes. Portsmouth, NH: Heinemann, 1987.

King, Martin Luther, Jr. "Letter from Birmingham Jail." In *The Dolphin Reader,* edited by Douglas Hunt. Boston: Houghton Mifflin Company, 1990.

Kogawa, Joy. *Obasan.* Boston: Godine, 1982.

Lessing, Doris. *The Fifth Child.* New York: Random, 1989.

———. "A Sunrise on the Veld." In *Stories from Central and Southern Africa,* edited by Paul A. Scanlon. Portsmouth, NH: Heinemann, 1983.

———. "To Room 19." In *The Norton Anthology of Literature by Women: The Tradition in English,* edited by Sandra M. Gilbert and Susan Gubar. New York: W. W. Norton, 1985.

Llosa, Mario Vargas. "Sunday." In *The Eye of the Heart: Short Stories from Latin America,* edited by Barbara Howes. New York: Avon Books, 1973.

Mason, Bobbie Ann. "Shiloh." In *The American Tradition in Literature,* edited by George Perkins et al. Seventh edition, vol. 2. New York: McGraw Hill, 1990.

Melville, Herman. *Billy Budd and Other Stories.* New York: Penguin, 1986.

Miller, Arthur. *Death of a Salesman.* In *The American Tradition in Literature,* edited by George Perkins, et al. Seventh edition, vol. 2. New York: McGraw Hill, 1990.

Mishima, Yukio. *The Sound of Waves.* New York: G. P. Putnam's Sons, 1956.

Momaday, N. Scott. *The Ancient Child: A Novel.* New York: Harper & Row, 1990.

———. *House Made of Dawn.* New York: Harper & Row, 1989.

———. *The Way to Rainy Mountain.* Albuquerque: University of New Mexico Press, 1976.

———. *The Ancient Child: A Novel.* New York: Harper & Row, 1990.

Nash, Roderick. *Wilderness and the American Mind.* New Haven: Yale University Press, 1982.

Ngũgĩ wa Thiong'o. *Weep Not, Child.* London: Heinemann, 1988.

Oates, Joyce Carol. "Where Are You Going, Where Have You Been?" In *The American Tradition in Literature,* edited by George Perkins et al. Seventh edition, vol. 2. New York: McGraw Hill, 1990.

Pearce, Roy Harvey. *Savagism and Civilization: A Study of the Indian and the American Mind.* Baltimore: Johns Hopkins Press, 1967.

Ruoff, A. LaVonne Brown. *American Indian Literatures: An Introduction, Bibliographic Review, and Selected Bibliography.* New York: Modern Language Assocation, 1990.

Salinger, J. D. *The Catcher in the Rye.* Boston: Little, 1951.

Sembene, Ousmane. *The Money Order.* London: Heinemann, 1987.

Shakespeare, William. *All's Well that Ends Well, Antony and Cleopatra,* and *King Lear.* In *The Complete Works of Shakespeare,* edited by David Bevington. New York: HarperCollins, 1980.

Shaw, George Bernard. *Candida.* New York: Penguin, 1950.

———. *Major Barbara.* New York: Penguin, 1950.

Silko, Leslie Marmon. "Lullaby." In *The Dolphin Reader,* edited by Douglas Hunt. Boston: Houghton Mifflin Company, 1990.

———. *Ceremony.* New York: Penguin, 1986.

———. "The Man to Send Rainclouds." In *Storyteller.* New York: Seaver, 1981.

Sophocles. *Oedipus Rex.* Oxford: Cambridge University Press, 1982.

Strensland, Anna Lee, ed. *Literature By and About the American Indian: An Annotated Bibliography for Junior and Senior High School Students.* Urbana, IL: NCTE, 1973.

Thoreau, Henry David. "Civil Disobedience." In *The Portable Thoreau,* edited by Carl Bode. New York: The Viking Press, 1975.

———. *Walden.* In *The Portable Thoreau,* edited by Carl Bode. New York: The Viking Press, 1975.

Tolstoy, Leo. *Anna Karenina.* Translated by Constance Garnett. New York: Macmillan, 1978.

Tremblay, Michel. *Bonjour, là, Bonjour.* Translated by John Van Burek and Bill Glassco. Vancouver and Los Angeles: Talonbooks, 1975.

Trevor, William. "The Distant Past." In *The Short Stories of William Trevor.* New York: Viking Penguin, 1989.

Tsao Hsueh-Chin. *Dream of the Red Chamber.* New York: Doubleday Anchor Books, 1958.

Tyler, Anne. "Average Waves in Unprotected Waters." In *The American Tradition in Literature,* edited by George Perkins et al. Seventh edition, vol. 2. New York: McGraw Hill, 1990.

Updike, John. "Separating." In *The American Tradition in Literature,* edited by George Perkins et al. Seventh edition, vol. 2. New York: McGraw Hill, 1990.

Walker, Alice. *Possessing the Secret of Joy.* New York: Harcourt Brace Jovanovich, 1992.

Welty, Eudora. "The Death of the Traveling Salesman." In *The Collected Stories of Eudora Welty.* Harcourt Brace, 1982.

———. *The Optimist's Daughter.* New York: Random House, 1978.

IV Intertextuality and Cultural Identity: Diversity in Related Texts

The essays in this section explore the perspectives of colonizer and colonized on such topics as the caste system in India (Ahlawat) and the Mexican Revolution (Espadas). Several of the essays deal with contrasting views of literary genre and tradition (Parkin, Lester, Hawkins) and with contrasts in the overall philosophy and world view of Western and non-Western cultures (Espadas, Egejuru, Ahlawat). Like Mary McCay in the preceding section, Neal Lester and Phanuel Egejuru explore responses to the cultural and literary chauvinism experienced by colonized groups and by America's ethnic minorities and women. The essays in this section bring these issues into sharp focus through a consideration of texts which are related through some form of intertextuality. The bibliographic essay examines questions of intertextuality more broadly, especially as they relate to issues of colonialism and national/cultural identity.

14 Crossing Cultural Bridges in Search of Drama: Aristotle and Zeami

Andrew Parkin
Chinese University of Hong Kong

At our stage in the history of entertainment, more people witness more forms of drama than ever before. This is true of live stage performances, although in most cultures these are now becoming the preserve of a relatively limited audience; but drama presented by means of film and television has such an immense audience that it pervades not only its "home" culture but many others around the world, as broadcasting networks buy each other's programmes. In terms of audience numbers it is clear that drama is the dominant genre. This vast, worldwide audience for drama is now familiar with a great number of directors and performers both in the theatre and recorded on film. This audience is also aware of an eclectic range of performance conventions and techniques ranging from naturalism to forms of nonrealistic presentation explored in opposition to and for the sake of novelty. Because most of the programming for television that is disseminated on a worldwide basis springs from Western studios, and many, though not all, of the touring groups taking live theatre to different audiences around the world are from Western countries, it is Western notions of drama, often realistic in mode, which are becoming universally understood, accepted, and imitated.[1] At the same time, movies and theatre tours from non-European based cultures are nevertheless making an impact on Western audiences and on artists.

Comparative study of Western and oriental drama is a rewarding direction in theatre research, as Yun-tong Luk (1990) recently demonstrated in regard to Chinese-Western drama. Years after the work of such pioneers as Edward Gordon Craig, Vsevolod Meyerhold, and W. B. Yeats, there are now, of course, influential directors such as Peter Brook who are well aware of many theatre conventions from all over the globe and who devise ways of integrating them into work where their use seems appropriate. Since these conventions do not arise from any one culture, and the theatre forms of many cultures have been explored and sometimes used in a practical way, our view of what constitutes drama and theatre must necessarily change; it cannot assume that any one culture's theatre and drama are self-evidently the norm. It is no longer tenable for Western critics or those of other cultures to contemplate Noh drama, for example, to discover that it is very static compared with plays exploiting actions full of conflict, and to describe it as therefore "undramatic."

Definition must account for the existing facts. Audiences have accepted Noh as a form of drama for hundreds of years and continue to do so. Noh must be taken into account rather than excluded when we attempt to define drama; otherwise we risk an ethnocentric and partial definition. That partial definition—taken as universal—persists and can be seen, for example, in Pfister's *The Theory and Analysis of Drama* (1977). Pfister's largely semiotic study founders at its very basis, where it distinguishes between narrative and dramatic works by maintaining that in dramatic texts there is no "mediating, fictional narrator" and thus no "stretching and shrinking of narrative time" nor "extension or restriction of locale." He concludes that in dramatic texts "the time-space continuum of the plot alone . . . determines the progress of the text within the individual scenic units" (Pfister 1977, 5). Apart from the shortcomings of a style cluttered with diagrams and pseudoscientific terminology, Pfister simply ignores the powerful narrators of Bunraku and the wonderfully subtle manipulation of time and place (without any controlling plot) that we find in the behaviour of *shite* (the main character, who appears twice, often as a ghost in the second appearance), *waki* (secondary actor, who is often a religious pilgrim), and chorus in the Noh drama. I assume, as does Schechner, that theatre is a performance genre, its text "understood as a key to action, not its replacement" (Schechner 1988, 28). To assist in his analysis of theatre action, Schechner invokes "mathematical and transactional game analysis" and "model-building" in the hope that such comparisons "between theater and related activities" would lead to a poetics of performance (27); I prefer here to discuss drama and theatre without recourse to other performed activities such as games, initiations, and rituals, since these, however close to the performance of scripted plays, are not the same thing, being *analogous* only. I am concerned with the performance of dramatic scripts as imitation and pretense. I have no moral objections to art as pretense. I see no reason to mix theatre as the imitation of action with real action. Such a mixture seems to me always crude and rarely artistically successful. Gladiatorial combat or live sex shows may be forms of entertainment, but they are not the same thing as a play, for their actions are real and irrevocable, forsaking one of the pleasures of dramatic performance, the knowledge that one is watching a skillful pretense. A great part of our admiration for and enjoyment of the Kabuki's female impersonators arises from the very fact that we know they are male, giving a *performed pretense* of being female characters in the play. Different again is the experience of seeing the Noh actor performing a wig part. Here the imitation is offered by a man whose male jowls, jaw, and voice are unmistakable. This works because the mask and other details of costuming combine with the actor's delicacy and grace to hint at and subtly reveal the feminine in both the role and the male.

For both Aristotle and Zeami, fathers respectively of the theory of European drama and Noh in performance, drama is founded on presenting, not merely reciting, an imitation. All art for them is an imitation, not reality itself.

Interestingly, the immense influence of Aristotle as a dramatic theorist begins with the Renaissance in Europe, at a time when all representational art was becoming increasingly realistic, and long after the original lectures he gave in Classical times. *The Poetics,* as Hutton (1982) remarks, is a modern book; its theory of drama reinforces the post-Renaissance tragedy; its assumptions about probability and necessity lead in the end to the most extreme form of realism, late nineteenth-century naturalism.

Zeami, the great actor, playwright, and theorist of Noh, turns out, like Aristotle, to be a very modern author. Writing at roughly the same time as Chaucer, Zeami kept his theory of Noh, *The Sixteen Treatises,* a secret for the use of his troupe only, just as Elizabethan writers were in no hurry to print their plays. Zeami's treatises had to wait until our own century to be printed and translated. What idea of the dramatic emerges from Zeami, father of a form of drama that has weathered six hundred years despite its reputation for being "undramatic"?

Whereas Aristotle thinks of drama as the imitation of an action, Zeami thinks of it as the imitation of things. Since Zeami's treatises are practical and theoretical guides to performance written by a performer and artist rather than an aesthetician, we must, I believe, give full weight to the performance implications of his remarks. The things imitated are *performable* things. In Noh the performable thing is often a character out of history, legend, or myth, and through such characters is conveyed an overpowering emotion, such as jealousy or desire for revenge, or the sorrow of lost love; or it is a place or object strongly associated with a significant event. Furthermore, Zeami classifies two kinds of imitation: realistic and symbolic. Noh uses both kinds, but its method and action are predominantly symbolic. To achieve that symbolic quality, the writing, staging, and performance concentrate on the essence of things imitated; austerity, economy of means, the hint, the nuance, the minimal sketch of the thing imitated, all are presented with perfect concentration aiming at symbolic resonance and strange beauty. These are what Noh offers its audience. It is not necessarily a complex action as in Greek or Elizabethan drama. Action is sometimes very minimal, as in Zeami's play, *Sekidera Komachi*, where the *shite* who plays Komachi hardly moves during the first hour of the play. A plot sequence moving through conflicts to climax and resolution is not necessary in Noh. Instead it relies, as Mae Smethurst puts it, on "the gradual intensification of verbal, rhythmic, and theatrical effects that reach a crescendo at significant moments within the play" (Smethurst 1989, 81). Most Noh plays leave out the building of complication and multiple conflict, if they present a conflict, and instead build up a concentration on place, atmosphere, and mood which can hold their own type of suspense. What Aristotle calls *anagnorisis* (recognition) becomes important; masking and unmasking are more often than not at the heart of Noh, but are not necessarily brought about by conflict. Intensities of connection between place, persons, past and present, atmosphere, mood, and appropriate rememberings of poetic tradition make up the fascination of the Noh as text and *mise-en-scène*. Because Zeami's theory of Noh is performance based, his analysis looks not only at the structure of the text but also at the performance aspects of that structure. Zeami, like Aristotle, insists on the inevitable beginning, middle, and end, which in Noh terminology is the *jo, ha, kyu* pattern, but with implications for performance: the *jo* is a fair-paced introduction which allows the audience to settle down; the slower *ha* offers some development with a strictly limited element of story to it; the *kyu* is climactic, faster in tempo, and designed to hold an audience's attention at a point when it could be lulled into inattention, or simply tired. The psychology of the actor-audience exchange that is basic to all theatre pervades Zeami's thinking. In line with the economy of Noh, the *jo, ha, kyu* pattern governs the arrangement of the five plays that make up a Noh performance, the structure of each play in that programme, and the structure of each *jo, ha,* and *kyu* taken individually. Furthermore, the same structure can be applied to the dance within a section of an individual play. But what effects are sought by the Noh performer? How can symbol be acted? How can it be termed "dramatic"?

Reading Noh texts and seeing the plays performed, we may well be struck not so much by a total lack of conflict, for at times it does appear, but by an *indifference* to it in some of the plays. Westerners, used to thinking of conflict as the essence of what makes any situation dramatic, find that quite often in Noh it is simply beside the point. The protagonist and antagonist of Greek drama, or the opposition between hero and villain in melodrama, cannot necessarily be applied to *shite* and *waki* in Noh. More often than not they play polite strangers who develop a kind of complicity. The drama, a highly symbolic drama, must be achieved, then, in many of the plays by means other than conflict.

According to Zeami, the Noh performer aims at *yugen, hana,* and *ran-i.*[2] Scholars usually translate *yugen* as "elegant and graceful charm"; Nogami (1955) reminds us that *yugen* was used originally to define the mood of "sentimental lonesomeness which evokes pensiveness" found in some of the best Japanese poetry. Later, in the Kamakura period (1184–1335), *yugen* still held the connotation of loneliness but with the idea of a delicate brightness as from the glitter of "swirling snow flakes." Later still, Seitetsu associated it with "beautifully attired ladies gathered in the garden of the South Palace resplendent with flowers" where brightness is all and loneliness banished (Nogami 1955, 53). At this stage in its development Zeami used *yugen* to refer to the elegance and grace of a performer who projects an effect of charm and beauty, attained by hard work and attention to posture. It becomes part of the critical vocabulary appropriate to an art of the stage in which an actor must move and dance with supreme control to give an effect of brilliant presence. The aim is to please and charm the audience. It is particularly stressed "with reference to a feminine role. That is the reason," says Nogami, "why the wig-drama is placed in the centre of a Noh program" (Nogami 53). But, whatever is being imitated, the performer should in Noh never lose sight of that elegance called *yugen,* for Noh is symbolic more than realistic, so that a ferocious demon, an old hag or a mad woman would not be grotesque, but always tinged with *yugen* in costume, mask, and performance. In such cases, *yugen* is not so much elegant charm as *brilliancy,* as in the case of the costuming for the ferocious ground spider. Whatever is imitated has to be made beautiful in some way, and then it will achieve its particular *yugen.* And to this end, *yugen* also controls the music of Noh. It is thus a central concept for performance at all levels, giving Noh a large part of its distinction. The rather shabby and dusty stage floors in many Western theatres are totally at odds with *yugen.* Noh stages in themselves are maintained as scrupulously clean and bright places, worthy settings for the brilliant appearance of the plays in performance. Furthermore, *yugen* becomes a structural feature of the Noh programme, in that it appears throughout a successful programme, but is most evident in the second play, usually a wig-drama. In sum, two basic features of Noh are its particular species of imitation of a symbolic view of reality and the finishing technique of achieving *yugen* to bring the *monomane* or imitation to as perfect a performance as possible. Nogami concludes that "different as they are in nature and use, these two (*monomane* and *yugen*) are one and inseparable in that they complement each other only when they are integrated" (Nogami 61).

Hana or "flower" is different from the previous two terms, because while they should be achieved as the constant basis of Noh performance, *hana* or flower is more elusive. It is reserved for those moments of supreme achievement in performance which are relatively rare: "We come across something like [an oasis in the desert] on the stage. That's the *flower*" (Nogami 62). It is a sophisticated weapon in the actor's campaign to hold the audience's attention and reveal to it the beauty of high art; it is not a crude or flashy effect of acting. It occurs when the actor performs an act which gives the audience "a feeling of strangeness" or of something unexpected, achieved by performing a set technique in an unusual context, or by making a change in emphasis in response to the way an audience is behaving. It is "bewitching the audience" to keep it in suspense by the power and resourcefulness of the performance (Nogami 66). Shakespeare, with a similarly mixed audience, offered in his roles for star actors many opportunities for "flower" or *hana;* he even applied the same principle in writing his minor roles, for many of them have at least one speech or scene when an actor can bring off something unusual or unexpected: Lady Anne in *Richard III* is but one example. The Duke of Burgundy in *Henry V* is another.

In his *Oral Instructions After Seventy Years of Age,* or *Returned Flower,* Zeami commented on "the most mysterious of all the secrets" of his art, which he wanted to impart only to his son Motomasa. This was the style of acting that comes in an actor's old age. This "returned style or flower," *kyakurai-ka,* derives from that penetration and spirituality of artistic understanding gained from long years of practice and attainment. Motomasa had said to his father about his approach to Noh: "I am determined not to do any useless thing." Zeami approved of this by acknowledging that the "spirit not to do any unnecessary thing is the key to Noh" (Nogami 68–69). We might add that it is the essence of all great drama, writing and performance alike. The restraint, austerity, and lack of self-indulgence in this approach to art cannot be achieved simply by technique; it is the returned flower of an acting sensibility fashioned by an actor's experience of art and life. There are no short cuts. It blooms from a sensibility that is ready to produce such blossoming.

It is closely connected with *ran-i* (or "fully matured . . . artistic sense that comes from an intense cultivation of skill and occasionally assumes a singular style of acting" [Nogami 68]). It is a new freedom and exhilaration in the actor, an expression of his spontaneity, and for that reason is not achieved by any special technique or training. It is nothing less than a psychic force or mental energy some great actors possess in their maturity. This *ran-i* may be translated as "attained skill"; in my view it is a special type of stage presence different from the magnetism of younger performers.

Zeami's concentration on performed drama is a fundamental necessity for any theory of drama. In the West, theory still concentrates primarily on the text. Relatively recently, academic critics and semioticians have been attempting theories of drama in performance. Unfortunately, some of these attempts are presented in a pretentiously pseudoscientific method and style, based, it seems, on a desire to achieve a new science of the stage, rather than upon a profound practical knowledge and experience of dramatic art. Therefore, bearing in mind the contrast between Zeami's approach to performance and that of Western critics, let us now return to Zeami's *Sekidera Komachi* to discuss its specifically dramatic qualities.

The play *is* totally undramatic if we define drama as it is usually defined in the West as action developing conflict, character study, and suspense. Yet Donald Keene's introduction to *Twenty Plays of the No Theatre* rightly describes the play as "incredibly moving" despite its lack of action. The situation is that "priests take a young disciple to hear from an old woman the secrets of poetry and gradually become aware she is the celebrated poet Komachi" (Keene 1970, 7). Why then is this a play and not merely a poem in the form of dialogue? The answer is apparent if we examine the rehearsed behaviour according to its own conventions.

The play opens with stage assistants bringing on a stylized hut with thatched roof. This simple structure is covered with a cloth. The Old Woman is inside. Immediately we are confronted with a form of *yugen:* the hut is not a decrepit shack and the cloth is no filthy old rag. The effect is neat and decorative. But something is hidden. The cloth masks the hut, the hut the Old Woman, her mask the actor who plays the role, and his maleness contains her femininity. This is very intriguing. There is already an element of suspense. Who or what occupies the hut? The thing imitated is the dwelling place of the Old Woman, and this is symbolic of her life itself.

Music accompanies the entrance of the Abbot, Priests, and Child. In the manner of medieval Western drama, the opening speeches establish time and occasion—Autumn and the Festival of Stars, Tanabata, celebrated on the seventh day of the seventh month. "Bamboo branches are decorated with five-coloured streamers and with slips on which poems have been written commemorating the lovers' meeting of the two stars" (Keene 1970, 78). They also give direct exposition of the identity of the travellers and their destination, together with the motive for the journey: to take young people to listen to poetry and learn.

The theme of poetry is also thus rapidly established. The simple gesture of turning to the Child captures in a brief moment of *performance* what would take many lines if one were to write a poem about the relation of youth to age, the need to pass on knowledge of poetry to the young, and the importance of contact between the beginner and the master of an art. And the Child is symbolic of all the novices, every young person who sets out on the journey to find truth, which always resides on a mountain. Even the master lives only at the foot of the mountain. Immediately after poetry has thus been established as the theme, the Priests allude to some famous lines by Po Chu-i which compare Autumn to the onset of old age in people: "We feel it in the wind and in our thinning locks" (Keene 1970, 69). The middle-aged, praying for poetic skill, initiate the young, seeking more knowledge from the Old Woman. Their journey from the Temple Garden to the hut at the foot of the mountain is performed by the simple convention that the Abbot "faces front, takes a few steps, then returns to his former position" (Keene 1970, 70). Like Shakespeare's stage, Noh has the great freedom to be anywhere and at any time. Miles are covered in a few feet, and centuries may elapse in the time it takes to say a few words. Conversely, a moment of extreme emotion or suffering may be prolonged by the deliberate slow pace of movement and dance to an almost unbearable amount of stage time, evoking the way some experiences can become centuries of purgatorial meditation.

Once everyone is kneeling at the hut, a stage assistant removes the cloth "revealing the Old Woman seated inside. Paper strips inscribed with poems hang from the crossbars of the hut frame. The Old Woman wears the uba mask" (Keene 70). This is the first unmasking. The effect is beautiful rather than realistic or repellent, as is the case with the removal of Hamm's cloth at the beginning of Beckett's *Endgame,* in which Hamm turns out to be composing a narrative during the course of the play. The discovery of the Old Woman leads without interruption to her first speech. She sketches her poverty-stricken existence (few make money out of poetry, especially those who know most about it: a good first lesson for the young aspirant); she contrasts two types of time, the cycles of nature and the brief linear span of human life; she yearns for her lost youth, as she confronts youth kneeling before her on the stage. This action is not conflict, but a dramatic confrontation of performed symbols, contrasting with one another. The entire effect is also enriched by her allusion to an anonymous Chinese poem: "The willows are tricked by the wind, / And their green gradually droops" (Keene 1970, 70). The bitter lesson that time deceives, cheating us of life and even talent, is unflinchingly there; it makes her weep. The drama comes not only from the contrast seen in the stage picture, but from the element of the unexpected: the knower, the teacher, is in wretched circumstances and her lesson is as much about the bitterness of life as it is about the art of poetry. And that is appropriate, for what is poetry but a vision of reality, not fake experience? The surprise is not only that of the pilgrims to this shrine of art; the Old Woman is surprised that anyone should make a journey to see her.

The next bit of suspense has not to do with action but with thought. The dramatic question is what will she reveal about the art of poetry? Her lesson is couched in nature imagery that inextricably links the external world, the inner, emotional world, and poetry:

> Just remember this: If you will make your heart the seed and
> your words the blossoms, if you will steep yourself in the fragrance
> of the art, you will not fail to accomplish true poetry. (Keene
> 1970, 71)

Her next revelation is that the poems the Abbot mentions, "The Harbor of Naniwa" and "Mount Asaka," are "the parents of all poetry" which should be an art for all people, "Even commoners like ourselves" (Keene 1970, 71). The dramatic dialogue here uses a technique by which the two speakers complete each other's thoughts. The effect is moving, and confirms as well as introduces the following chorus on the consolation of poetry:

> For poetry, whose source and seed is found
> In the human heart, is everlasting. (Keene 1970, 71)

The moment's drama comes not from a clash of wills or some form of conflict, but from complicity and faith in poetry as consolation in times of distress and suffering. We feel compassion for the old and for our own humanity, subject to the cruelty of time. Brief stage time itself becomes part of the dramatic effect: on stage we see the Old Woman, symbol of a long life, the Boy, symbol of the springtime of life, written poems on scraps of paper, symbols of a different order of time, the time of art, stretching beyond individual lives. We hear in the quotations from ancient poets—voices from time past, from the tradition. In the voice of the Old Woman in the eternal present of stage performance we hear the voice of that tradition too. So the play plays with time.

Its next unmasking is the revelation scene in which the Abbot realizes that the Old Woman is not only a teacher of the art of poetry, but the great Komachi herself. Her lament is taken over by the Chorus, another familiar Noh convention. The effect is powerfully dramatic. The Komachi poem the Abbot and Komachi quoted together is now repeated by a chorus of voices, the voices of all those who read and recite the poem that is now in the tradition. The expression of a woman's personal grief and shame at her humiliation by a fickle husband are now part of the tradition, performed first by one who remembers the poem, then by its author, played by an actor performing the role of Komachi, and then by a chorus, the voice of poetry's tradition, overheard by the Child on stage who represents the future of our human heritage. This is static, but it is foolish to call it undramatic. The revelation is very powerful, but not in the same way as the unmasking of a villain, or of some deception in a comedy of disguise. The element of surprise is part of its dramatic energy; Komachi herself is surprised by her feelings of shame, so powerful despite her great age. She is ashamed because she was put aside and ashamed to be seen as the withered old woman she has become.

Noh is a highly sophisticated form of drama; its simplicity of dramatic means is one sign of this. Komachi's shame at her frailty casts an ironic shadow across the previous assertions of the defeat of time by poetry. When it comes right down to it, Komachi, the great poet, is human, and cannot transcend her misfortune to become detached and superior to it. This brings with it another dramatic subtlety. Professional performance as skillful and elegant accomplishment is one of the pleasures of theatre. But as the *shite* actor who plays Komachi is about to stand up for the first time to begin the climactic dance, which is the *kyu* section of the play with a faster tempo, he comments on the grace of the Boy who has just finished his dance. Komachi confesses, "I have forgotten how to move my hands" (Keene 1970, 76). But Komachi was once an expert dancer. The *shite* has a supreme challenge: the role of an old woman who once charmed everyone when she danced, who now dances for the last time in extreme old age. For the aged Noh performer who will take the part, this is when not only *yugen* but also the most mysterious secret of performance must be drawn upon, *kyakurai-ka* or "returned flower." If the actor can show us that flower, he will have performed what the play has dramatized, Komachi's revelation to us of the last secret of the poet: the returned flower of the suffering heart which may express its longing in poetry, but cannot anaesthetize that longing for life. The two dances of youth and age form the two symbolic poles of the play and its themes: the long discipline of poetry, the brief discipline of life, the play of time, the persistence of suffering, the longing for lost youth, the shame of a woman cast off by a man, and the shame of genius decayed by old age.

This analysis of the dramatic qualities of the most static of Noh shows we must accept that the imitation of things and symbolic personages can be dramatic, just as the imitation of conflict is dramatic. Suspense arising from different sources, not merely danger, may be dramatic. Masking and unmasking too may bring many different kinds of revelation and recognition scenes as dramatic in their own way as such scenes in Western drama. *Sekidera Komachi* dramatizes the depths of a poet's mind and the relation of life or biography to poetry and drama. Noh is a tight form, but it is nevertheless a liberating one. It allows the dramatist to use the powerful shorthand of symbols, to dramatize the inner world of the dreaming dead, and to go beyond prose into verse, and beyond words into the sounds of the music, the concreteness and physicality of dance.

The realities imitated in drama may be long and complex conflicts or they may be different, not clashes of wills but, as John Peter puts it in *Vladimir's Carrot,* "pictures of the world" where the picture encapsulates "the world of the play with a lyrical power that burns it into the memory" (Peter 1987, 15). That is his definition of the modern element in drama. It is true of the most "static" and supposedly "undramatic" of Noh plays.

Notes

1. The widely accepted Western definition of drama at the end of the nineteenth century can be found, for instance, in "L'évolution de la Tragédie," a chapter in Ferdinand Brunetière's *Etudes Critiques:*

> Le *drame,* en general, c'est *l'action,* c'est l'imitation de la vie médiocre et douloureuse; c'est une représentation de la volonté de l'homme en conflit avec les puissances mystérieuses ou les forces naturelles qui nous limitent et nous rapetissent; c'est l'un de nous jeté tout vivant sur la scène pour y lutter contre la fatalité, contre la loi sociale, contre un de ses semblables, contre soi-même au besoin, contre les ambitions, les intérêts, les préjugés, la sottise,

la malveillance de ceux qui l'entourent; et de lè, le *drame* proprement dit. (Brunetière, 152–53)

Nowadays, many would accept that theatre occurs when people present themselves to others, whereas drama occurs when what is presented are imagined actions. Among recent books on drama as a genre, a clearly written account which covers examples of drama and dramatic theory from the Orient as well as the West can be found in Devlin (1989). Her basic definition is theatre as enacted human behaviour.

2. For Zeami's theories see Nogami (1955), Rimer and Masakazu (1984), and the excellent recent discussion of Sekine (1985).

References

Brunetière, Ferdinand. *Etudes Critiques sur l'Histoire de la Littérature Francaise.* Septieme serie. Paris: Hachette, n.d.

Devlin, D. *Mask and Scene: An Introduction to a World View of Theatre.* Metuchen, NJ: Scarecrow Press, 1989.

Hutton, James. *Aristotle's Poetics.* New York: Norton, 1982.

Keene, Donald, ed. *Twenty Plays of the No Theater.* New York: Columbia University Press, 1970.

Luk, Yun-tong, ed. *Studies in Chinese-Western Comparative Drama.* Hong Kong: The Chinese University Press, 1990.

Nogami, Toyoichiro. *Zeami and His Theories on Noh.* Translated by Ryozo Matsumoto. Tokyo: Hinoki Shoten, 1955.

Peter, John. *Vladimir's Carrot: Modern Drama and the Modern Imagination.* London: Andre Deutsch, 1987.

Pfister, Manfred. *The Theory and Analysis of Drama.* Translated by John Halliday. Cambridge: Cambridge University Press, 1988.

Rimer, Thomas J. and Yamazaki Masakazu, trans. *On the Art of the No Drama: The Major Treatises of Zeami.* Princeton, NJ: Princeton University Press, 1984.

Schechner, Richard. *Performance Theory.* New York: Routledge, 1988.

Sekine, Masaru. *Ze-ami and His Theories of Noh Drama.* Gerrards Cross: Colin Smythe, 1985.

Smethurst, Mae J. *The Artistry of Aeschylus and Zeami: A Comparative Study of Greek Tragedy and No.* Princeton, NJ: Princeton University Press, 1989.

15 Segregation in India: Forster's *A Passage to India* and Anand's *Untouchable*

Usha Ahlawat
St. Mary's College, University of London

"The problem of untouchability which pervaded India," said Gandhi, "repeated itself on the level of the Empire, with all of India in the role of the Untouchables."[1] Metaphorically, then, we can see the Indians in E. M. Forster's *A Passage to India* as untouchables in relation to the Anglo-Indians.[2] The novel is the product of Forster's two short visits to India in 1912–13 and 1921, and was published in 1924. It is Forster's most explicit statement on the imperial idea. He reflects a loss of confidence in the British Raj and a disillusionment in the traditional justification of imperialism, that the Indians are better off under English domination. Among other things, Forster emphasizes the racial discrimination between the Anglo-Indians and Indians in the colonial context, while Nulk Raj Anand, in *Untouchable,* portrays the untouchables' predicament in the age-old caste system in a traditional Hindu society.[3] It was Forster's portrayal of "the untouchable" in *A Passage to India* (1924) that inspired Anand to write *Untouchable* in 1935, which deals with the life of the outcaste Indians. Both novels portray segregation through the hide-bound nature of Anglo-Indians and Indians in India at the turn of the century. *A Passage to India,* while portraying the race relations between the Indians and the Anglo-Indians on the one hand, also deals with the segregation between the Hindus and Muslims. Nor does Forster overlook the dissent between the Anglo-Indians themselves as is evident from the different attitudes of Fielding, Mrs. Moore, Adela Quested, and the rest of the Anglo-Indian community. In *Untouchable,* Anand highlights the segmentation between the caste Hindus and the untouchables but also touches on the other divisions in Indian society.

In order to better understand these two writers, it might be well to consider in some detail the relationship between Britain and India on the one hand and the Indian caste system on the other. In India, unlike the other British colonies, the relationship between colonial power and the colonized was not simply that of the ruler and the ruled. India confronted the British with an older and more comprehensive civilization than the one they brought with them and the imperial idea underwent a real challenge and a test. For four thousand years before the introduction of British rule, there had existed indigenous cultural traditions of varying complexity. British colonialism, therefore, amounted to an occupation of an older culture which changed noticeably as a result of the British, but was not destroyed by it. As Inden remarks:

> India was remarkable, for the repeated conquests of that subcontinent did not bring an end to her civilization or even, for that matter, produce any fundamental change in it. (Inden 1990, 55)

What differentiated India from other colonies was this paradoxical fact: outsiders beginning with Aryans and ending with the British had conquered India again and again, but its ancient civilization had survived by continuously giving old meanings to new experiences. Another reason for this assimilation could be the fact that Indian society is organized more around its culture than around its politics. As Radhakrishnan observed in 1945, just before Indian Independence:

> The living contiguity of Indian life is to be seen not in her political history, but in her cultural and social life. Political obsession has captured India since the battle of Plassey. Today politics have absorbed life. The State is invading society, and the India of "no nation," as Rabindranath puts it, is struggling to become a "nation" in the Western sense of the term, with all its defects and merits. (Radhakrishnan 1945, 18–19)

However, one consequence of the frequent invasions was the peculiar development of the caste system. The first impulse came, no doubt, from the need of the first Indo-European settlers to preserve their way of life from contamination by the aboriginal inhabitants of India, but it has been sharpened over the centuries by the need to defend the identity of the race against successive waves of conquerors, first Muslims and then Europeans. What developed was a complexly and rigidly stratified society, in which each member's sense of himself was secured by the certainty of his place within the whole, and that society persisted—and persists—within an India that now makes quite different, even contradictory demands of its nation and citizens.

Anand responds to these changing needs of India in his first novel, *Untouchable,* in which he strongly attacks the injustice of the caste system and addresses the pertinent issues through Bakha's social segregation from the rest of the society. *Untouchable,* published in 1935, portrays the untouchables' predicament in the age-old caste system, in a traditional Hindu society. The caste system, the most distinctive and intricate feature of Indian culture, has remained the bedrock of the Indian social structure from ancient times to the present. Caste may variously be described as a system of institutionalized inequality, a social instrument of assimilation, an archaic form of "trade unionism," and an extension of the joint-family system reflecting the pattern of kinship interdependence upon a total social structure.

Even the most superficial consideration of the "India" construed by Western texts will show that the canon of historical, analytical, propagandist, and fictional writings devised a way of dividing the world which made British rule in India appear a political imperative and a moral duty. As Ronny Heaslop, in *A Passage to India,* informs his mother: "I am out here to work, mind, to hold this wretched country by force. . . . We're not pleasant in India, and we don't intend to be pleasant" (*API,* 69). He also says, "England holds India for her own good" (*API,* 124). The political theme, though secondary, is important to the understanding of the novel. Forster himself pointed out that "the political side of it was an aspect I wanted to express" (*Listener* 1959, 11). Forster's treatment of this subject is far from superficial; here he raises some essential questions about the meaning and validity of the imperial idea and also about how imperialism affects interpersonal as well as interracial relationships.

In the opening scene of *A Passage to India* the division between the Anglo-Indians and Indians is brought home with great clarity by the physical separation of the low-lying, squalid, and haphazardly built Indian section of Chandrapore from the clean and orderly civil station on the rise where the Europeans live like "little gods." The character of the two communities is skillfully suggested in the topography and structure of their respective residential areas which have nothing in common—the civil[4] station "shares nothing with the city except the overarching sky" (*API,* 32). As opposed to the Indian section, the civil station is "sensibly planned" with "a red-brick club on its brow" and bungalows disposed along "roads that intersect at right angles"—these roads, named after victorious British generals, are "symbolic of the net Great Britain had thrown over India" (*API,* 39). The details of the external setting thus suggest the division between the rulers and the ruled.

Forster studies the hide-bound nature of the Anglo-Indian society in *A Passage to India* in considerable detail. The Anglo-Indian officials regard themselves as living symbols of the Raj and behave as an army of occupation; they dislike and distrust Indians and do not want to have anything to do with them except for a master-servant relationship. The *memsahib's* attitude towards the Indians is even harder than that of many *pukka sahibs;* her strongest link with India is through her hordes of servants in a strictly feudal relationship. It would be appropriate to point out here that before the First Indian War of Independence (1857) things were more relaxed as there were not very many *memsahibs* around, and the Englishmen freely married or had liaisons with native women. Miscegenation was a common phenomenon of seventeenth-century British India. In 1687 the Directors of the East India Company offered financial incentives to encourage Englishmen to wed local women. It was convenient for a company struggling to secure its position in India to make lasting personal contacts with the indigenous population. It was not until administration became the cardinal concern of the British that social contact with Indians was felt to demean the ruler's authority. Imperialist attitudes changed during different periods, and the society described in *A Passage to India* is historically specific.

In this context it is thus quite natural for Mrs. Callendar to remark that "the kindest thing one can do to a native is to let him die" (*API*, 48). In response to Mrs. Moore's ironical query, "How if he went to heaven?" she replies with perfect candour: "He can go where he likes as long as he doesn't come near me. They give me the creeps" (*API*, 48). In this instance the Indians are seen as outcastes whose very presence is offensive to the Anglo-Indians.

At the same time Forster introduces the major issue of interracial relationships, with a group of Muslims discussing the problem of whether or not it is possible for Indians and English to be friends:

> "I only contend that it is possible in England," replied Hamdullah, who had been to that country long ago, before the big rush, and had received a cordial welcome at Cambridge.
> "It is impossible here. Aziz! The red-nosed boy has again insulted me in Court. I do not blame him. He was told that he ought to insult me. Until lately he was quite a nice boy, but the others have got hold of him."
> "Yes, they have no chance here, that is my point. They come out intending to be gentlemen, and are told it will not do. . . . They all become exactly the same, not worse, not better. I give any Englishman two years. . . . And I give any Englishwoman six months." (*API*, 34)

The placement of this scene so early in the book, before the plot proper has begun to be developed, shows how important Forster considered this issue to be. In common with other writings in the genre, *A Passage to India* articulates a strange meeting from a position of political privilege, and it is not difficult to find in phrases such as those which follow rhetorical instances where the *other* is designated within a set of essential and fixed characteristics: "Like most Orientals, Aziz overrated hospitality, mistaking it for intimacy" (*API*, 154); "the fundamental slackness that reveals the race" (*API*, 97); "this indifference is what the Oriental will never understand" (*API*, 130); "All unfortunate natives are criminals at heart" (*API*, 176); India is a "poisonous country" (*API*, 180); "Suspicion in the Oriental is a sort of malignant tumour" (*API*, 276). However, when Mrs. Moore, Fielding and Adela Quested make efforts to break free of standard Raj attitudes and desire to get to know real India and Indians, the entire Anglo-Indian community of Chandrapore is appalled. Ronny frankly tells his mother and Adela: "We don't come across them socially" (*API*, 49). The Bridge Party set, which attempts half-heartedly to meet some Indians, fails to bridge any social gap between the two sides. Mrs. Burton instructs Mrs. Moore to remember: "You're superior to them, anyway. Don't forget that you're superior to everyone in India except one or two of the Ranis, and they're on an equality" (*API*, 61). Perhaps, the myth of British superiority helped in sustaining the Raj.

The hub of social life for the Anglo-Indians in *A Passage to India* is their red-brick club—an almost "holy" institution where they learn the norms of behaviour in the caste-ridden society of India. The club, which was normally private, was one of the most interesting institutions developed by the Raj; it was, in the words of George Orwell, "the spiritual citadel, the real seat of the British power, the Nirvana for which native officials and millionaires pined in vain" (Orwell 1975, 17). Leonard Woolf writes that it is the "symbol and centre of British imperialism. . . . It had normally a curious air of slight depression, but at the same time exclusiveness, superiority, isolation. . . . The atmosphere was terribly masculine and public school" (Woolf 1961, 135). The club is a powerful symbol segregating the Indians and the Anglo-Indians. "Indians are not allowed into the Chandrapore Club even as guests," Aziz informs Mrs. Moore (*API*, 45).

In *A Passage to India*, the British-Indian connection is represented as the paradigmatic power relationship, and the encounters possible within the imperialist situation are perceived as grotesque parodies of social meetings. Notice for example the Indian ladies at the bridge party: they are presented as jittery, "adjusting their saris . . . uncertain, cowering, giggling, making tiny gestures of atonement or despair at all that was said, and alternately fondling the terrier or shrinking from him" (*API*, 62). A different kind of hierarchy exists here, based on class. Mrs. Burton will not shake hands with ordinary Indians: "I refuse to shake hands with any of the men, unless it has to be the Nawab Bahadur" (*API*, 61).

The strategy of discrimination and exclusion, in *A Passage to India,* can be further deduced from the meanings associated with the word *exotic*: dissimilar, unrelated, unconformable, untypical, eccentric, foreign, abnormal, deviant, outcaste, barbarous, bizarre, outlandish. Forster, for all his sympathy for Indians and his censure of the ignorance and heartlessness of colonial Englishmen, cannot escape from a certain residual racism. Consider first his Indian characters: Aziz is portrayed as both childlike and childish—the stock image of an Indian in Anglo-Indian fiction. Although he is professionally a doctor, his interest lies in sentimental poetry or religion. He is prone to tears, helpless in a crisis, and capable of great vindictiveness. Then there is mediocre, cowardly, and silly Dr. Panna Lal; the fatuous Nawab; and Professor Godbole, who is not so much profoundly spiritual as merely absurdly irrational. In the long run, the image of India seems all muddled, reflecting what the author himself terms "the celebrated Oriental confusion." The Indians, no matter how subtle and educated, are childlike—in keeping with the stereotyped image of Indians as construed by the West. Because they are children, the Indians can be emotional, sentimental, crude, and vindictive as they like, because such traits are expected of children. Given this outlook, a genuine friendship with an Indian is scarcely possible. This is the reason why, at the end of *Passage,* it is impossible for Aziz and Fielding to "be friends now." The simple fact is that Fielding and Aziz cannot be friends because of a perceived but unexpressed racial inequality that probably both unconsciously accept. The picnic arranged by Aziz to bring the Anglo-Indians and the Indians together has to be in the remote Marabar caves, suggesting a meeting point beyond the orbit of the two societies, and it ends on a bitter note, for there is nothing but disaster when "English people and Indians attempt to be intimate socially" (*API,* 174); Miss Quested finds that the "real India" she has so earnestly desired to discover is as hostile and painful as the cactus spines extracted from her flesh after her hysterical dash from the cave.

However, Forster touches on deeper levels of segregation between the Indians and the Anglo-Indians. If the relationships between the Anglo-Indians and Indians are strained, the Indian society is no harmonious whole. There is the Hindu Brahmin, Professor Godbole, who "took his tea at a little distance from the outcastes" (*API,* 89), the Eurasian chauffeur, Mr. Harris, who, "When English and Indians were both present . . . did not know to whom he belonged" (*API,* 106). Aziz, whose ancestors have been in India for several generations, has not yet accepted India as his home. He feels alienated until the end of the novel. In Mau, both Hindus and Muslims worship at the shrines to a Muslim saint who, in obeying his mother's injunction to free prisoners, had lost his head. "When Aziz arrived, and found that even Islam was idolatrous, he grew scornful, and longed to purify the place, like Alimgir. But soon he didn't mind, like Akbar" (*API*, 292). Like the mosque of Mau, "a flat piece of ornamental stucco, with protuberances at either end to suggest minarets" (*API*, 293), Islam has been transformed by India, so that the Muslim world in India appears as "a strange outcome of the protests of Arabia" (*API*, 293). Aziz becomes assimilated into the paradox of India; standing motionless in Mau in the rain he thinks, "I am an Indian at last" (*API*, 290), and it is a process of absorption which he simultaneously invites and resists.

It is through Aziz that we get the image of the Anglo-Indians in India. When the Muslims discuss the chilly English, the cold and odd nation whom Aziz thinks of as "circulating like an ice-stream through his land" (*API*, 88), a wintry surface covers their conversation. By temperament and choice the Anglo-Indians are hostile to India whether it be mosque, caves, or temple; participating in none, understanding none, resenting all. "They live amidst scenery they do not understand" (*API*, 188) and they sense that Indians hate them and feel India to be a poisonous country (*API*, 180, 209) intending evil against them. Already coarsened by their status in India, the crisis generated by Adela Quested's accusation against Aziz hurls them into cruder demonstrations of their hostility, some demanding holocausts of natives, others longing to inflict humiliating punishment. As if alert to India's syncretic powers and the fate of previous conquerors, "who also entered the country with intent to refashion it, but were in the end worked into its pattern and covered with its dust" (*API*, 215), the Anglo-Indians have contrived to guard against absorption:

> Meanwhile the performance ended, and the amateur orchestra played the National Anthem. Conversation and billiards stopped, faces stiffened. It was the anthem of the Army of Occupation. It reminded every member of the club that he or she was British and in exile. It produced a little sentiment and a useful accession of will-power. The meagre tune, the curt series of demands on Jehovah, fused into a prayer unknown in England, and though they perceived neither Royalty nor Deity they did perceive something, they were strengthened to resist another day. (*API*, 47)

The emblems of Anglo-India blazon a determination that they will not cross the threshold of any passage leading away from a censored consciousness into an emotional and spiritual anarchy: "Ronny's religion was of the sterilized Public School brand, which never goes bad, even in the tropics. Wherever he entered, mosque, cave, or temple, he retained the spiritual outlook of the Fifth Form, and condemned as 'weakening' any attempt to understand them" (*API*, 256).

If we now turn to Forster's characters in the novel to get a glimpse of India, we find that they have perhaps a fictional notion of India, as when Adela Quested, upon arriving in India says: "I want to see real India," as though there is an unreal India as well! To Fielding, India is provocative and baffling at the same time. In describing India to the newly arrived Miss Quested and Mrs. Moore, he says: "Aziz and I know well that India is a muddle" (*API*, 86). The dominant element in his image of India is its utter formlessness, since his taste is governed by the value of the Mediterranean as the "human norm."

To Forster, the struggle of one man to achieve intimacy with another exists in all places, but it is even more evident in India, where racial, imperial, and communal division seem to make personal relationships just about impossible. Peter Burra expresses the same viewpoint:

> The author's interest is in the clash of human beings, the struggle which any one individual must endure if he is to achieve intimacy with any other. The fundamental personal difference is again deliberately heightened by an external circumstance—the difference of race. (Burra [1924] 1986, 319–20)

The friendship of Aziz and Fielding at the heart of the plot, leads up to the last great passage in the novel which sums up his answer to questions about the possibility of good relations between the two races. The two friends ride together:

> "Clear out, all you Turtons and Burtons. . . . Down with the English anyhow. That's certain. Clear out, you fellows, double quick. . . . We shall drive every blasted Englishman into the sea, and then"—he rode against him furiously—"and then, . . . you and I shall be friends."
> "Why can't we be friends now?" said the other holding him affectionately. "It's what I want. It's what you want."
> But the horses didn't want it—they swerved apart; the earth didn't want it, sending up rocks through which riders must pass single file; the temples, the tank, the jail, the palace, the birds, the carrion, the Guest House, that came into view as they issued from the gap and saw Mau beneath: they didn't want it, they said in their hundred voices, "No, not yet," and the sky said, "No, not here." (*API*, 314–16)

Forster's portrayal of a divided India is historically accurate. The novel stresses the difficulty of friendship between races. The one moment in which India's fragmented cultural heritage comes together, uniting the Hindus and Muslims in a common bond, is produced by the need to drive the English out of India: "India shall be a nation! No foreigners of any sort! . . . We [Indians] may hate one another, but we hate you most" (*API*, 315–16). Whether India will remain one nation after the English have left is a question to be confronted later on, but for the time being "out with the English, double quick," as Aziz says to Fielding.

All other Indians in the novel including Aziz's poor relative, Mohammed Latif, belong, like Godbole, to a particular social level which, however complex, has evolved in one way or another, in contact with intelligible trends of civilization.

But the Indian who is seen as distinct from everyone else, from Indians belonging to society as well as from the British, is the man "of low birth," the outcaste Indian, who is employed to pull the punkah in the City Magistrate's Court.[5] Forster saw him as the India that would go on long after the untidy doings of the English had sunk into obscurity. He is humble, "splendidly formed," beautiful, and strong. He is shown sitting almost naked on the floor of a raised platform in the back of the Court. The proceedings of the trial are not understood by him; the social and political conflicts between the British and Indians do not touch his mind. Forster's portrayal of this unique figure in the Indian world is drawn with deep feeling, and it has a central relevance to the total outlook of the novel. He is drawn realistically, and also as a symbolic presence. By portraying him as he is—deprived and condemned by society—Forster draws attention to the one most enigmatic feature of the Indian social tradition, and also comments on the actual scene of social inequality, poverty, and deprivation in India: "This man would have been notable anywhere: among the thin-hammed, flatchested mediocrities of Chandrapore he stood out as divine, yet he was of the city, its garbage had nourished him, he would end on its rubbish heaps" (*API*, 226).

Symbolically, the punkahwallah's presence in the courtroom reflects on the meaninglessness of the communal and class conflicts in Anglo-India. Physically naked, he is presented in the novel as a man in his natural form, as the human individual, who is equal with all other individuals and higher than communities and religions. His presence points out, in the novel's local context, that the British in the days of their imperial power might have looked at Indians as equals; and in the wider context it points out the way that any individual human being might look at any other.

That Forster was deeply disturbed by the conditions of the untouchables in India is apparent in his preface to *Untouchable*, written eleven years after the publication of *A Passage to India*. He says:

> [Indians] have evolved a hideous nightmare unknown to the West: the belief that the products [of human waste] are ritually unclean as well as physically unpleasant, and that those who carry them away or otherwise help to dispose of them are outcastes from society. Really, it takes the human mind to evolve anything so devilish. No animal could have hit on it. (Forster 1935)

Untouchable, as the title suggests, deals with stratifications within the caste system between the caste Hindus and the untouchables at the turn of the century. An untouchable, by definition, is a member of a hereditary group believed to defile members of a higher caste on contact. The choice of the title without the definite article suggests that Bakha, the untouchable, represents millions of metaphoric untouchables who exist anonymously, not only in India but in all cultures and walks of life.

Through Bakha, Anand vividly conveys the sense of deeply felt life from an untouchable's point of view. The central theme of the novel is the age-old injustice committed by traditional Hindu society upon a whole class of people within its fold. Notice the similarity of the opening scene with *A Passage to India:*

> The outcastes' colony was a group of mud-walled houses that clustered together in two rows, under the shadow both of town and the cantonment, but outside their boundaries and separate from them. . . . There lived the outcastes from Hindu society. (*U*, 9)

Moreover:

> The outcastes were not allowed to mount the platform surrounding the well, because if they were to draw water from it, the Hindus of the three upper castes would consider the water polluted. (*U*, 22)

The emphasis is clearly on the physical exclusion of the untouchables from the caste Hindus. When Bakha's sister, Sohini, goes to the "caste-well," she counts on the pity of some caste Hindu to fill her pitcher. On the other side of the brook, the caste Hindu is armed with the feeling of six thousand years of social and class superiority.

The complexities of the Indian caste system are much deeper than they appear on the surface. In India, caste is the principle on which traditional Indian society relies for its stability. The practice of untouchability in the Hindu system arose out of the "ideas of ceremonial purity, first applied to the aboriginal sudras in connection with the sacrificial ritual and expanded and extended to other groups because of the theoretical impurity of certain occupations" (Ghurye 1961, 22). Originally, the caste system was divided into four divisions: *Brahmins,*

Kshtriyas, Vaishs, and the *Sudras.* The Brahmins were the priestly class and hence advisers to the ruling class. The Kshtriyas were the martial race who were the rulers. The Vaishs were the merchant class, and the Sudras did all kinds of menial jobs.

Over the centuries it got more complicated, and there grew further divisions and subdivisions within each caste. For example, Bakha's father is a *Jemadar* (head) of all the sweepers in town. But among the *Sudras,* i.e., the untouchables, there exists yet another hierarchy according to the work they perform in society (barbers, washermen, leather-workers, etc.). Bakha's caste is the lowest among the *Sudras;* his job is to clean the latrines of the caste Hindus.

The interactions between Bakha and the caste Hindus enhance the social divisions in the Indian society. When Bakha, on his way to sweep the streets in the town, stops to buy cigarettes from a shop, he is humiliated by the betel-leaf seller who flings a packet of cigarettes at him "as a butcher might throw a bone to an insistent dog sniffling round the corner of his shop" *(U,* 42). In another incident, a caste Hindu woman "flung . . . [a] paperlike pancake" at him from the second floor because Bakha's touch would pollute the stairs, and he had to pick up the bread from the "brick pavement of the gully" *(U,* 75–76). Such was the predicament of an untouchable in a Hindu society at the time Anand wrote *Untouchable.*

Early in the novel, Bakha is slapped by a caste Hindu for accidentally touching him and thereby polluting him. All the caste Hindus sympathise with the polluted man, whose anger knows no bounds. Bakha's

> first impulse was to run, just to shoot across the throng, away, away, far away from the torment. But then he realized that he was surrounded by a barrier, not a physical barrier, because one push from his hefty shoulders would have been enough to unbalance the skeletonlike bodies of the Hindu merchants, but a moral one. *(U,* 48)

Even after Bakha's repeated apologies, the polluted man and the army of other caste Hindus who join him in abusing Bakha will not stop calling him "a son of a dog . . . a careless, irresponsible swine." The consequences of pollution for the caste Hindu are serious. He will "have to bathe to purify" himself! There is an unmistakable hostility of society towards Bakha which painfully forces him to realise, "I am a sweeper, sweeper—untouchable! Untouchable! Untouchable! That's the word! Untouchable! I am an untouchable!" *(U,* 52). The only person who sympathizes with Bakha and doesn't mind touching him is the Muslim tonga-wallah, who is also an untouchable from the orthodox Hindu point of view. The Muslims, Christians, and soldiers who treat him like a fellow human being are outside the fold of Hinduism.

If the red-brick club is the ultimate symbol segregating the Anglo-Indians and the Indians, the temple and the village well in *Untouchable* are two powerful symbols Anand uses to bring out the sharply divided world of the untouchables and the caste Hindus. As stated earlier, the untouchables were not even allowed to mount the platform of the well. In another scene Bakha is humiliated for climbing the stairs to the temple. He had not entered the temple as such, but his very presence contaminated the service from a distance! Such is the polluting power of an untouchable among the Hindus. Similarly, when, at the temple, Sohini tells Bakha about the sexual intentions of the priest, his first reaction is: "I will go and kill him." The next moment, however,

> he felt the cells of his body lapse back chilled. His eyes caught sight of the magnificent sculptures over the doors extending right up to the pinnacle. They seemed vast and fearful and oppressive. He was cowed back. The sense of fear came creeping into him. He bent his head low. His eyes were dimmed. His clenched fists relaxed and fell loosely by his side. He felt weak and he wanted support. (*U*, 63–64)

Once again, it is the moral barrier which prevents him from clobbering the wily priest. When the temple priest tries to molest Sohini, she raises an alarm, but he reverses the situation by shouting "polluted, polluted!" and gets the support of the caste Hindus. Bakha knows the truth but feels unable to intervene, and the caste Hindus blindly believe the priest over Sohini. It is this collective power of the caste Hindus which intimidates Bakha. He resents his helplessness, but the servility of centuries, which is ingrained in him, paralyzes him even when he vaguely thinks of retaliation.

After the humiliating experiences Bakha returns home, crestfallen, and can do no more than rage against the brutalities of the upper castes. His father, Lakha, who accepts the laws of untouchability as a sacred creed, tries to assuage his feelings. In the afternoon, Bakha attends the wedding of the washerwoman's daughter, whom he used to adore secretly. He shares the sweets on the occasion and enjoys himself. Later, he receives a new hockey stick as a gift from Charat Singh. He plays the game against the rival team and scores a goal, which starts a fight in which a little boy is injured. Bakha carries the boy to his mother, who instead of being appreciative blames him for polluting her son. Bakha's misery reaches its peak when his father chastises him and turns him out of the house.

As a sequel to the events of the day, Bakha wanders homeless in the plains. Of the solutions hinted at to the problems in *Untouchable*—Christ, Gandhi, Marx, and the Sewage System (Machine)—Anand favours the last. As a committed artist, with a bit of the romantic, he sees the whole of life, and thus the novel does not end with "the negation of life."

To promote his social vision, Anand uses a second device—a spokesman figure, the young poet who is introduced in the last scene and explains the choice of possibilities to a section of the crowd that includes Bakha. Christianity is rejected because Bakha does not want to abandon his Hindu Gods—Rama and Krishna—whom his ancestors worshipped. He feels uncomfortable with the Christian concept of sin. Gandhi is revered by the poet as "the greatest liberating force of our age," but he suggests that India would suffer by rejection of the machine. Bashir, with whom the poet is talking, points out that the benefits of the machine are "greater efficiency, better salesmanship, more mass-production, standardization, dictatorship of the sweepers, Marxist materialism"—all possibilities that Anand desires for the new society. The poet's reply is, however, significant: "Yes, yes . . . all that, but no catch-words, and cheap phrases, the change will be organic and not mechanical."

In *Untouchable,* as in *A Passage to India,* the ruling class comes in for criticism. Anglo-Indians, after years in India, learn only some useful imperatives and swear-words. The missionary's wife, like Forster's Anglo-Indian *memsahib,* sums up the attitude of most Englishwomen towards the natives or "the blackies" (*U,* 132), an attitude which Orwell predicted would cost England her Indian empire. The missionary himself, for all his genuine efforts, has failed to transplant himself to the Indian soil, and the presence of his irreligious wife in his house makes a mockery of his attempt at proselytizing the heathens. But it is not the rulers that Anand is most concerned with, but the depravity that has infested Indian society since the first Aryan invasion.

Bakha is both isolated from and bound to his culture; it will not allow him fully to participate in the society and it cannot release him because of the essential service he performs for it. Thus his situation is classically colonial. Anand conceptualizes the whole colonial condition by describing a day in the life of a member of a recognised minority in the Indian society.

Towards the end of the day a feeling of powerlessness, of despair and resignation, replaces Bakha's anger and frustration. Withdrawing from his family and his friends, he vainly searches for an answer to the questions racking his mind: Why did people treat him in such an inhuman manner? What wrong had he done to deserve their scorn? Where would he find an explanation for society's refusal to see in him a human being whose very existence proved his right to live? Although used to both verbal and physical abuse, inarticulate as he is, Bakha's unprecedented fury and anguish at that slap nevertheless mark the beginning of a new awareness in him:

> Before now, Bakha had often borne the brunt of his misery with a resigned air of fatalism. He had quietly suffered his father's abuse and satire . . . with a calm that betokened his intense docility and gentleness. Today, however, he had had more than enough. The spirit of fire which lay buried in the mass of his flesh had ignited this morning and lay smouldering. A little more fuel and it flared up, like a wild flame. (*U,* 118–19)

Bakha himself has no idea of his future, and returns at the end of the day to his father's hut. Its cruelty is harshly apparent. But as Forster remarks:

> His Indian day is over and the next day will be like it, but on the surface of the earth if not in the depths of the sky, a change is at hand. (Forster "Preface to *Untouchable,*" 1935, viii)

Anand realises that "India" as a general concept is merely confusing, except for the geographer or the economist. It cannot be imagined, and thus he depicts the limited, the specific, and the concrete. Into this novel, Anand has infused felt experiences, a social vision, and a "prophecy" for a better society.

Both *Untouchable* and *A Passage to India* end on optimistic notes. Forster acknowledges that an Englishman and an Indian in a colony do not usually connect. However, he leaves open a possibility of reconciliation between races in a politically independent India. *Untouchable* ends with Bakha proceeding homewards, to his polarized world, pondering now on the message of the Mahatma, now on the machine. Gandhi's recognition of untouchability as a social evil sounds affirmative:

> While we are asking for freedom from the grip of [a] foreign nation, we have, for centuries, trampled under foot millions of human beings without feeling the slightest remorse for our iniquity. . . . I regard untouchability as the greatest blot on Hinduism. (*U,* 146)

The caste system is shown not as a static structure, but as a system of social intercourse. The final "thesis" is that profound social changes are on the way. With independence in 1947, the official sanction for the caste system disappeared; only the untouchables remain entitled to some form of protection by the state.

Notes

1. Gandhi quoted in Erik H. Erikson, *Gandhi's Truth: On the Origins of Militant Nonviolence* (New York: W. W. Norton, 1969), 374.
2. E. M. Forster, *A Passage to India* (1924; reprint, Middlesex: Penguin Books, 1986). All further references will be made from this edition, using *API* as an abbreviation.
3. Mulk Raj Anand, *Untouchable* (1935; reprint, Middlesex: Penguin Books, 1986). All further references will be made from this edition using *U* for an abbreviation.
4. In most Indian cities and towns where the English lived, the streets were called "Civil Lines"!
5. Forster told Miss Rama Rau (October, 1961) that the pankahwallah was "most important of all." Quoted by Mary Lago in "A Passage to India on Stage," *Times Literary Supplement* 22 February, 1985.

References

Anand, Mulk Raj. *Untouchable.* 1935. Reprint. Middlesex: Penguin, 1986.

Burra, Peter. Introduction to *A Passage to India,* by E. M. Forster. 1924. Reprint. Middlesex: Penguin, 1986.

"E. M. Forster on His Life and Books." *Listener* 61 (1 January 1959): 11.

Forster, E. M. *A Passage to India.* 1924. Reprint. Middlesex: Penguin, 1986.

———. Preface to *Untouchable,* by Mulk Raj Anand. 1935. Reprint. Middlesex: Penguin, 1986.

Ghurye, G. S. *Caste, Class and Occupation.* Bombay: Popular Book Depot, 1961.

Inden, Richard. *Imagining India.* Oxford: Basil Blackwell, 1990.

Orwell, George. *Burmese Days.* London: Penguin, 1975.

Radhakrishnan, Sarvepalli. *The Heart of Hindusthan.* Madras: G. A. Nateson, 1945.

Woolf, Leonard. *Growing: An Autobiography of the Years 1904–1911.* New York: Harbrace, 1961.

16 "The King Will Come": Laye Camara's Response to Kafka's World Vision

Phanuel Egejuru
Loyola University

Laye Camara[1] of Guinea published his first autobiographical novel, *L'Enfant Noir,* in 1953. In that novel, later published in English as *The Dark Child,* he presented the rich, unspoiled culture and civilization of the Mandinka people of West Africa. The book shows how as a boy growing up in a world infused with spiritual values, Camara was nurtured by the authentic and thriving African civilization whose existence had long been disregarded by Europeans.

In 1954, Camara published his second novel, *Le Regard du Roi,* translated as *The Radiance of the King.* In this novel, he continues to "teach" Europe about Africa and his people. To effectively accomplish his goal, Camara takes Franz Kafka's worldview as a point of departure in his comparison/contrast of African and European worldviews. Thus, on the title page of his novel, we find "Le seigneur passera dans le couloir, regardera le prisonier et dira: celui-çi il ne faut pas l'enfermer a nouveau, il vient a moi" (Camara 1954, title page). "The Lord *will pass* down the corridor, look at the prisoner and say: this one should not be locked up again. He is coming to me" (emphasis and translation are mine). This epigraph comes from one of Kafka's "Reflections," which reads in part "The Lord *may chance* to pass" (emphasis mine). Camara's alteration of the wording of the sentence signals his intention to respond to Kafka's European vision with an alternate view of experience.

When the book was published, some critics, who apparently did not understand this alternate vision, regarded Camara's work as unduly derivative in its use of Kafka's ideas and techniques. However, a few critics, such as Harold Scheub, understood Camara's intention of responding to, not imitating, Kafka's vision. In an article entitled "Symbolism in Camara Laye's *Le Regard du Roi,*" Scheub comments on Camara's explicit intention to carry the banner of Negritude. This article clearly demonstrates that Clarence's fate should not be compared to that of his counterparts in European literature:

> Like Sisyphus and the Ancient Mariner, he seems condemned— but Clarence's ultimate destiny is not that of the suffering Corinthian, nor is it that of the wandering Jew. Nor, though the novel resounds with echoes of Kafka, is his fate that of K. Clarence's is a journey which finally tears him from the last vestiges of civilization, the final remnants of an externally imposed morality and his own half-conceived notions of destiny and justice, until he is left naked, in fact and in spirit, exposed and vulnerable, ready to be delivered [by the African King]. (Scheub 1970, 26)

In the African novel, the idea of permanent suffering for the hero is absent. The seeming desperation of Clarence at missing the king initially is in some ways parallel to K.'s torments and fruitless endeavors to meet his ostensible employer and owner of the castle. But the final results of the heroes' trials are quite different.

By inserting an epigraph from Kafka's works at the beginning of his novel, Camara was indeed inviting the reader to compare and contrast his world with Kafka's. Moreover, as Camara himself suggests, critics who only pick out the similarities between him and Kafka should also look for the differences, because therein lie his originality and authenticity. This study will highlight these differences between the two writers through a pairing of their styles, themes, characters, incidents, settings, and scenes.

Style

Kafka's style is tedious and quite inaccessible to the average reader. Scholars and critics often need more than one reading to understand the surface meaning, let alone the symbolism in his works. As Camus observed:

> The whole art of Kafka consists in forcing the reader to reread. His ending or absence of endings, suggest explanations, which however are not revealed in clear language, but before they seem justified, require that the story be reread from another point of view. Sometimes there is a necessity for two readings. This is what the author wanted. (Camus 1962, 14)

Unlike Kafka, Camara's style epitomizes simplicity in the art of narration. Camara's novels are taught in high schools, whereas Kafka's works are difficult even for professors and college students. Camara's *The Radiance of the King* tells a simple, humorous story of a stranded white man's bizarre adventure in a particular corner of Africa. Although the novel calls to mind the technique and symbolism of Kafka, especially the notion of man's quest for God or for the self, Camara renders the same notion in a direct, straightforward, and entertaining fashion. Whereas Kafka tends to purposely frustrate the hero and the reader, Camara delights his reader with his simple presentation of profound ideas.

The inaccessible nature of Kafka's style is a direct reflection of his vision in *The Castle* and *The Trial* where the hero's world is marked by utter despair and unrelieved frustration. The reader of Kafka's works is frustrated along with K. or with Joseph K., not only because of what happens to them, but by the sheer effort of trying to follow the narrative. In contrast, Camara's narrative technique reflects his simple and optimistic world vision. The reader is entertained as he follows Clarence through his adventures and escapades.

Theme

Both Kafka and Camara deal with the central theme of the quest. However, the process and outcome of the quests differ significantly. In *The Castle,* K. spends his whole stay in the village trying to make contact with the owners of the castle who he claims have employed him as a land surveyor. K.'s efforts are frustrated by other officials and residents of the village. He dies without meeting his employer or doing the job. Even as K. lies dying, he is told that he has no legal rights to remain in the village. Throughout the story there is no relief from the torment and frustration which K., and indeed the readers, undergo through the illogical world of *The Castle.* Camus describes K.'s hopeless quest: "Each chapter is a new frustration and also a new beginning. It is not logic but consistent method. The scope of that insistence constitutes the work's tragic quality" (Camus 1962, 151).

In *The Radiance of the King,* Clarence has come from Europe expecting to spend some happy time in Africa. However, when Clarence finds himself penniless after gambling away his money in the European quarters of the African city of Adrame, he is forced to seek employment to pay for his debts. His search for employment, which takes him to the African sector, turns into a search for the king, the master of the land and the people. Contrary to K., who is denied lodging and an interview with the castle officials, Clarence is provided with his own hut—along with an "official" wife while he waits for the king. In addition, he is "kept" by the king's vassal, who makes sure that all his needs are met. Indeed, instead of being cast out, Clarence is tricked into becoming a member of the community by unknowingly sleeping with the Naba's wives and fathering their babies. Clarence, in the end, meets the king, who physically enfolds him into his bosom, welcoming him as a member of his society and his world.

The outcome of the quest in each work is embodied in the philosophic vision of each writer. In Kafka's "Reflection," from which Camara took his epigraph, one of the first signs of dawning insight is the desire to die, the view that this life is intolerable if any alternative can be attained. One asks to be let out of the accustomed cell which one hates and to be taken to a new one which one has yet to learn to hate. Although a vestige of faith persists that during the transfer the Lord *may* chance to pass along the corridor, this faith is tempered by the note of uncertainty manifest in the words, "the Lord may chance to pass." In *The Castle* the Lord never passes, and K. dies without meeting him. In contrast, Camara's alteration of the Kafka passage to state categorically that "the Lord will pass" changes Kafka's pessimistic anxiety into a confident and optimistic expectation. And Clarence's expectations are more than fulfilled in the end. This attainment of the hero's ultimate goal is what Camara claims to be the most outstanding difference between his work and Kafka's. Camara writes:

> I have never experienced angst, or a life of torment and despair. My characters know this angst, torment and despair better than I do, but the moment always comes when they attain happiness, and when they do so, they attain it fully, while Kafka's characters, on the other hand, attain it only in part or not at all, and even when they imagine they are attaining it, do so only provisionally. (Camara, *Dimanche Matin* 1955, n.p.)

Clarence does not receive the humble employment which he set out to secure, but is instead accepted into the society by being absorbed into the mystic body of the king. Clarence's reception by the quasi-divine king is Camara's demonstration to Europe that Africa, which is symbolized by the king, is not a world that rejects or alienates man, but a world that is ready to admit and nurture all who come to her and accept her as she is.

Character, Setting, Imagery

Other comparisons in characters, settings, and images reveal this same contrast in the authors' overall view of human experience. One such parallel between K. and Clarence is the tendency of the two characters to be asleep or drowsy most of the time. Here again the differences outweigh the similarities. Worn out by long travel in search of the castle, K. is found asleep on his first night at a corner in the bar. His drowsiness, which is made much of, is seen when he stumbles into Burgel's room at night by mistake. But Burgel takes advantage of his drowsiness and proceeds to tell him that officials are more inclined to grant interviews at night when the official barriers are removed. He then urges K. to take advantage of that night and to push his case. At the end of his long speech, K. is asleep, impervious to everything that is happening. In this incident, it appears that K.'s drowsiness costs him an opportunity which might have resulted in his making contact with the Castle. But given the general tendency of the officials to play games with K., it is more likely that it is another ruse to raise his hopes which Burgel knows will never be fulfilled.

In *The Radiance of the King,* Clarence seems to be in a perpetual state of drowsiness, if not totally asleep. Indeed, the service which he is required to render for his keep demands that he be drowsy so that he will not know that he sleeps with a different woman each night. To ensure that Clarence is kept drowsy, he is feted with palm wine during the day; at night the potent fragrance of the flowers and herbs brought by the women who sleep with him leave him semiconscious, and in that state he mates with them. In this case, Clarence's sleepiness ironically helps him perform his duty, a duty which symbolically makes him a part of the community through the children he fathers. When he goes to consult the seer Dioki about the time of the king's arrival, he falls into a trance and has a vision of what he has become. From that vision he sees himself as having sunk to the lowest level of bestiality. At this point he is so thoroughly ashamed of himself that he declares, "I don't want to go back to my hut! I never want to see Akissi again." "When you've had a drink of mulled palm wine, you'll feel differently," says Samba Baloum. "Never! I'll never feel any differently! Do you hear, Baloum, I'll never change my mind" (*Radiance,* 205). Up to this point, Clarence has refused to acknowledge that he has been through a systematic degradation and humiliation needed for his purification in readiness for his deliverance. Thus, his drowsiness which leads to a vision serves the purpose ironically of awakening him to what he has become. From this awareness, he concludes that he is unworthy to be received by the king. This vision then prepares him to receive the final lesson from Diallo, to the effect that in the world where he now finds himself none is worthy, but all receive favor from the king. Here, one detects a strong overtone of Christian belief in God's boundless love and benevolence towards undeserving humanity. Indeed few readers fail to notice the positive godlike qualities of Camara's king, whom many critics compare to the Christian God in his relationship with humanity.

Apart from the obvious use of sleep and drowsiness to make Clarence perform his duty of a "cock" or "stud," Camara creates a unique stylistic device out of the sleepwalking and dream motifs that pervade the novel. On the esplanade, when Clarence is waiting in the crowd to catch a glimpse of the king, he is so overcome by the heat and human odor that he falls asleep standing. The dancing boys wake him up, and he briefly catches a glimpse of the frail adolescent king. But as soon as the king disappears into the palace, Clarence falls back into his dreamlike state as the boys give him conflicting interpretations of the fresco scene. "I'm dreaming, I'm dreaming, but I'm going to wake up soon. The drums are speaking. This is just a bad dream. Who would have believed such nightmares were possible?" ("Introduction" *Radiance,* 43). The boys again jolt him out of the torpor to watch the king descend the staircase again for a final salutation to the crowd, but before it is over Clarence's vision is blurred.

This stylistic device of the sleep and dream motif is noted by Albert Gerard, who states that Camara uses the device to "provide objective correlatives for Clarence's deepening uncertainties in an alien culture whose underlying premises and inner logic he fails to grasp." Gerard further expounds on Camara's sleep/dream motif by comparing it to some aspects of Shelley's transcendence and spirituality ("Introduction" *Radiance,* 14–15). Clearly Camara goes beyond Kafka's occasional episodes of sleep and drowsiness in *The Castle* to create a persistent motif that gives practically all episodes in his novel a dreamlike quality.

The resemblance between K.'s assistants and the two dancing boys have incurred much attention. Yet, despite the close resemblance in the two pairs of characters, there are still marked differences. Whereas Jeremiah and Arthur are more of a hindrance than a help to K., Noaga and Nagoa help Clarence towards achieving his goal. Although Clarence calls them rascals, rogues, and other derogatory names, he often admires the brazen way they handle delicate situations. Furthermore, K. says that he has been expecting his assistants, but Noago and Nagoa just appear in the crowd and end up travelling with Clarence and the beggar to Aziana, where Clarence is sold to the Naba, who happens to be the grandfather of the two boys. Thus Camara again goes beyond the superficial resemblance between Noaga and Nagoa and K.'s assistants to create characters who play a crucial role in the development of the protagonist.

Much has been made also of the parallel between the castle and the king's palace. Here again the resemblance is slight, despite Soyinka's disparaging remark that "it is merely naive to transpose the castle to the hut" (Soyinka 1963, 387–88). Here is a short description of the castle as K. saw it:

> On approaching it he was disappointed in the castle; it was neither an old stronghold nor a new mansion, but a rambling pile consisting of innumerable small buildings closely packed together; if one had not known that it was a castle one might have taken it for a small town. The tower above him here—the only one visible. (*The Castle,* 15)

In *The Radiance of the King,* the palace is described as follows:

> The palace reared against the sky its tremendous mass of red stone. At first sight, it looked like a long-crenellated wall surmounted at intervals by thatched roofs, as if various main buildings were attached to it. The whole was dominated by a central tower whose staircase constructed on the outside, seemed to give access to the sky itself. . . . One would have been more inclined to say that the palace disdainfully refused to look down upon the esplanade or the crowd. . . . Yet in total impressiveness it surpassed by a long way both the esplanade and the crowd upon it, perhaps by reason of its dignity, or its mystery, or some other fact. . . . The general impression was that of sturdiness and strength. The building had more the air of a fortress than of a palace, and its proportions even gave one the feeling that it was a fortified city rather than a mere fortress. (*Radiance,* 40–41)

Unlike Kafka's castle, which is described in negative terms, Camara's palace is invested with dignity as well as an aura of mystery. Moreover, Camara's palace is very approachable, despite Clarence's illusion of its fading away. Several passages also suggest that the king's palace seems to follow him wherever he goes. Thus, Clarence recognizes some of its features even in the dense forest of the South. He also has a vision of it during his consultation with Dioki, the seer.

Just as the palace is compared to the castle, the king is also compared to the owner of the castle. The physical appearances of the king, who is regarded by his subjects as a quasi-divine being, is meticulously described. Above all, it is love that holds him down with the people. This figure is quite different from the invisible owner of the castle, referred to briefly as Count West West. Our view of Klamm, whose name is not to be mentioned when children are around because there is something indecent about him, contrasts sharply with our vision of Camara's king—inspired by Camara's mystical concept of the universe in which the person of the ruler is fused with the deity.

Though several passages related to Camara's palace and its ruler were inspired by Kafka's *The Castle*, Camara so elaborated on his borrowings that he created his own peculiar scenes from those passages. Camara also drew inspiration from Kafka in his presentation of the squalid premises and corridors in Adrame and Aziana, as well as some of what took place in the courts. For instance, in one scene in *The Trial*, Joseph K. presents himself to the priest, who says, "You are Joseph K.," and warns him of the bad prospects of his trial; K. replies: "Yet I am not guilty.... We are all human beings here, every one of us." "True," replies the priest, "but this is how the guilty tend to speak" (*Trial*, 232). A similar episode is found in Camara's novel when Clarence and the beggar are apprehended because the inn-keeper accused Clarence of stealing back his coat which he had relinquished to the inn-keeper in exchange for his lodging fees. Clarence finds himself before "a man crouched over a table, telling his beads." The man stares at Clarence for a while and says: "So this is the culprit?" "I am not guilty," cries Clarence. "They all say that when they're brought here, you can't think how sick I am of hearing it!" (*Radiance*, 77).

In another scene Joseph K. tries to intercede on behalf of a culprit who is being mercilessly whipped, but the whipper tells K., "I refuse to be bribed. I am commissioned to whip, and whip I shall" (*Trial*, 97). In *The Radiance of the King*, Clarence intercedes on behalf of the Master of Ceremony, who is being whipped for "blabbering" before Clarence that he has been purchased to serve as cock for the Naba's wives. The Naba accepts Clarence's plea for the culprit, but the people who have gathered to enjoy the spectacle, including the culprit who is rescued, are angry with Clarence for interrupting the course of justice: "You've offended their sense of justice," Baloum tells him. The people's complaint against Clarence's interruption of justice resembles in a way the whipper's insistence to K. that he is commissioned to whip; therefore, K. is obstructing justice by trying to stop the whipping. One finds also a close resemblance in the reaction of K. and Clarence to the whipping. In *The Trial*, two warders are being whipped because K. has complained to the magistrates that they have tried to steal his clothes. When he returns the next day and finds the flogging still going on, he slams the door shut and beats with his fists against it, running away almost in tears. Camara, however, juggles incidents so that Clarence is accused of stealing his own coat from the inn-keeper. However, his reaction to the flogging of the Master of Ceremony is almost the same as K.'s towards the flogging of the warders.

Certainly, the mockery made of justice at Adrame and Aziana recall that of *The Trial*, just as Camara's descriptions of the courtyards and corridors remind one of the corridors and doors in *The Castle*. During one of his wanderings in the Naba's court yard with Nagoa and Noaga, Clarence encounters again the corridors, which remind him of the ones he saw in Adrame:

> Clarence had a fleeting glimpse of a room no less encumbered with debris and rubbish of all kinds than those at Adrame. The next door opened on to a room neither less derelict, nor less wretched; "Have I come back to Adrame? Or could it be that the sordid justice of mankind can only be meted out in foulness and filth?" (*Radiance*, 165)

By making justice synonymous with filth, Camara echoes Kafka's concept of justice as a sordid institution that mocks our sense of fairness. However, even though the two authors share the same concept, the tone of their treatment of this concept differs greatly. In Kafka's presentation of the sordidness of justice, one feels a deep revulsion and rage. On the other hand, Camara brings humor to his presentation. Clarence may feel angry at what he considers a cruel punishment, but this is mainly because he comes from a different society where the same kind of offense is handled differently and perhaps more cruelly than at Aziana.

One may find reflections of Kafka in almost every line of *The Radiance of the King;* however, these reflections serve to highlight the differences in the outlook of the two authors. Camara himself differentiates his world from Kafka's in this way:

> Kafka's world is not mine. If like Kafka, I believe that nothing exists outside the spiritual world, it is because that world has been mine from childhood; and because I have never made any distinction between the visible and invisible. In Africa, I was as is natural immersed in this spiritual world. I remained within it in Europe, and I cannot conceive of ever leaving it. Death itself can only integrate me into it more fully. In contrast to Kafka and his characters, I have never felt myself isolated or abandoned in the spiritual world. On the contrary, I have always felt myself closely and affectionately surrounded in it. And I live in it with all men of my race accepted by them and in unity with them. . . .
> (Camara, *Dimanche Matin*, 1955, n.p.)

Unlike K., who is rejected to the very end by the world of the Castle, Clarence is accepted and encouraged to become a part of Aziana once his trials have provided him with the necessary understanding.

Much as critics like to emphasize the structural similarities between the two authors, serious considerations must also be given to the ways they apprehend their world, because their perceptions affect their approaches to similar ideas. If it is true that every artist is inspired by the world in which he is born and raised, Camara's claim is indisputable. He had not lived in Kafka's world of despair, and he could never have been inspired by it. Camara portrays a universe in which the individual integrates peacefully into his world. His world is so accommodating that even a total stranger from an alien culture can integrate into it as long as he can adapt to it. Thus, Camara has successfully presented an alternate vision of life in a world in which many of the frustrations inherent in Kafka's European, modernist vision can be removed. In doing so, Camara has created an authentic and original masterpiece, giving a vision conditioned by his world, nurtured by his environment, and defined by his culture.

Note

1. Editor's note: Usually presented in the West as Camara Laye.

References

Camara, Laye. *The Radiance of the King.* Translated by James Kirkup. "Introduction" by Albert Gerard. New York: Macmillan, 1971.

———. *Dimanche Matin.* 2 January 1955.

———. *Le Regard du Roi.* Paris: Plon, 1954.

Camus, Albert. "Hope and the Absurd in the World of Franz Kafka." In *Kafka: A Collection of Critical Essays,* edited by Ronald Gray. Englewood Cliffs, NJ: Prentice-Hall, 1962.

Egejuru, Phanuel. *Towards African Literary Independence: A Dialogue with Contemporary African Writers.* Westport: Greenwood, 1980.

Flores, Angel. *The Kafka Debate.* New York: Gordian, 1977.

Heller, Erich. *Franz Kafka.* New York: Viking, 1975.

Kafka, Franz. *The Castle.* New York: Penguin Modern Classics, 1957.

———. *The Trial.* New York: Penguin Modern Classics, 1953.

Lukacs, Georg. *The Theory of the Novel.* Cambridge, MA: Massachusetts Institute of Technology Press, 1971.

Neumeyer, Peter. *The Castle: 20th-Century Interpretations.* Englewood Cliffs, NJ: Prentice-Hall, 1969.

Robertson, Ritchie. *Kafka, Judaism and Literature.* Oxford: Clarendon, 1985.

Soyinka, Wole. "From a Common Backcloth: A Reassessment of the African Literary Heritage." *The American Scholar* 32, no. 3 (1961): 387–96.

Scheub, Harold. "Symbolism in Camara Laye's *Le Regard du Roi.*" *Ba Shiru* (Spring 1970): 24–36.

17 Carlos Fuentes's Tribute (and Reply) to Ambrose Bierce in *The Old Gringo:* A Unique Example of Inter-American Dialogue

Elizabeth Espadas
Wesley College

Carlos Fuentes's recent novel, *The Old Gringo* (1985), provides an excellent opportunity to expose students to a work which confronts different cultural values, religious beliefs, views of society, of the world, and of the self. Furthermore, *The Old Gringo* demonstrates the interrelatedness of all literature through its assimilation of both Western and non-Western literary heritages, which are molded into a creative critique of the lack of intercultural communication and understanding. In this essay, I will explore aspects of this interrelatedness by examining Fuentes's use of intertextuality, focusing on (l) his creative use of the life and works of his title character, Ambrose Bierce, in the bicultural elaboration of *The Old Gringo;* (2) the major thematic commonalities and differences between Fuentes's novel and Bierce's works *The Devil's Dictionary* and *In the Midst of Life,* and (3) the other Western and non-Western literary and historical elements that create a dynamic intertextual play throughout Fuentes's novel. Suggestions for classroom discussion and for further reading, as well as film and video titles, complete the overview.

The narrator of *The Old Gringo* is Miss Harriet Winslow, a spinster schoolteacher from Washington, D.C., who sits alone and remembers how years earlier she went to Mexico to be the governess to the children of a wealthy landowner, Miranda. Although the Mexican Revolution caused the family to flee before her arrival, she decided instead to stay on to teach the Mexican revolutionaries, their followers, and the peasant families. There she met two men who became powerful shaping forces in her life: the sensual young revolutionary, Tomás Arroyo, and a mysterious gringo journalist, a bitter old man who, pursuing his last illusion, had come to Mexico to die heroically. As she comes to know them, she learns the colonel is the landowner Miranda's illegitimate son, who has occupied the former estate, while the gringo is the

American writer Ambrose Bierce (who, in fact, went to Mexico to cover the story of the Mexican Revolution in Pancho Villa's forces and who disappeared there about 1914).

Inevitably, the two men clash, as a result of which Arroyo shoots the Old Gringo in the back for having destroyed the documents proving the legitimacy of his people's claim to the land. Despite, or perhaps because of, having been awakened to passion and to the sensuality of life by the vibrant Arroyo, Harriet denounces the murder to the authorities, and Arroyo is in turn executed by order of his commander, Pancho Villa. In the face of possible conflict with the U.S. authorities, the Old Gringo is subsequently given a second, honorable execution by Villa himself, just as he had wanted, before his body is claimed (fraudulently) by Harriet, who has him buried in Arlington Cemetery as her long-lost father. She then returns to the United States to sit alone, to recreate these events in her memory, and, through the novel, to give voice to what she has learned from her experience.

Harriet's remembrances, in which events of her early life in Washington freely intermingle with those of her stay in Mexico, bring to light the many conflicts she encountered or observed—the painful search for self-discovery and identity undertaken by all three main characters, the difference of philosophical and religious views, and the dynamics of interpersonal relationships across racial, social, national, gender, and generational lines, giving voice to what was formerly suppressed (see Bumas). As each of the main characters acts to resolve these conflicts, he or she, in essence, crosses a border, be it of a cultural, psychological, spiritual, or national nature.

It has often been noted that the different varieties of boundaries are indeed at the heart of the narrative in *The Old Gringo:* the geopolitical, the cultural, and the inner or spiritual borders (García Núñez 1988, 41; Zavala 1988, 128–30; Buchanan 1988, 244–46; Schaffer 1988, 276). The border is, by definition, a dialogic, bicultural marker, one that is intimately related to Fuentes's longstanding concern with United States-Mexican relations, and one which is a driving force in *The Old Gringo.*

Bierce's *The Devil's Dictionary,* which appears in Fuentes's novel both directly (67, 147) and indirectly through oblique allusions as well as in the spirit of Fuentes's book, is well known for its challenges to widely held assumptions. In that work, Bierce cynically defines a border as an "imaginary line between two nations, separating the imaginary rights of one from the imaginary rights of the other" (242). Fuentes reminds us that even the river that forms the border between the United States and Mexico is neither viewed nor named the same. For Mexicans, it is the "Río Bravo"; for citizens of the United States, the

"Rio Grande." This relatively minor difference is indicative, however, of the important yet little-understood cultural differences between the two peoples, a theme that dominates the spirit of Fuentes's novel. The questioning process is sparked by the presence in Fuentes's text of numerous issues that serve to foreground individual, interpersonal, societal, national, and universal dilemmas, the resolutions of which illustrate Latin American perspectives and reveal both commonalities and differences between the cultures of the United States and Mexico.

The deep divisions that have come between the United States and Latin America are presented and critiqued in Fuentes's novel, beginning with Manifest Destiny and the Monroe Doctrine:

> "Your father went to Cuba and now you're going to Mexico. What a mania the Winslows have for back yards."
> "Look at the map of our back yard: Here is Cuba. Here is Mexico. Here is Santo Domingo. Here is Honduras. Here is Nicaragua."
> "I will never be able to understand our neighbors. We invite them to dinner and then they refuse to stay and wash the dishes."
> (44)

The gringos' "back yard" is kept under control by economic power and by the force of military intervention when deemed necessary (Murray 1990, 22–23).

Although the Old Gringo is admired for his bravery and even loved by many of those who surround him, there is nevertheless an ambivalence that transcends individual relationships, as Inocencio Mansalvo reminds the Old Gringo's corpse: "Haven't you ever thought, you gringos, that all this land was once ours? Ah, our resentment and our memory go hand in hand" (9). The Rio Grande is not only a border, but a scar defacing the land (185).

Crossing frontiers has been, in fact, a part of the United States' mentality: "They spent their lives crossing frontiers, theirs and those that belonged to others, and now the old man had crossed to the south because he didn't have any frontiers left to cross in his own country" (5).

Through the experiences of Harriet Winslow, Fuentes presents a potential model for U.S.-Mexican (or Latin American) relations. Harriet comes to Mexico with all her Anglo-Saxon-Protestant values in full bloom, and when faced with the Miranda family's sudden exit, she turns her efforts to the guerrilla band and its hangers-on. But while she comes to educate, to change and transform her Mexican charges, she finds that it is she who learns from them. From Tomás, she acquires a vision of the passion and sensuality that are missing from her life;

she learns a concept of religion that greatly differs from her Methodist and Bierce's Calvinist backgrounds; and she experiences a mode of life with a different rhythm of eating, sleeping, and interacting. Only then can she understand and perhaps forgive her father and come to peace with herself.

Even though her understanding of life has changed, this change does not lead to a traditional "happy ending":

> For them all, it could be, but never for her, it could never have a meaning, a prolongation, a continued presence in her own future, whatever that might be. . . . She had known this world and could never be a part of it and he [Tómas] knew it, yet he gave it to her, let her taste it but knew that nothing could keep them together forever. (197)

But the experience and memory of the events that changed her life are what gave her the courage to live out the rest of it. As she claims the body of her "father," the Old Gringo, she becomes a national celebrity, expected as such to mouth the stereotypical platitudes: gringos are needed to bring progress and democracy to Mexico and to intervene in their affairs. The measure of Harriet's new knowledge is her reply: "No! No! I want to learn to live with Mexico, I don't want to save it. . . . What mattered was to live with Mexico in spite of progress and democracy, that each of us carries his Mexico and his United States within him, a dark and bloody frontier we dare to cross only at night." She realizes that this land will always be a part of her (187).

As Fredric W. Murray observes, ultimately each character is impelled to reflect on the respective philosophical orientations toward life and death, including the basic socio-ethical value system of each culture. Harriet's increasing repugnance at the tone and substance of the reporters' questions demonstrates her greater comprehension of how misguided North American policies toward Mexico have been in the past and how little the two countries understand each other. In short, she has learned to accept Mexican culture as different, not inferior.

In creating *The Old Gringo*, Fuentes also crosses a cultural and literary border by choosing as his subject Ambrose Bierce, whose enigmatic demise occurred some fourteen years before Fuentes's birth. Bierce's life was eventful but not altogether happy in his personal relationships; although famous, neither was he totally successful in his professional accomplishments. Born in Ohio in 1842, Bierce experienced a childhood dominated by conflict with his strict father. His initiation into journalism began in Indiana where, after his first year of high school, he became a printer's devil. In 1861 he enlisted in the 9th Indiana Volunteers and saw action in several Civil War battles, including

Shiloh and Chickamauga. He was wounded in 1864, at Kennesaw Mountain, and served until early 1865. Returning to journalism, he rose through the ranks in San Francisco periodicals, becoming editor of the *News Letter* in 1868, shortly after which he published his own first story, "The Haunted Valley," in 1871. His success took him to England, shortly after his marriage to Mary Ellen Day, where he wrote for the British magazines *Fun* and *Figaro* and published three books. It was in London (1872–75) that he apparently acquired the nickname "Bitter Bierce" for his sardonic wit and cynicism. Upon returning to San Francisco, he was associate editor of *The Argonaut* and editor of the *San Francisco Wasp*, with an unsuccessful try at mining in between. From 1887 to about 1907 he was associated with William Randolph Hearst's *San Francisco Examiner*, an often tumultuous relationship that introduced him firsthand to Mexico and to the problematic relationship of the United States and Latin America. In 1896 he moved to Washington, D.C., again active in journalism and writing. Although attractive to women, his personal life was troubled by his estrangement from his family: he separated from his wife and lost one son to a violent death and another to suicide. Disillusioned and frustrated by tendencies in American life, in 1913 he left to cover the Mexican Revolution under Pancho Villa and subsequently disappeared without a trace, probably in early 1914, though there have been various theories speculating upon his end (see Ruffinelli's *John Reed*).

Bierce, as a literary author rather than journalist, has been relatively neglected until an upsurge of interest in his writing in recent decades. As in many facets of his life, he was a writer who went against the current of his times, resulting in a delayed appreciation of his literary techniques and, especially, of his experimentation with the concept of postmortem consciousness. Nevertheless, it is notable that he has had a direct impact on American authors such as Ernest Hemingway and on Latin American authors such as Borges and Cortazar as well as sharing a remarkable affinity with the novelists of the Latin American writers of the "Boom" who began writing in the late 1950s and 1960s: Juan Rulfo, Gabriel García Márquez, Alejo Carpentier, and Fuentes himself, just to name a few. The debt that contemporary Latin American writers owe to Bierce is only now beginning to come to light, thanks to the analyses by Cathy N. Davidson (*Experimental Fictions*, 124–34) and Howard Fraser ("Points South . . . "). It is clear, however, that Fuentes is knowledgeable about his subject and source material and that he draws directly from *In the Midst of Life* and *The Devil's Dictionary*, as well as from correspondence, journalism, biographies, and even literary criticism.

Fuentes's intertextual references and borrowings are too numerous to survey fully here, but representative examples will permit a preliminary assessment of the nature and types of such intertextuality.

Although the Old Gringo is not named as Ambrose Bierce until the concluding section of the novel (192), textual clues alone reveal his true identity. Allusions to the "bitter old man" and the "bitter books" he carries are a clear allusion to his nickname, "Bitter Bierce" (Saunders 1985, 22). His frequent asthmatic attacks, his profession as a newspaperman, his physique and coloring, his painful relations with his children (54–56, 83), the feat with the Colt .44 that resulted in the gift of a Mexican sombrero, and the desire to die in Mexico and to be remembered as he was (Wilson 1962, 633) all recreate Ambrose Bierce, the historical personage, effectively if not totally accurately (Ruffinelli 1986, 127–30).

Fuentes enriches his borrowing with near-literal quotes from several of Bierce's works, but he carefully integrates them into the context of his own work, as in the following example: "At this early desert hour the mountains seem to await the horsemen in every ravine, as if they were in truth horsemen of the sky" (79). The "horsemen of the sky" motif is threaded throughout the novel (56, 79, 139, 145), and it reinforces the civil war theme and the parricidal motif. Moreover, the Old Gringo's dream "that his father was serving in the Army of the Confederacy, against Lincoln" made him decide to fight for the Union: "He wanted what he had dreamed: the revolutionary drama of father against son" (54), a further duplication of the plot line of Bierce's "A Horseman in the Sky" which blurs fiction and reality. The final line of the story ("Good God!") becomes a refrain in *The Old Gringo* (142).

Other texts from *In the Midst of Life* are cited similarly: allusions to the experience of fragmented consciousness from "An Occurrence at Owl Creek Bridge" appear repeatedly (139, 145). A description of the deaf-mute child's father in "Chickamauga" appears intact in *The Old Gringo* in a reference to Bierce's own father: "He had been a soldier, he had fought against naked savages and followed the flag of his country into the capital of a civilized race to the far south" (6, 76), which opens up questions on the possible autobiographical dimensions of Bierce's original narrative. Pigs scavenge among the fallen soldiers, as in "Coup de Grace" (88–89, 191). The coup de grace motif itself becomes a unifying device in the deaths of the Federal colonel, Arroyo, and the Old Gringo himself (24, 90, 177–78, 181). Other parallels with Bierce are found throughout: the description of the Old Gringo's corpse resembles that of Jerome Searing in "One of the Missing" (52); the Old Gringo identifies himself as a topographical engineer, the same as the narrator of "Killed at Resaca" (58); and Harriet's gray eyes (103) recall those of Peyton Farquhar in "An Occurrence at Owl Creek Bridge" (22), of Lieutenant Brayle in "Killed at Resaca" (54) and Captain Coulter in "The Affair at Coulter's Notch" (62), eyes associated with bravery and personal qualities of the highest order.

The Old Gringo shares with "Tales of Soldiers and Civilians" (*In the Midst of Life*) three individual preoccupations: the idea of duty, the nature of heroism, and the process of death and dying. Characters probed in these narratives are under great stress in a time of civil war, which places each of them in situations that test them and sometimes break them. Both authors question the traditional, easy stereotypes, which provide a basis for class discussion or essays on the meaning of duty and the definition of heroism then and now.

A starting point might be "Bitter" Bierce's definition of "Duty" in *The Devil's Dictionary:* "that which sternly impels us in the direction of profit along the line of desire" (227). Duty becomes the central obsession of "A Horseman in the Sky," in which Carter Druse, the only child of well-to-do Virginians, decides to join a Union regiment during the Civil War. His father's reaction is "Well, go, sir, and whatever may occur, do what you conceive to be your duty" (11). Further into the war, while serving as sentinel not far from his home, the young man is placed in the position of having to decide whether to fire on a gray-uniformed horseman who is observing the movements of Union troops from a cliff, a presence that jeopardizes the lives of all his companions. Druse experiences intense emotion as he wrestles with his decision to kill the foe, but is finally guided by his concept of duty, sending horse and rider sailing through the air to their doom below. He later reports to the sergeant that he had shot at the horse and that his father was on it. This representation of soldierly duty portrayed by Bierce can be compared to events in *The Old Gringo* such as Villa's remorseless execution of Tomás Arroyo for his attempt to return home, despite the fact that Arroyo was a trusted officer and long-time associate, because in circumstances of war no one is allowed that privilege.

Bierce's "The Affair at Coulter's Notch" also illustrates the individual's dilemma when faced by duty. Captain Coulter is ordered by his general to fire on a house, and he complies with that duty, only to be found later in the basement of the battered residence embracing his dead wife and child. All of these episodes speak to the loss of individual privilege and the human price of war. Although the reader does not know the motivation for the general's order—whether it was a test of Captain Coulter's sense of duty, the mere desire to eliminate a civilian Secessionist sympathizer, or an honest mistake on his part—the devaluing of human life in times of civil strife in the name of duty is a common thread.

This may lead to a broader examination of the themes of death and dying in the two texts. The circumstances and causes of death are varied in the "Tales of Soldiers and Civilians": as a direct consequence of the brutality of war in "A Horseman in the Sky," "Chickamauga," "An Occurrence at Owl Creek Bridge," "A Son of the Gods," "The Affair at Coulter's Notch," "Coup de Grace" and "Parker Adderson, Philosopher"; as the result of supernatural forces in "One of the Missing" and "A Tough Tussle"; or as the result of failed relationships with women in "Killed at Resaca" and "An Affair of Outposts." The Old Gringo, on the other hand, comes to Mexico to find death and encounters it in the person of the man who becomes his surrogate son. General Tomás Arroyo, in his fury at the burning of his treasured documents that constitute legal proof of the usurpation of the traditional Indian lands by his father, the abusive landowner Miranda, shoots the Old Gringo in the back. Later, as Harriet Winslow reclaims the body of her "father," she becomes a modern-day Antigone, giving him the proper rites and burial in Arlington National Cemetery in a tomb marked "Captain Winslow." The Old Gringo is given a second death by firing squad, the brave and heroic death he had dreamed of. Heroism is subjected to penetrating enquiry through the presentation of conflicting motives for bravery. The Old Gringo deliberately sought death ("To be a gringo in Mexico—Ah, that is euthanasia!" [9]). Arroyo wished to die young, so that the ideals of the Revolution might be preserved. Both Bierce and Fuentes present and question circumstances in which young men are forced by war to kill their loved ones.

Heroism can also be examined from a Jungian perspective in the context of the quest for self-knowledge and self-realization. Arroyo's own quest for identity and destiny begins with the granting of the hacienda, which becomes a symbolic initiation to a mission he sets out to fulfill (Buchanan 1988, 246). His encounters with the Old Gringo and with Harriet serve multiple purposes; for example, the union with the virginal Harriet is integral to the myth of the hero. Their dialogue, however, also forces him to re-examine his ideals and to redefine himself (Buchanan 248–49). Harriet and Tomás both desire to change their lives and are driven in their obsession to achieve their goals, without regard for other concerns, much as Antigone was in the classical myth.

Bierce and Fuentes present individuals who are troubled, and often overwhelmed, by conflictive interpersonal relationships mainly of two types: father-child and male-female. In Bierce, the American Civil War is cast not just as brother against brother, but more commonly as son against father. Carter Druse, observing his father astride the horse, observes that "magnified by its lift against the sky and by the soldier's testifying sense of the formidableness of the enemy, the group [horse and rider] appeared of heroic, almost colossal size" (12). He realizes that this soldier must be killed or the entire camp will be endangered. Only the remembrance of his father's words to do what he conceives as his duty gives him the calm to carry out the task. Fuentes recreates this act of parricide in the Old Gringo's imagination as he celebrates his feeling of liberation in the Mexican desert, "from the parenticides who circle around a famous writer like the ubiquitous buzzards of Mexico, and leaving those who admired him not the memory of a decrepit old man but the suspicion of a horseman in the sky" (145).

The Old Gringo confides in Harriet his pain over the deaths of his children, saying that "he had surrounded his family with a hatred alien to them. 'Maybe my children are the proof that I didn't hate the whole universe. But they hated me, anyway' " (144). Harriet reveals her secret to the Old Gringo, the story of the beloved father who, after years of an extramarital relationship with a lonely black woman in Washington, D.C., abandoned his wife and daughter during his service in the Spanish-American War to live with another black woman in Cuba. By declaring him "missing in action," the women were led to "kill" him for the sake of a monthly pension that allowed them to live. Arroyo also was abandoned by a father who refused to recognize him and denied him his identity. Thus, Harriet and Tomás share the pain of being the children of fathers who sexually exploited servants in patriarchal structures that replicate those of the larger social unit. Harriet and Tomás, as a result of their father's lack of family devotion, inattention or self-centeredness, are orphans "through death or unawareness" (162). Harriet must witness the death of the Old Gringo, now her surrogate father as well, at the hands of her lover Tomás. "She had screamed at Arroyo to stop him: Think, in making love to each other they had known who they were, they each bid farewell to an absent father, but also to their youth; she, consciously; he, by pure intuition; in the name of their lost youth, she begged him not to kill the only father either of them had ever known" (162–63).

The father-child relationship can thus be explored in various dimensions: Carter Druse kills his father in "A Horseman in the Sky" not for his mother, but for his mother country. In *The Old Gringo*, each protagonist at a particular moment duplicates a characteristic of the father and identifies with him at that time (Chrzanowski 1989, 14). Part of Ambrose Bierce's fame rests precisely on his pre-Freudian portrayal of the Oedipal conflict in "The Death of Halpin Frayser" in his collection *Can Such Things Be?* (Wiggins 1964, 33) to which Fuentes alludes in Tomás Arroyo's visions of his mother and of his father's wife. In both Bierce and Fuentes, the father figure is problematic, often treated with irony and frequently replaced by a surrogate, literally or symbolically, providing the basis for attention to Freudian approaches in class discussion.

Male-female relations in Bierce's fiction are complex and troubled. His war stories are understandably masculine in orientation, and moreover their depiction of women is problematical. The mother in "A Horseman in the Sky" is sick, dying, incapable of mediating the father-son conflict. Women are seen as often being the cause of the soldier/protagonist's death in the war. For instance, in "Dead at Resaca," Marian Mendenhall's hatred of cowardice made the distinguished Lieutenant Herman Brayle totally disregard his personal safety, leading to his death. His friend, the topographical engineer (alter ego of Bierce), visits Miss Mendenhall to return her love letter found on his body, bloodstained by his mortal wound. Repulsed by the sight of blood, she throws his letter into the fire, causing the narrator to remark that the Lieutenant had been "bitten by a snake" (60). Perhaps significantly, the only noble images of wives are in "An Occurrence at Owl Creek Bridge" and "The Affair at Coulter's Notch"; in the first, the sight of the beautiful wife is only a figment of the soldier's fragmented consciousness in the moments preceding death. In the latter, the wife and child are already dead, victims of the attack he himself led. After the raging battle in which her home was destroyed, the wife/mother portrayed in "Chickamauga" is not only found dead but grotesquely disfigured. In short, in "Tales of Soldiers" the only good women are dead women.

Bierce's misogynistic bent is reversed in Fuentes's novel, as he creates in Harriet Winslow an attractive, complex, and vital character who not only comes to terms with herself but also provides solace for the Old Gringo in his last days and rekindles his spirit again to face life before facing death. As the survivor of both the Old Gringo and the young Mexican fighter (and of the Mexican Revolution itself), she will embody memory: she is the one who now sits alone and remembers (the leitmotif most associated with her in the novel), forever changed by what she experienced in Mexico.

Lacanian analysis of the mirror stage can be utilized to trace Harriet's growing union of the self through contact with the Other: the fragmentation of that self, followed by a regaining of it through memory. Another approach posits an interpretation of Harriet as a renovation of the myth of woman as a vehicle between men and cultures, counterposed to that of Malinche (the companion of Hernán Cortés and symbolic beginning of Mexican mestizo society). Harriet may be seen as a sacrilegious Antigone or as the embodiment of the eternal feminine (Méndez and Hernandez Palacios 1988, 116). Thus, in the portrayal of male-female relationships, although both authors expose the facades of patriarchy in a dramatic way, Fuentes delves more deeply into the role of women as he critiques the patriarchal structures that produced a gender-divided society in prerevolutionary Mexico.

Social problems, such as slavery, racism, and the inferior status of women, are of concern to both authors and become threads woven into their narratives, though they gain greater prominence in Fuentes's novel. In Bierce's "Chickamauga," the six-year-old deaf-mute child, in his march with the retreating soldiers, attempts to ride horseback on one of the wounded, crawling soldiers, just as he had done many times with his father's slaves (30). Fuentes, in contrast, portrays an entire people enslaved by the repressive remnants of the colonial structures in Tomás Arroyo's story:

> We worked this land for a thousand years before the surveyors and the lawyers and the army came to tell us, This land is not yours, this land has been sold, but stay here anyway, live here and serve the new owners, for if you don't, you'll die of hunger.... Pray God this revolution never ends, but if it ends, we'll go fight in a new revolution, fight till we drop in our graves.... We never knew anyone outside this region, we didn't know there was a world beyond our maize fields, now we know people from all parts.... It's all ours now because we took it, girls, clothes, money, horses.... [We were] beaten if we weren't on our feet by four in the morning to work until sundown, beaten if we spoke to each other while we worked, beaten if they heard us making love, the only times we escaped being beaten was as babies crying, or as old men dying.... The worst master was the one who said he loved us like a father, insulting us with his compassion, treating us like children, like idiots, like savages; we're none of those things; in our minds we know we're none of those. (163–64)

Tomás's own origin—his mother was a defenseless young girl who was raped by the powerful landowner—in essence is a reenactment of the beginnings of Mexican society, the forcible penetration of the Indian civilization by the white conquerors who usurped Indian lands and virtually enslaved that population. The subsequent colonial structures depended on the continued subjugation of the masses of people, primarily through their landless condition. The failure to reverse colonial abuses following independence in the nineteenth century led to the outbreak of revolution in 1910 against the dictatorship of Porfirio Díaz, becoming the first social revolution of the twentieth century and the major event that has shaped modern Mexico (see Eckstein, Reed, Riding, and Womack).

The Mexican Revolution is, in all the literature that it spawned, a whirling force that catches men, women, and children up in its grasp and awakens them from centuries of drugged sleep to reclaim what is theirs. Here, comparisons with other texts of the Mexican Revolution can be drawn: Jack Reed's *Insurgent Mexico,* from the point of view of a sympathetic American first-hand participant; Mariano Azuela's *The Underdogs;* Juan Rulfo's *Pedro Paramo,* or Fuentes's own *The Death of Artemio Cruz* would provide many avenues of discussion on the nature of civil strife and the role(s) of foreign observers.

In the Midst of Life and *The Old Gringo* both fall generally into that broad category of literature known as "historical fiction," which represents another approach to the texts (see Balderston, Domínguez Michael, and González Echevarría). Bierce, in *The Devil's Dictionary,* defines "history" as "An account, mostly false, of events mostly unimportant, which are brought about by rulers mostly knaves, and soldiers mostly fools" (261). In this light, one might discuss the decisions taken in "Chickamauga," "The Affair at Coulter's Notch," "A Tough Tussle," "Parker Adderson, Philosopher," and "An Affair of Outposts." Fuentes, in his book of essays *Myself with Others* (1988), defines the novel as "the transformation of experience into history" (23). History is, for him, "also the things that men and women have dreamed, imagined, desired, and named," not just the "official, documented history of the times" (193), a concept which recalls the driving theme in the Colombian Nobel Prize recipient Gabriel García Márquez's *One Hundred Years of Solitude.* Bierce's presentation of the experience of the Civil War from the point of view of a member of the dominant Union forces and Fuentes's portrayal of the Mexican Revolution from the perspective of the dispossessed offer radically different examples of the intersection of Literature and History, which can be related to each writer's concept of their meaning.

Two thematic concerns stand out in these two authors' interests in the history of their nations: the use of a troubled family relationship to depict by metaphor or analogy a troubled national situation (including a personal quest for identity that replicates the national one) and the questioning of how personal motives impact the larger issue of patriotism. Bierce's fiction does not directly address the economic or political causes of the Civil War, but rather concentrates on the portrayal of its horror, destructiveness, ironies, human loss, and the peculiar alienation they produce. "A Son of the Gods," for example, includes a passage that describes the soldiers' view of the enemy as Other:

> Nothing appeared quite familiar; the most commonplace objects... everything related something of the mysterious personality of those strange men who had been killing us. The soldier never becomes wholly familiar with the conception of his foes as men like himself; he cannot divest himself of the feeling that they are another order of beings, differently conditioned, in an environment not altogether of the earth. The smallest vestiges of them rivet his attention and engage his interest. He thinks of them as inaccessible; and catching an unexpected glimpse of them, they appear farther away, and therefore larger, than they really are— like objects in a fog. He is somewhat in awe of them. (34–35)

Although the reader may assume that the point of view is that of a member of the Union army, no clues are given to define which side is friend or foe in the above passage.

Families are divided by Union and Confederate loyalties in many of the narratives of *In the Midst of Life:* there is a Confederate father and Union son in "A Horseman in the Sky"; the Searing brothers are on opposite sides in "One of the Missing"; the Union Captain Coulter's wife is a Secessionist sympathizer in "The Affair at Coulter's Notch." All of these ruptures cause great pain and grief. Bierce seems intrigued with the figure of the man of Southern birth who chooses to serve the Union cause (Captain Coulter, Carter Druse, Captain Armisted in "An Affair of Outposts"). Perhaps significantly, one of the two family members (often the Confederate one) in each of these works does not survive the ordeal. In "One of the Missing" the Searing family had been split up by Adrian's breach of discipline that caused him to flee his native Europe and land in New Orleans; in "The Affair at Coulter's Notch" the Coulter family was sacrificed to gain the military objectives set out by commanding officers; the Druse family in "A Horseman in the Sky" seems destined for extinction as a result of the son's slaying of the father and the mother's imminent death. Unlike the nameless enemy of the battlefields in "A Son of the Gods," the Confederate family members are portrayed sympathetically: Mrs. Coulter as a "good wife and highbred lady" (66) and the elder Druse as dignified and majestic, a fact which heightens the irony and poignancy of their sacrifices.

Among the participants in the revolutionary struggle of Mexico, the situation of the divided family was far less common as, at least broadly speaking, the major divisions were along lines of race and class. Tomás Arroyo, as the illegitimate son of the powerful Miranda, chose to serve in the forces of Pancho Villa; had he not been a bastard, he would not have fought alongside those who, as a class, had for generations been dispossessed by the unequal and illicit distribution of wealth and power in that country. They came together because Arroyo had been denied his heritage and identity as an individual, just as they had been as a class.

The enemy in the Mexican Revolution is also portrayed very differently than that in the Civil War struggle, primarily due to the greater social disparity. The federal troops cut a ridiculous figure, dressed in French Foreign Legion uniforms with kepis on their heads. As graduates of the French military academy, they want to fight in formal combat according to the "rules of war" when they are faced with Pancho Villa's rag-tag but determined and experienced group of guerrilla fighters (77, 83). But the concept of divided families (other than the case of the legitimate versus the illegitimate branches of it) never comes to the surface, presenting a striking contrast to Bierce's narrative.

Consideration of the social and economic differences between the two opposing sides, then, could lead to interdisciplinary discussion of the two wars as different varieties of civil strife. For example, whereas the American Civil War was waged over some very specific political and economic principles in an industrialized society, the Mexican Revolution began as an amorphous reaction against the overly extended dictatorship of Porfirio Díaz (1876–1910) and, until its waning days (if then), largely lacked an articulated ideology ascribed to by a majority of the participants. Mexico was, indeed, a very different nation from its northern neighbor, with a large Indian and mestizo population that was, more often than not, disenfranchised, landless, and victimized by residual colonial structures. One of the effects of the Revolution—that sweeping force described alternately as a whirlwind, a storm, or a rolling ball—was to accomplish both social upheaval, allowing some of those who had been on the bottom to rise socially, politically, and economically, and a vindication of Mexico's indigenous past (traditionally ignored and despised), by placing it above or at a par with the Hispanic past.

The portrayals of Tomás Arroyo, Pancho Villa, La Luna, La Garduña, Inocencio Monsalvo, General Frutos Garcia, and others reflect the social change that was occurring during the twentieth century's first social revolution. Over and over again, allusions to Tomás's blend of the Indian and the Hispanic and his performance as a General, albeit an illiterate one, make him the prototype of those who fought for the righting of injustices and the extension of opportunity to the dispossessed classes as he, too, sought to prove what was rightfully his. Ironically, his prized documents that reflected the Spanish Crown's own judgment that the land rightfully belonged to the Indians are things he cannot read. And the Old Gringo's act of provocation, in burning them, is what leads to his murder, despite his new role as Arroyo's surrogate father.

The reading/illiteracy paradigm is central to the development of the plot in *The Old Gringo,* from Harriet's arrival as a schoolteacher to the wealthy to her decision to teach those who have been deprived of education, and from the Old Gringo's livelihood in writing and journalism to his decision to live out a literary role as an American Don Quixote (see Carrillo, Huerta, Lorente-Murphy, Schaeffer, and Tittler). The act of reading is a motif developed through the second most important source of intertextual play: Cervantes's *Don Quixote,* one of the three books carried by the Old Gringo on his trip to Mexico.

While the historical Bierce's familiarity with this novel is unknown, Fuentes's interest in it is of long standing, as can be verified in his "Cervantes, or the Critique of Reading," an essay which also establishes the rationale for the work's prominent role in *The Old Gringo.* For Fuentes, "the modern world begins when Don Quixote de la Mancha, in 1605, leaves his village, goes out into the world, and discovers that the world does not resemble what he has read about it." Moreover, Don Quixote "illustrates the rupture of a world based on analogy and thrust into differentiation. He makes evident a challenge that we consider peculiarly ours: how to accept the diversity and mutation of the world, while retaining the mind's power for analogy and unity, so that this changing world shall not become meaningless" (Fuentes 1988, 49–50). Fuentes comments specifically on the use of active dialogue and its Erasmian themes of "the duality of truth, the illusion of appearances, and the praise of folly" (Fuentes 1988, 51–52), all of which become important themes in *The Old Gringo.* For Fuentes, *Don Quixote* is

> the most Spanish of all novels. Its very essence is defined by loss, impossibility, a burning quest for identity, a sad conscience of all that could have been and never was, and, in reaction to this deprivation, an assertion of total existence in a realm of the imagination, where all that cannot be in reality finds, precisely because of this factual negation, the most intense level of truth. . . . Art gives life to what history killed. Art gives voice to what history denied, silenced, or persecuted. Art brings truth to the lies of history. (Fuentes 1988, 62)

Fuentes draws on these Cervantine principles extensively in *The Old Gringo,* but not without warning. Tomás Arroyo's affirmation, shortly after meeting the Old Gringo, "I know who I am," (31) is one of the most often-cited lines of *Don Quixote* (part I, ch. 5). Harriet tells of being (re)created and locked into being Mr. Delaney's "ideal woman" (51), much like Don Quixote's Dulcinea, while the mirror motif is closely associated with Don Quixote's antagonist, Sansón Carrasco, known as "The Knight of the Mirrors" in his attempt to beat Don Quixote at his own game (part II, ch. 15). In the Old Gringo's imagination, the horseman in the sky becomes fused with Sancho's imagined "flight" on the wooden horse, Clavileño (107), and the Old Gringo himself suggests a Don Quixote, as a white knight on a white horse at whom the Mexicans stare as he rides into camp, much as the goatherds and serving girls looked at Don Quixote "when he came poking into their villages without being invited, riding a boxy old nag and with his lance charging armies of sorcerers" (21).

But even more striking is the development he gives to the Cervantine themes of the quest for identity ("the sad conscience of what could have been but never was") and the assertion of total existence in the realm of the imagination.

All three main characters participate fully in these dimensions: the Old Gringo, as he becomes the heroic figure that replaces the disillusioned, bitter old man, finds in his surrogate children an opportunity to relive his paternity and to live more fully in the face of death; Harriet chooses to be what she was not and, as a result, learns what could have been with Tomás, and then asserts her total existence through her dreams and memory; Tomás meshes his personal identity with that of his people and discovers the impossibility of going home again, yet he achieves a sense of fulfillment in the realm of the imagined through a symbolic meeting with the "brother" from the south who had brought Miranda to popular justice. Harriet perhaps most fully embodies the Cervantine concepts, as she learns from those whom she had intended to change and to "save," for the first time experiencing life in all of its dimensions, which she will carry with her and relive in her memory forever.

Fuentes draws from many sources in the abundant and often complex literary allusions. The attentive reader will find concepts and images that confirm Fuentes's assimilation of European, North American, Latin American, and his own Mexican heritage. To name only a few, he draws on the central thesis of Thomas Wolfe's novel *You Can't Go Home Again;* and on Borges's use of mirrors, labyrinths, and human existence as the projection of the dream of the Other (the theme of his "The Circular Ruins"). The image of the ubiquitous circling buzzards recalls the short story by the Spanish writer Ramon J. Sender, "El

Buitre" from the Aztec-inspired *Mexicayotl.* The idea that nothing is seen until the writer names it (146) recalls the founding of Macondo in *One Hundred Years of Solitude* by Gabriel García Márquez. Tomás Arroyo's explanation of the centrality of death in Mexican culture (134–35, 188–89) encompasses many aspects of José Gorostiza's poem "Muerte sin fin" as well as Octavio Paz's *Labyrinth of Solitude* in the twentieth century. This attitude toward death can perhaps be traced even to its Nahuatl sources (Alurista 1988, 211–14). Even the character of the Old Gringo had appeared previously, with that name, in the Mexican writer Fernando del Paso's *Palinuro de México* (see Corral 1987, 32). From a different medium, the avenging angel (70) brings to mind Luis Buñuel's film "El ángel exterminador" (1962), shot in Mexico and also a favorite of Fuentes (*Myself with Others,* 131–33). Fuentes's observation that "the theme of necessity is profound and persistent in Buñuel" and his comment that Buñuel's films "repeatedly reveal the way in which a man and a woman, a child and a madman, a saint and a sinner, a criminal and a dreamer, a solitude and a desire need one another" (31) reveal some important affinities with this novel.

Fuentes's intertextual play even includes borrowing from his own novels in the conception of the two male characters: the enigmatic disappearance of an historical personage, such as that of Bierce, was treated earlier in *Cumpleanos* (1969), and Tomás Arroyo shares many characteristics with the title character in *The Death of Artemio Cruz.*

Through such intertextuality Fuentes challenges his readers and encourages them to span as many of the physical, cultural, and psychological borders as possible. He clearly urges his readers from the United States to set aside their preconceived notions about their neighbor to the immediate south in favor of a direct and immediate communication as one human being to another. He also demonstrates his own virtuosity in bicultural understanding and makes a significant contribution toward the reassessment of the life and works of an underrated American writer, Ambrose Bierce. But, perhaps most importantly, in the creation of his character Harriet Winslow, Fuentes presents a new voice for inter-American dialogue, respect, and harmony that is a meaningful tribute to the legacy of Ambrose Bierce, the "Bitter Bierce" who always urged his readers to question and to redefine their most deeply held assumptions.

References

Primary Texts by Ambrose Bierce

The Collected Writings of Ambrose Bierce. Introduction by Clifton Fadiman. New York: The Citadel Press, 1946.

In the Midst of Life and Other Stories. Afterword by Marcus Cunliffe. New York: Signet Books, 1961.

Secondary Texts on Ambrose Bierce

Barrett, Gerald R. and Thomas L. Erskine. *From Fiction to Film: Ambrose Bierce's "An Occurrence at Owl Creek Bridge."* Encino, CA: Dickenson, 1973.

Berkove, Lawrence I. "The Man with the Burning Pen: Ambrose Bierce as Journalist." *Journal of Popular Culture* 15, no. 2 (Fall 1981): 34–40.

Crane, John Kenny. "Crossing the Bar Twice: Post-Mortem Consciousness in Bierce, Hemingway and Golding." *Studies in Short Fiction* 6 (1968): 361–65.

Davidson, Cathy N. *Critical Essays on Ambrose Bierce.* Boston: G. K. Hall, 1982.

————. *The Experimental Fictions of Ambrose Bierce: Structuring the Ineffable.* Lincoln: University of Nebraska Press, 1984.

Fajardo, José Manuel. "El diccionario del diabolico Ambrose Bierce." *Cambio 16* 760 (23 June 1986): 149.

Fraser, Howard M. "Points South: Ambrose Bierce, Jorge Luis Borges and the Fantastic." *Studies in Twentieth-Century Literature* 1 (1977): 173–81.

Grenander, M. E. *Ambrose Bierce.* New York: Twayne Publishers, 1971.

Saunders, Richard. *Ambrose Bierce: The Making of a Misanthrope.* San Francisco: Chronicle Books, 1985.

Wiggins, Robert A. *Ambrose Bierce.* University of Minnesota Pamphlets on American Writers no. 37. Minneapolis: University of Minnesota Press, 1964.

Wilson, Edmund. *Patriotic Gore: Studies in the Literature of the American Civil War.* New York: Farrar, Straus and Giroux, 1962.

Primary Texts by Carlos Fuentes

The Death of Artemio Cruz. Translated by Sam Hileman. New York: Farrar, 1964.

The Old Gringo. Translated by Margaret S. Peden and the author. New York: Harper and Row, 1985.

Myself with Others: Selected Essays. New York: The Noonday Press, Farrar, Straus and Giroux, 1988.

Secondary Texts on Carlos Fuentes

Alurista. "La muerte y el *Gringo viejo.*" In *La obra de Carlos Fuentes: Una visión múltiple,* edited by Ana María Hernández. Madrid: Pliegos, 1988.

Boling, Becky. "Parricide and Revolution: Fuentes' 'El día de las madres' and *Gringo viejo.*" *Hispanófila* 95 (January 1989): 73–81.

Brody, Robert and Charles Rossman. *Carlos Fuentes: A Critical View.* Austin: University of Texas Press, 1982.

Bumus, Ethan. "Away from Silence: The formation, transmittal, and implication of voice in *The Old Gringo.*" In *Interpretaciones a la obra de Carlos*

Fuentes: Un gigante de las letras hispanoamericanas, edited by Ana María Hernández. Madrid: Ediciones Beramar, 1990.

Buchanan, Rhonda Dahl. "El mito del héroe en _Gringo viejo._" In _La obra de Carlos Fuentes: Una visión multiple,_ edited by Ana María Hernández. Madrid: Pliegos, 1988.

Camacho-Gingerich, Alina. "_Gringo viejo:_ Viaje de la imaginación." In _La obra de Carlos Fuentes: Una visión múltiple,_ edited by Ana María Hernández. Madrid: Pliegos, 1988.

Carrillo, Germán D. "_Gringo viejo_ o un 'quijote' en el país de los espejos." In _La obra de Carlos Fuentes: Una visión múltiple,_ edited by Ana María Hernández. Madrid: Pliegos, 1988.

Castillo, Debra A. "Tongue in the Ear: Fuentes' _Gringo viejo._" _Revista Canadiense de Estudios Hispánicos_ 14, no. 1 (Fall 1990): 35–49.

Chrzanowski, Joseph. "Patricide and the Double in Carlos Fuentes' _Gringo viejo._" _International Fiction Review_ 16, no. 1 (Winter 1989): 11–16.

Corral, Will H. "Gringo viejo/ruso joven o la recuperación dialógica en Fuentes." _Cuadernos Americanos_ 1, no. 6 (November-December 1987): 121–37.

Dobrian, Susan Lucas. "Re-membering the Body: Fuentes' _Gringo viejo._" In _Confluencia_ 6, no. 2 (Spring 1991): 67–73.

García Núñez, Fernando. "La frontera norte de México en _Gringo viejo_ de Carlos Fuentes." _Plural_ 198 (March 1988): 41–44.

González, Alfonso. _Carlos Fuentes: Life, Work and Criticism._ Fredericton, NE: York Press, 1987.

Gyurko, Lanin. "The Quest for and Terror of Identity in Fuentes' _Gringo viejo._" In _Estudios en homenaje a Enrique Ruiz-Fornells,_ edited by Juan Fernández-Jiménez, José J. Labrador Herraiz and L. Teresa Valdivieso. Erie, PA: ALDEEU, 1990.

Hernández de López, Ana María. "_Gringo viejo_ y la Revolución Mexicana." In _Interpretaciones a la obra de Carlos Fuentes: Un giante de las letras hispanoamericanas,_ edited by Ana María Hernández de López. Madrid: Ediciones Beramar, 1990.

Huerta, Albert. "El lugar de Don Quijote: Miguel de Unamuno, Graham Greene y Carlos Fuentes." _Religión & Cultura_ 32, no. 153 (August 1986): 427–51.

Lemaitre, Monique. "Territorialidad y transgresión en _Gringo viejo_ de Carlos Fuentes." _Revista Iberoamericana_ 53, no. 141 (December 1987): 955–63.

Lorente-Murphy, Silvia. "_Gringo viejo_ y la búsqueda de un destino." In _La obra de Carlos Fuentes: Una visión múltiple,_ edited by Ana María Hernández. Madrid: Pliegos, 1988.

Mathieu, Corina S. "La frontera humana en: _Gringo viejo._" In _Interpretaciones a la obra de Carlos Fuentes: Un gigante de las letras hispanoamericanas,_ edited by Ana María Hernández. Madrid: Ediciones Beramar, 1990.

Meachem, Cherie. "The Process of Dialogue in _Gringo viejo._" _Hispanic Journal_ 10, no. 2 (1989): 127–37.

Méndez, Luis and Esther Hernández Palacios. "_Gringo viejo:_ La frontera salvaje." _Nuevo Texto Crítico_ 1, no. 1 (1988): 115–21.

Murray, Frederic W. "The Dynamics of Inter-Cultural Dissonance in *Gringo viejo.*" *Chasqui* 19, no. 1 (May 1990): 19–23.

Ortega, José. "El problema de la identidad en *Gringo viejo* de Carlos Fuentes." *La Palabra y el Hombre* (January–March 1989): 169–71.

Roffé, Reina. "Carlos Fuentes: Estos fueron los palacios." In *Espejo de escritores.* Hanover, NH: Ediciones del Norte, 1985.

Ruffinelli, Jorge. "Carlos Fuentes: Del Mito y la Historia: Una lectura de *Gringo viejo.*" In *La escritura invisible,* 119–31. Xalapa: Universidad Veracruzana, 1986.

———. "*Gringo viejo* o el diálogo con la otra cultura (Antiponencia sobre Fuentes/Bajtín)." In *La obra de Carlos Fuentes: Una visión múltiple,* edited by Ana María Hernández. Madrid: Pliegos, 1988.

Salamon, Linda Bradley. Review of *The Old Gringo. Latin American Literary Review* 15, no. 29 (January–June 1987): 219–31.

Schaeffer, Susan C. "El gringo viejo como héroe quijotesco." In *La obra de Carlos Fuentes: Una visión múltiple,* edited by Ana María Hernández. Madrid: Pliegos, 1988.

Seabrook, John. "One of the Missing." *The Nation* (January 1986): 54–56.

Shoris, Earl. "To Write, To Fight, To Die." *New York Times Book Review* 27 (October 1985): 1.

Tittler, Jonathan. "*Gringo viejo/The Old Gringo:* The Rest Is Fiction." *Review of Contemporary Fiction* 8, no. 2 (Summer 1988): 241–48.

Valdés, María Elena de. "La trinidad femenina en *Gringo viejo* de Carlos Fuentes." *Revista Canadiense de Estudios Hispánicos* 14, no. 3 (Spring 1990): 415–30.

Villordo, Oscar H. "Carlos Fuentes, *Gringo viejo* y la America Latina." *Suplemento Literario de La Nación* (Buenos Aires, 24 May 1987), 1.

Zavala, Lauro. "Forma y mito en *Gringo viejo.*" *Nuevo Texto Crítico* 1, no. 1 (1988): 123–31.

Related Literary Texts

Anzaldúa, Gloria. *Borderlands/La Frontera: The New Mestiza.* San Francisco: Spinsters/Aunt Lute, 1987.

Azuela, Mariano. *The Underdogs.* Translated by E. Munguia, Jr. New York: Signet Books, New American Library, 1962.

Hinojosa, Rolando. *Rites and Witnesses.* Houston: Arte Publico Press, 1982.

Paredes, Americo, ed. *"With his pistol in his hand": A Border Ballad and Its Hero.* Austin: University of Texas Press, 1958.

Rulfo, Juan. *Pedro Paramo.* Translated by Lysander Kemp. New York: Grove Press, 1959.

Yanez, Agustin. *The Edge of the Storm.* Translated by Ethel Brinton. Austin: University of Texas Press, 1971.

Related Secondary Sources

Balderston, Daniel, ed. *The Historical Novel in Latin America: A Symposium.* Gaithersburg, MD: Ediciones Hispamerica, 1986.

Dominguez Michael, Christopher. "Notas sobre mitos nacionales y novela mexicana (1955–1985)." *Revista Iberoamericana* 55.148 (July–December 1989): 915–24.

Eckstein, Susan. *The Poverty of Revolution: The State and the Urban Poor in Mexico.* Princeton, NJ: Princeton University Press, 1977.

Garcia Nunez, Fernando. "La frontera norte en la novela mexicana." *Cuadernos Americanos.* 2.4 (1988): 159–68.

Gonzalez Echevarria, Roberto, ed. *Historia y ficcion en la narrativa latinoamericana: Coloquio de Yale.* Caracas, Monte Avila, 1981.

Maciel, David R. *El Norte: The U.S.-Mexican Border in Contemporary Cinema.* San Diego: Institute for Regional Studies of the Californias, San Diego State University, 1990.

Mora, Carl J. *Mexican Cinema: Reflections of a Society.* 1896–1988. Berkeley: University of California Press, 1982.

Reed, John. *Insurgent Mexico.* New York: Penguin Books, 1983.

Riding, Alan. *Distant Neighbors: A Portrait of the Mexicans.* New York: Alfred A. Knopf, 1985.

Robinson, Cecil. "A Kaleidoscope of Images: Mexicans and Chicanos as Reflected in American Literature." In *Bilingualism in the Southwest.* Edited by Paul R. Turner. Tucson: University of Arizona Press, 1973.

Ross, Stanley R., ed. *Views Across the Border: The United States and Mexico.* Albuquerque: University of New Mexico Press, 1978.

Ruffinelli, Jorge. *John Reed, Villa y la Revolucion Mexicana.* Mexico, 1983.

Valdes, Maria Elena de. "Fuentes on Mexican Feminophobia." *Review of Contemporary Fiction.* 8.2 (Summer, 1988): 225–33.

Womack, John, Jr. *Zapata and the Mexican Revolution.* New York: Random House, 1968.

Related Films

Buñuel, Luis. *El angel exterminador.* 1962.

Enrico, Robert. *An Occurrence at Owl Creek Bridge.* 1962.

Fuentes, Fernando de. *Vamonos con Pancho Villa.* 1935.

Leduc, Paul. *Reed: Mexico Insurgent.* 1971.

Paz, Octavio. "Art and Revolution in Mexico." n.d.

Puenzo, Luis. *The Old Gringo.* 1990.

Vidor, Charles. *The Spy.* (Also called "The Bridge"). 1931–32.

Young, Robert. *The Ballad of Gregorio Cortez.* 1983.

18 African American Renderings of Traditional Texts

Neal A. Lester
University of Alabama

When T. S. Eliot, in a 1944 lecture to the Virgil Society, cited Shakespeare, Christopher Marlowe, William Congreve, Michel de Montaigne, Thomas Malory, Thomas Hobbes, Joseph Addison, and Jonathan Swift as "mature" writers, he clearly indicated that "traditional" literature, or the "classics," are indeed Eurocentric and white-male centered. The realities presented in these "traditional" texts are alleged "universals" which transcend racial, cultural, national, and even historical boundaries. Anyone coming to the "classics" whose experience, lifestyle, language, and values are not Eurocentric and characteristic of white middle-class males is expected to accept and embrace a potentially alienating reality as one's own. Hence, texts written about the experiences of minorities become relatively insignificant margins around the canon or mainstream. If these texts are even discovered by the dominant culture, they are most often less valued. For the minority individual bombarded by constant reminders that greatness is embodied by cultural, racial, and gender experiences foreign to his or her own, the result can be not only socially crippling but perhaps more importantly psychologically handicapping, ultimately affecting that individual's sense of self-worth. This process begins early, as the works most often regarded in our culture as children's classics—from Mother Goose to Grimm to Disney—do not depict alternative realities for people of color and other minorities.

Problematic in addressing African American renderings of traditional texts is whether the African American revisionist automatically acknowledges the place that Euro-texts hold in the cultural hierarchy of high art or whether revising Western texts, hence Western realities, empowers the revisionist to supply a version that is more meaningful individually and collectively, ultimately shaking the foundation of the classics. Indeed, to rewrite, revise, or adapt a classical text does not necessarily mean that the revisionist has accepted unquestionably that

239

alleged standard of greatness. African American author Ntozake Shange, in her essay "How I Moved Anna Ferling to the Southwest Territories, or My Personal Victory over the Armies of Western Civilization," explains how and why she became involved in some of this revisionist work (*See No Evil*, 1984). After seeing a New York Public Theater production of Shakespeare's *Coriolanus* with Black and Latin actors, she decided to revise a classical text to fit the cultural realities of people of color. Such a revision presented some inherent artistic and personal concerns for Shange:

> i had & still grapple with the idea of classics in the lives & arts of third world people. we [artists and writers of color] have so much to do, so much to unearth abt our varied realities / on what grounds do we spend our talents, hundreds of thousands of dollars, unknown quantities of time, to recreate experiences that are not our own? does a colonial relationship to a culture / in this case Anglo-Saxon imperialism / produce a symbiotic relationship or a parasitic one? if we perform the classics / giving our culture some leeway in an adaptation / which is the parasite? why aren't the talents & perspectives of contemporary third world artists touted in the same grand fashion successful revivals of dead white artists are? (textual irregularities are the author's; Shange 1984, 35)

While such a project presented a potential conflict for Shange, it offered at least two exciting rewards. First, it was a chance to "combat the irrationality of racism that assaulted such benign adaptations as *Carmen Jones* [and] *The Wiz*," which reiterated the racist stereotype of blacks as solely singers and dancers with frivolous lives as compared to white people's.[1] Secondly, Shange admits that the exercise satisfied a personal need to "make the demon [a Eurocentric classic] bend to her will" (Shange, 1984, 35–36). Of this empowerment objective, she writes:

> now i wd move what waz sacred to them / to something sacred to me. manipulation of symbols is not unlike big game hunting. learning the habits, expectations & reflexes of other animals allows us to slay them. i wd have my chance to hunt the cherished words of dead white men & using all my Afro-American reservoirs of magic, hate, & understanding of my people / undo one myth & replace it with my own. (Shange 1984, 36)

This empowerment has prompted artists to revise the classics for African Americans through restructuring language, changing physical and sometimes temporal settings, and even ignoring specific textual realities in the original that exclude that minority. Transforming a Euro-text into a meaningful African American experience also includes adding historical details that document the uniquely African American experience in the New World—the particular struggles of feeling like and being recognized as full human beings. Additionally, transformations include documentation from African American popular culture and mythology—the music, the dances, the foods, the heroes, the tales.

Generally, adaptations have been within the drama and have been met with varied receptions, depending upon the kind and degree of the specific changes made to the original text. These changes range from nontraditional casting of black actors in white roles, to minor textual adaptations, to thoroughgoing adaptations which reflect more fully the realities of African American culture. Revisions that have often not worked for audiences or critics are those that make no effort to redefine the experiences of the characters in terms of the racial realities of the actors. Conversely, some of the most successful in terms of popular and critical reception have been those that offer no overt threat to prescribed social and racial boundaries, those that for the most part retain segregated casts or characters that are publicly segregated. As Bonnie Allen asserts in her review of Shange's *Mother Courage,* "Performing classic Western drama has of course always presented a unique problem for Blacks in that by virtue of our very presence on stage, we introduce cultural interpretations that [do] not exist in the original work" (Allen 1980, 20). Such realities become particularly evident when classical Euro-texts are performed by black actors.

Some of the early work of the 1930's Federal Theatre Project involved revising classics for African American casts and audiences. One of the first productions was an all-black *Macbeth,* in which "the black actors and actresses of the Harlem unit wanted to prove that they could perform the classics as well as portray servants" (Haskins 1982, 95). In revising the play, the locale was moved from Scotland to Haiti, "famous for its 'voodoo' and witchcraft, allowing the black-magic theme of the drama to be played to the hilt" (Allen 1980, 20). Of the effectiveness of this change of locale, drama critic Brooks Atkinson explains:

> The witches have always worried the life out of the polite tragic stage. . . . But ship the witches down to the rank and fever-stricken jungle of Haiti, dress them in fantastic costumes, crowd the stage with mad and gabbing throngs of evil worshippers, beat the jungle drums, raise the voices until the jungle echoes, stuff a gleaming naked witch doctor into the cauldron, hold up Negro masks in baleful light—and there you have a witches' scene that is logical and stunning and a triumph of theatre art. (Allen 1980, 96)

Ironically, Atkinson's comments would suggest that this example of cross-casting may have been critically acclaimed primarily because it served to reinforce pre-existing racial stereotypes.

An African American production of George Bernard Shaw's *Androcles and the Lion* was another effort by the Federal Theatre Project to make the classics more meaningful for a black audience. Unlike Eugene O'Neill, who allegedly "resented blacks presenting his plays" (Allen 1980, 99), Shaw willingly released the performance rights to all of his plays to a black theatre unit. One particularly notable change in this African American revision of Shaw's play was the substitution of black gospel songs for Shaw's hymns. Identified as "uniquely black" (Allen 1980, 99), the revision had 104 performances.

Both Theodore R. Browne and Zora Neale Hurston revised Aristophanes' Greek comedy *Lysistrata*. Browne's *Lysistrata* is "an anachronistic adaptation (African version) of the Aristophanes farce about a successful demonstration against war, led by women, on the steps of the Acropolis at Ebonia" (Hatch and Abdullah 1977, 31). The play was produced at a theatre in Seattle, Washington in 1931. According to James Haskins, "The reason for the production's fame was that it was forced to close after opening night (the wife of the state WPA director decided it was 'obscene')" (Haskins 1982, 102). A typescript is available at the George Mason University Library of Congress Collection of Federal Theatre Plays.[2]

Hurston's *Lysistrata* is "a Negro *Lysistrata* updated and located in a Florida fishing community, where the men's wives refuse them intercourse until they win their fight with the canning company for a living wage. Apparently, it scandalized both the left and right by its saltiness" (John Houseman as quoted by Perkins 1989, 78). Neither a script nor a record of a production of this play exists.

An example of a particularly problematic revision is New York playwright Kathleen Tolan's *An American Doll's House,* which ran at Atlanta's Alliance Theatre from February through March of 1987. All of the actors in Tolan's version are, with one exception, black. While Director Timothy Near admits that she had no initial motive for casting blacks as the lead characters, the talent of the black actors who auditioned convinced her that the play's "universality"—the imprisoning of individuals by gender roles—would indeed work with a "nontraditional" cast. Near explains:

> The stakes for a black family who got the chance to dream the American Dream were very high. . . . After all, who knows more about oppression and socially pre-determined roles than members of American black culture? . . . I have a feeling that the survival of the theatre in America depends on the artists' attempt to find out what is *really* American—not just white American.[3]

As for the issue of non-traditional casting—only Dr. Rank, the sickly doctor romantically interested in Nora and the only source of confirmation of her equality in the real world, is white—one reporter found the racially-reversed casting refreshing. She submits: "Non-traditional casting tends to jar both white and black patrons. As a rule, whites do not assign to blacks the full range of human emotions they assign to themselves. The very notion of blacks playing parts that don't focus on race or racism—or parts that don't feature streetwise humor like Eddie Murphy's—seems vaguely unacceptable" (Tucker 1987).

Other critics, such as Linda Sherbert of *The Atlanta Journal/The Atlanta Constitution,* objected to the non-traditional casting. Sherbert writes: "Ms. Near integrated the cast somewhat unrealistically by using a white actor to play Dr. Rank, the Helmers' closest friend" (Sherbert *Doll's House*). The objections of critics such as Sherbert to the non-traditional casting reflect the very particular racial and social history and climate of America—particularly in the South, where too many deem it socially "improper" for a white male to be a close companion of a black married couple or for a white male to reveal his romantic interest in a black female.

Indeed, Tolan's presentation, some maintained, was not an adaptation of Ibsen's text at all, but instead a kind of cosmetic updating of the play because the original text was adhered to so closely, so much so that the language, even for educated Northern blacks, was stiff and artificial. Marc Levy echoes Sherbert's notion that the updating needed to be revised too. He contends that when Nora remarks on "how rosy her black children's cheeks and noses have become from being out in the cold," the playwright "flaunts the cardinal rule of theatre, that whatever one changes, one must not then deny the new reality that one has created." He adds, "Frankly, I find it easier to believe in nineteenth century Norwegians than a black lawyer and bank manager in the late fifties who is named Torvald Helmer, lives in a house with his old nursemaid and presumably (since Nora does no housework) other servants" (Levy 1987). Such criticism seems to be grounded in the very racial stereotypes Near's play attempts to contest. Perhaps Levy sees all blacks as having the same skin tone; however, the line about rosy cheeks could in fact work credibly given the different skin tones of the actors. Levy's last assertion seems to confirm Near's comments that in the 1950s black professionals were "almost invisible to the average white middle-class person" (Sherbert "Breaks Ground"). Although Near warned that "audiences wouldn't get 'pure Ibsen' in Tolan's *A Doll's House* but rather the essence of Ibsen" (Rakoczy 1987), the mixed critical reception to the production highlights the many problems attending adaptations which attempt to present the particular reality that invariably comes with such nontraditional casting.

A number of other productions at Atlanta's Alliance Theatre have also been Afrocentric adaptations of traditional Euro-texts, even at the risk of alienating conservative Southern white patrons. Described by Paula Couch as "perhaps the most innovative and adventuresome work the Alliance has ever staged" (Couch 1984), Kent Stephens's *The Threepenny Opera* (February–March 1984) is a black version of Bertolt Brecht and Kurt Weill's *The Threepenny Opera* (1928). While technical and aesthetic emendations worked, the nontraditional casting created quite a disturbance for the sensitive Southern white theatregoers. The production, consisting primarily of black actors, is set in 1933 Harlem, against the backdrop of the inauguration of Mayor Fiorello LaGuardia. The music itself, a significant part of the play, is appropriately jazz, blues, ragtime, and Dixieland.

While some reviewers found that Stephens's adaptation "put some oomph in . . . Brecht's dreary play" (Sandberg-Wright 1984), that the Harlem setting captured the original seediness of the characters, and that the Afro-American music of the 1930s provided a pleasurable and appropriate musical context for the adaptation, the racially mixed casting had some theatregoers protesting by walking out of the production after the first act and by writing letters to the Atlanta newspapers. A bi-racial cast introduced a distinctly racial aspect to the play that a Southern American audience would have to confront. That a black "master criminal (killer, thief, and bigamist) weds a white piece of fluff" (Sandburg-Wright 1984) created the flurry of protest. This public display of interracial intimacy, however contextualized by the willing suspension of disbelief, registered too close to the South's deep-rooted racial tensions and stereotypes.

Reviewer Jan Avgikos, however, recognizes that the added racial dimension offers the play a complexity that moves beyond the political and the economic; she writes: "In this production Stephens portrays the theme of social structure in racial terms" (Avgikos 1984). Avgikos suggests that the black-white casting reiterates effectively that the distinctly American race problem is but one manifestation of the greater socioeconomic enemy: "In the play, black and white alike are caught in the same morass. The racial struggle is a foil to the greater social and economic crises that pervade their lives, making the artificiality and transitoriness of all social superstructures apparent" (Avgikos 1984).

Asserting that the alleged "radicalism" of Stephens's production created a healthy stir, Tom Teepen, Editorial Page editor of *The Atlanta Constitution,* maintains: "Brecht would approve. . . . A theater that only confirms audiences in their predispositions and never rattles them might as well take out membership in the Chamber of Commerce, like another shopping-mall shoe store." According to Teepen, "At *Threepenny*'s center is a simple, naive yearning for a realization among people of the basic humanity we share, and a just fury at systems that play instead on our differences."

Another successful adaptation of a play by Bertolt Brecht is Ntozake Shange's *Mother Courage,* mentioned earlier in the introductory comments to this essay. Shange recognized parallels in dramatic theories and personal politics between her own and Brecht's: "His love of the complexity of ordinary people / his commitment to a better life for all of us / his use of politics and passion / music and monologues / were not so different from my own approaches to the theater" (Shange 1984, 37).

Shange's *Mother Courage* begins with the first thirty years of blacks' emancipation from slavery and their efforts to become Americans with rights equal to those of whites. She explains the relevance of this particular historical context,

> the first thirty years of our [African-Americans'] culpability in the genocidal activities of the cavalry, the exploitation on non-English speaking peoples, the acceptance of the primacy of the dollar. if i must come to terms with being a descendant of imperialist assimilationists who were willing if not eager to murder & destroy other people of color, in the name of a flag that represents only white folks, then let me use a vehicle conceived in the heartland of one of history's most cruel ideologies, Nazism. being Afro-American does not excuse our participation in the hoax of the myths of the western pioneers. (Shange 1984, 37)

Hence, Shange grounds the play in the particular experiences and the language of African-Americans in the New World.

Attacking white Americans' treatment of ex-slaves and American Indians, Shange's *Mother Courage* was produced at the New York Shakespeare Festival's Public/Newman Theater during May–June 1980; it had forty performances and twenty-two previews, and received the Obie Award for Outstanding Adaptation. Using miscegenated characters who are Creole, black, white, mulatto, seminole-Negro Indian and Latino, Shange moves her play from Europe during the Thirty Years' War (1618–1648) to the American frontier—the Southwest territories of Texas and Oklahoma—ten years after the Civil War when black and white troops were recruited to fight Indians, whites, and former slaves. Mother Courage is Anna Fiercesome, an emancipated slave from Charleston, South Carolina. She peddles her goods to troops during the wars against the Indians.

The reviews of the production were decidedly mixed. Calling Shange's adaptation "a venturesome feat of reinterpretation," Mel Gussow of *The New York Times* notes: "Scene by scene, almost line by line, [Ms. Shange] has translated Brecht into a black idiom, names, places, slang and aphorisms, without losing the essence of the play or of the heroine" (Gussow 1980, 80). Edith Oliver recognizes the impact of the specific politics of Shange's presentation, adding that "nineteenth-century skirmishes between whites and blacks and Indians still cut very close to the bone" (Oliver 1980, 77). Clearly, as John Simon notes, Shange does make a "value judgement: Blacks and Indians are felt superior to whites, though why they massacre one another is not quite gone into" (Simon 1980, 80). While Brecht's focus seems to be antiwar, Shange's focus is clearly on the racial tensions between Indians, blacks, and the white cavalry. Many reviewers thought Shange's play would have worked more effectively had she abandoned Brecht altogether and written a play solely on the treatment of blacks and Indians by whites after the Civil War; for some critics, the mixing of racism and militarism did not make for the smoothest aesthetic presentation.[4]

Shange also adapted British playwright Willy Russell's award-winning romantic comedy, *Educating Rita* (1983). The latest in a long line of adaptations of the Pygmalion myth which include Shaw's *Pygmalion* and Lerner and Lowe's *My Fair Lady,* this adaptation changes Russell's story of a brash lower-class English white woman's move (through literature and the arts) toward positive selfhood with the help of a boozing and burnt-out white English teacher to that of a poor black hairdresser from the ghetto (somewhere close to Cleveland, Ohio) who seeks knowledge of the "cultured" world, which in racial and cultural terms translates to white world. While Shange seems not to make radical statements here, the play's casting of a white English professor who teaches Rita Brown (the name is not coincidental) the "classics"— Blake, Yeats, Eliot, E.M. Forster, D.H. Lawrence, Shakespeare, and Joyce Carol Oates—inherently introduces the issue of assimilation and identity for "educated" African-Americans. Hence, Rita's move from the uneducated ghetto lifestyle to a more "cultured" existence transforms Rita "Brown" into Rita "White," a Rita whose language is no longer slang and black idiomatic expressions but is "correct" and adheres to the standards of the white patriarchy. Rita's rather superficial definition of being educated and refined means knowing what clothes to wear, what wine to order at dinner, what plays to see, what newspapers and books to read, how to sit with her legs together, and how to dress in pearls. All of these cues to "culture" she has observed not in her own black community but in the larger white society.

In Shange's version, Rita teaches Frank about black culture though she personally does not find much positive in that culture. Still, she speaks specifically of the history of American racism, mentioning Ku Klux Klan rallies, segregation, lynchings, and cross-burnings. Her job as a hairstylist allows her to speak comically and realistically about black hair, specifically about the mythologies surrounding black hair care and the racist attitudes toward hair (its texture and length) within the black community.

A potential inconsistency exists in Shange's presentation of Rita as one who knows African American literature; specifically, she discusses Ralph Ellison and Claude McKay with Frank, who is obviously ignorant of the works of African American authors. That Rita seems so displeased with her black cultural identity registers a note that Russell's play does not. And certainly the veiled romantic attraction between Frank and Rita introduces, by virtue of the casting, the interracial aspect. Although this element of romance is built into both plays, this racial recasting offers a distinctly different dimension to the play. Frank finds Rita irresistible, ravishing, funny, delightful, and refreshing in her rebellion against the establishment; she thinks he is intellectually brilliant. Perhaps unrealistically, neither character mentions the interracial realities that must be dealt with in the American historical and social context. That Frank, an English professor, knows little to nothing about African American literature but is allegedly "brilliant" in Rita's eyes, is just as telling as Rita's efforts to lose her "refreshing" rebelliousness that defines her blackness so as to be more like the establishment Frank detests and against which he quietly rebels. While the reversal in cultural ideals exists in both plays, the racial angle not found in Russell's play presents an inherent political subtext concerning the nature of American education and the African American identity struggle with assimilation.

About her adaptation, Shange submits: "The trick of adapting someone else's play is 'to understand the characters and submit to their reality.' Then I just change the language.... It's almost like translating. It becomes a rhythmical thing like weaving, once you get started" (Smith 1983). Russell authorized Shange to Americanize his play because he felt "that American audiences would better understand what he wanted to say if Rita had a minority, rather than a working class, background and if Frank and Rita had to confront racial in addition to social and educational differences" ("Studio Theatre" 1983). About her decision to adapt this play, Shange explains: "I liked the play right away. It's about real people who change and grow. Racism and class distinction are two problems we haven't yet solved in America. This play deals with them without being didactic and rhetorical"

("Ntozake" 1983). An interview with Helen C. Smith of *The Atlanta Journal/The Atlanta Constitution* reveals how Russell's play worked itself into Shange's own political arena:

> At first Ms. Shange, whose commitments are "to prove there is an Afro-American culture and to talk to everyone (of whatever race) who is a descendant of a slave," was "very concerned about why Willy wanted a black woman from a ghetto in his play."
> Why not have Frank be an educated black professor, and the girl be a white from Appalachia, she wondered.
> "But then I came to terms with it.... Since this is America, and there is a real race problem here, why not deal with it? I once said I'd never put white people in my plays because they've been talking too much already. I was rather worried I was going back on my word, but then I decided you can't cut off half the people in America because they ain't black." (Smith 1983)

Shange's *Educating Rita* (an unpublished manuscript is available) met with a generally favorable reception, and its ethnic flavor enhanced the audience's enjoyment of the play.

One of the most successful African American revisions, *The Gospel at Colonus,* is an adaptation by Lee Breuer, with music by Bob Telson, and is based on Sophocles' *Oedipus at Colonus. The Gospel at Colonus* is the story of Oedipus's suffering and search for salvation as told through the eyes and voices of a congregation in a black Pentecostal church service. Breuer reshapes Sophocles' story into a mixture of black gospel, Greek tragedy, and Japanese Kabuki theatre. The production itself presented a cast of such black gospel legends as Clarence Fountain and the Five Blind Boys of Alabama, J. J. Farley and the Original Soul Stirrers, and the J. D. Steele Singers.

In an interview with Lorna Gentry, adaptor Lee Breuer explains his decision to blend two seemingly different cultural traditions: "I've always been frustrated by the fact that American classical theatre is really a colonization of English classical theatre. [For] a long time I've been looking for an indigenous American style" (Gentry 1986). Breuer recognizes parallels between the communal religious experiences of the black Pentecostal service and of Greek tragedy in 400 B.C., which Breuer sees as "basically a religious, political experience." He notes that the black church in America has always nurtured political leaders as well as religious leaders and thus also combines these two arenas of life. Breuer also notes parallels in the cathartic experience of Greek drama and that found in African-derived Christianity. He writes:

> True catharsis in the church sense, turns from this kind of . . . cathartic tension [to] something really sublime and really joyful. . . . Our instinct is that perhaps the Greek catharsis did the

same thing, and what we tried to [achieve in the final moments
of *Gospel* was] a kind of catharsis that is closer to church catharsis,
not an all-white catharsis . . . intended to be pity and terror, etc.
But something really more joyful . . . the kind of thing that happens
when someone gives testimony. (Gentry 1986)

Breuer adds, "I'm really anxious to find an American classical form,
and I don't think it should be neo-colonial Elizabethan." He points
out that "all the great classical forms came from the church. Such as
opera, out of the catholic mass," and asks, "Why shouldn't the classical
form come out of the Pentecostal church?" (Gentry 1986).

In "reconceiving" Sophocles' play, Breuer renders not the actual
play text but rather a telling of Oedipus's story which becomes the
Biblical text in the black Pentecostal revival setting. As mentioned, the
casting of the play is also one of its most celebrated features. Specifically,
actual members of the church are characters in the play. The play's
action is framed by the Messenger, a visiting minister who reads the
story of Oedipus and conducts the church service. The preacher also
speaks as Oedipus's intellect, a singer represents his spirit, and the Five
Blind Boys offer the physical embodiment of Oedipus's past. An assistant
pastor reads the character of Theseus. An evangelist reads the character
of Antigone, and an audience member assumes the role of Polyneices.
A fifty-five member black gospel chorus, dressed in bright, multicolored,
African-inspired robes with toga-styled sashes, replaces the classical
Greek chorus. J. J. Farley and the Soul Stirrers are cast as church
deacons. In addition, a couple of the actors playing churchmen are
actually ministers.

Working within the idiom of African American music, composer
Bob Telson incorporates tambourine-shaking gospel, soul-soothing ballads, and rousing rhythm and blues. Indeed, it is the music that carries
this production. To reinforce the story-telling and narrative format of
the play, various parts of the original text are rendered as prayers,
hymns, and testimonials. Breuer suggests that the authentic casting and
setting help to achieve the distinctly African and African American
element of the audience as emotional participants rather than intellectual observers. The call-response atmosphere that defines much of the
black American church tradition is recreated effectively and completely
when audience members willingly and instinctively clap and wave their
hands, stomp their feet, and offer spontaneous verbal responses to the
performers. Interestingly, reviewer Steve Murray observes another historical parallel in that "the plot—a history of torment sweetened by
the promise of a gentle fate—parallels the oppressed past of American
blacks and the role of Christianity" (Murray 1986).

Without doubt, much of the success of *Gospel* results from its ability to conjoin two almost polarized cultures: "The components of Greek tragedy are [allegedly] elite culture, intellect, formal poetry, and paganism; the elements of Gospel music are mass culture, intense emotional expression, folk music, common speech, religious ecstasy and Christianity" (Cornwall). "A cross-cultural wedding of European sensibilities with those of black Americans and their African heritage, a cross-historical blurring of the ancient with the contemporary and a cross-racial use of black actors to tell a story nurtured by white literary traditions," *Gospel* proved that the human spirit of middle-class American blacks and whites can transcend, however momentarily, social, racial, and cultural boundaries that work to define unnecessarily separate existences (Sherbert 1986).

Recognizing a similar need, feminists, in works such as Douglas W. Larche's *Father Gander Nursery Rhymes* (Santa Barbara: Advocacy Press, 1985), have shaken the very foundation of the male-dominated, monocultural fairyland by revising fairy tales and nursery rhymes to more accurately reflect social realities. That sexism and racism exist as near-inseparable companions is no revelation. And just as *Mother Goose* needs rightfully to share her shelf space with *Father Gander Nursery Rhymes,* so too do the classics and their monolithic versions of reality with their revisionist counterparts.

Indeed, our attention to *Mother Goose* is not coincidental if we are addressing the classics. If there are no images of African Americans in traditional *Mother Goose* and *Grimm's Fairy Tales* texts, there is little surprise that the Encyclopedia Britannica's newly-revised edition of *Great Books of the Western World* contains no black authors. Once again, the key to addressing this exclusion is defining first what constitutes the "classics" or great works, a decision that is indeed culturally, racially, and politically subjective. That everything from aesthetics of beauty to standards regarding the English language are Eurocentric and Anglo-middle class white male-oriented in American society leaves little wonder that *Great Books'* Editor, Philip Goetz, would endeavor to "justify" the exclusion of African-American authors from this multi-volume work by maintaining that "Blacks generally only write one to two item (idea) books, but *we* don't consider those to be great in the sense that the others are" (emphasis mine, McCalope 1990, 14). *Great Books* Editor-in-Chief Mortimer Adler adds: "I think probably in the next century there will be some Black that writes a great book, but there hasn't been so far" (McCalope 1990, 14). Despite Adler's optimism, his very deliberate justification of the minority exclusion highlights the obvious racial and cultural bias at the heart of determining what constitutes a "classic."

Despite successful adaptations, however, black writers obviously have not concentrated their energies solely in this direction. African American literary scholar Nellie McKay reminds us that "few black writers have attempted to simply rewrite traditional Euro-texts from a black perspective. . . . Black writers have an enormous wealth of mythology of their own, both from their African and American experiences, and have also always had an agenda of their own to push in their writing. I don't think re-writing other people's texts has been high on their agenda" (Personal letter, November 26, 1990). However, until the monolithic social realities presented in literary works regarded by our culture as "classics," from nursery school to graduate school, are replaced by literature which represents the multicultural realities of American life, such adaptations in one form or another will be needed. Until racism and sexism no longer exist and hence oppress socially and psychologically, there will always be a need for people of color and women to reshape the images and realities that separate them from those that render them virtually nonexistent in the dominant culture. And strides are being made on every level. Becoming aware that such biases exist and recognizing the potential psychological impact they can have on the development of positive selfhood and identity are steps in that direction. Reshaping the classics presents a broader political and social issue: the ultimate questioning of tradition and the past, and the need to create what is more representative of America's complex multicultural realities.

Notes

1. This same attack on the banality of *Carmen Jones* (1955) is recognized in James Baldwin's essay "*Carmen Jones:* The Dark Is Light Enough" in Baldwin's *Notes of a Native Son* (Boston: Beacon Press, 1984). Baldwin maintains that "the fact that one is watching a Negro cast interpreting *Carmen* is used to justify their remarkable vacuity, their complete improbability, their total divorce from anything suggestive of the realities of Negro life" (49). And in a *New York Times* interview explaining why she wanted to make *A Raisin in the Sun* (1959), Lorraine Hansberry explains:

> One night, after seeing a play I won't mention, I suddenly became disgusted with a whole body of material about Negroes. Cardboard characters. Cute dialect bits. Or hip-swinging musicals from exotic sources. [Take for example] *Carmen Jones.* Now there's reality for you. . . . An all-Negro musical written by two white men from

a French opera about gypsies in Spain (Nan Robertson, "Dramatist Against Odds," *New York Times,* 8 March 1959, sec. 2).

2. There are two published finding aids to the Library of Congress Theatre Project Collection: *The Federal Theatre Project: A Catalog-Calendar of Productions* (New York: Greenwood Press, 1988) and *A Register of the Library of Congress Collection of U.S. Work Projects Administration Records at George Mason University* (Washington, D.C.: Library of Congress, 1987).

3. "An Interview with Timothy Near," *The Alliance Preview,* 7 Feb. 1987.

4. For a more detailed analysis of Shange's parallels with and movements away from Brecht's text, see Frank Rich's "Stage View: *Mother Courage* Transplanted," *New York Times,* 15 June 1980.

References

Allen, Bonnie. "Theater: A Home Instinct." *Essence,* August 1980, 20.

Eliot, T. S. "What Is a Classic?" In *The Informed Reader: Contemporary Issues in the Disciplines,* edited by Charles Bazerman. New York: Houghton Mifflin, 1989.

Gussow, Mel. "Stage: *Mother Courage*/Brecht in the Old West." *New York,* 26 May 1980, 80.

Haskins, James. *Black Theater in America.* New York: Thomas Y. Crowell, 1982.

Hatch, James V. and Omanii Abdullah, eds. *Black Playwrights, 1823–1977: An Annotated Bibliography of Plays.* New York: R. R. Bowker, 1977.

McCalope, Michelle. "Blacks Furious over Exclusion from New Great Books of the Western World." *Jet,* 19 November 1990, 14–18.

Oliver, Edith. "The Theatre/Off Broadway." *The New Yorker,* 26 May 1980, 77.

Perkins, Kathy A. *Black Female Playwrights: An Anthology of Plays before 1950.* Bloomington: Indiana University Press, 1989.

Shange, Ntozake. *Mother Courage and Her Children.* December 1979. Unpublished manuscript.

———. *See No Evil: Prefaces, Essays and Accounts (1976–1983).* San Francisco: Momo's Press, 1984.

Simon, John. "Avaunt-garde and 'Taint Your Wagon.'" *New York,* 26 May 1980, 80.

Newspaper Sources

Avigkos, Jan. "Threepenny Opera." *Creative Loafing,* 10 March 1984.

Cornwall, Pamela. "Lee Breuer and Bob Telson's *The Gospel at Colonus:* Historical Background," n.d.

Couch, Paula. "Innovative *Threepenny* a Feast of Superb Sights, Songs at Alliance." *Atlanta Constitution,* 24 February 1984.

Gentry, Lorna. "Alliance Theatre Company Interview with Bob Telson and Lee Breuer, Creators of *The Gospel at Colonus.*" 8 July 1986.

Levy, Marc. "Theater: Thoroughly Modernism." *Open City,* March 1987.

Murray, Steve. "Theatre: Shout." *Southline,* 3 September 1986.

"Ntozake Shange Adapts Comedy at the Alliance." *Atlanta Daily World,* 28 April 1983.

Roakoczy, Rebecca. "Director Sidesteps Tradition in *House.*" *Gwinnett Daily News,* 19 February 1987.

Sandberg-Wright, Mercy. "Theater Review: *The Threepenny Opera.*" *Creative Loading.* 10 March 1984.

Sherbert, Linda. "*American Doll's House* Breaks Ground." *Atlanta Journal.* 24 February 1987.

———. "*Doll's House* Fails to Fulfill Expectations." *Atlanta Journal.* 29 March 1987.

Smith, Helen. "*Rita* Adapts to Life in the States." *Atlanta Journal.* April 1983.

"Studio Theatre Premiers American Adaptation of British Award-Winning Drama." *Alliance Theatre News.* March 1983.

Teepen, Tom. "Radicalism in a Pretty Ribbon." *Atlanta Constitution.* 15 March 1984.

Tucker, Cynthia. "Black or White, Nora's Still Nora." *Atlanta Constitution.* 18 March 1987.

19 Politics and the Poet in Baraka's *The Slave:* Turning and Turning in Yeats's Gyres

Maureen S. G. Hawkins
University of Lethbridge

African American authors, as James Weldon Johnson pointed out as early as 1928, face the special problem of addressing an audience divided between white America and black America, each with "differing and often opposite points of view" as to how blacks should be portrayed. Although black writers might want to respond, "Damn the white audience!" (Miller 1987, 301–02), social and economic considerations make doing so difficult. This problem has been especially severe for African American playwrights. Their black audience is smaller than that for black novelists and poets because, as Pawley said as late as 1971, the black community has no tradition of theatre-going (Pawley 1987, 314–15). Furthermore, as Miller says, it is more sensitive about the dramatic representation of African Americans than about their fictional or poetic portrayal, being willing to accept the realistic dramatic depiction of blacks as having both virtues and vices only if that depiction is not staged for white audiences (Miller 1987, 302).

One response to this problem was the black nationalist dramatic movement of the 1960s and 1970s, spearheaded by LeRoi Jones/Amiri Baraka.[1] This movement sought, successfully, to enlarge the black theatre audience and often addressed both black and white audiences, with different messages for each. Its goal *vis-à-vis* the black audience was to engage, arouse, and unify it "by confronting it with an image of its own acquiescence [in white oppression] or by elaborating myths of a heroic past or a revolutionary future" (Bigsby 1985, 381); its goal *vis-à-vis* the white audience was, Baraka wrote, to make them "cower . . . [to] teach them their deaths" (Costello 1970, 212). Like many of Baraka's plays of this period, *The Slave* (1964) addresses both audiences in these terms, presenting an image of a future black revolution designed to unify and empower blacks and frighten whites. However, again like many of his other works during this period, it also addresses a *third* audience—his former, mostly white, "literary peers"

(Lacey 1981, *x*). Through a complex structure of quotations from and allusions to the poetry, drama, politics, and historical theories of W. B. Yeats, Baraka justifies his movement from what he calls in his *Autobiography* a would-be "white intellectual" to "a black nationalist" (Jones 1984, 328)—a justification which includes an implicit plea to his former colleagues and to all whites not to force blacks into the revolution which *The Slave* depicts.

Because Yeats is one of the major figures of twentieth-century European poetry and drama, and a favored literary model for Baraka and his former literary colleagues—the Beat poets—Baraka's treatment of his work may at least partly reflect what Harold Bloom calls the "anxiety of influence." As Lacey points out, even Baraka's earliest poetry displays Yeats's technical influence (Lacey 1981, *vii*), and his "Crow Jane" poems, written during the four years before he wrote *The Slave,* respond even more directly to Yeats's work. In them, Benston says, Baraka "deliberately inverts or, as Harold Bloom would say, creatively misreads" (116) Yeats's "Crazy Jane" poems in order to examine questions of "tradition and influence" and the "relation of [his] poetic voice to the competing forces of Western and African-American culture" (Benston 1976, 115). The "Crow Jane" poems display many of the same techniques Baraka employs in *The Slave:* in them, Benston says, "He appropriates a classic Euro-American form, inverts its imagery and themes, and molds it into a new structure by wedding furious critique to traditional African American expressions" (Benston 1976, 119).

That Baraka should respond to Yeats is not surprising, for the parallels between the two writers are many. Philosophically, both espouse unity of art and action. Yeats idealizes Byzantium as a locus in which "religious, aesthetic and practical life were one" (Yeats 1962, 279); Baraka agrees with Wittgenstein that "ethics and aesthetics are one" (Benston 1976, 47). Romantics, both assert the artist's literally creative power: Yeats in "The Tower" (Yeats 1956, 196) and Baraka in "Black Art, Nationalism, Organization, Black Institutions" (Baraka 1971, 98). As colonized[2] Romantics, both view "history as degeneration from an idealized past and [tend] to assume a cyclical, often apocalyptic movement towards change" (Innes 1978, 15). Both regard the colonizer as materialistic and their own colonized peoples as spiritual (Innes 1978, 17; Baraka 1971, 24)—though Yeats eventually rejects this formulation. Caught, as Yeats puts it in "Under Ben Bulben," "between . . . two eternities / That of race and that of soul" (341), the colonized condition of their peoples forces both to choose between political commitment and political detachment. Furthermore, at least initially, their personal, artistic, and political careers followed similar paths: they began as apolitical artists, dedicated to art for art's sake, then became nationalist poets, playwrights, and theatre managers, concerned, in the contexts of their respective colonial situations, to create new, empowering images for their peoples and to shape their postcolonial identities; indeed, Baraka cites Irish writers, including Yeats, as models for methods of "function[ing] inside and outside" the colonizer's society (Jones 1966, 165). Within their respective nationalisms, each must choose between revolutionary and nonrevolutionary means, and, torn between the demands of nationalism and art, both, as Yeats puts it in "The Choice," must "choose / Perfection of the life, or of the work" (242) and decide whether, as Yeats says in "A Dialogue of Self and Soul," to pursue their chosen perfections by ascending "the winding ancient stair" of Yeats's tower or by wielding Sato's sword (230–31). Finally, as an artist, Baraka asserts his need, like Yeats, "to propose his own symbols, erect his own personal myths, as any great literature must" (Benston 1976, 57), and, like Yeats, draws many of them from his own life.

However, Baraka's treatment of Yeats's work in *The Slave* reflects not only the similarities between the two authors but also significant divergences between them. An Anglo-Irishman, descended from Cromwellian English colonizers of Ireland, Yeats exemplifies Memmi's "colonizer who refuses" but discovers that he cannot "be identified with [the colonized] and [that] they cannot accept him" (Memmi 1967, 19, 39), leading him to fight a rearguard action to defend both the Irishness of his class and their right to restored hegemony in an independent Irish nation. Baraka, on the other hand, exemplifies Memmi's colonized "intellectual [who, having] live[d] . . . in cultural anguish," revolts when he finds that he is "unable to change his condition in harmony and communion with the colonizer" (Memmi 1967, 120, 127). Over time, Yeats became increasingly right wing; towards the end of his life, he even wrote marching songs for Ireland's fascist party. Baraka, on the other hand, became increasingly left wing and, a decade after *The Slave*, declared himself a Marxist-Leninist-Maoist. Yeats projects his desire for unity of art and action into idealized past societies, such as Byzantium and renaissance Italy; Baraka projects his into a revolutionary future. Forced to choose between "race" and "soul," sword and tower, political commitment and political detachment, revolutionary and non-revolutionary nationalism, nationalism and art, and perfection of the life or perfection of the work, Baraka chooses the former, Yeats the latter. However, each rationalizes his decision in terms which allow him to reconcile the two options rather than rejecting one for the other.

Thus, even where they come together, such as in choosing—as Yeats ultimately did—involvement in life over detachment, they diverge in their definition of terms. For Yeats, involvement is personal, for Baraka, political—yet, for both, it is the basis of art and, therefore, the artist's only proper choice.

It is these divergences and the definitions of art and the role of the artist emerging from them which form *The Slave*'s message to Baraka's former colleagues, and, by extension, to his entire white audience. They render the play both Baraka's *apologia pro vita sua* and a plea for help to avert the horrors of the future civil war which it dramatizes, though, since Baraka couches it in the context of Yeats's historical gyres as described in *A Vision* and "The Second Coming," one must wonder if it *can* be averted. Such a possibility would seem to be denied by the work's two-part, cyclical structure of prologue and play, each part embodying the other's antithetical gyre before being transformed into its own antithesis. Walker Vessels, the prologue's aged philosopher/field slave, becomes his antitype, Walker Vessels, the play's mature black poet *cum* rebel leader who stumbles offstage at the play's end, becoming once again "the old man at the beginning of the play" (Jones 1964, 88). Yet, *The Slave* is subtitled "A Fable in a Prologue and Two Acts," and a fable is, among other things, a story with an instructional, moral purpose, as field-slave Vessels suggests when he tells the audience that "ideas . . . need judging" (44), thus inviting us to judge what we are to see. As rebel-poet Vessels admonishes us, "there doesn't have to be" a civil war if whites do "anything concrete to avoid" it (74).

Baraka establishes *The Slave*'s Yeatsian context from the outset, opening the prologue with old Vessels's being awakened by a child's faint crying, an action which suggests the rousing of Yeats's "rough beast" in "The Second Coming" or, for that matter, the inception of each two-thousand-year era by the conception of a child[3] whose "rocking cradle" (185) eventually awakens that age's antithetical gyre.[4] This suggestion is reinforced by the play's ending with the sound of "a child . . . crying and screaming as loud as it can" (88) as rebel-poet Vessels once more becomes the field slave. In both incarnations, Vessels is a poet: the field slave offers the audience a "poem" (45) which proves to be the body of the play in which rebel-poet Vessels twice quotes the second part of Yeats's "News for the Delphic Oracle," first claiming the lines as his own, then attributing them to Yeats in a dialogue with Easley that ensures that the title and author of Yeats's poem are both repeated (Jones 1964, 50–51; Yeats 1956, 323–24). The dramatized "poem" also includes several other references to Yeats and his work. Rebel-poet Vessels affects "*an imprecise 'Irish' accent*" (53). Yeats's

"Lapis Lazuli" is echoed twice—in both works, a "town" is "beat[en] flat" (Jones 1964, 58; Yeats 1956, 292) or "flattened" (Jones 1964, 49). The relationship between Vessels and Grace demonstrates the results of what Yeats calls "The folly that man does / Or must suffer, if he woos / A proud woman not kindred of his soul" (Yeats 1956, 232). But, most of all, *The Slave* is, itself, a "ritual drama," as Easley calls Vessels's poetry. In his own death at Vessels's hands (56, 81) and, in Vessels's killing of Easley and his revolution's responsibility for Grace's death, the play inverts Yeats's ritual drama about the poetic process. In Yeats's *The King of the Great Clock Tower*, the poet must die by the king's orders that his blood may fecundate the queen, his muse, and create both art and poetic immortality.

It is not, however, only the rebel-poet Vessels whose words and actions recall Yeats's work and suggest that Vessels's two aspects may be Yeatsian mask and anti-mask; the prologue's Vessels calls being old an "embarrassment" (45), which suggests Yeats's description in "The Tower" of old age as "tied to me / As to a dog's tail" (192). Echoing Yeats's poems "The Tower" and "Death," Vessels declares, "We invent death" (43), and he implies that his "poem" will show us a "dream" (43), a term Yeats frequently uses, as in "The Tower," to refer to the artist's literally creative power which makes his "ideas" reality. Field-slave Vessels's resemblance to the aged, wise Aherne in Yeats's "The Phases of the Moon" suggests that we may yet escape the cycling gyres if we will listen to rebel-poet Vessels, who resembles the soul "at the crumbling of the moon" who "would be the world's servant . . . / Choosing whatever task's most difficult" (Yeats 1964, 163).

Yet rebel-poet Vessels appears to be trapped in the role of Yeats's "rough beast," as the close match between his character and Yeats's description of the approaching "antithetical gyre" suggests (Yeats 1962, 263). Like the embodiment of that gyre, Vessels aims at "imminent power" and is highly "expressive." He represents "hierarchical" social organization, as is demonstrated when Easley and Grace call him "Jefe" (49), "illustrious leader" (58), and "commander-in-chief of the forces of righteousness" (62)—however sarcastically they may intend these titles. He is "multiple," as is emphasized by Grace's insistence that he is "split so many ways" (61), always shifting from role to role (or mask to mask). That he is "masculine" is established by his phallic gun and by the fact that he has begotten two children. He is, as Yeats says the next age will be, "harsh"; he pistol-whips Easley, has no compunction about killing him, and may even have killed his daughters despite his love for them—an indication that he is also "surgical," capable of cutting out of his society and his life whatever might weaken his revolution or his resolution. The deaths of his two daughters, whether by his own hand or as a result of the shelling, free him to devote himself totally to the war. Thus, he becomes a skewed analogue of Agamemnon and his revolution an analogue of the Trojan War, both of which figure prominently in Yeats's account in "Leda and the Swan" of the beginning of the last pre-Christian gyre, the classical era. Like the Trojan War, rebel-poet Vessels's revolution produces "the broken wall, the burning roof and tower" (211); however, as an Agamemnon figure, he is not killed by his Aegisthus and Clytemnestra, but effects (directly or indirectly) *their* deaths, though *his* war requires the sacrifice of not one but both his daughters, as well as of all personal or family life. Thus, whether "rough beast" or field slave, Vessels is a vessel for cyclical historical forces which deny him freedom and render him the "victim" that Baraka calls him (Jones 1966, 211).

Easley and Grace similarly display the characteristics which Yeats ascribes in *A Vision* (263) to the present era (Yeats 1962, 263). That both are "feminine" is supported by Vessels's continual aspersions on Easley's masculinity and Easley's failure to beget children of his own. As liberal humanists, they are "humane," with "peace [their] means and end," though Baraka treats these qualities as effete in their expression. Their democratic principles, which, in Yeats's antidemocratic terminology, make them "levelling" and "unifying," are symbolized by Grace's maiden name, Locke, but manifest themselves only as a thin veneer of "concern for minorities" (52). This veneer, which consoles the white conscience without requiring it to do "anything concrete" (74) to relieve oppression, cracks under pressure to reveal an inherent racism. Easley, an English professor, is especially "dogmatic" about art, which he rejects if it does not conform to European formal conventions, and about the role of the artist, whose sole valid goal, he insists, is a Yeatsian "perfection of the work."

Their flaws, however, do not deny Easley and Grace—or the values they represent—all worth; in fact, Vessels declares that he "would rather argue politics, or literature, or boxing, or anything, with . . . Easley" (67) than lead this revolution. But he has no choice because white, middle-class, liberal American society has let itself be "used too often," made too many "intellectual compromise[s]," traded "whatever chance we had" for "liberal lip service to whatever was the least filth," and, worst of all, stopped trying to actualize or even believe in its own values (74–76). "The best," as Yeats says in "The Second Coming," "lack all conviction" (185), and therefore, as Vessels tells Grace and Easley, they and all they represent will die, whether he leads a black revolution or not.

Nor can Vessels promise that his revolution will do more than "at best . . . change . . . the complexion of tyranny" (66). As in "The Second Coming," "the worst / Are full of passionate intensity" (185), whether they be whites like the "cracker soldier" (52) to whom Easley threatens to betray Vessels or whether they be Vessels's own black officers, whom he condemns as "ignorant motherfuckers who have never read any book in their lives," and who eagerly drag "darkies out of their beds and [shoot] them for being in Rheingold ads." What the revolution has required of him, he tells Grace and Easley, has "helped kill love in [him]," is killing him "in [his] head," and has deprived him of "soul or heart or warmth," while his "murderous philosophies have killed for all times any creative impulse [he] will ever have" (66–67). Yet his only alternatives are to die with the tainted Western liberal tradition that Grace and Easley represent or to try to end the "three hundred years of oppression" that he and his people have suffered, even if he can do this only by transforming the oppressed into oppressors—an alternative which at least has some justification, since, even if "innocent" whites such as the morally compromised Grace and Easley will suffer, so will "those [whites] who we can speak of, even in this last part of the twentieth century, as evil" (72–73).

Given such alternatives, one must ask whether art of any kind is possible. Rebel-poet Vessels says that his activities have destroyed his creativity, but Easley's Yeatsian definition of art as an "anarchic relationship between . . . man and his work" (75) is based on the same withdrawal from public life which Baraka portrays as having vitiated white Western liberalism. It denies art any moral, social, or political function and is therefore, by the standards Baraka shares with Wittgenstein, a false aesthetic which, by absolving the artist of moral, communal, and political responsibility, takes him "too far away from the actual meanings of life" to produce valid art. The prime exemplar of Easley's aesthetic, Louie Rino, "hat[ed] people who wanted to change the world"; and denied the poet's literally creative power, retreating "into some lifeless cocoon of pretended intellectual and emotional achievement" (75–76). If "ethics and aesthetics are one" and, as Vessels says, "right is in the act" (75), even the violent or destructive act, if it be against "ugliness" (75), can be art, a conclusion validated by Vessels's early experience of "strik[ing] and know[ing] from the blood's noise that [you're] right, and what [you're] doing [is] right, and even *pretty*" (53). So action—even the destructive actions of Vessels's revolution— not Rino's "tired elliptical little descriptions of what he could see out the window" (76), constitutes art—or at least as much art as is possible, given Vessels's alternatives.

Thus, *The Slave* dramatizes what Baraka sees as the choices open to Vessels, and all African American artists, including himself. It justifies Vessels's choice of Sato's sword over Yeats's tower, even if that choice means that he will turn and be turned in Yeats's gyres, enslaving the whites and thus setting the stage for *their* future revolution against the blacks which will, once more, make him a field slave. If doing so is the only way he can create true art, Vessels will, again and again, "relive [his] death" with the "innocents" from Yeats's "News for the Delphic Oracle," and create revolutionary art's "intolerable music." *His* "News for the Delphic Oracle" is that, though he could, like Yeats's Plotinus, free himself from life's pain and suffering—in his case, by choosing "perfection of the work" and withdrawing from the world—he refuses to do so (Jones 1964, 50–51; Yeats 1956, 324).

However, there is still hope for an even better alternative, one which will let both blacks and whites break free of Yeats's gyres to join the "nymphs and satyrs" from "News for the Delphic Oracle" (*The Slave,* 51; Yeats 1956, 324) in their "choir of love" (Yeats 323). "Love," as the prologue's Vessels says, "is an instrument of knowledge" (45), and, if the audience has attended to his dramatic "poem" with sufficient love, they may have learned how to choose that better alternative. The "ideas" which the prologue's Vessels tells us we must judge are not merely concepts, but, as he says, "heavy worlds" with which we "stone possible lovers" (43). His imagery suggests that they may be the supersensual neo-Platonic forms which, according to Yeats, are stored in the *Spiritus Mundi* ready to be actualized (see Jeffares 239–43) but capable of being glimpsed in visions, such as that which allows Yeats to see briefly the "rough beast" of "The Second Coming" before it emerges into the material world. Normally, however, Vessels says, we do not see them because we demonstrate "a stupid longing not to know . . . which is automatically fulfilled. . . . Automatically makes us killers or foot-dragging celebrities at the core of any filth." Therefore, we must be forced to see and judge them—even if they are right, for "the very rightness stinks a lotta times" (43–44). Only by becoming conscious of history's cyclical progression have we any hope of escaping it; if we do not do so, we will have what Vessels's "poem" demonstrates: a revolution such as that which Yeats's "The Great Day" prophesies, one which will involve a mere changing of places between oppressors and oppressed, justified only on the grounds that, as poet-rebel Vessels says, "you had your chance, darling, now these other folks have theirs" (73). But if we do learn the lesson of the "poem" and use our ideas to remake our society so that we do not use them to "stone possible lovers" (43), we can after all create a true revolution which will free us from the gyres and produce "more love ... beauty ... [and] knowledge" (73).

Notes

1. Reflecting his changing sense of his identity, beginning in 1969, LeRoi Jones changed his name to Ameer Baraka or Imamu Ameer Baraka, then to Imamu Amiri Baraka; in 1984, again re-evaluating his identity, he published his *Autobiography* under the name LeRoi Jones/Amiri Baraka. He will hereafter be referred to as Baraka, though bibliographic entries to his works are listed under the names under which he published them.

2. It is important to note that, though Yeats is frequently treated as a British writer, he perceived himself as an *Irish* writer and Ireland as a colony (or, after 1921, an ex-colony) of England. The writings of Frantz Fanon, Albert Memmi, and other Third World anticolonialists strongly influenced Baraka and other black nationalists, who saw the position of American blacks as analogous to that of Third World peoples and declared their solidarity with them.

3. As he explains throughout *A Vision,* Yeats thought that the classical era began when Zeus, in swan form, impregnated Leda, just as the Christian era began when the Holy Spirit, in dove form, impregnated Mary. Believing, in accordance with classical astrology, that each era is approximately two-thousand-years long, he anticipated the imminent beginning of a new era which would, presumably, be inaugurated in similar fashion.

4. Yeats did not conceive of primary and antithetical gyres as simple mirror-images of one another. Thirteen primary and thirteen antithetical gyres, each with its own variations on the basic pattern of "revers[ing] the previous] era and resum[ing] past eras in itself" are required to complete a Platonic Great Year, and, between each of these gyres, "the *Thirteenth Cone,* the sphere, the unique intervenes" (Yeats 1962, 263), ensuring that there is no mechanical repetition.

References

Baraka, Amiri [LeRoi Jones]. *Raise Race Rays Raze: Essays Since 1965.* New York: Random House, 1971.

Benston, Kimberly W. *Baraka: The Renegade and the Masks.* New Haven, CT: Yale University Press, 1976.

Bigsby, C. W. E. *A Critical Introduction to Twentieth-Century American Drama, 3: Beyond Broadway.* 3 vols. Cambridge: Cambridge University Press, 1985.

Costello, Donald P. "Black Man as Victim." In *Five Black Writers: Essays on Wright, Ellison, Baldwin, Hughes, and LeRoi Jones,* ed. Donald B. Gibson, 206–14. New York: New York University Press, 1970.

Innes, C. L. "Through the Looking Glass: African and Irish Nationalist Writing." In *African Literature Today,* ed. Eldred Durosimi Jones, 10–24. Vol. 9: Africa, America and the Caribbean. London: Heinemann, 1978.

Jeffares, A. Norman. *A Commentary on the Collected Poems of W. B. Yeats.* Stanford: Stanford University Press, 1968.

Johnson, James Weldon. *The Book of American Negro Poetry.* New York: Harcourt, Brace, 1931.

Jones, LeRoi/Amiri Baraka. *The Autobiography of LeRoi Jones/Amiri Baraka.* New York: Freundlich, 1984.

Jones, LeRoi [Amiri Baraka]. *Home: Social Essays.* New York: William Morrow, 1966.

———. *The Slave: A Fable in a Prologue and Two Acts.* In *Dutchman and The Slave,* 39–88. New York: William Morrow, 1964.

Lacey, Henry C. *To Raise, Destroy, and Create: The Poetry, Drama, and Fiction of Imamu Amiri Baraka (LeRoi Jones).* Troy, NY: Whitson, 1981.

Memmi, Albert. *The Colonizer and the Colonized.* Boston: Beacon, 1967.

Miller, Adam David. "It's a Long Way to St. Louis: Notes on the Audience for Black Drama." In *The Theatre of Black Americans,* ed. Errol Hill, 301–06. New York: Applause, 1987.

Pawley, Thomas D. "The Black Theatre Audience." In *The Theatre of Black Americans,* ed. Errol Hill, 307–17. New York: Applause, 1987.

Yeats, W. B. *The Collected Plays of W. B. Yeats.* London: Macmillan, 1966.

———. *The Collected Poems of W. B. Yeats.* New York: Macmillan, 1956.

———. *A Vision.* London: Macmillan, 1962.

20 Intertextuality and Cultural Identity: A Bibliographic Essay

Maureen S. G. Hawkins
University of Lethbridge

Elizabeth Espadas rightly says that all literature is interrelated. Moreover, as the articles in this collection demonstrate, its interrelationships are multiple, creating a complex intertextual web which links writers, literary works, readers, and societies. Even the most reclusive authors, such as Emily Dickinson, do not write in isolation. Deliberately and otherwise, all writers literarily incorporate, (mis)interpret, respond to, communicate with, influence, and otherwise interact with a multitude of texts from both their own times and cultures and from those of others. Furthermore, as Michael Worton and Judith Still note, contemporary critical theories expand the term "text" to encompass any " 'signifying structure' from *the spectacle of nature to social codes*" (viii), so such "texts" may include a work's economic, socio-political, literary, and linguistic, visual, and oral contexts (1990, 5–7).

Deliberately responding both to one or more narrowly defined "texts" *and* to one or more broadly defined ones is an ancient practice, dating back at least to Vergil's drawing on Homer's *Iliad* and *Odyssey* to validate Roman political and cultural hegemony in the *Aeneid*. The practice still thrives. As Espadas demonstrates, the response of Carlos Fuentes to the works and life of Ambrose Bierce *and* to the impact of American neoimperialism on Mexico provides intertextual subtexts for *The Old Gringo*. Similarly, Malcolm Lowry's novel, *Hear Us O Lord from Heaven Thy Dwelling Place,* incorporates Coleridge's marginal gloss to *The Rime of the Ancient Mariner* as a marginal gloss to the "Through the Panama Canal" section, which also includes cross-references to Conrad's novel *Youth,* thus rendering Lowry's voyage as mystical, expiatory, and redemptive as that of Coleridge's sailor and as connected to the relationship between maturation and imperial expansion as that of Conrad's protagonist. In Brian Friel's *The Freedom of the City,* the American sociologist, Dodds, discusses the political consciousness of the trapped Civil Rights marchers in words taken from

Oscar Lewis's *La Vida,* thereby linking Northern Ireland's poor with those of Puerto Rico. Friel's Hugh, in *Translations,* anachronistically quotes from George Steiner's *After Babel,* thus linkinq nineteenth-century colonized Ireland with the postmodern condition.

Muriel Rukeyser's poem "Myth" responds both to Sophocles' *Oedipus Tyrannos* and to the social code—common both to the ancient Greeks and to Rukeyser's own modern Western culture—that privileges males by treating "man" and "human" as synonyms. Rukeyser portrays sexism as Oedipus's fundamental *hamartia;* when he answered her riddle, the Sphinx says:

> "You didn't say anything about woman." "When you say Man,"
> said Oedipus, "you include women too. Everyone knows that."
> She said, "That's what you think."

Malawian Felix Mnthali expands such intertextual practice in his poem "The Stranglehold of English Lit" to encompass the entire *ouevre* of Jane Austen; the leisurely lives of Austen's characters, his poem asserts, depend on Britain's exploitation of its colonies, and her novels' "elegance of deceit" seduces Africans educated in the British tradition into acquiescing in their own oppression. A more complex example is Chinese American dramatist David Henry Hwang's *M. Butterfly,* which uses Puccini's opera, *Madame Butterfly* (itself adapted from John Luther Long's short story of the same title) to explore the intersection of patriarchal, imperialist, and racist discourse in the West's "feminine" image of the Asian, and the effects of that intersection on both East-West relations and Western concepts of gender identity.

As the overt literal intertextuality of these examples suggests, writers are, first and also, readers—a fact which students may initially fail to recognize (but which, once recognized, may stimulate them both critically and creatively). Even if one limits the term "text" to "a literary work," all texts have an intertextual dimension: their authors are affected by at least some of the works which they have encountered and, consciously or unconsciously, interact with them in their own works, as critics from Aristotle and Plato on have pointed out.

Many of the articles in this section demonstrate that writers relate their works to those of others in intricate ways which often become even more complex in colonial situations. For example, Usha Ahlawat's examination of the relationship between Forster's *A Passage to India* and Anand's *Untouchable* shows that a work by a colonizer that is set in a society which his or her culture has colonized may spur a colonized writer to recognize a parallel broadly defined "text" *within* his own society. This insight fruitfully expands the concept of "colonizer" and "colonized": it shows that "colonized societies" may be conventionally colonized nations or groups, but they may also be groups, such as women and minorities, which exist in a "colonial" or "neocolonial" relationship to the dominant culture—or "colonizer"—within their own nations.

On a more obvious level, Ahlawat also shows that colonized writers may both emulate the colonizer's work and "correct" his or her vision by portraying the colonized society from within. For example, Chinua Achebe writes that Joyce Cary's focus on Rudbeck's road-building project in *Mister Johnson* encouraged his own centering of *Arrow of God* on Wright's construction of the Umuwaro-Okperi road:

> It was clear to me that [Cary's] was a most superficial picture of—not only of the country, but even of the Nigerian character and so I thought if this was famous, then perhaps someone ought to try and look at this from the inside. (qtd. in Pieterse and Duerden 1972, 4)

The phenomenon of the "corrective" response may be far more broadly based than that seen in Achebe's reaction to Cary's novel. For example, as the articles by Egejuru and Hawkins demonstrate, even when the precursor is not a member of the immediate colonizer's society, the fact that his or her work (or works) forms part of the matrix of its metropolitan culture may be sufficient to invite "corrective" response.

Going further, many nontraditional works provide countervisions to those prevalent in metropolitan literature as a whole. For example, much postmodern Western literature has a dark and, at best, ambiguous view of the human condition; of humanity's ability to survive, much less correct, its own mistakes; and of the possibility of any form of salvation or redemption. Postmodern works by women, Third World writers, and minority authors, however, often provide a hopeful, affirmative, redemptive vision, and that vision may affect even the structure of the works in question. Many postmodern works by male writers lack closure, leaving their protagonists, at best, to face an open-ended, doubtful future (as in Salinger's *The Catcher in the Rye*), or, at worst, in a circular hell of their own devising (as in Sartre's *No Exit*, Beckett's *Waiting for Godot*, or Flann O'Brien's *The Third Policeman*). Many nontraditional works, on the other hand, provide positive, even triumphant, closure which affirms the possibility of salvation, often by self-empowerment and united action. Thus in Gloria Naylor's *The Women of Brewster Place*, the women can unite to tear down the wall which segregates them and African American men from dominant white American society once they learn to disregard differences of local origin, class background, religious orientation, and sexual preference.

Nor do African American women writers alone espouse such visions. In America and Europe, white women writers have created similar ones. For example, the lesbian relationship in Elizabeth Lynn's fairy tale, "The Woman Who Loved the Moon," and the relationship between the sisters in Beth Henley's play (and the film made from it), *Crimes of the Heart,* provide images of female mutual love, solidarity, and empowerment. In Britain, contemporary plays by male playwrights often offer either increasingly blackly comedic, anarchic visions, as in Joe Orton's *Loot,* or increasingly despairing ones, as in John Osborne's *Look Back in Anger,* Edward Bond's *Saved,* and David Hare's *Plenty.* But similar works by British women dramatists, like Caryl Churchill's *Top Girls, Fen,* and *Cloud Nine,* or Timberlake Wertenbaker's *Our Country's Good,* suggest solutions which can save society, male and female, from what these writers see as constrictive, destructive sociopolitical constructs (e.g., war, capitalism, sexism, and imperialism).

Many female African writers also offer positive visions. For example, in Ama Ata Aidoo's play *Dilemma of a Ghost,* an orphaned African American woman finds a new home and a new mother in Ghana. African male authors often do likewise, whether their visions are as mystically redemptive as Laye's in *The Radiance of the King* or as tentative as that found in the ending of Kenyan novelist Meja Mwangi's *Going Down River Road.* Mwangi's conclusion implies that African men and women may yet reunite, despite the dehumanizing effect of post/neocolonial urbanization, and restore family structures under the *aegis* of traditional village values.

Besides author-generated intertextuality, Worton and Still add, some contemporary theories treat readers as "co-producing" a given work with its author in that "the reader's experience of some practice or theory unknown to the author may lead to a fresh interpretation" of it by adding implications which would have been unknown to the original author but which validly interact with it (1990, 2)—as shown by the response of gender-conscious readers like Rukeyser to works which treat "man" and "human" as synonyms. Andrew Parkin's article shows us that adding a knowledge of theoretical approaches from non-Western cultures to the reading of Western texts may also be illuminating. For example, he suggests that a knowledge of Zeami's dramatic theories can provide an interpretational dimension for seemingly "static," or "conflictless" Western works—from medieval pageants to modern antirealistic works by dramatists like Strindberg, Yeats, Beckett, Pinter, Arrabal, Ionesco, and Shange—whose power is not adequately accounted for by Aristotle's *Poetics.*

Furthermore, juxtaposing literary texts which bear on one another—even ones by authors ignorant of one another's works—in the light of broader "texts" can produce valid "intertextual" readings of both narrowly and broadly defined "texts." For example, relating the dramatic representation of gender to socioeconomic context can illuminate our understanding of the images of woman as wife and woman as prostitute in Chikamatsu's *joruri* (puppet-play) *The Love Suicides at Amijima* and Aphra Behn's *The Rover,* plays produced in the similar socioeconomic contexts of Genroku Japan (c. 1673–1735) and Restoration England. That understanding may be further expanded by juxtaposing these plays to modern Western works, such as Ibsen's *Hedda Gabler* or the film *Pretty Woman,* which also dramatically represent (or refer to) woman as wife and prostitute in the contexts of contemporary capitalist, patriarchal cultures.

One may go even further by applying this "text" to works like the film *American Gigolo* which reverse the gender roles of prostitute and patron, or one may add to it such factors as racism and imperialism as Joy Kogawa does in her novels *Obasan* and *Itsuka* and Caryl Churchill does in her play *Cloud Nine.*

Such "texts" could also be explored in works which treat interracial sexual relationships, such as Spike Lee's film, *Jungle Fever,* Shelagh Delaney's play, *A Taste of Honey,* or Stephen Frears's film, *Sammy and Rosie Get Laid.* Further, one could expand these "texts" by relating Hwang's *M. Butterfly* to Frear's film, *My Beautiful Launderette;* in both, the interracial relationship is a homosexual one. Because sexuality, gender identity, and national identity frequently interact intertextually, expecially in works by colonized writers, one could further juxtapose any of these works to French Canadian Michel Tremblay's plays, such as *Hosanna,* in which the relationship is homosexual, or *Bonjour, là, Bonjour,* in which the incestuous relationship between Serge and Nicole may be read as a justification of Quebecois separatism.

However, valid intertextual readings often also require an understanding of the aesthetic codes governing conscious intertextuality in the culture in which a work was produced. For example, medieval Western writers so valued "auctorite" that many sprinkled their texts with references to (often unnamed) sources to lend them weight. Many premodern Japanese and Chinese works—especially poetry and Noh plays like Zeami's *Komachi at Sekidera*—exist in an intertextual matrix of allusions to earlier works and to the circumstances of their composition because such allusiveness was considered a mark of high art. Similarly, many African writers, especially playwrights (who often write for both a literate global audience and a partially illiterate local one), draw on the resources of their native oral culture, liberally sprinkling their texts with traditional proverbs which add metaphoric significance and ground their works in their indigenous culture as well as in the Western literary traditions from which they adopt some of their literary forms.

Modern Western writers are frequent practitioners of conscious intertextuality, too. The common use of biblical and classical allusion is the most obvious example of such practice, but more exotic examples also abound: Eliot's heavily annotated references to Sanskrit sources in *The Waste Land,* his adaptation of the medieval morality play genre in *Murder in the Cathedral,* Yeats's free adoption of Japanese Noh form for many of his plays, and Richard Murphy's English-language "versions" in *The Mirror Wall* of Old Sinhalese *Sirigiri* poetic graffiti are but a few. Indeed, Eliot asserts that "the most original parts of a work may be those in which the dead poets, [the author's] ancestors, assert their immortality most vigorously" (1941, 24), and the free interplay of multiple texts in Joyce's *Finnegan's Wake,* perhaps the quintessential modern novel, suggests that conscious intertextuality may be a hallmark of much modern Western literature.

However, for most writers in any society, what Harold Bloom calls "anxiety of influence"—the fear of being merely derivative of and overshadowed by a highly valued literary precursor (1973)—is a significant factor in determining how (and how openly) she or he uses other texts. Such anxiety is an old and pervasive problem, but it may play an especially important part in the works of many writers from "colonized societies," whose "anxiety of influence" extends not only to the works and writers to which they respond, but also to the cultures which produced those works and writers, if such are identified with the "colonizer." Drawing on a metropolitan work seemingly privileges it, its author, and its author's culture, calling into question the identity and authenticity of the colonized writer's work, self, and society, and thus implicitly undermining his or her nation's cultural autonomy, even when it has achieved political independence.

This problem, and that of the related issue of the identity of the colonized, is exacerbated for the author who writes in the language of the colonizer rather than in that of his or her indigenous culture, especially since, in such cases, the colonizer may "co-opt" the cultural identity of favored colonized writers. The practice of treating Yeats as an English writer, despite his efforts to assert an independent *Irish* identity, is a classic example of this phenomenon, and Canadians frequently complain that Margaret Atwood has similarly been "co-opted" by American critics. Many colonized writers have adopted various strategies to avoid or resist being so treated, even when doing so potentially limits their audiences. Major examples include Northern Irish poet Seamus Heaney's refusal to allow his poetry to be printed in *The Oxford Anthology of English Poetry;* Irish poet Micheal Hartnett's decision, signaled in his collection *A Farewell to English,* to write in both English and Irish; and Kenyan novelist Ngugi wa Thiong'o's abandonment of English for Gikuyu.

This problem is greater for colonized writers who do not speak their native culture's language and must rely on that of the colonizer, as Stephen Dedalus reflects in *Portrait of the Artist as a Young Man* when listening to the English-born dean of studies: "His language, so familiar and so foreign, will always be for me an acquired speech. I have not made or accepted its words. . . . My soul frets in the shadow of his language" (189). It is quite likely that a similar linguistic identity crisis affected Joyce's later "interlingual" as well as intertextual experimentation in *Finnegan's Wake,* just as it may affect the linguistic experimentation of such diverse African American writers as Langston Hughes, LeRoi Jones/Amiri Baraka, Don L. Lee, Nikki Giovanni, Lucille Clifton, and Gwendolyn Brooks.

The problem may be even more serious for writers from colonized societies whose ethnic heritage is that of the colonizer but who find themselves unable to identify fully with either the colonizer or the colonized, like the French Algerian Albert Camus or such European-South Africans as Alan Paton, Nadine Gordimer, André Brink, and Athol Fugard. Anglo-Irish writers, like J. M. Synge, Sean O'Casey, and Samuel Beckett, have the same problem, which may affect the linguistic inventiveness of Synge and O'Casey as well as Beckett's choice of French over English *or* Irish as his primary language of composition.

Paradoxically, however, as Neal Lester demonstrates, directly and openly adapting the work of an earlier writer from another, often dominant, culture is a major intertextual strategy which colonized writers frequently exploit to defuse the potential devaluation of their own culture inherent in intercultural intertextuality. Although it privileges the author and culture from which the original derives, such adaptation reciprocally privileges the adaptation and implicitly asserts its superiority as an "improvement" over the original.

Nor need the adapter be militarily colonized to adapt this strategy. In adapting a work like Euripides' *Hippolytus* as *Phaedra,* Seneca acknowledged Greek cultural prestige, but he also appropriated it and asserted *Roman* cultural superiority by "improving" his source according to Roman models. Jean Racine later did the same for French Enlightenment culture and Jansenist Roman Catholicism through his

Phaedra, and, later yet, Eugene O'Neill adapted the same story in *Desire Under the Elms,* thus imputing heroic tragic stature to the American experience (as he did in *Mourning Becomes Electra,* his revision of Aeschylus's *Oresteia*). However, O'Neill's revison of the Hippolytus myth also inverts Euripides' values: *his* Phaedra and Hippolytus *do* become lovers, thus prioritizing youth, new life, new values, and the New World over age, authority, the weight of tradition, and the Old World. Brian Friel similarly inverts Euripides' values in *Living Quarters,* his version of the myth; thus he grants Frank Butler—his Theseus and the representative of Ireland's resident colonizers—tragic dignity at the same time that he metaphorically strips him and his people of power and authority.

Such adaptation of classical Greek works has become a literary tradition. In *Antigones,* George Steiner discusses nearly fifty revisions of Sophocles' *Antigone,* many of which have political agendas. In a colonial or post-neocolonial context, the act of adapting a source which a writer from the metropolitan culture has also adapted allows the colonized adapter to assert cultural independence and equality by bypassing the colonizer's culture. Furthermore, such adaptation allows the adapter to directly comment on his or her own society, adding the prestige of the classic source to the commentary. For example, besides repudiating the colonizer's cultural hegemony, Jean Anouilh's French *Antigone* protests the Nazi occupation of France; *The Riot Act,* Northern Irish Tom Paulin's version of Sophocles' *Antigone,* protests British occupation of Northern Ireland; and South African Athol Fugard's incorporation of Antigone's trial scene into *The Island* protests the injustice of apartheid. Similarly, Nigerian Ola Rotimi's African adaptation of Sophocles' *Oedipus Tyrannos* as *The Gods Are Not to Blame* is a covert allegory of European culpability for the Biafran War; Nigerian Wole Soyinka's *The Bacchae of Euripides* indirectly comments on the African postcolonial internecine conflicts which are as destructive as the Dionysian madness which led Agave to destroy her own son; and *The Cure at Troy,* Seamus Heaney's adaptation of Sophocles' *Philoctetes,* is a hopeful plea for reconciliation in Northern Ireland as well as an acknowledgment that reconciliation would, itself, involve pain.

J. M. Synge goes further, declaring Irish cultural independence from English models and asserting a European, not English, identity for Ireland by adapting or drawing on both Classical *and* European works. He acowledges the influence of Euripides' *Alcestis* and Cervantes' *Don Quixote* on *The Playboy of the Western World,* in which he scathingly comments on Ireland's (un)readiness to rebel against England, despite her revolutionary rhetoric. *The Playboy'*s Pegeen Mike may be seen as

Synge's version of Ibsen's *Hedda Gabler* as well as as an embodiment of Ireland: like Hedda, she has the artistic sensitivity and innate desire for freedom to recognize and love the independent artist-hero; like Hedda, she succumbs to public opinion and repudiates her artist-hero; but, unlike Hedda, she lacks the final courage to rebel against her self-chosen fate—as, Synge implies, Ireland does. Similarly, both Synge's *The Shadow of the Glen* and Sean O'Casey's *The Plough and The Stars* may be seen as adaptations of Ibsen's *A Doll House*—even to the names of the female protagonists—but the two Anglo-Irish plays impute to Irish males even less virility, courage, love, and self-knowledge than are shown by Ibsen's Torvald, suggesting that there is even less hope for Ireland's social and cultural regeneration than for Norway's.

Soyinka's rewriting of Brecht's *The Threepenny Opera* (itself an adaptation of Gay's *The Beggars' Opera*) as *Opera Wonyosi* both denies British cultural hegemony over Nigeria by adapting a British work via a German adaptation, *and* criticizes corruption in postcolonial Nigerian society without directly blaming British imperialism for it. By drawing on two European sources, both critical of their *own* societies' corruption, Soyinka deflects any implication of Nigerian moral inferiority to England and counters the doctrines of the primarily French West African Negritude movement by warning newly independent African societies that they have no innate moral superiority to assure their salvation.

As Christopher Innes points out, African and Caribbean writers have frequently looked to Irish writers for models of empowering intertextual strategies (1978). This is because the Irish have had a longer history of colonization—including exposure to metropolitan culture, colonial "anxiety of influence," consequent identity problems, and post-neo-colonial experience—than most other colonized or previously colonized societies. Some African and Caribbean writers have even adapted Anglo-Irish works to their own cultural contexts, thus circumventing the colonizer and declaring solidarity with the colonized without abandoning the advantages of drawing on metropolitan culture. For example, among Caribbean writers, Mustapha Matura has adapted Synge's *The Playboy of the Western World* as *The Playboy of the Islands,* and Derek Walcott has adapted Synge's *Riders to the Sea* as *The Sea at Dauphin.*

Moreover, African, Caribbean, and, as Neal Lester says, African American writers have not confined themselves to Irish or other European models. Many firmly have grasped the nettle by adapting the major works of their colonizers, whether British or Euro-American. Among the most significant of such adaptations are the many rewritings of Shakespeare's *The Tempest* from the viewpoint of the colonized (usually conceived of as Caliban, though Uruguayan José Enrique Rodo's novel *Ariel* casts Ariel in that role). As Rob Nixon's "Caribbean and African Appropriations of *The Tempest*" demonstrates, responses to *The Tempest* have played a major role in the development of African and Caribbean anticolonialism. Literarily, it has been revised in Martiniquen Aimé Césaire's play *A Tempest*, Zambian David Wallace's play *Do You Love Me Master?*, Barbadian George Lamming's allegorical novel *Water with Berries*, Barbadian Edward Braithwaite's poem "Caliban," and Sierra Leonean Lemuel Johnson's volume of poems, *highlife for caliban.* Shakespeare's works have also been adapted by writers from other cultures. For example, modern British dramatist Edward Bond's *Lear* applies *King Lear*'s allegory of social disintegration and internecine violence to modern British society, and Akira Kurosawa's film *Ran,* though set in Sengokujidai Japan (c. late sixteenth century), applies it to modern Japanese society. Kurosawa's film *Throne of Blood* is, similarly, an adaptation of Shakespeare's *Macbeth,* as is Eugene Ionesco's untranslated *Macbett;* the former, though set in Kamakura Japan (c. thirteenth–fourteenth century), allegorically applies Shakespeare's vision of the socially destructive effects of greed and ambition to post-World War II Japan, just as the latter applies it to post-World War II Europe. Indeed, so richly does Kurosawa's *ouevre* intertextually relate to Shakespeare's that his film *Kagemusha,* set just before and during the 1575 Battle of Nagashima, suggests the kind of film that Shakespeare, were he a filmmaker dramatizing Japanese history, might have made. Not only does it, as Donald Richey says, "continue the director's reflections on the nature of power and consequently war" (204)—one of Shakespeare's major themes, as well—but it mixes tragedy, comedy, and spectacle in distinctly Shakespearian fashion.

Kurosawa has drawn on other Western (as well as non-Western) writers than Shakespeare, however, and some of his films have, in turn, been adapted by Western filmmakers. *The Idiot* is his Japanese adaptation of Dostoyevsky's novel, and *The Lower Depths* is his Japanese adaptation of Gorky's play. Conversely, his *The Seven Samurai* has been remade by American John Sturges as *The Magnificent Seven;* Italian Sergio Leone pirated his *Yojimbo* as *A Fistful of Dollars* (thus initiating the "spaghetti Westerns"), and American Martin Ritt remade *Rashomon* (itself based on two of Akutagawa Ryunosuke's short stories, "Rashomon" and "In a Grove") as *The Outrage.* Despite artistic differences, any one of his historical films and its Western adaptation could be fruitfully juxtaposed in the context of post-World War II culture(s), their relations to the past, and their artists' attempts to influence the present and the future by dramatically reconstructing that past.

Kurosawa, Sturges, Ritt, and Leone are far from the only filmmakers to adapt previous works, and such works can fruitfully be compared with their precursors to encourage a generation of students raised on film and television both to read more and to recognize the ramifications of intertextuality. Thus, *The Warriors,* a film about modern American gang culture, gains both new dignity and cultural depth when compared with its precursor, Xenophon's *Anabasis,* leading students to examine such questions as the nature of heroism and whether it can exist for the disadvantaged in the modern, materialist West. A much more complexly intertextual "cult" film, Brian de Palma's *The Phantom of the Paradise* draws on the spiritual implications of Marlowe's *Doctor Faustus* and Wilde's *The Picture of Dorian Gray* as well as on the Romanticism/romanticism of Goethe's *Faust* and Gounod's *Faust,* all of which it incorporates into a savagely satirical film, full of wickedly funny parodies of popular rock groups, about the contemporary music industry and the perennial theme of the costs of artistic and personal ambition.

Given the pervasiveness of literary intertextuality, each section of this book provides fruitful suggestions for intertextually relating works from traditional and nontraditional sources which illuminate the issue of identity, whether colonial, personal, or both. For example, Ronald Ayling's comments about the relationship between childhood and the colonial condition lead quite naturally to an examination of the role of children in works by colonized writers. Ken Goodwin points out that "the image of a new-born child . . . seems apt for a new land and a new nation" and so is frequently used to symbolize and define "the individual, the land, society, and the nation" (1988, 15) in Commonwealth literature, in which the child's survival or failure to survive implies hope or lack of hope for the nation's survival. He adds that the various incarnations of this literary "nation-child" share similar characteristics: "a prolonged process of birth, often painful; . . . a confused sense of parentage involving adoption or mystification," danger of abortion or death, "magic . . . or an elevated . . . significance surrounding the child; . . . and a sense of a new beginning or rebirth" (1988, 16).

His description fits numerous children in Commonwealth literature—one may instance the Half-Child in Soyinka's play for Nigerian independence, *A Dance of the Forests;* the aborted first child and hope for a second child in Canadian Margaret Atwood's novel, *Surfacing;* the orphaned Metis (Native American-European) sisters, Cheryl and

April, in Canadian Beatrice Culleton's novel, *In Search of April Raintree;* Rose's daughter in Australian Patrick White's novel, *Voss;* and the miraculous, telepathic children in Pakistani Salman Rushdie's novel, *Midnight's Children.* However, this pattern is not limited to Commonwealth literature, but appears frequently in post-neocolonial works of all provenances. For example, in Anglo-Irish drama, such a child is successfully born at the end of Denis Johnston's *The Moon in Yellow River,* but the child which is born at the beginning of Brian Friel's *Translations* dies as the British troops begin to ravage the land at the play's end.

One of the earliest such nation-children may be Pearl in Hawthorne's *The Scarlet Letter,* which reminds us that Hawthorne's United States, like modern Commonwealth nations, was a post-/neocolonial society and that its literature may, therefore, have much in common with theirs. Hawthorne's Pearl shows many of the characteristics Goodwin speaks of and, like the children he discusses, she is linked to the land and its aboriginal gods through her preference for the forest over the town and her isolation from the Puritan settlers.

Since Pearl and Hester both go to England, *The Scarlet Letter* may also be one of the first in a long line of colonial and post-/neocolonial novels about emigration, immigration, and/or the "been-to" experience (i.e., that of individuals from colonized or once-colonized societies who have "been to" the metropolitan center and returned home)—experiences which may occasion a greater identity crisis than the colonized would have otherwise experienced. Many of Henry James's works might be read in this light; although, like the protagonists of most such Commonwealth works, his heroines seldom make the transition as successfully as Pearl does.

Such works are very popular among colonial and post-/neo-colonial writers, whose works often demonstrate the cultural conflicts caused by the intersection of colonialism and expatriatism. For example, although expatriate Indian novelist Nirad Chaudhuri's *A Passage to England* (whose title suggests that it is a response to Forster's *A Passage to India*) records his negative impressions of England, many of his other works depict India in the colonizer's terms: as a backward, superstitious, dead society. On the other hand, John Pepper Clark does not denigrate his native Nigeria in his description of his temporary expatriation to the United States in *America, Their America,* a work whose unflattering look at the United States may have the valuable effect of opening the eyes of American students to the way they may be perceived by others.

Works about "been-to's" are especially popular and ubiquitous. In some, such as Balachandra Rajan's novels *The Dark Dancer* and *Too Long in the West* and Arun Joshi's novel *The Foreigner,* the return to the homeland is successfully accomplished, but, more often, it proves difficult. George Moore's short story "Home Sickness" and his auto-biographical *Hail and Farewell* record hopeful, nostalgic returns to Ireland, but both works' protagonists eventually accept the colonizer's stereotype of their native lands as backward and leave with relief. The heroine of Leena Dhingra's *Amritvela* is similarly disillusioned with India, but, though she leaves, she plans to return. Such works provide an interesting juxtaposition to works like Alex Haley's *Roots* which, to some extent, romanticize the ancestral homeland.

However, for some the return to the homeland is impossible. For example, the protagonists of Santha Rama Rau's autobiographical *Remember the House* and David Mura's *Turning Japanese,* like Thomas Wolfe's protagonist, find that they can't go home again; they no longer fit in. The same pattern is found in Anglo-Irish works such as Friel's plays, *Philadelphia, Here I Come!* and *The Loves of Cass McGuire,* in which "returned Yanks" are portrayed as deracinated individuals who have lost their Irish identity yet have not found and/or do not expect to find a satisfactorily compensatory identity in the United States. In African works, the resulting disconnection from native society may even prove fatal, as it does for Obi Okonkwo in Achebe's *No Longer at Ease* and for Freddie Namme in Kenyan Cyprian Ekwensi's *Jagua Nana.*

Recently, however, some expatriate writers, like Northern Irish Brian Moore and Indian Bharati Mukherjee, have begun treating emigration as a positive choice, a pattern particularly marked in Mukherjee's *Jasmine.* Some of Moore's protagonists follow careers which mirror Moore's own peripatetic one: the protagonists, respectively, of *The Luck of Ginger Coffey, An Answer from Limbo,* and *Fergus* are Irish immigrant writers in Montreal, New York, and Hollywood. All three initially feel dislocated but eventually embrace their new lives and lands.

The personal context of autobiography and autobiographical fiction may interest students in the interaction between historical, cultural, sociopolitical, and literary "texts" which might otherwise seem geo-graphically and/or chronologically "foreign" to them. Such diverse Western works as Augustine's or Rousseau's *Confessions,* Goethe's ostensibly autobiographical *The Sorrows of Young Werther* and *Egmont,* Byron's *Childe Harold's Pilgrimage,* Adams's *The Education of Henry Adams,* and Newman's *Apologia pro Vita sua* could, depending on the course level, be useful for demonstrating autobiography's many forms and dominant concerns, including education (whether formal or informal) and psychological, artistic, and/or spiritual maturation. However, juxtaposing them with autobiographical works from non-Western cultures could more clearly illuminate significant questions related to the liberating, socializing and/or oppressive effects of education, and the effects of gender, class, culture, political structure, ideology, and/or economics on one's definitions of maturity and/or sense of personal and communal or national identity.

Thus, the *Babur-nama,* the autobiography of Babur, the sixteenth-century founder of the Moghul dynasty in India, grants first-person insight into the personal, political, and military experience of a conqueror, as well as into the historical circumstances which surrounded his career. On the other hand, such autobiographical works as *The Black Obelisk,* Erich Maria Remarque's novel about post-World War I Germany; *Black Rain,* Ibuse Masuji's novel about the bombing of Hiroshima; or *Obasan,* Joy Kogawa's novel about the Japanese and Japanese Canadian experience in World War II, allow readers to share the experience of the conquered. This experience, as compounded by colonialism, may also be shared in autobiographical works such as South African Bloke Modisane's *Blame Me on History,* Barbadian Austin Clarke's *Growing Up Stupid Under the Union Jack,* Barbadian George Lamming's *In the Castle of My Skin,* or Egyptian Tâhâ Husayn's *An Egyptian Childhood* and *The Stream of Days.*

Many of these works bear out Ayling's observation that the pattern of growth seen in colonial (and post-neocolonial) autobiography may parallel that seen in an emerging nation, as do several Indian works, including Attia Hosain's *Sunlight on a Broken Column,* from Muslim India; Ved Mehta's *Mamaji* and *Daddy Ji,* from Hindu India; and Bapsi Sidhwa's *Cracking India,* which brings the two cultures, previously united by opposition to British rule, together in the context of the independence and subsequent partitioning of India, a seminal and traumatic experience for modern Indian and Pakistani history and identity. To Sidhwa's novel, in particular, one might add Sean O'Casey's autobiographies and Brendan Behan's autobiographical *Borstal Boy,* which recounts the experiences of an Irish teenager imprisoned in a British juvenile detention center for IRA bomb-making activities; both reveal that the partitioning of Ireland had a similar effect on Irish history and identity.

Ayling's observation may particularly fit African autobiographical literature which, James Olney writes, is "less an individual phenomenon than a social one" (1973, viii) because, as Thomas Knipp says, "Africans tend traditionally to see themselves not so much as individuals but as parts of the seamless whole of the community or tribe" (1986, 41). Thus, the African autobiographies mentioned by Ayling and Sarah Palmer, African novels about childhood and youth such as Cameroonian Ferdinand Oyono's *Houseboy* and Ngũgĩ's *The River Between* and *Weep Not, Child,* and even autobiographical poetry, like Nigerian Christopher Okigbo's collection, *Labyrinths,* tend to relate the growth and condition of the protagonist to that of his people. In them, alienation from the community is less marked and/or less sympathetically portrayed than in similar Western works about childhood such as Joyce's *Portrait of the Artist as a Young Man* or Salinger's *The Catcher in the Rye.*

However, it may be significant that Joyce's and Salinger's works deal with childhoods that are primarily urban. Many Western works which focus on isolated rural childhoods, like American Willa Cather's *My Antonia,* Canadian W. O. Mitchell's *Who Has Seen the Wind?,* and Canadian Ernest Buckler's *The Mountain and the Valley,* treat childhood and community as idyllically and nostalgically as many African and Indian works do, and their protagonists, though feeling more impelled to leave by their personal need for growth, demonstrate a similar regret for what is lost and a greater desire to maintain community with their people after departure.

Similar patterns appear in autobiographical and childhood narratives written by minority writers within North American culture. Though poor, the rural childhoods portrayed in works such as Canadian Metis Maria Campbell's *Half-Breed* have idyllic aspects. However, such pastoral Edens are often adversely affected by the intrusion of the dominant whites, a pattern which parallels that found in the works of colonized writers about village childhood, in which the effects of such intrusion range from social division, as in Ngũgĩ's *The River Between,* to torture and death, as in Oyono's *Houseboy,* to outright genocide, as in the Native American *Black Elk Speaks* or Vahan Totovents's *Scenes from an Armenian Childhood.*

Because, as Ayling points out, there are parallels between colonial and patriarchal oppression, relating the effects of gender on personal and/or communal identity to those of colonialism, urbanization, racism, and class further widens the broadly defined "intertextual" matrix of childhood narratives. One could explore this matrix by juxtaposing the works of women from different (sub)cultures. For example, works by non-Western women, such as those by the Indian writers Attia Hosain and Bapsi Sidhwa, could be related to those of North American minority writers such as J. California Cooper and Jade Snow Wong and/or to those by Western white women. The last group could include such American works as Sylvia Plath's *The Bell Jar;* Laura Cunningham's memoir of a Bronx girlhood, *Sleeping Arrangements;* or Beverly Donofrio's account of growing up as a "bad girl," *Riding in Cars With Boys.* Other such possibilities include British Antonia White's *Frost in May,* New Zealander Janet Frame's *To the Island,* and Canadian Alice Munro's *Lives of Girls and Women.* Even more light may be shed by juxtaposing such texts to works about male childhoods. For example, in both Baldwin's *Go Tell It on the Mountain* and White's *Frost in May* the protagonists also struggle against their fathers' repressive religions to achieve autonomy, and in both Baldwin's and Munro's works patriarchal figures attempt to control the protagonists and other children through physical and emotional violence.

Because colonial, minority, and women's experiences do not end with childhood, an even broader context can be developed by reading autobiographical works which do not limit their focus to it. *Black Elk Speaks,* Sean O'Casey's autobiographies, and Kwei-Li's *Golden Lilies,* the purported memoirs of a turn-of-the-century Chinese noblewoman, are but a few examples of such works. One could add such diverse minority autobiographical texts as *Before Freedom: Forty-Eight Oral Histories of Former North and South Carolina Slaves; Gemini,* Nikki Giovanni's account of her life as an African-American poet; *Soul on Ice,* Eldridge Cleaver's narrative justification of the events which led to his imprisonment for raping white women; *The Autobiography of Malcolm X,* which recounts his rejection of white society and its codes, including Christianity; Le Ly Hayslip's *When Heaven and Earth Changed Places,* her account of her transition from Vietnamese war-child to founder of a relief organization; or Joy Kogawa's sequel to *Obasan, Itsuka,* which chronicles her protagonist's personal, emotional, and political growth through her gradual involvement with the movement for redress for Japanese Canadians.

Because several of these works chronicle the processes by which their authors learned to question, protest, and/or rebel against both the social codes that restricted their lives and the laws that enforced them, they could also be juxtaposed with such otherwise dissimilar works as *The Man Died,* Wole Soyinka's record of his imprisonment for opposition to the Biafran War, or Ron Kovic's autobiographical novel (and the film made from it), *Born on the Fourth of July,* which documents how a patriotic young American who volunteered for duty in Vietnam became a Vietnam War protester.

Born on the Fourth of July, however, also documents another kind of marginalization: the experience of being physically handicapped. In this respect, it could be juxtaposed with such works as Helen Keller's *The Story of My Life,* Irish author Christy Brown's *My Left Foot* and/ or Brown's fictionalized version of it, *Down All the Days*—either of which could be paired with the film of *My Left Foot.*

Autobiographical writing relates well to historical literature, for, as Hugh says in Brian Friel's *Translations,* "it is not the literal past, the 'facts' of history, that shape us, but images of the past embodied in language" (1984, 445). Historical works can be about any "past" which is significant to writer and audience. Whatever their subject, however, they are intrinsically intertextual in the broad sense (and often in the narrow sense, too) because, as Christopher Murray says of historical drama, such works are "always . . . concerned with power, identity, and the national consciousness" (1988, 296). Although they often have other agendas as well, they attempt to influence the national consciousness by creating a shape for the past which justifies the author's view of how the nation should be defined and of who should hold power within it.

Such politically oriented literary rewriting of history has a long history. For example, Euripides' *Medea* greatly revises the original legend of Medea in order to rehabilitate the reputation of the city of Corinth and its rulers. Similarly, there is abundant evidence that many of Shakespeare's history plays dramatize the politically expedient Tudor "revision" of the history of the War of the Roses.

Examining dramatic works with historical themes is particularly useful from the viewpoint of broadly defined "intertextuality." Because they are aided by what Anthony Roche calls the "then-as-now in the perpetual present of the theatre" (1988, 230) and because they do not require literacy to be understood, these works address a larger local audience than most historical poetry or prose can reach. They are, therefore, especially popular in nations which have experienced cultural imperialism. In countries which have experienced other forms of imperialism, the colonial identity crisis strikes hardest at the literate minority who have been educated in the colonizer's educational system; in such countries, historical fiction is more prevalent than historical drama. But in nations which have experienced cultural imperialism, the colonial identity crisis is more wide-spread and requires a communal art form, accessible to literate and illiterate alike, to address it. Therefore, historical drama and film frequently most directly address the political and social issues most relevant to the community at large, using the past to validate the author's view of what the "nation's" political structure, methods, and goals should be. Such works attempt to reappropriate the people's past from their colonizers, and thus to reform the communal present and future.

Historical drama can include a broad diversity of forms, all of which can be linked intertextually through their political purposes. The heyday of medieval mystery plays was the fourteenth century, just as the first intimations of the Renaissance and the Reformation were beginning to be felt. Within this context, the complaints of the shepherds at the beginning of *The Second Shepherd's Play* take on a politically radical coloration which is not really ameliorated by the play's ending, for it is the poor, who can least afford it, who display *caritas* and establish their *bona fides* as true Christians, not the rich, who, the shepherds lament, oppress them. Such a levelling subtext matches well with the focus of Caryl Churchill's *Light Shining in Buckinghamshire*, written during Britain's postwar economic decline about seventeenth-century Britain, or with Margaretta D'Arcy and John Arden's *The Non-Stop Connolly Show*, written during the same period, which partially borrows the medieval cycle form to create a socialist mystery play about the life of Irish nationalist labor leader, James Connolly. However, the tendency of established religion to support the *status quo* in wartime also produces countertexts which portray religion as a repressive force during such periods, as may be seen in Shaw's *Saint Joan*, Arthur Miller's *The Crucible*, and Brecht's *Mother Courage*.

Because the achievement of peace after civil war or independence after foreign domination brings great social, political, and economic change, such periods tend to prolifically produce historical drama, usually written by playwrights who wish to grant history's *imprimatur* to their own visions of the shape of the newly emerging nation. Widely varied works from such periods attempt to create images of an idealized past according to which the renascent nation should reform itself and/ or warnings about the dangers which it may face if it takes what the dramatist considers a wrong turn. Such works include Shakespeare's history plays, which celebrate the unifying virtues of Tudor and/or Jacobean revisionary history and warn of the dangers of renewed Civil War should the ruler fail to provide a legitimate heir. Restoration historical tragedies like Otway's *Venice Preserv'd* similarly warn of the danger to liberty should the "wrong" party gain power. German Romantic historical tragedies like Schiller's *Wallenstein* celebrate the image of a unifying hero and warn of the dangers of failing to support one. Less optimistically, Soyinka's play favoring Nigerian independence, *A Dance of the Forests*, rejects the celebration of Africa's past glories if they do not include an honest recognition of her past faults which may, if ignored, lead to corruption and the stillbirth of the emerging nation. Soyinka's *Death and the King's Horseman,* on the other hand, assesses the deep cultural wounds inflicted on African culture by British imperial rulers, even when (or perhaps particularly when) they were well-meaning, and suggests that restoring past traditions is no longer possible now that the chain of legitimacy has been broken.

The history and mythological history plays of the Anglo-Irish Yeats and Lady Gregory, written just before and after Irish independence, and the historical films of the samurai-class Kurosawa, written after the end of America's postwar occupation of Japan, share a common political "text." All three writers are from classes which previously ruled their countries but which had been losing power for the better part of a century, and all three would like to see their classes' power restored in a newly independent nation. Thus, all exalt aristocratic ideals, portraying them as the only hope for their nation to become united, independent, and spiritually whole—and all three are gradually forced to admit the defeat of their hopes in increasingly dark works as their countries diverge more and more widely from their dreams.

The current troubles in Northern Ireland have produced a wide variety of historical plays about Ireland, each, however, with its own agenda and its own audience. These include two works which use Celtic Britain under the Romans as a metaphor for British domination of Ireland: British Howard Brenton's *The Romans in Britain* and Protestant Northern Irish David Rudkin's *The Saxon Shore.* While Northern Irish Catholic Frank McGuinness's *Observe the Sons of Ulster Marchinq Towards the Somme* sympathetically portrays the plight of Protestant loyalists, Rudkin's *Cries from Casement as His Bones Are Brought to Dublin* asserts the "Irishness" of Northern Protestant republicans. However, Northern Irish Catholic Brian Friel's historical plays, *The Enemy Within, The Freedom of the City, Translations,* and *Making History,* which range from the fifth century to recent history, provide one of the most wide-reaching, subtle analyses of the Northern Irish problem.

Historical poetry also lends itself to intertextual analysis or comparison. For example, many scholars think that the completed form of the Irish epic, *Tain Bo Cuailgne* ("The Cattle Raid of Cooley") was influenced by Vergil's *Aeneid*—itself an intertextual work which draws on Homer's *Iliad* and *Odyssey.* Other important examples include the three great Sanskrit epics—the *Mahabharata,* which Milton Foley discusses; the *Ramayana,* an account of Rama's heroic activities (which also appear in condensed form in the *Mahabharata*); and Kalidasa's fifth-century *Raghuvamsa,* an account of the history of Rama's dynasty. Like the *Iliad,* the *Odyssey,* and the *Aeneid,* they form an intertextual triad of epics which relate to one another in sophisticated literary and political fashion. For example, the last work in each triad shifts the focus from heroic to dynastic history, thus mirroring the growth of political complexity and the resulting need to celebrate and/or assert dynastic legitimacy over heroic action.

On the other hand, some historical verse laments the loss of past glories. Among them, one might count *Beowulf,* whose Geats are doomed to extinction, the Welsh poems attributed to Llywarch Hen, Tennyson's *Idylls of the King* and Longfellow's *Evangeline,* both influenced by the rapid cultural change of the nineteenth century, and H. I. E. Dhlomo's *The Valley of a Thousand Hills,* which laments the subjugation of South Africa's Black inhabitants.

Historical fiction frequently engages the intersection between historical, cultural, sociopolitical, and literary "texts" more directly and accessibly than the other historical genres. Compared to autobiographical works, for example, family chronicle novels grant the reader access to a wider variety of viewpoints as well as to a longer span of time, both of which allow greater complexity in the treatment of historical events and their effects. Western works which provide such perspectives, such as Trollope's Barsetshire series, which chronicles the effects of important changes in England during the period of its empire, can be profitably set against such works as Chinua Achebe's trilogy—*Arrow of God, Things Fall Apart,* and *No Longer at Ease*—about the changes which that same empire creates in a Nigerian family. Similarly, the decline of a family, mirroring the social conditions in which it lives, appears as a major theme in Ts'ao Chan's Chinese classic *The Dream of the Red Chamber* and Colombian Gabriel García Márquez's *One Hundred Years of Solitude,* in which the Buendia family's experience allegorically reflects the historical experience of Colombia and/or much of Latin America. This theme appears as well in Maria Edgeworth's *Castle Rackrent,* which chronicles the colonized's gradual reappropriation of power from the colonizer in seventeenth- and eighteenth-century Ireland with the aim of warning the Anglo-Irish that they risk losing control of Ireland through their own weaknesses and self-indulgence. From a very different perspective, the struggle between the generations in Chinese anarchist novelist Pa Chin's *Family* mirrors the political conflict between traditional China and the Chinese leftists who eventually made modern China a socialist state.

Another grouping could include works about war, including civil wars and rebellions. Some such works focus on prominent historical figures from significant conflicts in their culture's history and, in doing so, lend themselves to an examination of the complexities of the relationships between colonizer and colonized. For example, *The General in His Labyrinth,* García Márquez's novel about Simon Bolivar, the South American leader who freed much of South America from Spain, provides an illuminating contrast, both politically and stylistically, to Canadian Rudy Wiebe's realistic novel, *The Scorched-Wood People,* about Metis leader Louis Riel, whose 1884 rebellion to secure the rights of Metis and Native people in Saskatchewan ended in failure and execution.

Another focus could be on historical narratives which address the lot of more ordinary people in such conflicts. Stephen Crane's novel about the American Civil War, *The Red Badge of Courage;* Ernest Hemingway's novel about the Spanish Civil War, *For Whom the Bell Tolls;* and Erich Maria Remarque's German novel about World War I, *All Quiet on the Western Front* concentrate on the inglorious and dehumanizing effect of the battlefield experience; the last provides an especially interesting parallel text to Wilfred Owen's poems, such as "*Dulce et Decorum Est,*" which present a British view of the same war.

Remarque's novel and Owen's poems may fruitfully be juxtaposed to Jennifer Johnston's Anglo-Irish novel about World War I, *How Many Miles to Babylon?,* which like Frank McGuinness's play about the same war, *Observe the Sons of Ulster Marching Towards the Somme,* also addresses the relationship between colonizer and colonized. In it, Anglo-Irish Lieutenant Alexander Moore discovers that, in British eyes, he is as "Irish"—and therefore as "untrustworthy"—as his native Irish tenants, whom he has been taught to despise, and he is forced to decide where his loyalties—and his identity—lie. The relationship between colonizer and colonized under circumstances of war against an external enemy portrayed in Johnston's novel could profitably be related to that portrayed between whites and African Americans in the film *Glory.* Other examples include the relationship between non-Vietnamese tribesmen and Americans during the Vietnam War in Francis Ford Coppola's film *Apocalypse Now* (itself adapted from Joseph Conrad's *Heart of Darkness*) and the relationship between whites and Japanese Canadians during World War II in Joy Kogawa's *Obasan.*

The theme of inhumanity in the context of colonial wars for independence is developed in Frank O'Connor's short story "Guests of the Nation" and Albert Camus's "The Guest," both of which advance shared humanity as a higher value than nationalism. On the other hand, populist and/or radical revolutionary perspectives are provided in Ngugi's *Petals of Blood,* set in the context of Kenya's Mau Mau Rebellion, and *Shui-hu Chuan,* Shih Nai-in's fourteenth-century Chinese classic novel about Sung Chiang's rebellion during the Sung dynasty

(960–1280), which was translated into English by Pearl Buck as *All Men Are Brothers.*

The ways, as this entire collection suggests, in which works are intertextually related and/or can be intertextually examined are as limitless as the reading and experience of readers and writers alike. To heed the more zealous and/or anxious adherents of *either* the "canon" or "political correctness" would, in effect, be to throw the baby out with the bath, for both traditional and nontraditional writers have always refused to be limited by such orthodoxies. Furthermore, both speak to today's multicultural audience, and that audience should be encouraged to listen and respond so that the ages-long, ongoing, intertextual multi-logue (if I may be permitted a neologism) which constitutes the world's great literary tradition may continue.

References

Because many primary texts which are referred to in this article are also referred to in other articles, bibliographic entries for them are not repeated here.

Print Sources

Adams, Henry. *The Education of Henry Adams.* New York: Random House, 1990.

Anouilh, Jean. *Anouilh: Five Plays.* Vol. 1. Mermaid Dramabook Series. New York: Hill and Wang, 1958.

Ashcroft, Bill, Gareth Griffiths, and Helen Tiffin. *The Empire Writes Back: Theory and Practice in Post-Colonial Literatures.* New York: Routledge, 1989.

Atwood, Margaret. *Surfacing.* New York: Fawcett, 1987.

Augustine. *The Confessions of Augustine.* Translated by W. R. Connor and John Gibb. Latin Texts and Commentaries Series. Salem, NH: Ayer, 1979.

Babur. *Babur-Nama in English: Memoirs of Babur.* Translated by Annette S. Beveridge. 1921. Reprint. New York: South Asia Books, 1989.

Beckett, Samuel. *Waiting for Godot.* New York: Grove-Weidenfeld, 1984.

Before Freedom: Forty-Eight Oral Histories of Former North and South Carolina Slaves. Edited by Belinda Hurmence. New York: New American Library, 1990.

Behan, Brendan. *Borstal Boy.* Boston: Godine, 1982.

Behn, Aphra. *The Rover (The Banished Cavalier).* Swan Theatre Plays. London: Methuen, 1986.

Beowulf. Translated by Michael Alexander. New York: Penguin, 1973.

Bloom, Harold. *The Anxiety of Influence: A Theory of Poetry.* Oxford and New York: Oxford University Press, 1973.

Bond, Edward. *Lear.* New York: Hill and Wang, 1972.

———. *Saved.* Methuen Modern Plays Series. New York: Heinemann Educational Books, 1988.

Braithewaite, Edward. "Caliban." In *Islands.* Oxford and New York: Oxford University Press, 1969.

Brecht, Bertolt. *Mother Courage and Her Children.* Translated by Eric Bentley. New York: Grove-Weidenfeld, 1987.

———. *The Threepenny Opera.* Translated by Eric Bentley and Desmond Vesey. New York: Grove-Weidenfeld, 1964.

Brenton, Howard. *The Romans in Britain.* Revised edition. New York: Heinemann Educational Books, 1988.

Brown, Christy. *Down All the Days.* New York: Stein and Day, 1970.

———. *My Left Foot.* New York: Simon and Schuster, 1965.

Buck, Pearl. *All Men Are Brothers.* Translation of *Shui-hu Chuan.* New York: Grove Press, 1957.

Buckler, Ernest. *The Mountain and the Valley.* Toronto: McClelland and Stewart, 1961.

Byron, George Gordon. *The Complete Poetical Works of Byron, Vol. 2: Childe Harold's Pilgrimage.* Oxford and New York: Oxford University Press, 1980.

Campbell, Maria. *Halfbreed.* Lincoln: University of Nebraska Press, 1982.

Camus, Albert. *Exile and the Kingdom.* New York: Random House, 1965.

Cary, Joyce. *Mister Johnson.* Revised Modern Classics Series. New York: New Directions, 1989.

Cather, Willa. *My Antonia.* Boston: Houghton Mifflin, 1973.

Césaire, Aimé. *A Tempest.* Translated by Richard Miller. Ubu Repertory Theatre Publications Series: No. 14. New York: Ubu Repertory, 1986.

Chaudhuri, Nirad C. *A Passage to England.* New York: Random Century, 1990.

Chikamatsu Monzaemon. *Four Major Plays of Chikamatsu.* Translated by Donald Keene. New York: Columbia University Press, 1961.

Churchill, Caryl. *Cloud Nine.* New York: Routledge, Chapman, and Hall, 1985.

———. *Light Shining in Buckinghamshire.* New York: Routledge, Chapman, and Hall, 1982.

———. *Softcops and Fen.* Methuen Modern Plays Series. New York: Heinemann Educational Books, 1988.

———. *Top Girls.* New York: Heinemann Educational Books, 1988.

Clark, John Pepper. *America, Their America.* New York: Holmes and Meier, 1969.

Clarke, Austin. *Growing Up Stupid Under the Union Jack: A Memoir.* Toronto: McClelland and Stewart, 1980.

Cleaver, Eldridge. *Soul on Ice.* New York: McGraw-Hill, 1967.

Coleridge, Samuel Taylor. *Coleridge: Poems and Prose.* Penguin Poetry Library. New York: Penguin, 1985.

Conrad, Joseph. *Youth and Heart of Darkness.* World's Classics Paperbacks Series. Oxford and New York: Oxford University Press, 1984.

Culleton, Beatrice. *In Search of April Raintree.* Winnipeg: Pemmican, 1983.

Cunningham, Laura. *Sleeping Arrangements.* New York: A. A. Knopf, 1989.

D'Arcy, Margaretta, and John Arden. *The Non-Stop Connolly Show: A Dramatic Cycle of Continuous Struggle in Six Parts.* London: Methuen, 1986.

Dhingra, Leena. *Amritvela.* New York: Woman's Press, 1988.

Dhlomo, H. I. E. *The Valley of a Thousand Hills.* Durban, South Africa: Knox, 1941.

Donofrio, Beverly. *Riding in Cars with Boys: Confessions of a Bad Girl Who Makes Good.* New York: Morrow, 1990.

Dostoyevsky, Fyodor. *The Idiot.* Translated by David Magarshack. New York: Penguin, 1956.

Edgeworth, Maria. *Castle Rackrent.* New York: Norton, 1965.

Ekwensi, Cyprian. *Jagua Nana.* African Writers Series. New York: Heinemann Educational Books, 1987.

Eliot, T. S. *Murder in the Cathedral.* San Diego: Harcourt Brace Jovanovich, 1964.

————. *Points of View.* London: Faber and Faber, 1941.

————. *The Waste Land and Other Poems.* New York: Harcourt Brace Jovanovich, 1955.

Friel, Brian. *The Loves of Cass McGuire.* New York: Farrar, Straus, and Giroux, 1967.

————. *Selected Plays.* Irish Drama Selections 6. Washington, DC: The Catholic University of America Press, 1984.

Fugard, Athol, John Kani, and Winston Ntshona. *Statements: Three Plays.* New York: Theatre Communications Group, 1986.

Gay, John. *The Beggars' Opera.* New York: Penguin, 1987.

Giovanni, Nikki. *Gemini: An Extended Autobiographical Statement on My First Twenty-Five Years of Being a Black Poet.* New York: Penguin, 1976.

Goethe, Johann Wolfgang. *Egmont: A Play.* Translated by Charles Passage. New York: Ungar, 1985.

————. *Faust.* Translated by Walter Arndt. New York: W. W. Norton, 1976.

————. *The Sorrows of Young Werther and Selected Writings.* Translated by Catherine Hutter. New York: New American Library, 1962.

Goodwin, Ken. "The Image of the National Child in the Work of Atwood, Rushdie, Soyinka, and White." In *Literature and Commitment,* edited by Govind Narain Sharma, 15–25. Toronto: TSAR, 1988.

Gorky, Maxim. *The Lower Depths and Other Plays.* Translated by Alexander Bakshy and Paul S. Nathan. New Haven, CT: Yale University Press, 1959.

Hare, David. *Plenty.* New York: New American Library, 1985.

Hartnett, Michael. *A Farewell to English.* Dublin: Gallery Press, 1975.

Hawthorne, Nathaniel. *The Scarlet Letter.* New York: New American Library, 1959.

Hayslip, Le Ly. *When Heaven and Earth Changed Place.* New York: New American Library, 1990.

Heaney, Seamus. *The Cure at Troy.* New York: Farrar, Straus, and Giroux, 1991.

Hemingway, Ernest. *For Whom the Bell Tolls* New York: Macmillan, 1982.

Henley, Beth. *Crimes of the Heart.* New York: Penguin, 1987.

Hosain, Attia. *Sunlight on a Broken Column.* East Glastonbury, CT: Ind-US, 1981.

Husayn, Tâhâ. *An Egyptian Childhood.* Translated by E. H. Paxton. London: G. Routledge, 1932.

———. *The Stream of Days: A Student at Azhar.* Translated by H. Wayment. Revised edition. New York and London: Longmans, Green, 1948.

Hwang, David Henry. *M. Butterfly.* New York: New American Library, 1989.

Innes, C. L. "Through the Looking Glass: African and Irish Nationalist Writing." In *African Literature Today,* edited by Eldred Durosimi Jones, 10–24. *Africa, America and the Caribbean, Vol. 9.* London: Heinemann, 1978.

Johnson, Lemuel. *highlife for caliban.* Ardis New Poets in America Series. Ann Arbor, MI: Ardis, 1973.

Johnston, Denis. *The Dramatic Works of Denis Johnston.* Vol. 2. Washington, DC: The Catholic University of America Press, 1979.

Johnston, Jennifer. *How Many Miles to Babylon?.* New York: Avon, 1975.

Joshi, Arun. *The Foreigner.* Orient Paperback Series. East Glastonbury, CT: Ind-US, 1975.

Joyce, James. *Finnegan's Wake.* New York: Penguin, 1982.

Kalidasa. *Raghumvasa.* Translated by Gopal Raghunath Nandargikar. Delhi: Motilal Banarsidass, 1971.

Keller, Helen. *The Story of My Life.* New York: New American Library, 1988.

Knipp, Thomas R. "Poetry as Autobiography: Society and Self in Three Modern West African Poets." In *African Literature in Its Social and Political Dimensions,* edited by Eileen Julien, Mildred Mortimer, and Curtis Schade, 41–50. Washington, DC: Three Continents Press and The African Literature Association, 1986.

Kogawa, Joy. *Itsuka.* Toronto: Viking Penguin, 1992.

Kovic, Ron. *Born on the Fourth of July.* New York: Simon and Schuster, 1990.

[Kwei-Li]. *Golden Lilies.* New York: Viking Penguin, 1990.

Lamming, George. *In the Castle of My Skin.* New York: Schoken, 1987.

———. *Water with Berries.* New York: Holt, Rinehart, and Winston, 1972.

Lewis, Oscar. *La Vida: A Puerto Rican Family and the Culture of Poverty—San Juan and New York.* New York: Random House, 1966.

Llywarch Hen, poetry attributed to. In *Celtic Miscellany.* Translated by Kenneth Jackson. Classics Series. New York: Penguin, 1972.

Long, John Luther. *Madame Butterfly.* 1898. Reprinted in *Madame Butterfly, Purple Eyes, and Other Short Stories.* American Short Story Series. New York: Garrett Press, 1969.

Longfellow, Henry Wadsworth. *Evangeline and Selected Tales and Poems.* New York: New American Library, 1964.

Lowry, Malcolm. *Hear Us O Lord from Heaven Thy Dwelling Place.* New York: Carroll and Graf, 1986.

Lynn, Elizabeth. *The Woman Who Loved the Moon and Other Stories.* New York: Berkley, 1981.

McGuinness, Frank. *Observe the Sons of Ulster Marching Towards the Somme.* Winchester, MA: Faber and Faber, 1986.

Marlowe, Christopher. *Doctor Faustus.* Edited by John Jump. New York: Routledge, Chapman, and Hall, 1965.

Matura, Mustapha. *The Playboy of the West Indies.* New York: Broadway Play Publishing, 1989.

Mehta, Ved. *Daddy Ji.* New York: W. W. Norton, 1989.

———. *Mamaji.* New York: W. W. Norton, 1988.

Miller, Arthur. *The Crucible.* New York: Penguin, 1976.

Mitchell, W. O. *Who Has Seen the Wind?.* Toronto: McClelland and Stewart, 1991.

Mnthali, Felix. "The Stranglehold of English Lit." In *The Penguin Book of Modern African Poetry,* edited by Gerald Moore and Ulli Beier. 3rd ed. New York: Penguin, 1989.

Modisane, Bloke. *Blame Me on History.* New York: Simon and Schuster, 1990.

Moore, Brian. *An Answer from Limbo.* New York: Penguin, 1965.

———. *Fergus.* New York: Holt, Rinehart, and Winston, 1970.

———. *The Luck of Ginger Coffey.* New York: Dell, 1962.

Moore, George. *Hail and Farewell: Ave, Salve, Vale.* Washington, DC: The Catholic University of America Press, 1985.

———. "Home Sickness." In *The Untilled Field.* Gerrards Cross, England: Colin Smythe, 1976.

Mukherjee, Bharati. *Jasmine.* New York: Grove-Weidenfeld, 1989.

Munro, Alice. *Lives of Girls and Women.* New York: New American Library, 1974.

Mura, David. *Turning Japanese: Memoirs of a Sansei.* New York: Atlantic Monthly Press, 1991.

Murphy, Richard. *The Mirror Wall.* Winston-Salem, NC: Wake Forest Press, 1989.

Murray, Christopher. "The History Play Today." In *Cultural Contexts and Literary Idioms in Contemporary Irish Literature,* edited by Michael Kenneally, 287–308. Studies in Contemporary Irish Literature 1; Irish Literary Studies 31. Totowa, NJ: Barnes and Noble, 1988.

Naylor, Gloria. *The Women of Brewster Place: A Novel in Seven Stories.* New York: Penguin, 1988.

Newman, John Henry. *Apologia pro Vita sua.* New York: Doubleday, 1956.

Ngũgĩ wa Thiong'o. *Petals of Blood.* New York: Dutton, 1978.

———. *The River Between.* African Writers Series. New York: Heinemann Educational Books, 1965.

Nixon, Rob. "Caribbean and African Appropriations of *The Tempest.*" *Critical Inquiry* 13 (Spring 1987): 557–78.

O'Brien, Flann [Brian O'Nolan]. *The Third Policeman.* New York: New American Library, 1976.

O'Casey, Sean. *Three Plays.* New York: St. Martin's Press, 1969.

O'Connor, Frank. *Collected Stories.* New York: Random House, 1982.

Okigbo, Christopher. *Labyrinths: Poems.* New York: Africana, 1971.

Olney, James. *Tell Me Africa: An Approach to African Literature.* Princeton, NJ: Princeton University Press, 1973.

O'Neill, Eugene. *Three Plays.* New York: Random House, 1959.

Orton, Joe. *Complete Plays.* New York: Grove-Weidenfeld, 1990.

Osborne, John. *Look Back in Anger.* New York: Penguin, 1982.

Otway, Thomas. *Complete Works.* New York: AMS Press, 1926.

Owen, Wilfrid. *Collected Poems.* Revised edition. New York: New Directions, 1964.

Oyono, Ferdinand. *Houseboy.* Translated by John Reed. London: Heinemann Educational Books, 1974.

Pa Chin [Fei-Kan Li]. *Family.* New York: Gordon Press, 1976.

Paulin, Tom. *The Riot Act: A Version of Sophocles' Antigone.* Boston and London: Faber and Faber, 1985.

Pieterse, Cosmos, and Dennis Duerden, editors. *African Writers Talking: A Collection of Radio Interviews.* New York: Africana, 1972.

Plath, Sylvia. *The Bell Jar.* New York: Bantam, 1975.

Racine, Jean. *Phaedra and Other Plays.* Translated by John Cairncross. New York: Penguin, 1964.

Rajan, Balachandra. *Dark Dancer, A Novel.* Westport, CT: Greenwood Press, 1970.

———. *Too Long in the West.* East Glastonbury, CT: Ind-US, 1961.

Ramayana. Translated by William Buck. Berkeley: University of California Press, 1976.

Rao, Raja. *The Serpent and the Rope.* East Glastonbury, CT: Ind-US, 1968.

Rau, Santha Rama. *Remember the House.* New York: Harper, 1956.

Remarque, Erich Maria. *All Quiet on the Western Front.* New York: Fawcett, 1987.

———. *The Black Obelisk.* Translated by Denver Lindley. New York: Harcourt Brace Jovanovich, 1957.

Richey, Donald. *The Films of Akira Kurosawa.* Revised edition. Berkeley: University of California Press, 1984.

Roche, Anthony. "Ireland's *Antigones:* Tragedy North and South." In *Cultural Contexts and Literary Idioms in Contemporary Irish Culture,* edited by Michael Kenneally, 221–50. Studies in Contemporary Irish Literature 1; Irish Literary Studies 31. Totowa, NJ: Barnes and Noble, 1988.

Rodo, José Enrique. *Ariel.* Translated by Margaret S. Peden. Austin: University of Texas Press, 1988.

Rotimi, Ola. *The Gods Are Not to Blame.* London: Oxford University Press, 1971.

Rousseau, Jean-Jacques. *Confessions*. Translated by John M. Cohen. New York: Penguin, 1953.

Rudkin, David. *Cries from Casement as His Bones Are Brought to Dublin*. London: BBC, 1974.

———. *The Saxon Shore*. New York: Heinemann Educational Books, 1988.

Rukeyser, Muriel. "Myth." In *Breaking Open*. New York: Random House, 1977.

Sartre, Jean-Paul. *No Exit and The Flies*. Translated by Stuart Gilbert. New York: A. A. Knopf, 1947.

Schiller, Friedrich von. *Schiller's Works*. Translated by J. G. Fischer. 4 vols. Philadelphia: George Barrie, 1883.

Second Shepherds' Play. In *Stages of Drama: Classical to Contemporary Masterpieces of the Theatre*, edited by Carl H. Klaus, Miriam Gilbert, and Bradford S. Field, Jr. 2d ed. New York: St. Martin's Press, 1991.

Seneca, Lucius Annaeus. *Phaedra*. Translated by Frederick Ahl. Masters of Latin Literature Series. Ithaca, NY: Cornell University Press, 1986.

Shaw, George Bernard. *St. Joan, Major Barbara, Androcles*. New York: Random House, 1979.

Soyinka, Wole. *The Bacchae of Euripides: A Communion Rite*. New York: W. W. Norton, 1975.

———. *A Dance of the Forests*. Three Crowns Books. Oxford and New York: Oxford University Press, 1963.

———. *The Man Died: Prison Notes of W. S*. Noonday Series. New York: Farrar, Straus, and Giroux, 1988.

Steiner, George. *After Babel: Aspects of Language and Translation*. Oxford and New York: Oxford University Press, 1975.

———. *Antigones*. Oxford and New York: Oxford University Press, 1984.

Tain [*Tain Bo Cuailgne*]. Translated by Thomas Kinsella. Oxford and New York: Oxford University Press, 1970.

Totovents, Vahan. *Scenes from an Armenian Childhood*. Translated by Mischa Kudian. London: Oxford University Press, 1962.

Tremblay, Michel. *Bonjour, là, Bonjour*. Translated by John Van Burek and Bill Glassco. Vancouver and Los Angeles: Talonbooks, 1975.

———. *Hosanna*. Translated by John Van Burek and Bill Glassco. Vancouver and Los Angeles: Talonbooks, 1974.

Trollope, Anthony. *The Barsetshire Novels*. 6 vols. Oxford and New York: Oxford University Press, 1989.

Walcott, Derek. *The Sea at Dauphin*. New York: Noonday Press, 1991.

Wallace, David. *Do You Love Me Master?* Lusaka, Zambia: NECZAM, 1977.

Wertenbaker, Timberlake. *Our Country's Good*. The Royal Court Writers Series. London: Methuen, 1989.

White, Antonia. *Frost in May*. Boston: G. K. Hall, 1987.

White, Patrick. *Voss*. New York: Penguin, 1984.

Wiebe, Rudy. *The Scorched-Wood People*. Toronto: McClelland and Stewart, 1977.

Wilde, Oscar. *The Picture of Dorian Gray.* Oxford and New York: Oxford University Press, 1981.

Worton, Michael, and Judith Still, editors. *Intertextuality: Theories and Practices.* Manchester and New York: Manchester University Press, 1990.

X, Malcolm. *Autobiography of Malcolm X.* New York: Ballantine, 1987.

Xenophon. *March Up Country: A Modern Translation of the Anabasis.* Translated by W. H. Rouse. Ann Arbor: University of Michigan Press, 1958.

Films

Beresford, Bruce. *Crimes of the Heart.* 1986.

Coppola, Francis Ford. *Apocalypse Now.* 1979.

De Palma, Brian. *The Phantom of the Paradise.* 1974.

Frears, Stephen. *My Beautiful Laundrette.* 1986.

———. *Sammy and Rosie Get Laid.* 1987.

Hill, Walter. *The Warriors.* 1979.

Kurosawa, Akira. *The Idiot.* 1963.

———. *Kagemusha.* 1980.

———. *The Lower Depths.* 1957.

———. *Ran.* 1985.

———. *Rashomon.* 1951.

———. *The Seven Samurai.* 1954.

———. *Throne of Blood.* 1957.

———. *Yojimbo.* 1961.

Leone, Sergio. *Fistful of Dollars.* 1964.

Marshall, Gary. *Pretty Woman.* 1990.

Ritt, Martin. *The Outrage.* 1964.

Schrader, Paul. *American Gigolo.* 1980.

Sheridan, Jim. *My Left Foot.* 1989.

Stone, Oliver. *Born on the Fourth of July.* 1989.

Sturges, John. *The Magnificent Seven.* 1960.

V APPROACHES TO CHINUA ACHEBE'S *THINGS FALL APART*

The essays in this section explore a variety of pedagogical and theoretical approaches to Chinua Achebe's *Things Fall Apart*. Nigerian scholar Ndiawar Sarr examines the importance of the historical and cultural context to an understanding of the concepts of heroism reflected in Achebe's protagonist, Okonkwo. Bruce Henricksen examines the complexities and shifting perspectives with which readers may approach such a work, and Norman McMillan, Julian Wasserman, and Liam Purdon consider the values of teaching Achebe's novel in the context of Western "classics" such as *The Aeneid* and *Beowulf*. The bibliographic essay explores the implications of these various approaches to other such clusterings of both traditional and nontraditional texts, with special attention to feminine perspectives, and to the values of teaching fantasy, science fiction, and the sacred literatures of many cultures.

21 Chinua Achebe:
The Bicultural Novel and
the Ethics of Reading

Bruce Henricksen
Loyola University

Ostensibly, Marlow's narration, which constitutes all but a few paragraphs of Joseph Conrad's *Heart of Darkness,* functions as a corrective to the propagandistic rhetoric with which Europe justified its imperialistic enterprise in Africa. As the novel opens, a "framing narrator" has apparently just delivered a speech in praise of England's imperialist past, glorifying such adventurers as Sir Francis Drake and Sir John Franklin. Marlow speaks in response to this narrator, reminding him that England, too, has been a dark place (Conrad [1902] 1988). The corrective intentions of Marlow's narrative can be understood in terms of what Michel Foucault called "counter-memory," the memory which restores what official ideologies have repressed or conveniently forgotten (Thomas 1989). But, as numerous readers and critics have noticed in recent years, Marlow's own narration does not escape all of the assumptions of imperialism. Marlow, one might say, is "colonized" by imperialistic attitudes even as he attempts to critique those attitudes. Chinua Achebe has presented the strongest version of this revisionary reading of Conrad.

Achebe's essay "An Image of Africa: Racism in Conrad's *Heart of Darkness*" boldly attacks one of the most highly praised texts in the English tradition. Despite the deep skepticism that Conrad reveals concerning the validity of the imperialist enterprise, Achebe argues that Conrad's novel is the epitome of racism, an "offensive and deplorable book" which purveys the usual Western prejudices about the African while refusing to represent Africans and their culture in anything like their legitimate humanity (Achebe 1989, 14). One of Achebe's most telling observations is the fact that Marlow, Conrad's narrator, rarely even suggests that the Africans have languages of their own. At one point the cannibals grunt a few words in pidgin English about eating enemies, their only speech serving paradoxically to underscore their uncivilized natures.

> It is clearly not part of Conrad's purpose to confer language on the "rudimentary souls" of Africa. In place of speech they made a "violent babble of uncouth sounds." They "exchanged short grunting phrases" even among themselves. But most of the time they were busy with their frenzy. (Achebe 1989, 8)

To rob the other of a voice and therefore of the possibility of self-representation remains a pervasive form of domination. Teaching literatures originating in recently or currently marginalized cultures and societies is one way to respond to the ethical imperative of listening to the other's story—of acknowledging the rights of others to speak for themselves. Indeed, Achebe's *Things Fall Apart* can profitably be studied in conjunction with Conrad's *Heart of Darkness* as an attempt to restore the voices silenced by that earlier novel—as another perspective on roughly the same historical period depicted by Conrad. If Conrad's counter-memory was subtly inhabited by the ills it sought to diagnose, Achebe in his turn counters Conrad's memory. But for the Westerner with the standard training in English, European, or United States literatures—and therefore with some of the same ideological baggage Conrad brought to his representation of Africa—to "teach" Third World texts such as Achebe's and to listen to these other voices requires a willingness to acknowledge the limitations of one's own experiences and to make those limitations an aspect of the pedagogy. To listen to the other as though one is an authority on his or her discourse is to deny the very otherness to which one should be open. Among "other" things, then, our encounter with Third World literatures teaches an awareness of the constraints and limitations in force within our own community of interpretation.

The problem, more bluntly stated, is that many African writers either claim or intimate that Europeans and Americans are disqualified, by virtue of their positions as the heirs of colonialism, from criticizing the African novel. This issue is raised at the outset of Umbonal Ngara's *Stylistic Criticism and the African Novel,* and it is raised by Achebe himself as he castigates "colonialist criticism" in his essay bearing that title (Achebe 1989, 68–90). The extreme of this position is presented in *Toward the Decolonization of African Literature,* a book (published as recently as 1983) which is willing to find malicious, imperialistic attitudes in anything a Western reader or teacher might think to say about African literature. I quote from the "Introduction":

> The task at hand is to end all foreign domination of African culture, to systematically destroy all encrustations of colonial and slave mentality. . . . In Africa's present situation, Africa's prose literature is under attack from dominant and malicious eurocentric

criticism. Africa's poetry is being crippled by malicious praise. (Chinweizu 1983, 1)

While the claim to cultural uniqueness is one way in which a nation affirms its autonomy, it is not unproblematical. It is difficult to demonstrate, as Mary N. Layoun points out, "that there is something distinctly and unalterably Greek or Egyptian or Palestinian or Senegalese or whatever, essences waiting out there to be recognized and represented as *the* national identity and manifested in a (thenceforth fixed) national culture" (Layoun 1988, 60).

Achebe has chosen to write in English and has claimed, in his discussion with Phanuel Egejuru, that his intended audience includes anyone who reads English (Egejuru 1980, 16–19). While there are certainly assumptions a Western critic or teacher can make that are either insulting or simply wrong on a factual level, it would not be consistent for a writer to address an audience and then demand only respectful silence in response—silencing the other, after all, was Conrad's sin. And Achebe's essay does not attempt to silence all Western response, although it does enumerate certain kinds of "colonialist" (or, more appropriately, neocolonialist—the essay was published in 1975, years after Nigerian independence) responses that are objectionable in his view.

Perhaps a more subtly nuanced question would be whether the critical tools that have been fashioned for the understanding of Western literature by Western readers are appropriate for the reading of African novels. Or is African literature "an autonomous entity separate and apart from all other literatures" and therefore requiring its own critical tools (Chinweizu 1983, 4)? If for no other reason than his choice of titles, taken from Western poetry, Achebe seems to posit a certain relationship with Western fiction rather than the radical difference many other Third World authors have insisted upon.

One tool Western criticism has found useful for analysis of Western fiction is the distinction between the *story* and the *discourse;* the story is the totality of fictional events that we pretend "really" happened, while discourse refers to all the effects of telling—the ordering or plotting of the events, the choice of a point of view, of levels of diction and style, and so on. If story is the object, discourse is the lens through which it is viewed and which gives it its shape and appearance. A careful analysis of the elements of discourse in any given work enables one to see how the effect of a narrative results from artistic choices— from aspects of narrative form, and not simply from the objective nature of the reality being represented (Chatman 1978). One might observe, for instance, that while Achebe's discourse in *Things Fall Apart* serves to make the world of the novel seem familiar to a Western reader, his story, in crucial ways, remains distanced from the Western experience. In other words, *Things Fall Apart* seems to have been designed to offer such a Western community a tolerable, medicinal dose of the Ibo's difference, while at the same time creating areas of familiarity. This movement between familiarity within the discourse and difference within the story is one aspect of the novel's biculturalism.

The novel opens with the question of reputation, of reprehensible laziness versus economic success, and it suggests that Okonkwo is driven by an Oedipal desire to outdo his failed father. Thus, Achebe creates a socially and psychologically familiar world for the Western reader, whereas Conrad's Marlow had repeatedly referred to his African journey as a journey into a prehistoric past or even another world where one lost all bearing: "Going up that river was like travelling back to the earliest beginnings of the world" (Conrad [1902] 1988, 35). Achebe's style assures that we do not have perceptions like Marlow's. Thus, key Ibo terms are defined, as when we are told that the *ndichie* are the elders, or that one's *chi* is one's personal god (Achebe 1959, 16, 20). Elsewhere Achebe pauses to explain to the reader the function of the god Ani in the lives of the people, and the Ibo myth reported at most length, concerning the bird and the tortoise, is remarkably close to a fable Westerners have all heard (Achebe 1959, 37, 91). Finally, when he refers to one person's role as "the town crier" and another's role as "share cropping," he lends the world of the novel the folksy familiarity of the recent American past (Achebe 1959, 13, 25).

In addition to the familiarity of Achebe's language, the novel's mingling of the familiar and the "other" may be seen in the apparent superimposition of a tragic plot upon the representation of the impact of colonialism upon the Ibo. Okonkwo has many of the qualities of the tragic hero—a kind of stature mixed with a debilitating hubris— and the assumption here would be that this tragic plot, plotting also being an element of discourse, is typically Western. And, in support of this plotting, certain verbal choices, as when Achebe refers to the practice of consulting "the Oracle," seem to echo classical Western literature. The story of traditional Ibo culture is brought closer with the lens of tragic emplotment, which is already familiar to us. But these assumptions must be made tentatively, since the Western reader, in all probability, has no way to encounter the traditional oral myths of Ibo culture directly, and therefore this reader cannot be certain of how much of a foreign shape—foreign from the Ibo perspective—is being given to the Ibo way of experiencing time and history by virtue of Achebe's plotting of his story as a tragedy and by virtue of his choosing a Westernized discourse.

In *Black Time,* Bonnie J. Barthold argues that Third World peoples experience time in ways different from the linear, Western model, and one of her chapters concerns Achebe's *The Arrow of God.* But she does not notice that in *Things Fall Apart* one can see a linear movement toward an altered future, largely, but in Achebe's discourse not entirely, the result of the impact of the colonist. This linear time sense is superimposed upon the cyclical model of time that was in place in the agrarian community at the outset. Perhaps telling the Ibo story in a Westernized discourse replicates the impact of Western structures of thought, particularly of time and history, upon the Ibo. If so, the novel's subject matter, the encroachment of the West upon the Ibo, is subtly mimed or embodied in the problematics of the novel's form.

But if Achebe invites a comparison between certain aspects of Ibo and Western experience, the Western reader—and here is one of the points Achebe insists upon in "Colonial Criticism"—must resist essentialistic readings that universalize the African experience. American or English readers who praise the African novel for having characters and situations comparable to their own, and who conclude that the novel is about the "universal" aspects of human experience, may be committing a kind of cultural violence, since it is likely that these readers are actually taking what is local or Western as their measure of the universal. In other words, readings and arguments that posit universals and essences are given to ethnocentrism in unacknowledged ways.

Years ago Ferdinand de Saussure, the Swiss linguist, pointed out that the associations sanctioned by one's own language or system of representation—one's own "signs"—will appear to conform to reality, but that this appearance is misleading because these associations are arbitrary. In cultural terms, Saussure's principle of the arbitrariness of the sign means that different systems of representation will reveal the world differently and that no one system is necessarily more true or natural than another. Achebe objects to readings that take a Western system of representing the world—such as the conventions of the "realistic" novel—as natural and that praise foreign writers for finding universal truths when those writers seem to mime those Western conventions. The critic Achebe refers to in the following passage has praised an African novel by saying its characters could easily be imagined in American settings:

> Does it ever occur to these universalists to try out their game of changing names of characters and places in an American novel, say, a Philip Roth or an Updike, and slotting in African names

just to see how it works? But of course it would not occur to them. It would never occur to them to doubt the universality of their own literature. In the nature of things the work of a Western writer is automatically informed by universality. It is only other writers who must strain to achieve it. (Achebe 1989, 76)

While agreeing with Achebe, one might also point out that his own familiarizing discourse in *Things Fall Apart* may have helped to plant the trap of universalizing interpretations.

If one must resist universalizing readings, a roughly opposite temptation must also be critiqued, the temptation to see the other as mysterious, inscrutable, and exotic. It is the extreme version of this characterization that Achebe objects to in *Heart of Darkness,* with its reliance upon the myth of darkest Africa. As Martin Green argues, the adventure tale in English since Defoe's *Robinson Crusoe* (but one could certainly go back at least to Shakespeare's *The Tempest*) has been complicitous with the politics of imperialism, infusing "England's will with the energy to go out into the world and explore, conquer, and rule" (Green 1979, 3). A common element in the adventure tale is the representation of the other as an exotic zone, inviting quasi-libidinal exploration and conquest. This thesis is also found in Edward Said's *Orientalism,* orientalism being "a kind of Western projection onto and will to govern over the Orient" (Said 1979, 95).

The Commissioner at the end of *Things Fall Apart* finds merely curious the Ibo custom by which only strangers may bury the body of the person who died by suicide. He echoes, even in his fastidious, no-nonsense self-concept, the affiliation between imperialism and the impulse to exoticize. His projected book should be seen as an allusion to the essay on savage customs that Kurtz writes in Conrad's *Heart of Darkness.* The Commissioner's thoughts conclude Achebe's novel:

> The story of this man who had killed a messenger and hanged himself would make interesting reading. One could almost write a whole chapter on him. Perhaps not a whole chapter but a reasonable paragraph, at any rate. There was so much else to include, and one must be firm in cutting details. He had already chosen the title of the book, after much thought: *The Pacification of the Primitive Tribes of the Lower Niger.* (191)

Achebe's novel is the antithesis of the imperialistically affiliated adventure story, and the reader must resist any temptation to turn the act of reading into an adventure of reading—into an exoticizing of the African, which is to say into "interesting reading." *Things Fall Apart* is not a bit of exotica—a merely more sophisticated travel brochure. Indeed, the many ways Achebe familiarizes the story of Ibo life may be an artistic attempt to forestall such exoticizing readings. And the final words of the novel, the Commissioner's projected title, constitute a sort of framing device that perhaps echoes Conrad's use of a frame. Whereas Conrad ends by shifting our attention to the response of one of Marlow's auditors to his tale, Achebe concludes by shifting our attention from his own writing to our Western discourses (Conrad's among them) upon Africa.

Both the universalizing and the exoticizing readings, then, have affiliations with imperialist ideology, and both reveal a deafness to the actual voice of the other. An ethical reading must find a vocabulary that resists these tendencies, which have come to seem so natural in Western discourse.

Communication requires that the artist and the audience share certain beliefs and assumptions, and this sharing occurs in the discourse of *Things Fall Apart.* But Achebe's story maintains a sense of the difference and uniqueness of Ibo culture. In this regard, the religious ceremonies involving ancestor worship will appear strange to many Western readers, and the strangeness is enhanced by Achebe's refusal to translate all italicized Ibo terms. Further, the practice of killing twins as abominations and the ritual/political murder of the child, Ikemefuna, will seem, in the language of Conrad's narrator, "savage" and "unspeakable."

I do not think that the ethics of reading require one to withhold judgment of all of the tribal practices found within the story; at least the novel itself does not demand such an extreme of cultural relativism. Achebe utilizes narrative omniscience—an aspect of discourse—at the end of the seventh chapter to report on the dissolution of a cultural identity within Nwoye as a result of Ikemefuna's killing, and this suggests that things are beginning to fall apart even before the advent of the white man. Such killing no longer meets the needs of the people (Okonkwo, too, is tormented by his deed) and very likely would have been abandoned without the pressure of the colonists. One can question the violence of colonialism without naively approving of all the old practices of the colonized.

Be that as it may, Achebe set out to represent the people who were silenced—who were literally given no language—by a Western writer such as Conrad. The difficulty is that in choosing a Western language and a Western generic mode, he may have reinscribed some of the same problems he exposes in Conrad's text, just as Conrad's text reinscribed some of the blindnesses of colonialism it set out to critique. Conrad robs the African of language, but Achebe represents the African within a Western language and genre. The extent to which these forms of representation blur or distort the absent (to us) reality to which they refer is not precisely knowable. A cliché has it that all translation involves an element of betrayal. What, then, is the status of an "original" (Achebe's narrative of the Ibo past) that is *already* a "translation" (written in modern English and plotted as a Western tragedy)?

It may seem unsettling that the most appropriate response in a Western pedagogy is simply to raise such questions rather than offer definitive answers. Teachers are paid to know things. But what we must know in such cases is precisely the limits of our knowledge. To posit the other within our pedagogical discourses as entirely knowable is itself a form of violence, not unlike Conrad's simplified representations to which Achebe so forcefully objected. The ethics of our reading and our pedagogy demand, in the particular kinds of situations referred to here, the openness implied in deferring finalizing judgments.

And yet the preceding paragraphs rest upon a number of assumptions which may be wrong. Literary theory holds that all texts imply their ideal audience, for instance, and I have assumed that the Western reader is Achebe's intended audience. But this is an issue that has been widely disputed, and the ease with which I have assumed that the text implies a Western reader may itself be a form of imperialism—a reinstatement of the form of appropriation I ostensibly critiqued when discussing universalizing and exoticizing readings. To what extent, then, does reading always enact a ritual of appropriation, or how can it best be avoided?

Some of Achebe's Nigerian critics nave argued that to write of Ibo culture to a Western audience and in the language of the colonizer is to abandon what they claim is the artist's obligation to address his or her own people. *Toward the Decolonization of African Literature* announces that its companion anthology of African writings will exclude "off-track" works "directed either at no community at all, or to the wrong one" (Chinweizu 1983, 6). And even more recent, although not written in specific reference to Achebe, is the statement of Abdul R. JanMohamed and David Lodge in their "Introduction" to *The Nature and Context of Minority Discourse:* "Every time we speak or write in English, French, German, or another dominant European language, we pay homage to Western intellectual and political hegemony" (JanMohamed and Lodge 1990, 2). The difficulties are clearly dramatized by the fact that JanMohamed and Lodge make this statement in English, a language that various minorities have in common in spite of its historical affiliation with oppression. Although there would be politically valid reasons for addressing the Western reader about the societies that colonialism has so drastically altered, Achebe, sensitive to such criticisms and difficulties, has claimed that his intended audience is anyone who reads English, including the English-speaking Nigerian. And in his interview with Egejuru, Achebe denies that he offers explanations in *Things Fall Apart* that are aimed especially at foreigners. A healthy skepticism about such authorial claims is conventional in Western literary studies, but is it appropriate to read according to these conventions in such a highly politicized situation, when one's own reading runs so many dangers of becoming, like Marlow's supposedly oppositional discourse, just another form of imperialism? In any case, the issue of Achebe's audience can be partially defused by remembering that many Nigerians are not Ibo and might therefore require the same explanations as a Western reader.

At the least, one can foreground the assumptions that enable a reading, as I have tried to do, and acknowledge their tentative nature. It is essential to recognize the political issues involved in Achebe's choice of English and in the question of his implied audience, but it seems inappropriate for the Western reader to enter with too much energy a debate that originates elsewhere, in social and historical circumstances we have not known and that involve choices we have enjoyed the luxury of not having to make.

If the problematics of Achebe's own bicultural identity are implicit in the story/discourse opposition in *Things Fall Apart, No Longer at Ease* thematizes bicultural identity explicitly. And if justice demands that one acknowledge the right of the other to speak, analysis reveals the dependence of each person's speech and identity—the dependence of every "subject position"—upon the various discourses, viewpoints, and ideologies that constitute the network of forces within which people live. *No Longer at Ease,* which first appeared in 1960 shortly after Nigerian independence, offers a pessimistic analysis of the possibility of a morally coherent bicultural identity in a postcolonial society that is an unstable composite of traditional Nigerian and colonial attitudes, beliefs, and practices. It depicts Obi Okonkwo's fall from traditionally and communally defined identity into a particularly Western form of individualism.

Obi, the grandson of the protagonist of *Things Fall Apart,* has been educated in England and has returned to Nigeria to become part of the ruling elite. Achebe's reading of Western literature holds that it has played a particularly powerful role in promoting a form of individualism that sets the subject against his or her culture or community (Achebe 1989, 52–53). Thus, he makes his protagonist into a student of English literature. Obi is caught between the traditional values of his tribe and the imperfectly grafted mores of the West, and his initial shock at the corruption rampant in the civil service is eventually superseded by his own acceptance of a bribe. The novel is framed with references to his trial.

One of the more subtle effects of the novel lies in Achebe's refusal to rest with a simple opposition between the Westernized bureaucracy of the city and the traditional values of the town. Instead, we find that the tribe itself is also a site of social contradictions. They have invested in Obi's English education in hopes of benefitting from the governmental position it will earn him. They expect that Obi will use his position to give preferential treatment to people of Umuofia, and they are therefore disappointed in his decision to study literature. Obi's father, the Nwoye (now called Isaac) who adopted the Christian religion in the aftermath of Ikemefuna's killing in *Things Fall Apart,* nonetheless clings to traditional values in his refusal to accept Obi's engagement to an *osu.* And the final irony is that the tribe criticizes Obi not for becoming corrupt, but for accepting such a *small* bribe.

Lagos, the capital of Nigeria and the site of Obi's fall, is the unsatisfactory, even monstrous, offspring of a wedding between the values of the traditional Ibo village and the values of London. If in the village, for instance, transactions are accompanied by the giving of the kola nut, in London transactions involve the exchange of fixed payments. In some liminal space between these two exchange systems is the system of bribery in place in Lagos. Although, as we saw, the Umuofia of the novel's present is not untouched by the West, from the perspective of the village, Lagos—with its automobiles and bars— looms as a spreading cancer from the West. But from a London perspective Lagos seems primitive. Lagos is a corruption of the values of both London and of traditional Ibo culture.

In a society so deeply marked by contradictions, Obi lacks the ability to find an authentic position from which to speak and be. He is a product of what Mikhail Bakhtin called the "speech diversity" of his society. According to Bakhtin, the novel arose out of historical conditions in which ancient structures of authority gave way to a diversity of interests—in Bakhtin's terms, the "monologue" of authoritarian structures is replaced by "dialogue." The rich potential of the novel as a genre lies in its ability to represent the competing voices of a society in flux (Bakhtin 1981). *No Longer at Ease,* filled with clashing and hybridized idioms, almost seems to have been written to illustrate Bakhtin's point. In fact, many of the difficulties facing the new Nigeria were quite literally linguistic. Of Achebe's novel, Shatto Arthur Gakwandi writes:

> Within the city the author tries to capture the speech habits of the colonial officials, educated Nigerians such as Obi, urbanized laborers who have learnt a little English and a whole range of other groups who cannot easily be fitted into any of these categories. In the rural areas there are the Christians who have had to widen the traditional idiom to embrace new areas of experience and there are the other Ibos on whom modern life has had relatively little impact. The complexity of the situation is further complicated by the fact that there are many people who use English, Pidgin, and Ibo in varying circumstances. The language in which they choose to express themselves and the way in which they do so reflect their thoughts and their life-style. It is through their language that we are able to enter their world and to share their experience. (Gakwandi 1977, 33)

Conrad's colonial biases, in Achebe's view, caused him to repress the speech of the African in *Heart of Darkness.* Now, paradoxically, in *No Longer at Ease* the speech diversity of postcolonial African society, speech diversity being understood as a reflection of the ideological conflicts and contradictions within the society, problematizes the very identity of the hero, rendering him incapable of authentic speech. In England, Obi had delivered a speech on African politics to the Nigerian Students' Union and had written sentimental poems about his homeland. Later he is pompous in his verbal confrontations with corrupt members of the bureaucracy and even with his parents over the question of his marriage to Clara, the *osu.* This question has a particular symbolic power, since the *osu* was literally placed outside of communication with the rest of the tribe. Ultimately, Obi himself becomes the modern world's version of the *osu*, and the novel is in fact an analysis of how a postcolonial society produces its outcasts and criminals.

The culmination of Obi's decline and criminalization is symbolized by his crumpling of his patriotic poem, "Nigeria," and only a page later he is called a "beast of no nation" (Achebe 1960, 142–43). The novel opens with the trial scene, in which corruption is ironically reinscribed—workers have bribed their doctors to obtain medical leaves so they can attend Obi's bribery trial. Throughout this scene Obi himself is silent. This opening, from which the rest of the novel is a prolepsis or flashback, creates a kind of dramatic irony. As the reader subsequently watches Obi's decline, certain already of the outcome, Obi's silence at the trial presides, as it were, over all the talk of the novel. Obi is finally deprived of speech not by a colonial author like Conrad, but by his own inability to find an authentic voice in the speech diversity of his fractured world.

If *Things Fall Apart* seems to imply a Western reader, *No Longer at Ease* is aimed to a greater degree at the educated Nigerian elite. (Of course this was a small readership, and for a Nigerian writer to establish an authoritative voice he had of necessity to seek a wider audience.) Achebe's pessimism concerning the educated Nigerian's preparedness for the responsibilities of leadership is well known, and in his novels Western education (like Achebe's own) offers little hope for progress. In this regard one might contrast James Ngũgĩ's *The River Between,* where Western education seems to hold some real hope, despite Waiyaki's inability to make this message prevail in his own political circumstances. Paradoxically Ngũgĩ now writes in the language of his ethnic group, Gikuyu, out of a conscious desire to reject the notion of the prestige of English. It is interesting in another sense to compare Achebe's work to such novels as *A Bend in the River* and *In a Free State* by V. S. Naipaul. Naipaul displays a cynicism rather like Achebe's, doubting as he does both the African's preparedness for self-government and the efficacy of the new African's Westernized education. But Naipaul, who is a West Indian rather than an African, has been attacked for his allegedly imperialist and reactionary views (Cudjoe 1988, 185–92), even though he has tried to authenticate his critiques of the Third World by cultivating the image of the perennial exile and nomad who cannot be accused of ideological entanglements. From the standpoint of an ethics of reading, the question is whether (and how) our responses should vary depending on the author's and our own sites of enunciation. Does Achebe's own Nigerian birth legitimate a kind of critique that is deemed (appropriately?) racist when coming from the pen of someone who is not African? Must we necessarily read Naipaul's African writings differently than we read Achebe's because of Naipaul's "otherness"? And what site of reading grants one the right to label a critique such as Naipaul's "racist"?

A time-honored principle of liberal democracy holds that we should weigh the validity of what someone says without reference to his or her origins or ethnicity. A version of this notion within literary criticism was the formalist or New Critical dictum to read only the work itself, without reference to the author's supposed intentions. And yet the limitations of this principle come into view when the content of the utterance involves a representation—and all representations should be suspected of serving specific interests—of a marginalized group or people.

A related question concerns the representation of the European "other" within the text of the Third World or minority author. Are Achebe's representations of Europeans open to the same kind of criticism that he leveled against Conrad's representation of Africans? It could be argued, for instance, that both the Commissioner and Smith in *Things Fall Apart* are rather crude caricatures. And although the more positive portrayal of Brown restores a balance, Brown in turn is a caricature of the naive, benevolent missionary. In *No Longer at Ease,* Green is a quickly sketched and entirely two-dimensional version of the cynical colonialist mentality, and none of the Europeans is sympathetic in the sequel, *A Man of the People.* A writer from an empowered class or society representing less empowered people in such apparently superficial ways would be justifiably criticized. But is violent representation something of which only those in power can be guilty? Do the ethics of reading require that we grant a certain license to the writer who speaks for the marginalized, a license to represent people from empowered positions in ways that will serve the interests of the less empowered? If reading is a political act, can it be governed by general critical principles, or, in the language of Sartrean situation ethics, must one always improvise?

Reading is as much a form of representation as is writing, and in fact current theory has belabored the proposition that reading *is* writing. Whatever social or moral ends a writer may have intended to serve with his or her representations, every reading re-presents the text in terms of the reader's ends. The question of the aims of reading as a form of writing, and therefore as an exercise of power that must be governed by ethical considerations, is implicit in Achebe's choice of titles for the two novels I have discussed. Few would dispute the positions of Yeats and Eliot at the center of modernist literature in English, but how can Achebe have been reading these authors to appropriate their phrases for his titles? Neither was known for his sympathies with minorities or repressed peoples; Yeats flirted with reactionary politics and Eliot's anti-Semitism is as clear as Pound's (Howe 1991). In fact Yeats's "The Second Coming," from which Achebe's first title comes, can be read as a paranoiac response to the kind of historical change that would bring about the emergence of the Third World. The "center" which cannot hold in the poem is the European, imperialist hegemony. And Yeats's "rough beast" that is "slouching toward Bethlehem to be born" could be (in Yeats's prophetic imagination) Africa with its new and imperfectly grafted Christianity, or even Obi Okonkwo himself, the "beast of no nation."

Sharing the gloom of Spengler's *The Decline of the West* (1918), Yeats's poem is profoundly reactionary. And in its fear of change it deprives the other of language and humanity, depicting him only as a beast. Certainly this poem is as open to objection from Achebe's point of view as is Conrad's *Heart of Darkness.* One could argue that there is irony lurking in Achebe's title—that he is demonstrating that Yeats

308 · Approaches to Things Fall Apart

was wrong about the rough beast from other lands. But nothing really suggests this, and the effect of the title seems instead to point merely to the falling apart of traditional Ibo society—as though Yeats and Achebe simply agree: things fall apart. The point, then, is that Achebe's readings of these canonical Western texts are motivated by varying needs. At a certain historical moment it was politically desirable for a young Nigerian writer to attempt to occupy a position in relation to the canon of Western literature, and with his titles Achebe announces an affinity with two of the major authors in that canon. A reading that was blind to the objectionable aspects of Yeats's poem was strategically necessary. Later (Achebe's Conrad essay was first delivered as a lecture in 1975 and first published in 1977) the position and the audience that were established by virtue of the blind reading of Yeats were used to uncover what is racist or repressive in Conrad.

Although my primary theme has concerned the possibility and the ethics of a Western reading of Achebe, a secondary theme has concerned Achebe's reading of the West—explicitly of Conrad and of "colonialist" critics in his essays, implicitly of Western literature as he links it to Obi's weakness of character, and implicitly of high modernism as he (paradoxically?) affiliates himself with it in his choice of titles. It remains to ask whether my reading of Achebe's reading of Conrad, Yeats, and Eliot is a hostile one. Am I accusing Achebe of logical inconsistency, or worse, of an unethical opportunism? Although this question will ultimately be answered only in your reading of my essay, my answer is that all readings serve interests and are therefore "political." Achebe does what we all do. For instance, it was at one historical moment correct and appropriate to see the oppositional, anti-imperialist message in *Heart of Darkness;* it is just as correct and appropriate now to see its imperialist affiliations. Similarly, the question of whether the Western or the African reader should see African literature written in English as a branch of English literature or as a literature entirely different in kind does not admit ultimate or permanent answers. While national identity and independence are nourished by belief in a unique national culture, national identity and national culture are not eternal, Platonic essences, but rather matters of contestation and struggle. Alliances shift, old things do fall apart, and oppositions such as that between Africa and the West, which are so integral to the structure of the present moment, are perpetually rewriting themselves as the gyres of history turn.

Interpretations and readings are forms of the struggle for identity, and receive their validity from the social context in which they are made. The issue with which we began—the issue Achebe clarifies in his remarks on Conrad's depiction of the African—can stand as a guide, as texts, both African and Western, are continually recontextualized by historical change: that reading is ethical which does the most to acknowledge the right of all voices to speak.

References

Achebe, Chinua. *Hopes and Impediments: Selected Essays.* New York: Anchor Books, 1989.

———. *No Longer at Ease.* New York: Fawcet Primier, 1960.

———. *Things Fall Apart.* New York: Fawcet Primier, 1959.

Bakhtin, Mikhail. "Discourse in the Novel." In *The Dialogic Imagination,* edited by Michael Holquist, 259–422. Austin: University of Texas Press, 1981.

Barthold, Bonnie J. *Black Time: Fiction of Africa, the Caribbean, and the United States.* New Haven: Yale University Press, 1981.

Chatman, Seymour. *Story and Discourse: Narrative Structure in Fiction and Film.* Ithaca: Cornell University Press, 1978.

Chinweizu, Onwechekwa Jemie, and Ihechukwu Madubuike. *Toward the Decolonization of African Literature.* Washington, DC: Howard University Press, 1983.

Conrad, Joseph. *Heart of Darkness.* 1902. Reprint, edited by Robert Kimbrough. New York: W. W. Norton, 1988.

Cudjoe, Selwyn R. *V. S. Naipaul: A Materialist Reading.* Amherst: University of Massachusetts Press, 1988.

Egejuru, Phanuel Akubueze. *Towards African Literacy Independence: A Dialogue with Contemporary African Writers.* Westport, CT: Greenwood Press, 1980.

Foucault, Michel. *Language, Counter-Memory, Practice,* edited by Donald F. Bouchard. Ithaca: Cornell University Press, 1977.

Gakwandi, Shatto Arthur. *The Novel and Contemporary Experience in Africa.* New York: African Publishing Company, 1977.

Green, Martin. *Dreams of Adventure, Deeds of Empire.* New York: Basic Books, 1979.

Howe, Irving. "An Exercise in Memory." *The New Republic* 204 (March 11, 1991): 29–32.

JanMohamed, Abdul R., and David Lodge. "Introduction: Toward a Theory of Minority Discourse: What Is To Be Done?" In *The Nature and Context of Minority Discourse.* New York: Oxford University Press, 1990.

Layoun, Mary N. "Fictional Formations and Deformations of National Culture." *The South Atlantic Quarterly* 87 (Winter 1988): 53–73.

Ngara, Emmanuel. *Stylistic Criticism and the African Novel.* London: Heinemann, 1982.

Thomas, Brook. "Preserving and Keeping Order by Killing Time in *Heart of Darkness*." In *Heart of Darkness: A Case Study in Contemporary Criticism*, edited by Ross C. Murfin. New York: St. Martin's Press, 1989.

Said, Edward. *Orientalism*. New York: Vintage, 1979.

22 If the Shoe Fits: Teaching *Beowulf* with Achebe's *Things Fall Apart*

Julian Wasserman
Loyola University

Liam O. Purdon
Doane College

"Never take a course that includes *Beowulf*," Alvie Singer frantically warns Annie Hall. Those who love the poem, convinced of its beauties and wisdom, may laugh at this academic *caveat emptor*, but we must also wince a little at its truth for many students for whom the eighth-century epic is, to say the least, inaccessible. Indeed, the title of Stanley Greenfield's 1982 translation of the poem—*A Readable Beowulf*[1]— hints at the difficulty that modern readers often encounter when first reading the poem, even in translation. And that is not the least of student objections to the poem. Rendered readable, *Beowulf*—with its heroic code and treasure dealing, not to mention its monsters—often seems hopelessly remote from the modern world and daily concerns of contemporary readers.

Far from being inappropriate, these concerns are fundamental to the educational mission of the language and literature professor, not only because they raise the issue of identity and difference, which is central to the reading experience itself, but also because they situate one of the principal concerns of medieval studies—namely the simultaneous familiarity and alterity of the medieval text—in the context of the multicultural classroom. In fact, multicultural studies offer much to the medievalist who believes in the "medievalness" and, hence, otherness of the works we teach and study. Such renewed attention to cultural context serves as counterbalance to many developments in contemporary criticism which have challenged traditional ways of reading texts by placing more emphasis on the reader and, hence, less emphasis on both the writer and the culture in which the writer is situated.

311

Why, then, teach a text that is so impenetrable, so unknowable, so unreadable that the title of its recent translation has to reassure the reader that what is contained within is worth his or her trouble? Why study a work like *Beowulf,* even if it is readable, when it is a product of a culture that is so different from our own? Asking these questions, far from subverting the study of *Beowulf* or challenging its place in the canon, opens up an approach to the medieval text which has the advantage of considering the text's features in anthropological and cultural terms, issues foregrounded in multicultural classes.

The Integrity of Difference

To understand someone else, it is said, you first need to walk in their shoes, and, indeed, medieval shoes, as cultural artifact, provide a starting place for an understanding of the issues involved in the study of the poem. How, one might ask, would an "anthropological" reader "read" a cultural object such as medieval shoes, objects of both function and fashion?[2] Shown a number of slides of medieval footwear, students readily observe that medieval shoes tend to favor pointed toes.[3] Many students recognize the essential form as that of the pointed "pixie boots" of fairy tale characters. Moreover, what one notices in the selected illustrations of medieval footwear is that the points become longer as a matter of fashion rather than function. In fact, the points, as they become longer, were often supported by something analogous to the plastic collar stays fashionable in men's shirts in the 1950s and 60s (a period almost as remote to contemporary students as the Middle Ages). Still longer points were maintained by curling the toe upward as in the style most students associate with genies of Middle Eastern lore. Finally, in extreme cases, shoe points might be extended to a length that required that they be tied back to the shin with ribbons. From the instructor's point of view, the object of the presentation is to make these "medievals" seem as ridiculous, and hence alien and remote, as possible. They are, after all, people whose shoes we associate with pixies and genies, who aren't really people at all. "What has he to do with Hecuba, or Hecuba to him?" Hamlet asks. Indeed, what have we, students ask, to do with these people and their absurd footwear, people who lack our modern sensibility, not to mention sensible footwear?

The next step is simply to produce a slide of a "platform shoe" or even an evening shoe with a high, spiked heel, and the two essential questions that are necessary in any encounter with a text such as

Beowulf from which we are separated by wide gulfs of either time or culture become evident: How are its author and audience different from us? How are they like us? Medievals differ from us in aesthetics, preferring toes to soles or heels. They are like us in that, like most contemporary Americans, they believed "more is better." Rare is the student who will not admit to knowing perfectly well what drives one person to want a longer and hence more fashionable toe or heel than his or her neighbor. The desire to be fashionable, whatever its source, appears a human constant, a mirror in which we see the reflections of ourselves as well as these impossibly remote medievals. If the means of fashion differ over the ages, the ends, and perhaps the first causes, do not. Much of what bothers the modern student about *Beowulf* is, in fact, fashion—a verbal aesthetic different from our own in its love of alliteration or convoluted syntax—but many of the essential presumptions of the poem are as recognizable to today's reader as the fashion impulse we have just discussed.

Appreciating this difference concerning things medieval, however, does not simply result from its recognition. Recognition, to be sure, is the first step in the process. What becomes more important, once this step has been taken, is understanding the integrity of that difference, the value of the object taken in its own terms, apart from what it means or how it appears to a "modern" audience. Without this understanding, the study of *Beowulf* or any other comparable medieval text becomes an act of literary voyeurism, a gawking at the folks with the funny footwear, with the object of study left unacceptably remote. Indeed, the captivating strangeness that attracts so many students to courses in medieval literature can actually be self-defeating in that it can produce the effect of placing a living work in the equivalent of the museum case, protected from the wearing and distorting results of close contact with a human audience, like the mummy in glass case that becomes so remote that it becomes an artifact suggesting some invincibly remote religion of jackal-headed gods and cartouches rather than human remains that suggest the human activities that transcend cultural difference: loving, embarrassment, happiness, grief.

If, on the other hand, we are looking for sameness—perhaps even for human universals that underlie the many differences separating "them" from "us"—such as a need for belief, the problems of coping with death, or the pleasure of creating or perceiving the beautiful—the search to see ourselves in others is not without its own pitfall—that is, the danger of self-absorption, the Narcissus-like impulse not only to worship our own image but also to see it in all times and in all places, sometimes with a vision that is completely blind to difference.

The challenge, then, to the language and literature professor responding to questions like those posed at the outset of this paper is to discover
the means of counterbalancing the contrary totalizing impulses of
simple rejection and complete identification of either the familiar or
the foreign so that the integrity of the culturally different artifact may
be appreciated in its own terms as well as its relation to those of us
who do not share its culture. In the case of *Beowulf,* one fruitful way
of securing this means is to use what to contemporary American
students is an equally "alien" text, one which introduces comparable
presuppositions about difference and sameness as presented in the
Anglo-Saxon epic. Interestingly enough, such a text is available in the
African novel, Chinua Achebe's *Things Fall Apart.* There are probably
many other non-European texts like *Things Fall Apart* which might
have the same effect upon the reader's appreciation for a work like
Beowulf. No doubt as they become more available to students and are
incorporated in the global literary canon, their value in this regard will
be recognized. What distinguishes Achebe's novel now, however, is
Achebe's acute awareness of language theory and understanding of the
differences and similarities between oral and literate cultures and
between the artifacts which are products of those cultures.

Presumptions of Sameness, Presumptions of Difference

"Different from," "similar to": the spatial prepositions in these phrases
are significant locators of our emotional registers as well as indicators
of our intellectual recognitions of factual comparisons. We feel distance
from that which is different. We feel closer *to* that which is similar.
Reading *Beowulf* and *Things Fall Apart,* we not only attempt to measure
the text but to measure ourselves and our feelings of distance from/
closeness to the text, to see each work from a distance and to see it in
close proximity. For students in freshman and sophomore level "World
Literature" or "Introduction to Literature" courses in which *Beowulf*
or *Things Fall Apart* regularly appear, presumptions about differences
and sameness are often a source of resistance to texts. For *Things Fall
Apart,* there is the presumption of difference—say, from a society that
abandons twins in the woods or that is polygamous and, even, non-
urban—that leads students to assume an alterity that makes reading a
curiously detached exercise, with little commentary on our own society.
Interestingly enough, the opposite presumption, one of sameness,
frequently provides a barrier to reading *Beowulf.* There, the presumption
that these are our ancestors—that they are just like us, except less

technologically advanced—blinds us to the fact that theirs is an entirely different worldview, one that in some ways is no less remote than that of the Ibo of Nigeria who are the subject of Achebe's novel. Ironically, then, these two works, whose readers' presumptions in regard to difference and sameness are so divergent, may well shed light on each other. In particular, reading *Things Fall Apart* in conjunction with *Beowulf* works well to illuminate two particular aspects of medieval literature that are especially difficult for contemporary readers to appreciate but which are essential to understanding works like *Beowulf*. The first of these concerns the nature of oral cultures; the second, the nature of the pre- or non-romantic *Weltanshaung*.

Of course, using contemporary or nearly contemporary oral cultures as a way into medieval oral culture is not new. Alfred Bates Lord's famous studies of Balkan oral tradition contributed immeasurably to our understanding of the scop and Anglo-Saxon orality.[4] Jeff Opland has made direct comparisons between African oral culture and that of the Anglo-Saxons.[5] Yet *Things Fall Apart* is a particularly effective entré into questions of orality in the case of *Beowulf* because it inherently avoids the pitfall of cultural hubris implicit in comparing a nine-hundred-year-old English society to a turn-of-the-century non-English culture. That is to say, it makes it difficult for us to assume cultural superiority of our own civilization through the implication that the Ibo culture of 1900 is somehow a millennium behind our own. What prevents such an all-too-easy and false assumption is that in *Things Fall Apart* the essential tension is between the oral Ibo culture and that of the literate "civilizers" from the Colonial British government.[6] Indeed, in this struggle between the literate British and the oral Ibo, it is the literate point of view, limited by its inability to perceive the value of the culture it wishes to make over in its own image, that embodies both moral and linguistic corruption through a regime under which bribes are extorted and words distorted. If the modern American reader identifies with the literate British strangers, the novel methodically subverts the hierarchy presumed by students that privileges the literate culture over the oral one.

The method of that subversion is quite straightforward. The first half of Achebe's novel serves as a dispassionate if implicitly partisan introduction to Ibo culture. Almost acting the role of anthropologist, the omniscient narrator provides the reader with a picture of a society rich in poetry, art, and ceremony, and concerned with justice, order, and tradition. Having carefully documented the Ibo life as the object of study, *Things Fall Apart* then presents Europeans, whose acts of decoding what has been presented as the authorized version of Ibo culture comprise a set of normative models for "reading" cultural alterity. The Europeans' divergent perceptions of the established norm tell us more about themselves and their methods of reading culture than they do about the Ibo. As such, these models also serve as a means of revealing something about the student's own methods of reading cultural difference whether it be that of the Ibo or the early Anglo-Saxon.

Students who are convinced of the essential differences between themselves and the Ibo—that is, who are situated as outsiders residing in a foreign culture—do well to consider the actions of the novel's two missionaries, Mr. Brown and Mr. Smith. Neither is, of course, an anthropologist; neither makes a pretense of studying the Ibo for their own sake, for each has his own purpose: the conversion of the Ibo. But such purpose makes the missionaries ideal models for the student reader whose own purpose is not merely to read the different for its own sake but also to see likeness, to see oneself in the seemingly different, to convert the different to the like for our own purposes of pleasure and instruction.

To his credit, Mr. Brown is anxious to create a dialogue between himself and the Ibo and does walk among and talk to the people who are the reason for his errand into the wilderness. Indeed, to expedite the process of conversion, he even approaches the tribe's greatest and wisest man, for he knows that if Akunna agrees with him and he with Akunna, then the people will be ready and willing to accept the principles of his religion. In short, his is a search for identity, for likeness. As he discusses God with Akunna, he creates an intellectual common ground with the wise man by agreeing with Akunna that the Supreme Being and Chukwu are analogous. Yet the differences, as well as the common ground, become apparent as Brown tries to get Akunna to understand that belief in lesser gods like Akunna's Ikenga is merely idolatry: " 'There are no other gods,' he says, adding: 'Chukwu is the only God and all others are false. You carve a piece of wood like that one—and you call it a god. But it is still a piece of wood.' "[7] Akunna does not disagree with Brown, but rather points out that, because his *Ikenga* is made from stuff of the world which has been made by Chukwu, his *Ikenga,* in effect, has to be considered a messenger of Chukwu and so must be treated with the respect one would show a lesser god. Then he adds that Brown himself is like an *Ikenga* in that Brown is a messenger to the head of his church, who in turn represents the Supreme Being on Earth. Rather than comprehend the analogy with which Akunna provides him however, Brown, who has been given a glimpse of sameness in alterity, falls back on principles he knows, claiming it is wrong to anthropomorphize God, an obvious irony which Brown himself does not comprehend, and decides to proselytize among the young. Between Akunna and Brown, the perceptual divergence, as we shall see, is clear. Brown's monotheism and Akunna's polytheism are more than simply different religious tenets; they are indicators of the antithetical ways in which they perceive and, hence, construct their worlds. In their own ways, both Brown and Akunna become factotums for the resistant text that refuses to be made over in the eye of the beholder. To the Europeans for whom all things must conform to one measure, one truth, God is one and the Trinity is one. To the Europeans whose monoculturalism is as firmly established as their monotheism, there is only one set of values, one mode of administration—theirs—to be imposed. To the Ibo, both pluralistic and polytheistic, there are many truths, and the Trinity is three. What is good for one is not necessarily good for all. As Obierika's eldest brother notes, "What is good in one place is bad in another" (71). There is in the discussion between Brown and Akunna genuine intercultural dialogue, understanding of common ground and difference, if not conversion of the other's point of view. There is also a lesson here for the reader of a foreign culture attempting to view a religion from a vantage outside the closed circle of the faithful; that is, from the *logical* perspective of the scientist or student of culture. Without the leap of faith—belief—the Trinity is, from Akunna's quite logical point of view, three rather than one. Reason without belief, at best, leaves alien culture, as well as doctrine, quaint and, at worst, incomprehensible—as baffling as the Ibo custom is to the District Commissioner who fancied himself a "student of primitive customs" (189). And, unfortunately, reason or logic is almost all that the contemporary student has to unravel the mysteries of the closed cultural circles of either the Anglo-Saxon or the Ibo. Read with care, the theological dialogue between Brown and Akunna does not rob the student of that tool, but it does serve as a helpful warning that what we are viewing is being observed from without and that while the principles of logic may be universals, the presumptions—the articles of faith and culture—upon which those principles operate are not.

The second model for reading alterity is introduced when Mr. Smith succeeds Mr. Brown as chief of the mission. Smith enters further into Ibo culture than Brown but with far less openness or intellectual curiosity. The essence of Smith's engagement of the Ibo involves dismissiveness and repudiation. Smith rejects outright many of the actions or stories told by members of his congregation. He does not use the Ibo as a means of affirming his own belief, nor does he perceive any sameness underlying their differences; rather, he views the Ibo as possessing a difference to be condemned and eradicated. For him, they are merely a people who must respond to his religious ultimatum: perceive agreement in all things or else be cast out. Indeed, we learn that for Smith, there will be no new wine in old vessels (169). For him there are no analogies, such as Brown accepts with Chukwu. In his single-mindedness and his literalism, there are no metaphors, no "A is to B," only tautologies, "A is to A."[8] The Ibo are, in other words, a text for him—not one in which he sees his own prejudice confirmed but, rather, one which the force of his prejudice distorts in order to accommodate his belief.

Interestingly enough, the differences between Brown and Smith as cultural readers are paralleled within the Ibo in the persons of Enoch and Obierika. As violent a reader of alterity as Mr. Smith is, it is not he but Enoch, one of his mission's zealous converts, who acts out this basic literal-mindedness by unmasking the *egwugwu,* an ancestral spirit, during the annual ceremony held in honor of the earth deity (171). As a converted Ibo, Enoch is both text and reader, subject and object, in the reading of Ibo culture. He is also totalizing in both of these roles. His act is a literal-minded rejection of the metaphoricity of Ibo custom and culture in favor of the single-mindedness and narrow field of vision of his patron, Mr. Smith. Unmasking the *egwugwu,* in other words, is tantamount to "unmasking" or reducing meaning, a blow for strict denotation against the polysemousness that, as we shall see, characterizes the Ibo, as opposed to the foreigners', use of language. The second model within the community of the Ibo is Obierika, who, while clearly remaining Ibo, is self-aware enough to be critical of his clan's practice of abandoning twins in the Evil Forest. He is neither completely unchanged like Akunna, nor is he completely made over like Enoch.

For the student who has read *Things Fall Apart* and come to understand these very different approaches to the seemingly objective fact of Ibo culture, the question that arises is how might these models be used to understand the typical contemporary response to a work like *Beowulf.* In other words, when the student encounters the different or alien in the Anglo-Saxon epic, how is the student's response like the responses of Brown or Smith or even Enoch to Ibo culture? What is more, when we compare our own literate culture to our emerging concept of the nonliterate culture like that of the Ibo or of eighth-century Denmark and come to admire features of orality, do we scorn all written words and decry logocentrism, or do we act like Obierika whose cultural identity is strong enough to resist the force of the alien culture from without and flexible enough to profit by the self-scrutiny

from within? As such, he is, in many ways, a model reader for the
student who stands on the outside looking in at the cultures portrayed
in either of these two works.

The Hallmark of Culture

Of the readers of Ibo culture, the one who is perhaps most revealing
is the "logical" District Commissioner, who shows himself to be
infuriated by the Ibo elders' love of superfluous words:

> The Commissioner did not understand what Obierika meant
> when he said, "Perhaps your men will help us." One of the most
> infuriating habits of these people was their love of superfluous
> words, he thought. (189)

Ironically, it is the Commissioner, so given to verbal reduction, who
gets the last word in Achebe's novel when he considers how he will
treat Okonkwo's death, first, by giving the incident a whole chapter
and, then, by paring it down to a "reasonable paragraph," there being
so much else to include in a work of this sort:

> As he walked back to the court he thought about that book. Every
> day brought him some new material. The story of this man who
> had killed a messenger and hanged himself would make interesting
> reading. One could almost write a whole chapter on him. Perhaps
> not a whole chapter but a reasonable paragraph, at any rate. There
> was so much else to include, and one must be firm in cutting out
> details. (191)

As the verbally reductive Commissioner moves to progressively
shorter verbal units—from a chapter, to a paragraph and finally to a
title—Achebe manages to encapsulate the essential perceptual struggle
embodied in the book, between the expansive oral culture of the Ibo[9]
and the essentially reductive linguistic habits of the literate foreigners,
a perceptual concept already witnessed in the debate between the
monotheistic Brown and the polytheistic Akunna. Indeed, what the
Commissioner reduces to a "reasonable paragraph" has taken the
narrator an entire novel to relate. The cultural complexity of the two-
hundred-page portrait of the Ibo is summarized in the single word
"primitive" in the would-be author's title, *The Pacification of the
Primitive Tribes of the Lower Niger.*

We have already made mention of the rather remarkable title of
Greenfield's *A Readable Beowulf,* because the title itself recognizes one
of the essential cultural barriers between the modern student and the
medieval poem, a conflict that in part mirrors the barrier between the

reductive literate habits of the European "civilizers" and the verbally expansive orality of the Ibo. If the readability of Greenfield's translation is such a defining characteristic of his translation, what then makes others "unreadable"? As any teacher of *Beowulf* would readily recognize, basic speech patterns of the poem present not only the first challenge to the modern reader's expectations but also a real comprehensive difficulty to those used to speech patterns and rhetorical strategies of contemporary English.

Partly this difficulty is exacerbated by the fact that, contrary to student expectations, *Beowulf,* far from being an "action" poem dominated by the hero's struggles with monsters, dragons, and other embodiments of evil, is a poem of and about discourse and rhetoric, for the bulk of the poem is comprised not of battles but of speeches, often with their subject being the act of speaking itself. The poem is not an occasion or vehicle for descriptions of battles; rather, the battles are simply excuses for making speeches. Indeed, no self-respecting Anglo-Saxon warrior simply went to battle without speaking first, either through the heroic *beot,* or boast, to inspire his comrades or by *flyting,* or ritual insult, to his enemies. From the Anglo-Saxon perspective, the heart of the poem lies not in the three battles but in Hrothgar's great speeches (858–85, 1573–1670),[10] models of rhetoric and oratory that are comparable to those of the "powerful orator" Ogbuefi Ezeugo at the beginning of *Things Fall Apart* (14–15) and those by Uchendu on Okonkwo's arrival in and departure from exile (122–25, 154–56).[11]

The rhetorical strategies involved in all of these speeches are often baffling, if not annoying, to the modern student from a literate culture, taught to place the thesis up front and to proceed deductively, who finds her- or himself a stranger in a strange land of orality. The reason for this is that the strategy, one fundamental to oral culture, is indirect, the subtle evolution of the topic by means of circumlocution, the use of metaphor, and/or the act of renaming.[12] As an example, one might consider the Beowulf-poet's seemingly redundant renaming of the Divinity as he tells us that the afflicted Danes

> looked to hell,
> Not Knowing the Maker, the mighty Judge,
> Nor how to worship the Wielder of glory,
> The Lord of Heaven, the God of hosts.[13]
> 179–82

"Maker . . . Judge . . . Wielder . . . Lord . . . God"—superfluous, as in the "love of superfluous words" that so irritates the Commissioner, is clearly in the eye and ear of the receiver, and, no doubt, the English

Commissioner so bent on bringing British civilization to the "primitive" Umuofia would find the above passage from his own cultural roots as maddeningly inefficient as the roundabout locutions of the Ibo.

Such renaming on the verbal level is, however, merely the microcosm of the same strategy on the narrative level. The so-called Thyrth "digression" in *Beowulf* is likewise illustrative of this method insofar as it is used to develop the qualities and character of Queen Hygd by means of contrast. This strategy of indirection of course is likewise part and parcel of the language of the Ibo in *Things Fall Apart,* for they are a people for whom speech is not merely a secondary means to an end but an art form in itself, often more important than the information it conveys.[14] Enjoyed for its own sake, it is practiced with deliberation and without urgency or haste. Achebe underscores this distinction between form and content early in the book when describing the circumlocutory strategy of Okoye:

> Having spoken plainly so far, Okoye said the next half dozen sentences in proverbs. Among the Ibo the art of conversation is regarded highly and proverbs are the palm oil with which words are eaten. Okoye was a great talker and he spoke for a long time, skirting round the subject and then butting it finally. In short, he was asking Unoka to return the two hundred cowries he had borrowed from him more than two years before. As soon as Unoka understood what his friend was driving at, he burst out laughing. (10–11)

Like the Anglo-Saxon, the Ibo speaker is not given to making his points "in short"—a fact that makes the words of both less readable to the modern student who, like Unoka, may take some time to see what the speaker is "driving at."

As suggested, then, *Things Fall Apart* provides an excellent means of introducing students to oral culture, and a comparison between Achebe's novel and *Beowulf* helps to highlight which properties are not solely elements of Anglo-Saxon culture but are properties of oral culture in general. Perhaps the most obvious of these is the presence of proverbial lore, the "palm oil with which words are eaten," a linguistic trope that any reader of *Beowulf* would recognize as a *kenning,* a poetic compounding of words to form a highly imagistic metaphor.[15] There the sea is alternately the "swan's path" and "the whale's road"; swords were "foe hammers." To speak is "to open one's word hoard." "*Beowulf,*" itself, is a compounding of "bee" and "wolf," providing a kenning for "bear" or the honey-loving predator who stalks the bee. To be sure, Old English possesses the words "sea," "sword," and "bear"— "sae," "sweord," and "bera"—and, no doubt, an unarmed Anglo-Saxon thane unlucky enough to be hotly pursued by a bear would use the shorter forms to apprise his friends of his need to borrow a sword. But the use of such poetic description was the mark of the eloquent and respected speaker, not the harried one. For those who practice such verbal art, elaboration, rather than economy, becomes the hallmark of verbal acuity and, hence, good character.

For the Ibo, there is clearly a similar poetic sensibility. Brusqueness, or brevity to the point of rudeness, was to be avoided. Compounding, as in the Anglo-Saxon kenning, is for the Ibo the hallmark of even ordinary discourse of this people much given to poetry and poetic imagery, proverb and song. Among the Ibo, the rainbow is called the "Python of the Sky" (152). Ezinma is called "Crystal of Beauty" (158). Of the "efulefu," the "empty or worthless man," the narrator tells us, "The imagery of the *efulefu* in the language of the clan was a man who sold his machete and wore the sheath to battle" (133). Words, concepts, have "imagery" for the clan. So too do names such as Okonkwo's youngest child, Nwofia, "Begotten in the Wilderness."[16] Such imagistic richness in Ibo names stands in stark and deliberate contrast with the monosyllabic and equally monosemantic "Smith" and "Brown," neither of which actually has any real "meaning" in regard to its referent. Again, the richness of multiplicity stands starkly juxtaposed to the barrenness, or at the least the paucity, of oneness. Proverbs are, by their nature, parabolic; that is, open-ended and therefore subject to multiple interpretation and usable in myriad contexts.[17] It is little wonder, then, that the District Commissioner, given his literate preoccupation with verbal conciseness, becomes infuriated by the Ibo's failure to simply get to the point, a mark of rudeness in an oral culture. In many ways, then, the clash between the Ibo and the would-be chronicler of "primitive culture" is the juxta-position between the timeless self-indulgence of poetry and the ruthless efficiency of prose, between language that is subjective, mutable, and open, as opposed to language that is objective, fixed, and closed.[18] Nwoye, whose conversion to Christianity so offends his father Okonkwo, is, it should be recalled, attracted by "the poetry of the new religion" (137), although in the hands of Smith, it is clearly prose masquerading as poetry. For Brown and especially Enoch, the unmasker, there is nothing but unmetaphored prose.

Another property associated with orality, one often associated with the proverbial, is a highly developed concern with verbal etiquette and ritualized speech. In *Beowulf,* the Danish coastguard provides a most memorable example. He stops the arriving Geats' advance, both praising and interrogating them. He indicates he must know the reason for their presence; at the same time, however, it is equally important for him to know the seafarers' lineage. Beowulf cannot and does not simply arrive in the land of the Spear Danes and take on the task of ridding Heorot of Grendel. He must ask permission, and before even being allowed to attempt to demonstrate the strength of his arm, he must first prove his worthiness—that is, his wisdom—which he does first in his speech to the coastguard and later in replying to Unferth's challenge with words rather than physical violence. Similarly, Beowulf's verbal exchanges with Hrothgar are intended as models of proper discourse, intended as instruction for future thanes and lords. Proving himself a master at words, Beowulf is then allowed to demonstrate his courage and strength. Words come before; deeds, which follow, must live up to words. And when the deeds do come, then there are more words.[19]

Proverbs, politeness, verbal one-upmanship, ceremony—these are the hallmarks of oral culture, in *Beowulf* as well as *Things Fall Apart,* where a similar sensitivity to language and protocol is evident.[20] For the members of the clan, there is a proper way of addressing a snake as well as for addressing an ancestral spirit. There is a "polite" term to describe a leper. "During the negotiation over Akueke's bride-price, the men gather, share the palm-wine that Ibe, the suitor, has tapped, and talk about everything except the thing for which they had gathered" (69), a criticism that students have been known to make concerning the formal discourse of Beowulf. Once the wine is finished, the bride-price is determined by means of the bundle of broom sticks. Obierika presents the suitor's father, Ukegbu, with thirty sticks; once the latter has conferred with his family, he returns fifteen sticks. Obierika's response includes acknowledgement of his initial position regarding bride-price at thirty sticks and, then, modification of that position aphoristically by means of a proverb. He says to Ukegbu, "We had not thought to go below thirty. But as the dog said, 'If I fall down for you and you fall down for me, it is play.' Marriage should be a play and not a fight; so we are falling down again" (70).[21]

Clearly, then, for both the Anglo-Saxon and the Ibo, language is the hallmark of culture; its preservation the preservation of society, its destruction just the opposite.[22] This is why seemingly minor incidents in the linguistic struggle between the foreigners and the Ibo take on the dimensions of a struggle for survival—such as when the missionaries' messengers mispronounce the clan's word for "myself" so that it becomes *kotma,* or "Ashy Buttocks," a term—or kenning, if one will—that the Ibo find appropriate for the white interlopers.[23] As the harbingers not only of a new language but a new set of linguistic practices and etiquette, the missionaries are not only the "rough beast" of Yeats's

"The Second Coming" but are little different from Grendel whose seizure of the Feast Hall likewise threatens the central social ceremony that keeps that society from falling apart. "Does the white man understand our custom about land?" Okonkwo asks. To which Obierika replies, "How can he when he does not even speak our tongue?" When Obierika ends his speech by stating that the white men have "put a knife on the things that held us together and we have fallen apart" (162), the knot that has been cut is language (162). This is exactly the point made when Uchendu rises to thank Okonkwo for his hospitality and tells the assembly that the people no longer speak with one voice so that their cohesiveness as a people is severely undermined:

> You may ask why I am saying all this. I say it because I fear
> for the younger generation, for you people. . . . As for me, I have
> only a short while to live. . . . But I fear for you young people
> because you do not understand how strong is the bond of kinship.
> You do not know what it is to speak with one voice. And what
> is the result? An abominable religion has settled among you. (150)

When the unity of the clan dissolves, what is left is a collection of individuals.

The second area of consideration in which a text like *Things Fall Apart* can elucidate a work like *Beowulf* involves the pre- (or in the case of the Ibo, a non-) romantic world view in which the group is more important than the self, in which likenesses that generate classes or groups (and metaphors) are privileged over differences which produce individuals.[24] In Chaucer's *General Prologue,* for example, we are told that when the great renewal of April occurs plants turn green, birds mate, and people long to go on pilgrimages. Modern students schooled in the value of individual identity invariably report that three separate and, hence, individual events are taking place here in three separate unrelated realms—the vegetable, the animal, and the spiritual. From a medieval point of view, only one event, renewal, is taking place, but it is taking place in three worlds that reflect each other, worlds that are anything but separate. The same habits of perception may be seen in a modern student's reception of a typical page from a fifteenth-century *Biblia Pauperum,* or illustrated *Bible of the Poor,* which is divided into three panels: the right with Jonah emerging from the mouth of a whale; the left panel with Samson emerging from the City of Gaza whose barred gates he has broken; and the center panel with Christ emerging from a tomb.[25] Again, to the medieval eye, trained in the perception of identity rather than difference, there is here one story told three ways rather than the three distinct stories perceived by the modern reader. The modern student inured in the cult of the individual will ask why when Beowulf has slain Grendel does the scop sing the lay of Sigemund who slew the dragon. Why is the poet speaking of someone else at Beowulf's great moment? And the answer from the medieval point of view is that this is not someone else's story; Sigemund's story is Beowulf's story as well because he too has slain a monster and is now part of a great tradition which far outweighs the loss of individual identity. Of course, the same student might well also ask why the narrative of *Things Fall Apart* is interrupted by the parable of Eneke the Bird or the chapter-long tale of the lazy trickster, Tortoise.

In *Beowulf,* this fact of pre-romantic culture is evidenced in several ways, providing elements that seem alien and off-putting to the modern reader who automatically looks for the discrete or individual. *Beowulf,* for example, does not begin with Beowulf but with Scyld Scaefing and a long genealogy, loathsome material seemingly suitable only for pop-quizzes. In other words, the epic begins with the distant past. From the medieval point of view, such an opening, like the beginning of *Sir Gawain and the Green Knight,* which begins with the fall of Troy rather than Camelot, is far from being a digression, but instead is the very subject matter of the poem. For the poet of *Beowulf* or the *Gawain*-poet, the context of Beowulf, the generic man not the individual, or the context of Gawain, the knight, is the principal object of study. We are reminded of this perceptual tendency later in *Beowulf* when the Geat hero is asked his identity by the Danish coastguard. Beowulf responds by providing a "context" rather than an individual identity. He says he is the son of Ecgtheow and then, after a long locution incorporating Wulfgar's interview—that is, some eighty lines later—he offers the less important "My name is Beowulf."

What holds true for people is equally true for the objects that fill the pre-romantic world of the epic. Nothing stands alone. Everything has a context, whether swords, whose forges, owners, and battles are given, or even Grendel who is of the seed of Cain. To the modern reader, such histories are "superfluous" or in the case of the opening genealogy, distracting digressions. But to the reader schooled in the holistic rather than individualistic vision of the Anglo-Saxon, or for that matter the Ibo, there are no digressions in *Beowulf.* There can't be "digressions" in a world in which everything is connected, and that, in essence, is the point about polytheism that Akunna wishes to make to Mr. Brown concerning the *Ikenga.* The wooden gods are made of material created by Chukwu and as such cannot be separated from either their creator or the creation of which they are a part. To see them as separate is to see with the separatist eye of the literate European rather than the unitive eye of a member of an oral culture trained to see likeness rather than individuality, since language is a way of seeing the world as well as describing it. And that, to the sympathetic reader of Achebe's novel, is exactly what is so discomforting about the reductive perception of the District Commissioner with his passion to eliminate the superfluous and get down to the basic facts.

If the title of the District Commissioner's proposed book reveals much about his way of thinking, we must in the end turn to the titles *Beowulf* and *Things Fall Apart* as, themselves, indicators of cultural values of both their authors and their readers. The importance of context over the individual in *Beowulf* has to make one carefully reconsider the critical presuppositions implicit in the early editorial decision to entitle the work after one of its prominent characters. Approaching the poem from the "modern" point of view with its implicit privileging of the individual, Zupitza and other early editors of the poem gave little thought to any alternative but naming their editions of the untitled manuscript after its central character. *Things Fall Apart,* it has been noted, has as its hero, not an individual, but Umuofia, the Ibo homeland and implicitly its culture.[26] What, one might ask, might have happened if Achebe had been allowed to choose the title for the Anglo-Saxon epic? Might it have been named for Beowulf's clan, the Geats, or even for their demise? Read with the presumption of the importance of the individual indicated in its title, *Beowulf* is certainly a poem about the career of a great hero, but would the same reading be quite so evident were the reader to approach the same poem entitled *The Fall of the Geats?* Had Zupitza edited the untitled manuscript of Achebe's novel, would he have named it *Okonkwo,* and how would that title have shaped our expectations and thus our ways of seeing what follows? Showcasing the importance of expectation on the part of the reader, such questions reveal not only the essential indeterminacy of texts but also the central role of culture in shaping whatever determination there is, an essential lesson in cross-cultural reading. That the titles themselves are the products of our culturally induced expectation and presumption is but further proof of the lesson in the Commissioner's *The Pacification of the Primitive Tribes of the Lower Niger.*

Finally, if *Things Fall Apart* is deliberately not named after its central character, what then are we to make of Okonkwo, who is the focal point, if not the hero, of the novel? Our reading of Okonkwo's fate serves as a last lesson in the problem of cultural assumptions inherent in both the Anglo-Saxon epic and the Nigerian novel. It has been noted that Okonkwo, despite his self-image as the last faithful man to Ibo tradition, is himself guilty of violating Ibo law, as in his violence to his wife during "Peace Week," and more significantly in his consistent failure to place the group over the individual. From the very outset, his wrestling, like almost all of his actions, is generated for personal glory rather than the glory of the clan. Unlike his fellow clansmen, Okonkwo is a man of few words. Rather than being an orator, he stammers, a physical manifestation of his internal inability to communicate, to participate in the verbal activity that is the essence of Ibo culture. In despising his music-loving but ne'er-do-well father, Okonkwo in many ways rejects the poetry, the love of song and conversation that represent the best of the defining features of the culture he claims to champion. Okonkwo represents a type of selfish individualism that is in essence a threat to Ibo notions of clan, and culture. Okonkwo's demons are personal, private ones. He presumes that he, by acting alone against the advice of the clan, can be its personal savior, an ironic pose for a declared enemy of the Christian missionaries. His is consistently a failure to act with the group or its desires, usually in order to prove his individual manhood. Characteristically, he wishes to force his ideas of what is and is not appropriate on the rest of the clan. Okonkwo's pursuit of tribal ranks, a ruling passion in his life, is not to affirm the value of the clan's traditions but to set himself apart from others of lesser degree. Despite these obvious shortcomings, Okonkwo, in the minds of many contemporary students, is often a sympathetic character, more sinned against than sinning. Such students' final sympathy with Okonkwo usually seems to find its source in Okonkwo's status as victim of authority, as member of the oppressed who takes a stand by acting alone to kill the Commissioner's messenger. Yet such sympathy for the outsider/victim, a defining impulse of post-Romantic culture, runs exactly counter to the notion of the preeminence of the group, the clan that should speak with one voice.

If, indeed, the Commissioner is an oppressor, it is the Ibo as a group who are threatened, not the individual Okonkwo. The threat to Ibo custom from without embodied by the Commissioner is, in fact, reflected within the group in the person of Okonkwo. In the end, the cross-cultural sympathy for Okonkwo has much in common with the cultural misreading likewise apparent in student sympathy for Grendel as outsider. Interestingly enough, the description of Grendel as "lone-goer" is an equally apt portrait of Okonkwo's emotional relations with his wives, his children, and the rest of the clan. Both Grendel and Okonkwo are essentially antisocial in their aloneness. Grendel, it will be recalled, was first driven to his murderous raids on the feast hall by the sounds of men singing the "song of creation," his devouring of flesh and blood being not only a parody of communion but an attempt to silence the hall. Both Okonkwo and Grendel are together in their aloneness and their mistrust of song and communion. From the point of view of both the Anglo-Saxon and the Ibo, exile is a kind of damnation, a being cut off from defining origin, from the ritual and above all communication that defines humanity. Aloneness breeds monstrosity. In his heart, Okonkwo, like both Grendel and the impatient reader of *Beowulf,* shares much in common with the District Commissioner in his impatience with words and his preference for deeds rather than speeches.[27]

Viewed in this light, Okonkwo's individualism is far from heroic. If he seems tragic, it is because we feel awe at the magnitude of his error, as in the case of Faustus, rather than because we feel pity for a victim of his own virtue and forces of evil beyond his control. Hanged Okonkwo is not hanged Cordelia. Rather, viewed from the perspective of Umuofia as "hero," Okonkwo's personal demise represents a "comedic" confirmation of Ibo values by showing the price of departing from the spirit of custom. Remarkably, *Beowulf* ends with much the same point through the ending "Messenger's Prophecy" of invasion and annihilation when outsiders learn of the Geats' desertion of their leader in battle. By running away and deserting their lord for the sake of *personal* safety, the Geats have broken the heroic code that defines them as a group, and the fate of the Geats, like that of Okonkwo, provides a stark reminder of the price of losing or straying from tradition. In the end, both *Beowulf* and *Things Fall Apart* are conservative in that they both express a desire to conserve, to preserve, culture by warning that annihilation is the price of its abandonment. In the end, both *Beowulf* and *Things Fall Apart* have as their theme cultural survival, the preservation of ways of seeing, knowing, and speaking that are alien to their present American audiences. In the former, the threat is from within. The danger comes from the sleeping Grendel of individuality that lies dormant even in the best of men. The Geats fall victim to themselves. In the latter, the threat is from without, which makes the latter an effective analogy for interaction between students situated outside the culture of both works.

That such readings seem so hidden and even perverse to students whose cultural orientation and, hence, sympathies are closer to those of John Gardner's *Grendel*[28] is perhaps the final great lesson about culture and its role in shaping our reading that emerges from our comparison of these two unlikely literary companion pieces. One culture's hero is another's villain. As Obierika's brother noted, "What is good in one place is bad in another." The trick is to know "one" from "another"; that is, to recognize sameness and difference.

Conclusion

That two such different works might, through their similarities, fit together in odd combination leads us at last to the lion-bodied, human-headed sphinx in the poem from which Achebe takes his title. "The Second Coming," in fact, provides a final metaphoric analogy for the clash of cultures that has been the focus of our discussion of these two works. In Yeats's poem there is, of course, the juxtaposition of the Sphinx and rocking cradle of the infant Jesus, each an icon simultaneously familiar and comforting to the culture which spawned it, threatening to that which did not—a conflict that serves to remind us of the Trinity seen from both inside and outside the circle of faith. But those searching for a parable of the cross-cultural reader might rather turn to the poem's famous falcon in the gyre, the first sign that things are falling apart. The widening gyre is caused by the fact that the falcon cannot hear the falconer, a powerful sign that the natural order of things is breaking down; that is until one asks whether the taming of falcons for the sport of falconers is in fact the *natural* order of things. Or is it—like a preference for prose over poetry, for the individual over the group—an arbitrary presumption of the reader, a cultural imperative imposed from without? Students reading *Beowulf* for the first time have a natural tendency to "hood the falcon," to make it fly not on its own terms but on ours and, when it fails to do so, to find the results to be an "anarchy" worthy of the warning with which this paper began. Reading *Things Fall Apart* cannot, of course, curb that tendency, but it can help to lay it bare, to make the impulse as important a part of our understanding as the traditional content of these two works, something that turns disorder into "*mere* anarchy" and the dissolving Order into the less substantial "things." In another poem about collapse (and regeneration), "Lapis Lazuli," Yeats tells us that "all things fall and are built again, / and those that build them again are gay." To rebuild: that, in essence, is the task of reading, but especially reading works from cultures from which we are removed. And when we rebuild, we need to be aware that we do so in our own image. The ways we build are as much the point as what we think we have restored. *Beowulf* and *Things Fall Apart* teach us that our task will be gay if our goal is neither to confine these works to a museum case nor simply to trade in our own well-worn shoes for those designed for other souls.

Notes

1. Stanley B. Greenfield, *A Readable Beowulf, The Old English Epic Newly Translated* (Carbondale: Southern Illinois Press, 1982).

2. For a brief discussion of "anthropological" issues in cross-cultural studies and especially their relation to the study of orality, see David E. Bynum, "Myth and Ritual: Two Faces of Tradition," in *Oral Tradition and Literature: A Festschrift for Alfred Bates Lord,* ed. John Miles Foley (Columbus, OH: Slavica Publications, 1981), pp. 142–63. Also helpful in this regard is Lloyd W. Brown, "Cultural Norms and Modes of Perception," in *Critical Perspectives on Chinua Achebe,* eds. C. L. Innes and Bernth Lindfors (Washington, D. C.: Three Continents Press, 1978), pp. 22–36. Senior students may wish to consult Ernst Cassier, "An Essay on Man," in *An Essay on Man: An Introduction to Philosophy of Human Culture* (New Haven: Yale University Press, 1944).

3. There are a number of resources for illustrations readily available. The widely available Ellesmere portraits of the Canterbury pilgrims give some sense of the general trend in footwear, especially those of the Knight and Squire. Nancy Bradfield, *Historical Costumes of England, From the Eleventh to the Twentieth Centuries* (New York: Barnes and Noble, 1971), gives the best general overview of the broad changes in shoe fashion during the later Middle Ages. However, Bradford provides only modern drawings of medieval footwear. She does, however, provide an excellent drawing of "piked shoes" with the points tied back to the shin (pp. 42–43). Michael and Ariene Batterburg, *Fashion: The Mirror of History* (New York: Greenwich House), present several late medieval illuminations containing some splendidly extended points from the court of Philip the Good, Duke of Burgundy, known as "the cradle of fashion" (pp. 86, 89). Penelope Byrde, *The Male Image, Men's Fashion in Britain 1300–1970* (London: B. T. Batsford, 1979), contains an excellent photograph of a late fifteenth-century shoe with upturned toe (p. 194).

4. See Alfred Bates Lord, *The Singer of Tales* (Cambridge: Harvard University Press, 1960). For a brief and helpful overview of oral-formulaic studies, as well as a discussion of Bates's role in that development, see John Miles Foley, "The Oral Theory in Context," in Foley, *Oral Tradition,* p. 27.

5. Jeff Opland, *Anglo-Saxon Oral Poetry: A Study of the Tradition* (New Haven: Yale, 1980).

6. Many critics have recognized the linguistic themes, especially the conflict between the Ibo and their "civilizers," as central to the novel. C. L. Innes notes, "*Things Fall Apart* is a commentary on the ways in which language can become rigid and incapable of communication, but at the same time demonstrates the creative possibilities of language," in *Chinua Achebe* (Cambridge: Cambridge University Press, Cambridge Studies in African and Caribbean Literature, 1990), vol. I, p. 36. Also see, C. L. Innes, "Language,

Poetry and Doctrine in *Things Fall Apart*," in Innes and Lindfors, *Critical Perspectives*, pp. 111–25, as well as Julian N. Wasserman, "The Sphinx and the Rough Beast: Linguistic Struggle in Chinua Achebe's *Things Fall Apart*," *Mississippi Folklore Register,* 16 (1982), 61–70.

7. Chinua Achebe, *Things Fall Apart* (New York: Astor-Honor, 1959), p. 164. All citations are from this edition of the text.

8. Metaphors, themselves, require both similarity and difference. Metaphors, as signs, must be other than what they represent, as conventionally a "thing" cannot signify itself. At the same time there must be some identity between a metaphor and its referent. Such simultaneous identity and difference would appeal far more to Akunna than to Brown or the even more single-minded Enoch. Advanced students may find it useful to consult Paul Henle, "Metaphor," in *Language, Thought and Culture,* ed. Paul Henle (Ann Arbor: University of Michigan Press, 1958), pp. 173–95, as well as Paul Ricoeur, *The Rule of Metaphor: Multidisciplinary Studies of the Creation of Meaning and Language,* translated by Robert Czerny (Toronto: University of Toronto Press, 1977).

9. For a brief discussion of the difficulties of oral texts for literate audiences, see John Miles Foley, "Oral Theory in Context," in Foley, *Oral Tradition,* p. 7.

10. Unless otherwise indicated, line numbers refer to *Beowulf and the Fight at Finnsburg, Edited with Introduction, Bibliography Notes, Glossary, and Appendices,* 3rd ed., edited by Fr. Klaeber (Lexington, MA: D.C. Heath, 1950).

11. Phanuel Akubueze Egejuru has recently presented a paper—"Orhetory (Oka Okwu): A Neglected Technique in Achebe's Literary Artistry"—at the International Conference to mark Chinua Achebe's sixtieth birthday at the University of Nigeria Nsukka—in which she coins the term "orhetory" to describe a combination of oratory and rhetoric:

> On the one hand, we find in orhetory the cumulative repetition
> of actual facts or feelings which is a distinctive feature of oratory.
> On the other hand, we find an intellectualization of facts which
> is a distinctive feature of rhetoric.

We are especially grateful to Professor Egejuru not only for her generosity in sharing her presentations with us but with her willingness to share her ideas as well as her enthusiasm for Achebe's works.

12. For a brief discussion of the features of Anglo-Saxon poetry suitable for beginning students, see "Traditional and Oral Formulaic Features," in Alain Renoir's "Introduction" to Greenfield's *A Readable Beowulf,* pp. 7–14. For a much more detailed discussion more suitable for junior and senior students, see "Some Remarks on the Nature and Quality of Old English Poetry," in Stanley B. Greenfield, *A Critical History of Old English Literature* (New York: New York University Press, 1965), pp. 69–79. Still more advanced students may wish to consult Francis P. Magoun, Jr., "Oral-Formulaic Character of Anglo-Saxon Narrative Poetry," *Speculum 28* (1953): pp. 446–67.

13.   ... helle gemundon
   in modsefan, Metod hie ne cupon,

dæda Demend, ne wiston hie Drihten God,
ne hie huru heofena Helm herian ne cupon,
wuldres Waldend. (Klaeber, II. pp. 179–83)

The translation is taken from Charles W. Kennedy, *Beowulf, The Oldest English Epic* (New York: Oxford University Press, 1940).

14. The distinctive properties of Ibo speech are also those of the narrator. See Innes, *Achebe,* p. 33. Phanuel Akubueze Egejuru notes ways African novels differ from European ones: "loose plots, sketchy characterization, and lack of scenic or atmosphere description," *Black Writers: White Audience* (Hicksville, NY: Exposition Press, 1978), p. 192—qualities of orality equally evident in the style and structure of *Things Fall Apart.*

One of the most sensitive and enlightening readings of the style and texture of Achebe's prose is found in B. Eugene McCarthy, "Rhythm and Narrative Method in Achebe's *Things Fall Apart,*" *Novel* (Spring, 1985): pp. 243–56. McCarthy, through close readings of passages, notes how Achebe's prose style reflects the stylistic patterns and devices of oral works, including repetition, accumulation, and rhythm. Especially noteworthy are the discussions of the ways in which form and content/theme complement each other. While McCarthy's essay may be beyond freshman and sophomore students, it is remarkably clear in its presentation and analysis. We frequently make it required reading for advanced students of *Beowulf,* asking students to attempt similar stylistic analyses of short passages of that poem.

For Achebe's views on the suitability of English as a language for the African novel, see Chinua Achebe, "The African Writer and the English Language," in *Morning Yet on Creation Day* (Garden City: Anchor Press, 1975), pp. 91–104.

15. For a discussion of kennings appropriate for students at all levels, see Greenfield, *Critical History,* pp. 73–74. We do not, for purposes of this paper, find it necessary to make the distinction between a *kenning* and a *kent heti,* a similar compound metaphor, although the distinction is explained in the cited passage from Greenfield.

16. Consider, for example, the names given by Ekwefi to her children:

Her deepening despair found expression in the names she gave her children. One of them was a pathetic cry, Onwumbiko—"Death, I implore you." But Death took no notice; Onwumbiko died in his fifteenth month. The next child was a girl, Ozoemena—"May it not happen again." She died in her eleventh month, and two others after her. Ekwefi then became defiant and called her next child Onwuma—"Death may please himself." And he did (74).

17. For a discussion suitable for advanced students on the inclusive and exclusive strategies of parables as well as their openness, see T. D. Kelly and John T. Irwin, "The Meaning of *Cleanness:* Parable as Effective Sign," *Medieval Studies* 35 (1972): pp. 232–60.

18. Egejuru argues that the novel, in the context of African literature, is essentially a "borrowed form." The basis of this judgment is a juxtaposition of the novel and the epic. The former is presented as the story of an individual

while the latter is primarily concerned with the fate of society (*Black Writers: White Audience*, 193–94). The former is more suited to an oral society while the latter is more suited to a literate one. Citing Lukacs, Egejuru notes "the epic is the product of a solid society with a harmonious vision of the world. The novel is the product of a dislocated society with a disintegrated image of the world" (193). Such a juxtaposition of genres exactly captures the divergent perceptions of the Europeans and the Ibo.

19. Consider, for example, the coastguard's speech, in which Beowulf is told "a seasoned warrior must know the difference between words and deeds" (Kennedy, I, 283). In this light, the difference is clear between Beowulf, who avoids violence by answering Unferth's slander with words rather than physical action, and Okonkwo, who, we are told, "Had a slight stammer and whenever he was angry and could not get his words out quickly enough . . . would use his fists" (8).

20. See Elizabeth Isichei, *The Ibo People and the Europeans: The Genesis of a Relationship, to 1906* (New York: St. Martins, 1973), especially pp. 27–43, as well as M. M. Green, *Ibo Village Affairs* (New York: Frederick A. Praeger, 1964), pp. 5–12 for discussions of Ibo verbal practices and the relationship between Ibo language and identity.

21. One of most interesting ritual exchanges, combining verbal grace and the politics of politeness, is between Obierika and Okonkwo in regard to the latter's statement, "I don't know how to thank you":

"I can tell you," said Obierika. "Kill one of your sons for me."
"That will not be enough," said Okonkwo.
"Then kill yourself," said Obierika. (131–32)

22. For Achebe's views on the relationship between language and culture, see Chinua Achebe, "Language and the Destiny of Man," in *Morning Yet on Creation Day*, pp. 47–59.

23. It is tempting to see a wordplay here that reinforces the linguistic themes of language and identity: when my language ("myself") is corrupted, I become Kotma, the white man. Corruption of language is therefore the corruption of self. Word play is often a feature of oral culture as it obviously is for the Ibo in this case.

24. For a discussion of Romantic and post-Romantic misreadings of premodern literature, especially in light of the former's emphasis on the individual, see D. W. Robertson, Jr., *A Preface to Chaucer, Studies in Medieval Perspectives* (Princeton: Princeton University Press, 1962), especially pp. 3–51.

25. See *Biblia Pauperum, Facsimile Edition of the Forty-Leaf Blockbook in the Library of the Esztergom Cathedral* (Corvina Press, 1967), p. 29 or *Biblia Pauperum, A Facsimile Edition*, edited by Avril Henry (Ithaca: Cornell University Press, 1987), pp. 104, 106.

26. For a discussion of Umuofia as "hero," see Egejuru, *Black Writers: White Audience*, p. 196. Egejuru, however, also sees Okonkwo as "the most outstanding character of the novel . . . who is the embodiment of the social values of Umuofia community" (195).

27. C. L. Innes, in *Achebe,* explicitly links Okonkwo and the District Commissioner in their mutual rigidity and refusal to acknowledge feelings, p. 22.

28. Modern students, viewing the creative act from the perspective of the primacy of the individual, of necessity privilege "invention" (read: breaking rules and convention) and "self-expression" as the chief virtues in art. Given this perspective, they find the formulaic nature of oral poetry, an essential element of its conservatism, disturbing. For an excellent discussion of the issues of the counterbalancing demands of artistic freedom/creativity and tradition, see M. Ngal, "Literary Creation and Oral Civilizations," *New Literary History* 8 (Spring 1977): 335–44, especially pp. 335–38. While primarily intended for an advanced audience, the above issue of *New Literary History,* devoted entirely to "Oral Cultures and Oral Performances," contains much of interest to students of Achebe and *Beowulf.* An excellent summary of the volume's content is presented in Robert Kellog's final essay, "Literature, Nonliterature, and Oral Tradition," pp. 531–34.

23 An African Turnus: Heroic Response to Colonialism in Vergil's *Aeneid* and Achebe's *Things Fall Apart*

Norman McMillan
University of Montevallo

Reading literature which originates from outside the Western tradition not only provides the joy of discovering exciting new works in places few of us would have thought to look a few short years ago, but at the same time it offers us the possibility of looking afresh at works which have nourished many of us for years. The richness of Chinua Achebe's *Things Fall Apart,* a Nigerian novel published in 1959, has by now been experienced by countless readers, among whom are many whose reading of traditional texts has been deepened by the experience. For example, David Carroll, in a recent book on Achebe, points out that an old classic like Thomas Hardy's *The Mayor of Casterbridge* might profitably be read afresh in light of similarities in character between the impressive, wrongheaded heroes of the novels, Henchard and Okonkwo (Carroll 1990, 58–59).

In this paper I will discuss thematic similarities between *Things Fall Apart* and Vergil's great epic, the *Aeneid.* Certainly it is not time, place, culture, or custom which connect these works. While we are interested in these matters, we are more drawn to the works because they address questions which seem general to the human condition, no matter what the time and place. Vergil, while drawing heavily on his knowledge of Roman culture and history, writes a work which is, as Viktor Pöschl puts it, "a poem of humanity, not a political manifesto." He goes on to say that "the tragedy in the *Aeneid* is a symbol not only of the tragedy in Roman history, but in human life, as well" (Pöschl 1962, 23–24).

Achebe, too, depicts universals in his work, as he himself tells us. To begin with, he confesses to having some worries about Western critics who look for universality in everything because quite often they impose a narrow interpretation of universality on the rest of the world. He especially finds it galling that some of these critics seem so shocked to find universality in an African work while "it would never occur to them to doubt the universality of their own literature" (Carroll 1980, 25). Besides that, Achebe believes that the writer has the obligation at times to educate or re-educate his readers, in the case of his own writing to make them see that the "[Ibo] past—with all of its imperfections was not one long night of savagery from which the first Europeans acting on God's behalf delivered them" (Carroll 1980, 26). But despite his interest in depicting the Ibo culture as accurately as possible, in all its distinctive qualities, he says that "the writer's duty is not to beat the morning's headlines in topicality; it is to explore the depth of the human condition." He adds, "Like any other, African fiction will achieve universality through both a sensitive reading and interpretation of its own culture and through transcending the purely local conditions which occasion it" (Killam 1969, 10–11).

What, then, is the universal human concern which yokes the *Aeneid* and *Things Fall Apart* together? Perhaps it would best come into focus by casting it as a question: How should persons react when their lands are invaded by outsiders who not only feel superior but also feel destined to rule over the native people? Both the Trojans coming into Latium in Vergil's work and the British establishing a colonial presence in Nigeria force the local people into difficult and even tragic choices.

As the towers of Troy fall around him, Aeneas learns that his destiny will take him to Italy, where he will "found" Rome. His attitude toward the Italian people he will encounter is shaped by the prophecies he hears during the first six books of the epic. When his father's ghost tells him, "In Latium you must fight a race of savages" (V, 730–31), the expectations of both Aeneas and the reader are set.[1] Both his father Anchises and Zeus use the word *pacify* to describe what the Trojans must do to the Italians. For most readers, I imagine, this description conjures up an image of a chaotic situation which must be brought under control. Instead, we find a kindly, gentle old king in Italy who has "grown old in years of peaceful reign" (VII, 46) as well as a walled city with many of the customary trappings of civilization—a council, a temple, a palace, feasts, athletic contests. Where, one questions, is the savagery? Who, we ask, needs pacification? The supreme paradox is that the need for pacification occurs only because the pacifiers precipitate the disorder. Pacification, ironically, has a history of being a very unpeaceful procedure. As Aeneas says, "[Italy] must do us homage and wear our yoke today / else, burn it; level its towers with the ground" (XII, 561–69). Either way, wearing the yoke or burned to the ground, Italy will be pacified—a Hobson's choice before there was a Hobson.

Achebe's novel takes up the question of pacification even more directly. At the very end of *Things Fall Apart,* after the main character Okonkwo has become so thoroughly humiliated by the colonists that he commits suicide, the point of view shifts abruptly to the British District Commissioner, who reacts to the death:

> The story of this man who had killed a messenger and hanged himself would make interesting reading [in the book he would write on bringing civilization to Africa]. One could almost write a whole chapter on him. Perhaps not a whole chapter but a reasonable paragraph, at any rate. He had already chosen the title of the book, after much thought: *The Pacification of the Primitive Tribes of the Lower Niger.* (Achebe 1959, 191)[2]

The callousness of these words is chilling, and the same question we asked about Italy occurs again: did the village of Umuofia need pacification until the missionaries, government people, and traders arrived from Britain? Did the British deeds and attitudes in any way precipitate the disorder?

The British view of the Ibos was pretty much the same as the general European view of African culture and history which accompanied imperialism: Africans stagnated in primitive savagery with no sense of order, no sense of ethics, no principles of conduct—attitudes which became the justification for conquest and exploitation. The missionaries, who came first, dismissed the value of traditional religion, their objections becoming more strident as time went on. They told the Ibos that their gods were idols, that their ceremonies, their marriage customs (including polygamy), their ancestor worship (a practice shared with the ancient Romans), and their non-Christian names were wrong. The actions of the missionaries in *Things Fall Apart* are consistent with the philosophy clearly expounded in this statement from a spokesman of the International Missionary Council during the period of colonization:

> The Missionary is a revolutionary and has to be so, for to preach and plant Christianity means to make a frontal attack on the beliefs, the customs, the apprehensions of life and the world, and by implication (because tribal religions are primarily social realities) on the social structures and bases of primitive society. (Coleman 1960, 97)

The destruction of the existing culture was quite consciously undertaken, not only by the missionaries, but also in an even more brutal way by the traders and government administrators who followed them. The British politicians asserted that the decentralized system of political power found in clan life was primitive and that their rules were worthless, and the traders responded similarly to their economic systems.

Just as was the case in the *Aeneid*, the British view of Umuofian society is not altogether borne out by what we see. Much of *Things Fall Apart* describes life in the clan before the arrival of the Europeans, so we have a much more thorough picture of Ibo society than we have of the invaded people in the *Aeneid*. In Umuofia we find a complex family life, clan life, and religious life. The people have their laws and their courts, an oral literature, a highly developed oratorical style, and their feasts and festivals. Life is not, however, idyllic. The clan sanctions the exposure of twins to certain death, the mutilation of the stillborn child to discourage its reentry into the womb, the murder of persons outside the clan, and other unsavory practices, but, despite these things, the Umuofians are far from the benighted savages the British take them to be.

The sudden disruption of the lives of both the Italians and the Ibos was largely unexpected. The responses of the invaded to these invaders begins with some disbelief, but slowly the Latins and the Ibos must face the painful reality of the power of their invaders. When the Trojan emissaries sent by Aeneas to the Italian King Latinus approach the town, the Latins are engaged in athletic contests on the outskirts of the city. The Trojans are sufficiently distinct in appearance to cause one Italian participant to leap astride his horse and gallop off to report to the king that "tall men dressed in foreign garb [are] coming." Later, the Italians taunt the Trojans about their appearance and way of life. One young Latin yells, "your coats are scarlet trimmed with gold! You / love amusement, luxury, the dance, sleeves to your / wrists, a bonnet, ribbons to tie it. Men of the East? / No: women!" (IX, 614–17). Turnus later prays that in battle he may be able "to tear [Aeneas's] corselet from him, rip it off— / our Phrygian laddy—and foul his pretty curls / crimped with hot iron and dripping with perfume" (XII, 98–100). We see here a sense of superiority over the decadent Trojans. But, over all, the differences in Trojans and Italians are minimal. Contrasts in religion, in the mechanism of government, and in basic social structures seem rather unimportant to the Italians, both to those who accept Aeneas and those who reject him. The chief issue here is more *who* will control the society than how it will be operated.

This is not at all the case with the Ibos. The differences go to the very heart of what is acceptable behavior within a society. The arrival of the Europeans is a far, far stranger, a far more shocking thing than the arrival in Italy of the Trojans, who, according to legend, come from good old Italian stock sometime in the long past anyway.

When he hears of the arrival of the first white man in the African village of Abame, Okonkwo is incredulous: a *white* man—not a man made white by leprosy, not an albino, but a real white man—one who rides into town on an iron horse (i.e., a bicycle) and has no toes (i.e., wears shoes). He tries to communicate with the curious people who cautiously approach him and finally work up the nerve to touch his strange skin. The villagers do what they normally do when they have a problem which defies normal human wisdom: they consult their oracle, who tells them that "the strange man [will] break their clan and spread destruction among them" (128). So they kill the man and tie his bicycle to a sacred silk-cotton tree so that it cannot "run away and call the man's friends" (128). The oracle here is just as true as those prophecies predicting Aeneas's role in the future of Rome. The white men do come and murder almost all of the inhabitants of Abame—men, women, children—in a surprise attack, making no attempt to identify the guilty, an action called collective punishment which was officially sanctioned by British policy (Wren 1980, 27). This news is more than Okonkwo can take in. His friend, Obierika, jokes with Okonkwo, saying, "Who knows what will happen tomorrow. Perhaps green men will come to our clan and shoot us." Okonkwo answers innocently, "God will not permit it" (131).

But the Trojans and British are there, and they mean to stay. The last halves of the *Aeneid* and *Things Fall Apart* chronicle the response to this presence when it can no longer be denied.

In Italy, the Trojan presence is given the validity not only of Aeneas's divine revelations, but also of King Latinus's own revelation. He has learned from the oracle that a foreigner will come who will be united with his daughter in marriage, will rule the country, and will initiate the march of history which will produce the future glories of Rome. Latinus lacks a male heir, so that is no barrier to his accepting Aeneas, and, as an old man, he wants nothing to interrupt the long-standing peace. With almost no questioning of whether Aeneas is really the man who has been prophesied to come to Latium, Latinus embraces the Trojan. Others do as well. A less noble embracer of the Trojans is the character Drances, who argues for an eternal bond of peace with the Trojans at all costs. This man especially infuriates Turnus, who tells him, "You always flood us, Drances, with your talk, / when warfare cries for action" (XI, 378–79). He also taunts him with charges of cowardice and bastardy.

In Umuofia there are also people who accept the colonists. At the outset these are the *efulefu,* the worthless men who "in the language of the clan [sell their machetes] and [wear] the sheathe[s] to battle" (133). The *osu,* who were outcasts in the clan, also quickly gravitate toward the Christian church. As time goes on, people of more worth and position in the tribe join the Christians. Among those who do not actually join the missionaries are some who counsel making peace rather than fighting. There is a Drances figure in *Things Fall Apart,* Egowanne, whom Okonkwo sees as a coward, as one whose "sweet tongue can change fire into cold ash" (143). When Egowanne speaks, Okonkwo says, "He moves our men to impotence. If they had ignored his womanish wisdom . . . we would not have come to this" (184). Drances and Egowanne are both seen as representing feminine weakness, which Turnus and Okonkwo believe will in the end destroy their worlds. In their view, only violent, masculine response is appropriate in responding to aggression.

As is already obvious, Turnus and Okonkwo are the central figures around whom the negative response to the outsiders collects. They represent extremely well those who cannot abide the interlopers, who see dangerous implications in their presence, and who ultimately want to destroy them. In sum, both represent the heroic response to the threat of the imminent destruction of all that is dear and sacred.

Before the arrival of their adversaries, both Turnus and Okonkwo have already established themselves as exceptional people with impressive qualities. Both are physically imposing and are well known for their athletic and military prowess. They are considered the bravest and boldest of men, worthy of high honor. Both are industrious; both seem forthright and honest, and both have not accomplished what they have aspired to. Turnus wants to be king and Okonkwo wants to take the fourth (and highest) title of his clan. It is true that both have big egos and a high sense of their importance in the scheme of things, that both are ambitious and have a lust for glory, and that neither suffers fools gladly, but they both so value their own cultures that they are willing to fight to the death to preserve them. Neither is an altogether likeable man, but each is a great man, and readers find sympathy with them and admire them.

The flaws in the characters of Turnus and Okonkwo are evident before the arrival of the Trojans and the British. We know much less of Turnus because the first half of the epic focuses on the exploits of Aeneas, but we do know that Turnus is capable of a great deal of resentment and has come into conflict with the king and the oracle because he is unwilling to consider the idea of a foreign husband for Lavinia. We also know that he is quite full of himself and can treat inferiors with great scorn.

Of Okonkwo we know far more. His character is well-established before the arrival of the British, and what Frances M. Sibley says of him is undoubtedly true: "Granted his inability to adjust to colonialism, he is equally unable to adjust to his own society" (Sibley 1975, 320). He commits several offenses—offenses which grow out of an extreme anger, an unyielding spirit, and an impetuous, unreasoned, violent response to frustration. With these flaws is coupled an unhealthy concern for what the clan thinks of him. The following passage gives an excellent insight into his character:

> Okonkwo ruled his household with a heavy hand. His wives, especially the youngest, lived in perpetual fear of his fiery temper, and so did his little children. Perhaps down in his heart Okonkwo was not a cruel man. But his whole life was dominated by fear, the fear of failure and of weakness. It was deeper and more intimate than the fear of evil and capricious gods and of magic, the fear of the forest, and of the forces of nature, malevolent, red in tooth and claw. Okonkwo's fear was greater than these. It was not external but lay deep within himself. It was the fear of himself. (16–17)

He is especially afraid that people will find him like his father, a ne'er-do-well who valued pleasure over duty and never amounted to much in the eyes of the clan.

Okonkwo's anger flashes in all directions. In holding himself above others, he feels entirely justified in treating inferiors with brusqueness. He beats one wife for not cooking her portion of his evening meal, thereby committing the serious offense of breaking his tribe's celebration of the Week of Peace, and he shoots at another of his wives. His fear of being thought weak leads him to deal the killing blow to the young boy Ikemafuna, a boy whom he has kept and loved as a son for three years but one whom the oracle has said must be sacrificed. Later Okonkwo grieves for this action, and his friend Obierika tells him that he should not have joined the group who took Ikemafuna out to execute him. When Okonkwo says that it was necessary to carry out the bidding of the oracle, Obierika says, "This is true. But if the Oracle said that my son should be killed I would neither dispute it nor be the one to do it" (64–65). These contrasting points of view reveal a great deal about Okonkwo's character. He sees things simply, clearly, rigidly, purely. He can never see the conditional nature of things, can never admit to dilemma.

The heroic qualities of Turnus and Okonkwo, both positive and negative, are magnified after the arrival of the Trojans and the British. They now have a greater focus for their rage, a cause which is more intense than anything they have previously experienced. The very survival of their societies is threatened.

Turnus is immediately maddened at the arrival of the Trojans, ordering his men to arms and saying that he will guard Italy and beat her enemies off, even if he has to fight some fellow Latins first. He is outraged that anyone calling himself a Latin could be taken in by these sweet-talking liars who sue "for peace in ships festooned with spears" (X, 80). Okonkwo is likewise maddened, but his initial knowledge of the arrival of the white man is not firsthand. He is in exile (having been cast out of his own village for a serious infringement of its rules) when he hears of the destruction of the village of Abame, and he says that the inhabitants were fools. "They had been warned that danger was ahead," he said. "They should have armed themselves with their guns and machetes even when they went to market" (130). When he first hears of the white men's religion, he is convinced that they are mad, and when he sees them gaining converts in the town of his exile he argues that until the abominable gang is chased out of the village with whips there can be no peace. When others appease the British, Okonkwo says:

> Let us not reason like cowards. If a man comes into my hut and defecates on the floor, what do I do? Do I shut my eyes? No! I take a stick and break his head. This is what a man does.

"This [is] a womanly clan" (148), he thinks; they pretend not to see what is going on. He cannot believe that his own village of Umuofia would react so timidly.

Okonkwo's hope for a more "manly" response by his hometown to the British is an empty dream. During the seven years he is in exile, the British become entrenched. The missionaries have gained more and more converts, the British administration is firmly in place, and the traders have won over a great number of citizens to the new system of trade. As time goes on, the converts become more actively antagonistic to the old ways and look for occasions to confront unconverted tribesmen with acts which indicate what they have come to regard as the foolishness, falseness, ineffectiveness, and powerlessness of the native culture. One such act is a Christian's unmasking of an *uwugwu*—that is, an ancestral god—during a ritual dance celebrating the tie with ancestors. This is an egregious act of great sacrilege and sets off the heroic response of Okonkwo and other like-minded Umuofians.

Okonkwo, like Turnus, has powers as a leader, and he manages to convince others of the need for swift, decisive action in the face of such aggression. Like Turnus in his foray against the Trojan forces, Okonkwo, in the retaliatory destruction of the Christian church, is at first encouraged by his success, but his happiness is short-lived. Neither he nor Turnus has properly reckoned with the power of the imposing forces or the inroads they have made with the natives. Turnus says that he will move against the townsmen who join the Trojans, but Okonkwo's culture will not allow him to destroy one of his own. As time goes on, their confederates fall away, and both Turnus and Okonkwo determine that they must proceed alone. They mourn for a time when men were men. Turnus cries, "Oh for some vestige of our native honor" (XI, 415), and Okonkwo complains that "worthy men are no more" (184). The two heroes assume that fighting is the only recourse.

Neither Turnus nor Okonkwo can singlehandedly reverse the tide of events in which he is caught. Their roles become tragic as we see them realize the odds against them. As Povey beautifully puts it, we move here "into the very painful heart of human experience where human honor and determination seem to be toys of immeasurable forces that play with mankind's pretensions and struggles, turning heroism and honor into folly... [a place] where personal strength and integrity are as nothing when unimaginable social forces develop their own impetus towards uncontrollable changes" (Povey 1972, 105–06). The heroes, both Turnus and Okonkwo, wind up alone, cut off from consolation, estranged even from their gods, in despair.

Turnus sees the vision of his end. He asks his sister, "What turn of fate could save me now?" (XII, 637). He says that he will see his land destroyed. But he will not let the land see Turnus run. Pathetically, he asks, "Is it so bad to die?" (XII, 646), and in the question we see an essential aspect of his character: death is better than to live having lost everything. Okonkwo, likewise, sees his end and that of his clan. He begins "to suspect himself to be in the grip of an overriding destiny he cannot control" (Killam 1969, 25). When he learns that his own son, Nwoye, has gone over to the Christians, he gets a glimpse of the future:

> [H]is son's crime stood out in its stark enormity. To abandon the gods of one's father and go about with a lot of effeminate men clucking like old hens was the very depth of abomination. Suppose when he died all his male children decided to follow Nwoye's steps and abandon their ancestors? Okonkwo felt a cold shudder run through him at the terrible prospect, like the prospect of annihilation. He saw himself and his fathers crowding round their ancestral shrine waiting in vain for worship and sacrifice and finding nothing but ashes of bygone days, and his children the while praying to the white man's god. (142)

The ashes here are reflected in his vision of his own end. As he muses ironically on his nickname, "Roaring Flame," his eyes are opened and he sees the whole matter clearly: "Living fire begets cold, impotent ash" (143). Finally, when the ancestral spirit is unmasked, an act of unspeakable horror, "it seemed [to him] as if the very soul of the tribe wept for the great evil that was coming—its own death" (171–72).

Despite these visions of the end, the two heroes continue their efforts. Turnus moves out alone to meet Aeneas face to face in battle, knowing he will die. Okonkwo and five others are arrested for burning the church, and while in jail they are brutally treated by the agents of the British administrator. Bent on revenge once he is released, Okonkwo calls a meeting to decide what the next move of the clan should be. During the meeting, messengers from the British District Commissioner come to break up the meeting. So inflamed by this impertinence is Okonkwo that he pulls his machete from his sheath and beheads one of the messengers. When his fellow clansmen allow the other messengers to escape, Okonkwo knows that he is alone.

At the end, Turnus is cut down by Aeneas; Okonkwo goes home and hangs himself. Death seems the only way out for both. The anthropologist Ernest Becker points out that "short of natural catastrophe, the only time that life grinds to a halt or explodes in chaos is when culture falls down on its job of constructing a meaningful hero system for its members" (Becker 1971, 112). In effect, this is what Okonkwo experiences. He fights the good fight, but he sees that he has no further outlet for heroic action. Ironically, in committing suicide he goes against a tabu of the culture he has attempted more heroically to save than anyone else. His death, like Turnus's, has a strong element of tragedy. In pursuing their ideals so singlemindedly, so uncompromisingly, they achieve a sort of greatness, but also horrible deaths.

More than anything, it seems to me that Vergil and Achebe use Turnus and Okonkwo as examples of what happens when persons lack the ability to live in a world which is constantly presenting the unexpected, no matter what form it takes—colonization, revolution, social change, technology—whatever. Both writers demonstrate the destructive nature of rigidity. Achebe takes his title from Yeats's poem, "The Second Coming," a poem which addresses the inevitability of historical change. D. S. Izevbaye points out that Achebe's work demonstrates that "all important social and historical change is drastic and tragic, and it is necessary to adapt or be destroyed" (Izevbaye 1974, 145). It is quite true that figures like Turnus and Okonkwo do not ask to be presented with such horrible choices, and we must sympathize with their frustration. Yet at the same time, we know that those Italians who finally give in to Aeneas ultimately will be incorporated into the new order. Zeus says this, describing the future of Rome:

> Italians shall keep their fathers' ways and
>   speech,
> yes, and their name; except in blood

commingled,
Trojans shall sink from sight, I'll teach our
　Latins
new rite of worship; one tongue shall serve
　for all.
From Italy's mingled blood one folk shall
　rise,
surpassing god and man in righteousness.

(XII, 834–39)

Certainly we are not left with such a picture for the future of Umuofia, and yet we do have the case of Okonkwo's friend Obierika, who manages to keep a sense of integrity and identity in the face of the great changes his village faces. And although Achebe says of the effects of the colonial experience that "in terms of human dignity and human relations the encounter was almost a complete disaster for the black races," he also says, "I am not one of those who say that Africa has gained nothing from the colonial period . . . we have gained a lot" (Killam 1969, 4). Yet we are keenly aware that the tragedy of both *Things Fall Apart* and the *Aeneid* is, in part, the tremendous cost inflicted by the inability to adjust to the sweep of history.

In closing I wish to quote a statement of Paul Roche made in 1958 in an introduction to his translation of Sophocles' Theban plays, a statement as applicable, I believe, to a Turnus or an Okonkwo as to those inhabitants of the great house of Thebes:

> We need to be told that man is but a limited and contingent creature, subject to sudden disrupting forces. Success is not finally to be measured by fame and or material prosperity. Human greatness consists ultimately in nobly accepting the responsibility of being what we are; human freedom, in the personal working out of our fate in terms appropriate to ourselves. Though we may be innocent, we are all potentially guilty, because of the germ of self-sufficiency and arrogance in our nature. We must remember always that we are only man and to be modest in our own conceits. Our place in the total pattern of the cosmos is only finite. That is not to say that it may not be glorious. Whatever our circumstances, we can achieve and endure through to essential greatness. It is not what fate has in store for us that matters, but what we do with it when it comes. . . . The seeming caprice and unfairness of life, striking some down and pampering others, is only the beginning of the Great Encounter. Both the choice and destiny are ours. (Roche 1958, vi)

Notes

1. Unless otherwise stated, the quotations from Vergil are from *The Aeneid*, translated by Frank O. Copley, 2nd ed. (Indianapolis: Bobbs-Merrill Educational Publishing, 1975).

2. Unless otherwise stated, the quotations from Chinua Achebe are from *Things Fall Apart* (New York: Fawcett Crest, 1959).

References

Achebe, Chinua. *Things Fall Apart.* New York: Fawcett Crest, 1959.

Becker, Ernest. *The Birth and Death of Meaning.* 2nd ed. New York: The Free Press, 1971.

Carroll, David. *Chinua Achebe.* 2nd ed. New York: St. Martin's Press, 1980.

———. *Chinua Achebe: Novelist, Poet, Critic.* New York: Macmillan, 1990.

Coleman, James S. *Nigeria: Background to Nationalism.* Berkeley: University of California Press, 1960.

Izevbaye, D. S. "Nigeria." In *Literatures of the World,* edited by Bruce King. London: Routledge and Kegan Paul, 1974.

Killam, G. D. *The Novels of Chinua Achebe.* New York: Africana Publishing Co., 1969.

Pöschl, Viktor. *The Art of Virgil: Image and Symbol in the Aeneid.* Ann Arbor: University of Michigan Press, 1962.

Povey, John. "The Novels of Chinua Achebe." In *Introduction to Nigerian Literature,* edited by Bruce King. New York: Africana Publishing Co., 1972.

Roche, Paul. "The Great Encounter." *The Oedipus Plays of Sophocles.* New York: New American Library, 1958.

Sibley, Francis M. "Tragedy in the Novels of Chinua Achebe." *Southern Humanities Review* 9 (1975): 359–73.

Vergil. *The Aeneid.* 2nd ed. Translated by Frank O. Copley. Indianapolis: Bobbs-Merrill Educational Publishing (The Library of the Liberal Arts), 1975.

Wren, Robert M. *Achebe's World: The Historical and Cultural Context of the Novels.* Washington, D.C.: The Three Continents Press, 1980.

24 The Center Holds: The Resilience of Ibo Culture in *Things Fall Apart*

Ndiawar Sarr
Université de Saint-Louis

Written about the past of Africa by a novelist who sees himself as a "teacher," *Things Fall Apart* encompasses several worlds, several experiences, sometimes complex, all altered or mixed. Achebe is never a mere reporter of public events. Talking of *Things Fall Apart,* he said: "I now know that my first book was an act of atonement with my past, the ritual return and homage of a prodigal son" (Achebe 1975, 70). The past that Chinua Achebe describes so beautifully in *Things Fall Apart* is a past that Achebe himself had to rediscover. It is a past that was largely lost as a result of twentieth-century Europeanization. This rediscovery of the suppressed past is an act of faith and religious revival. Achebe, like the majority of African writers today, wants his writings to be functional, to serve as oral literature did in traditional Africa, reflecting the totality of actual experience. As David Cook tells us:

> Close study of a passage from *Things Fall Apart* out of context is particularly likely to lead to pedantic fault-finding and to have little relation to the full impact the novel makes upon us since . . . the achievement of this work is essentially an epic achievement in which the whole is greater than the parts and in which the parts cannot be appreciated properly when separated from the whole. (Cook 1977, 65)

John Mbiti similarly sees the holistic and communal nature of African culture in his statement: "I am because we are and since we are therefore I am" (Mbiti 1970, 141). This communal sense makes it necessary to see Okonkwo as something other than just a tragic hero in the usual Western sense—a lonely figure who passes moral judgment on the group.

The "we" of Achebe's story is the Ibo society of Umuofia, which has no centralized authority or king. The tribal setup is very different from most tribal societies in Africa, because of its respect for individ-

347

ualism and its rejection of any inherited or hierarchical system of authority. The Ibo people's highly individualistic society may have developed partly because of geography, for they lived in forest areas which were difficult to penetrate, and each village lived separated from the next. These natural obstacles are described by another Ibo writer, Elechi Amadi, in his novel *The Concubine:*

> Only the braves could go as far as Alyi. It was a whole day's journey from Omokachi. The path went through forests and swamps and there is no knowing when and where headhunters would strike. When there was any message to be relayed to Alyi two strong men ran the errand. (Amadi 1984, 9)

In spite of its isolation, Umuofia society is proud, dignified, and stable. It is governed by a complicated system of customs, traditions, and rituals extending from birth through marriage to death. It has its own legal, educational, and religious system and conventions governing relations between men and women, adults and children, and the various generations. The first part of the book allows us to see the customs, rituals, and traditions of Umuofia (e.g., consultation of oracles, the Week of Peace, the New Yam Festival) and to see the myths operating in the clan (e.g., Ogbanje, or a child that repeatedly dies and returns to the mother to be reborn, the exposure of twins, and taboos about shedding the blood of one's clansmen).

In addition, we are shown a society that is competitive and materialistic. A man's prestige is in direct proportion to the size of his barns and his compounds, to the number of titles he has taken. As *Things Fall Apart* shows the first impact of European invasion upon the old Ibo society, Achebe presents, in a very fair and objective way, the strengths and weaknesses of this society. Contrary to the views of the District Commissioner who plans to write a book, *The Pacification of the Primitive Tribes of the Lower Niger,* Achebe presents an Ibo culture which is neither "primitive" nor "barbaric." Even though his ambition to prove that "African peoples did not hear of culture for the first time from Europeans" might seem to cast doubt on his objectivity, he does not romanticize the Ibo society, but reveals instead the bad side as well as the good. He acts as the conscientious teacher he wants to be. Nothing is left aside.

To his credit, Achebe does not merely describe these traditions, values, and customs; he brings the ceremonial to life, presenting events and conversations dramatically. In so doing, he presents convincingly a rich Ibo culture which is not static, but clearly in a state of transition. Outwardly, Umuofia is a world of serenity, harmony, and communal activity, but inwardly it is torn by the individual's personal doubts and fears. At times, the reader is faced with contradictions. For example, although the child is valued more than any material thing in Umuofian society, an innocent child named Ikemefuna is denied life by traditional laws and customs which demand his life in return for that of a Umuofian who was killed by his people. But Ibo society is full of contradictions. It is a world in which the spiritual dimension is a part of daily life, but also a world in which a man's success is measured by his material goods. It is a world which is at once communal and individualistic, a world in which human relations are paramount, but in which old people and twins are left in the forest to die. It is a male-dominated society, in which the chief goddess is female and in which proverbial wisdom maintains "Mother is supreme." This sustained view of the duality of the traditional Ibo society intensifies the wider tragedy and reveals the dilemma that shapes and destroys the life of Okonkwo.

We likewise have a dualistic view of Okonkwo and thus have sympathy for him despite our moral revulsion at some of his violent, inhuman acts. At all points of his destiny, Okonkwo is shown to be highly conscious of the beliefs of his community. Achebe shows how the code of values of the society is designed to respond strongly to any threat, no matter how small, to the overall stability of the clan. Okonkwo adheres closely to this attitude, which he is willing to put into practice all the time, even to the point of alienating himself from his surroundings. Throughout the novel, Okonkwo is presented as a man whose life is ruled by an overriding passion: to become successful, powerful, and rich, and to found a dynasty. Okonkwo has been driven to achievement by shame for his father's failure. Unoka, his father, was a weak man who preferred music, pleasure, and debt to social responsibility. Okonkwo's character is partly determined by the need to be everything that his father was not.

In his concern about his daughter's illness and in his secret grief over the death of Ikemefuna, Okonkwo shows another, softer side of his character. However, thinking it weakness to show emotion openly, except it be anger, Okonkwo appears a cold, dehumanized person. He treats unsuccessful men like dirt. His entire life (both public and private) is dominated by the obsession of proving his manliness:

> He ruled his household with a heavy hand. His wives, especially the youngest, lived in perpetual fear of his fiery temper, and so did his little children. (Achebe 1958, 108)

No episode in the novel dramatizes Okonkwo's desire to assert his manliness more clearly than the killing of Ikemefuna, the child hostage who had lived as Okonkwo's foster child while the clan waited for the oracle to decree his fate. This event illustrates also in a dramatic way Okonkwo's alienation from the best traditions of his inherited culture. After all, the elder Ezeudu says clearly to him: "I want you to have nothing to do with it [the sacrifice of Ikemefuna]. He calls you father" (Achebe 1958, 108). And yet it is Okonkwo himself who delivered the fatal blow to the child. This violent act, so contrary to the traditional concept of the family in Africa, is not excused by anyone in the novel.

For the most part, Okonkwo resorts to such violence in order to maintain control of a situation and to show his manliness. Even in his relationships with his *chi,* or personal god, Okonkwo exerts force to mold his *chi* to his will. He therefore violates the conventional harmonious relationship one has with his personal god. On all levels, then, Okonkwo must dominate and control events. By sheer force—and, if necessary, brutality—Okonkwo tries to bend to his will his family, his clan, and his *chi.* According to the narrator, Okonkwo was not a man of thought but of action in whose rigid view, any brooding, introspection, questioning, or show of joy is a sign of weakness. For Okonkwo the opposition between private self and public man is the conflict between the feminine and masculine principles. For him one is either a man or a woman; there can be no compromise, no composite. Okonkwo is inflexible, and his action allows no room for reflection. Such a rigid commitment to a code of behavior and design for action thwarts Okonkwo's personal development; he does not grow and change with age and experience. In rejecting compromise and flexibility and in repressing all feminine influences, Okonkwo thus rejects the values of the society he determines to champion. All his life, Okonkwo has tried to negate ordinary human feelings, and consequently has failed to achieve a balance of strength and sensibility.

The failure of such an attitude is obvious when we consider his relationship with his son Nwoye. The divorce between father and son became inevitable after the killing of Ikemefuna. In killing the foster brother Nwoye loves and admires, he alienates his son, who then seeks refuge in Christianity, the new religion. Christianity appeals to Nwoye; he is "captivated" by the poetry of the new religion. Has not Nwoye been presented all along as a sensitive boy, a romantic being? However, this conversion to Christianity is perceived by Okonkwo as utter treason, a will to annihilate his family line:

> Now that he had time to think of it, his son's crime stood out in its stark enormity. To abandon the god of one's father and go about with a lot of effeminate men clucking like old hens was the very depth of abomination. (Achebe 1958, 108)

Unwilling to change, Okonkwo also rejects change in others, in the people of Umuofia. Herein lies the downfall of the hero; he is unaware of his lack of harmony with his people, with some basic principles of the clan. We have evidence that the social code of Umuofia is responsive to change. When people find elements of the code contradictory, they will alter them, provided such a modification does not conflict with the will of the gods. They have proverbs such as "Let the kite perch and the eagle perch too. If one says no to the other, let his wing break" or "The world has no end and what is good among one people is an abomination with others."

This incapacity of the hero to comprehend certain values of his society as reflected in the proverbs, enhances his tragedy. Many of the qualities which to Okonkwo are marks of femininity and weakness are qualities which society respects and recognizes as signs of greatness. This is why we can hardly agree with Eustace Palmer when he declares, "Okonkwo is what his society has made him, for his conspicuous qualities are a response to the demands of his society" (Palmer 1972, 53).

Although it is true that Okonkwo does champion many of the beliefs and principles of his society, his responses to specific situations prove his misunderstanding of this society. His society, of course, demands achievement, but it nevertheless admires less heroic deeds which contribute to the perpetuating of the society. Okonkwo's responses are limited, however, by the obsession of proving his manliness. No doubt Okonkwo loves his society, but I would rather believe that characters such as Ezeudu or Obierika, who espouse the way of compromise, of blending the masculine and feminine, represent better and more aptly the traditional Ibo way of life. Okonkwo is not more heroic than these characters, for these latter are more human; they show feeling and care, as the society wants. They also have that quality essential to any social progress: the capacity to adapt themselves to their environment, a capacity which can be considered as a sign of intelligence.

As noted above, males and their problems dominate in the active Ibo society, but the religion, associated with female life, sustains and judges it. While in exile in Mbanta, his mother's land, Okonkwo is lectured by his uncle on the importance of those principles. The Ibo people have a saying "Nnekka," which means "Mother is supreme." This high status of the woman among the Ibo is enhanced by Achebe through the positive role of the goddess Ani, the ultimate judge of morality and conduct:

> A man belongs to his fatherland when times are good and life is sweet. But when there is sorrow and bitterness he finds refuge in

his motherland. Your mother is there to protect you. (Achebe 1958, 94)

Okonkwo is unable to see the balance inherent in the nature of the Ibo clan; the apparent weakness of the female principle hides a real strength which is the source of perpetuation of life. Even during his exile, Okonkwo could not see the importance given by this society to deep thinking and human consideration. This is why he could not, like his good friend Obierika, entertain the changes which are unavoidable with the coming of the white man. In fact, it is only people as calm and thoughtful as Obierika who can pass judgment, as is seen in this statement:

> The white man is very clever. He came quietly and peaceably with his religion. We were amused at this foolishness and allowed him to stay. Now he has won our brothers, and our clan can no longer act as one. He has put a knife into the things that held us together and we have fallen apart. (Achebe 1958, 124–25)

Disregarding Obierika's wise assessment of the situation, Okonkwo thinks that he can return to the same Umuofia he has known. Thus, he is disappointed by his clan's permissive attitude and readiness to accommodate the new situation. Okonkwo believes only in solving problems by force and violence. He shares this view with a white character in the novel, Reverend Smith, whose Manichean vision of life—black being the absolute evil for him—leads to violent clashes between his church and the Ibo people.

Such clashes are also central to the story of Okonkwo, which unfolds around five actions of violence and desecration. Each action calls for expiation rather than judgment, and for the restoration of social order; each has tragic implications for the community. The interrelation between Okonkwo's actions and his society is a close one. With each phase of the story, Okonkwo and the society move in a widening circle:

1. Violence occurs first in his household, directed against the family unit of wives and children.

2. Then, with the death of Ikemefuna, violence moves into the village in its relationship with Ikemefuna's home, Mbaino.

3. The circle extends to Mbanta and surrounding Ibo communities when Okonkwo is responsible for the accidental death of a clansman and must go into exile for seven years.

4. After his return to Umuofia, the conflict with Europeans leads to Okonkwo's killing a white governmental employee as he confronts the international representatives of colonialism.

5. Finally, Okonkwo's suicide introduces an abomination of the earth itself.

With this progressive widening of the circle we have a technique which shows once more Achebe's craftsmanship. A man is always connected to others and to the universe through its various "fragments."[1] Okonkwo, though a strong individual by himself, will miss the significance of his life because he fails to consider the paramount status of the group. Even when he is convinced that he is just securing the interest of the group, he should not go against the general view. How can he ignore the evil he is bringing upon himself and his family by committing suicide at the conclusion of the novel? Obierika says,

> It is an abomination for a man to take his own life. It is an offence against the Earth, and a man who commits it will not be buried by his clansmen. His body is evil, and only strangers may touch it. (Achebe 1958, 147)

In a communal society, nothing is more painful than being rejected, excluded by the group. So even in his stoic death, Okonkwo falls alone, and his spirit, according to the beliefs of the society, will wander restlessly in the supernatural world. In other words, Okonkwo is a lonely character, doomed to constant isolation. He is not the prototype of the African elder in his communal society; instead Okonkwo is the individual asserting himself against tribal norms *and* the encroachment of Christianity. He lacks the subtleties that one would wish from a character witnessing and taking part in the processes of change. With the arrival of the Christian missionaries in the Ibo villages, there was no dramatic confrontation, no sudden conversion, but rather a number of different responses in the community and divergent attitudes within the culture itself. Okonkwo is not in touch with this diversity.

In providing a context for interpreting Okonkwo's relationship with his society, the novel's use of proverbs plays an important role. They reveal the clan's dependence upon traditional wisdom and help to present the whole way of life. Many critics have demonstrated the power of proverbs in the work of Achebe in general and in *Things Fall Apart* in particular.[2] Bernth Lindfors sums up the role of the proverbs in Achebe's fictions when he declares:

> Proverbs can serve as keys to an understanding of his novels because he uses them not merely to add a touch of local color but to sound and reiterate themes, to sharpen characterization, to clarify conflict, and to focus on the values of the society he is portraying. (Lindfors 1973, 77)

Such an understanding of the subtleties of language by the reader is possible only through personal effort linked with open-mindedness. It is, unfortunately, those elements which are lacking among many of the characters in the novel and which have led also to cultural misunderstanding among its readers. Achebe is using English, a worldwide language, to translate African experience. In other words, English, a tool in the hands of all those who have learnt to master it, can be submitted to different kinds of use. Critics of African literature must keep this fact in mind and try to grasp all the riches of the Ibo language and rhetoric that Achebe, as a son of the tribe, has tried to translate. With such an attitude, the critic will contribute to consolidating and widening our experience, the human experience. Hasn't the reader grown into accepting, for instance, that the natural world is penetrated by the supernatural, thanks to Achebe's ability to make us live (with the characters) the various stages of their cultural life?

Things Fall Apart, the title of which is an allusion to W. B. Yeats's poem "The Second Coming," is a novel in which Achebe is interested in analyzing the way things happen and in giving language to the Ibo experience. He offers a larger view of history and of individual life:

> No civilization can either remain static or evolve forever towards a more inclusive perfection. It must both collapse from within and be overwhelmed from without, and what replaces it will appear most opposite to itself, being built from all that it overlooked or undervalued. (Stock 1978, 86)

The novel, therefore, celebrates stability in human affairs despite its apparent "anarchy" (to use a word from Yeats's poem). Ibo culture, even while changing, is very much alive. Despite the tragic loss of Okonkwo, the society of the Ibos, because of its flexibility, survives. Despite the loss, "the center holds."

Notes

1. We have in mind the novel by Ayi Kwei Armah, *Fragments,* in which we can read: "Each thing that goes away returns and nothing in the end is lost. The great friend throws all things apart and brings all things together again."

2. We can mention articles such as "The Palm Wine with Which Achebe's Words Are Eaten," by Bernth Lindfors; or "Language and Action in the Novels of Chinua Achebe," by Gareth Griffiths; or "Language, Poetry and Doctrine in *Things Fall Apart*," by C. L. Innes.

References

Achebe, Chinua. *Things Fall Apart*. 1958. Reprint. London: Heinemann, 1984.

———. *Morning Yet on Creation Day*. London: Heinemann, 1975.

Amadi, Elechi. *The Concubine*. 1966. Reprint. London: Heinemann, 1982.

Armah, Ayi Kwei. *Fragments*. London: Heinemann, 1974.

Cook, David. *African Literature: A Critical View*. London: Longman, 1977.

Innes, C. L., and Bernth Lindfors, eds. *Critical Perspectives on Chinua Achebe*. Washington, D. C.: Three Continents Press, 1978.

Lindfors, Bernth. *Folklore in Nigerian Literature*. New York: Africana Publishing, 1973.

Mbiti, John. *African Religions and Philosophy*. Garden City, NY: Anchor Books Doubleday, 1970.

Palmer, Eustace. *An Introduction to the African Novel*. London: Heinemann, 1972.

Stock, A. G. "Yeats and Achebe." In *Critical Perspectives on Achebe,* edited by C. L. Innes and Bernth Lindfors. Washington, D.C.: Three Continents Press, 1978.

25 Approaches to *Things Fall Apart:* A Bibliographic Essay

John Lott
University of Montevallo

Sandra Lott
University of Montevallo
(with the assistance of Rita Sparks, Wenona High School)

The critical essays on Achebe's *Things Fall Apart* stress the fact that it is possible to lead students to an understanding of unfamiliar literary works by examining works with similar themes and methods in other cultural and historical contexts. One can find universal concerns in Achebe's novel and use these concerns both to make the novel accessible to contemporary students and to make clear what is specific to Ibo culture of the late nineteenth century. One can come to know that culture and to respect it without trying to erase the differences—as cultural relativism might tempt us to do.

Professor Henricksen's essay deals with the methods with which the student or critic reads the bicultural novel, one which depicts conflicts when cultures come into contact with each other. As Henricksen notes, the student or critic is always reading from within a cultural and historical context, and must consciously attempt to understand the voices with which people of other times and places have spoken and also the voices which these "others" have heard. For this reason, rich novels like *Heart of Darkness* and *Things Fall Apart* justify multiple rereadings and may be seen differently as the reader's context changes. Hispanic American works such as Lorna Dee Cervantes' "Refugee Ship" and Rolando Hinojosa's *The Valley* and his *Rites and Witnesses* also lend themselves to this approach to cultural conflicts. In addition, this approach would lead to profitable rereadings of such "canonical" works as Conrad's *Lord Jim*, Dostoevsky's *Crime and Punishment*, and Cervantes's *Don Quixote* from the vantage point of changed cultural or critical perspectives.

356

Poetry, such as that of the seventeenth-century metaphysicals or the nineteenth-century romantics, likewise repays rereading in the light both of the cultural changes the poets were responding to and the cultural changes which have occurred since. The work of these poets might well be studied in relationship to poetry from China and Japan which also grows out of strong cultural and literary traditions, or in relationship to the work of such Hispanic poets as Julia de Burgos, Etnairis Rivera, Sandra Maria Esteves, and Alma Villaneuva.

Professor McMillan's essay shows us the universal pattern in tragic figures like Turnus and Okonkwo who maintain the values of a culture in spite of the inevitable forces of history which are threatening to submerge that culture. The possibilities of showing that pattern repeated are multiple—from the Biblical narrative of Jeremiah, who counseled maintenance of the Covenant relationship in the heart even as the Jewish state and its culture fell to the conquering Babylonians, to such contemporary works as *Cities of Salt* by Syrian author Abdelrahman Munif, and *Midaq Alley* by Egyptian Naguib Mahfouz. *Cities of Salt* chronicles the shock to the oasis-centered, family-oriented culture of an unnamed Persian Gulf sheikdom as the American oil companies and their workers overwhelm the local society. A character such as Miteb Al-Hathal is like Turnus and Okonkwo in his refusal to be assimilated. In *Midaq Alley* the inhabitants of a Cairo street fight to maintain their small world.

These themes are seen as well in the European canon. For example, in Chekhov's play *The Cherry Orchard*, Madame Lyubov Ranevskaya attempts to hold on to the aristocratic values of an older Russia. The passage of time, political changes, and the freeing of the serfs doom these values as inevitably as the economic forces doom the symbolic cherry orchard.

Other non-European works which reflect this kind of struggle to retain cultural values in the face of historical forces include works such as Jose Maria Arguedas's *Yawar Fiesta* and Rolando Hinojosa's *Korean Love Songs*, Federico Garcia Lorca's *The House of Bernardo Alba*, Carlos Solorzano's "Doña Beatriz." This theme is central as well in works by Japanese authors such as Yukio Mishima and Junichiro Tanizaki. In his tetralogy, *The Sea of Fertility*, Yukio Mishima, uses the concept of reincarnation to explore the quest for the ideal within the context of modernization and cultural transition. *The Makioka Sisters*, a novel by Junichiro Tanizaki, depicts four sisters growing up amid the cultural changes brought by modernization in Japan. *Some Prefer Nettles*, also by Tanizaki, shows these cultural changes in the context of the breakup of a traditional marriage. The impact of cultural conflict and change in a Latin American setting are explored in Gabriel García Márquez's *One Hundred Years of Solitude, No One Writes to the Colonel,* and *The Autumn of the Patriarch. The Death of Artemio Cruz,* by Mexican author Carlos Fuentes, is another treatment of this theme. Because of Fuentes's innovative use of style and point of view, and his concern with the impact of the past on the present, this work might well be taught in conjunction with works by William Faulkner such as *The Sound and the Fury; Absalom, Absalom!;* and "A Rose for Emily." This theme is also evident in many of the novels and short stories of Flannery O'Connor and Eudora Welty, such as O'Connor's "Everything that Rises Must Converge" and "The Enduring Chill" and Welty's "The Demonstrators." There are a number of works from South Africa, such as *A Walk in the Night* by Alex Laguma and *"Master Harold" and the Boys* by Athol Fugard, which depict the struggle for cultural reform and personal fulfillment, a struggle which is also depicted in *The Unbearable Lightness of Being* by Czech author Milan Kundera. This quest for personal fulfillment in the context of oppression and social change is also central to James Baldwin's *Go Tell It On the Mountain,* Toni Morrison's *Song of Solomon, Beloved,* and *Jazz,* and Ralph Ellison's *Invisible Man.*

The theme, which is central to much modern literature, has found strong expression in poetry from the Victorian Age to the present. The speaker in Matthew Arnold's poem "Stanzas from the Grande Chartreuse" describes himself as "between two worlds, one dead, the other powerless to be born" (lines 559–62). Many of Arnold's poems, like the poetry and novels of Thomas Hardy, deal with the inability of persons to "unlearn" their culture and to accept a "new world." T. S. Eliot writes of the loss of tradition in poems such as "The Wasteland" and "The Hollow Men," and of the quest for renewed meaning in his religious poetry such as *The Four Quartets.* Poems such as William Butler Yeats' "Lapis Lazuli," "The Second Coming," and "Leda and the Swan" explore the ceaseless process of destruction and creation which Yeats sees as an inevitable part of the cycles of history. These works might be paralleled with Latin American works dealing with the difficulty of cultural transition, a theme reflected in texts such as Romula Gallegos's *Doña Barbara* and Carlos Fuentes's *Change of Skin,* a work which deals also with the ceaseless process of destruction and creation.

Poems by America's ethnic writers are especially strong in their handling of the themes of cultural conflict and change. Particularly useful to teachers are collections such as *I Am the Darker Brother* and *Celebrations,* both edited by Arnold Adoff, and *Settling America,* edited by David Kherdian. In this last volume, Kherdian has collected poems by America's immigrant poets, representing a wide range of ethnic backgrounds, some of which are unpublished elsewhere.

Professor Wasserman's essay points to the use of Achebe's novel to bring alive for contemporary students the concept of orality in literature and to serve, thus, as an introduction to a work like *Beowulf,* which seems impossibly remote to them. The same orality lies behind the Homeric epics and much of the literature of the Pentateuch, the New Testament, and the Koran. A similar approach to Wasserman's could illumine for students the story of Joseph as it is found in Genesis and as it is found in Surah XII of the Koran. (One might consider in addition Thomas Mann's series of novels on *Joseph and His Brothers.*) One might also examine the near sacrifice of Isaac in the Bible or Ishmael in the Koran as they relate to the sacrificial death of Ikemefuna in *Things Fall Apart.* A similar orality in style and method lies behind the poetry of Whitman and such Faulkner narratives as *Absalom, Absalom!* and *The Bear.* It is found as well in more recent literature such as Luis Rafael Sanchez's *Macho Camacho's Beat* and Latin American border corridos such as "The Ballad of Gregorio Cortez," collected by Americo Paredes.

Professor Sarr's essay points to Okonkwo's failure to understand "feminine" qualities which underlie some of the values of the society of Umuofia. Other works which reflect this theme include Lorna Dee Cervantes' "Uncle's First Rabbit" and "Visions of Mexico" and Isabel Allende's *The House of Spirits* and *Of Love and Shadows.* A literature teacher might well compare these works with such a standard of the European canon as Flaubert's *Madame Bovary.* Emma Bovary is overwhelmed by excesses of the so-called "feminine" traits of emotion and poetic sensibility which Professor Sarr finds lacking in Okonkwo. Like Okonkwo, Emma is influenced by changes taking place in her society, although she has difficulty assimilating them into her own view of life. Other possible comparisons would be with Ibsen's Hedda Gabler, a female character who exhibits some of the same qualities of rigidity and fear of weakness as Okonkwo, and with Shakespeare's Othello, whose fear of public humiliation and weakness causes him to lose faith in Desdemona's loving nature.

Other works in which the masculine hero's conformity to conventional values of money and power and social conformity are shown to have made life empty and meaningless are Tolstoy's *The Death of Ivan Ilych,* about a dying Russian bureaucrat's gradual realization of ways in which his life has been "most simple, most ordinary, and therefore, most terrible" (1215), and Japanese director Akira Kurosawa's *Ikiru,* a film with very close parallels to Tolstoy's work. *Ikiru* depicts the last days of an outwardly successful Japanese man who, dying of cancer, attempts to find meaning in his life by building a playground for children.

As noted in the section of this text on "Cultural Diversity in Related Texts," such works can lead to a better understanding of the different forms of heroism and to a re-examination of such concepts as the tragic hero and the tragic flaw in the light of gender studies and multicultural awareness. Latin American works which deal with masculine and feminine views of heroism and tragedy include Mario Vargas Llosa's *The War of the End of the World,* Teresa de la Parra's *Ifigenia,* and Jorge Luis Borges' "Emma Zunz" and "The Other Death."

Study of *Things Fall Apart* in the context of these and other works, such as Alice Walker's *The Color Purple,* Toni Morrison's *Sula,* Buchi Emecheta's *The Joys of Motherhood,* and Sophocles' *Antigone* can illuminate questions of gender and other cultural issues discussed in Professor Sarr's essay.

Such questions may also be illuminated by an examination of *No Longer At Ease,* Achebe's third novel about Okonkwo's family and community. In this work Okonkwo's grandson, Obi Okonkwo, expresses views of tragedy and heroism which seem counter to Okonkwo's "masculine" vision.

> Conventional tragedy is too easy. The hero dies and we feel a purging of the emotions. A real tragedy takes place in a corner, "in an untidy spot," to quote W. H. Auden. The rest of the world is unaware of it. (43–44)

These words from *No Longer at Ease* are relevant as well to *Things Fall Apart.* Okonkwo's death is certainly "an important failure," one that deserves more than a paragraph in the Commissioner's superficial book; however, the reader may just as earnestly concern himself with the fate of Obierika. Analysis of the characters of Okonkwo and Obierika in Chinua Achebe's *Things Fall Apart* raises questions about the nature of true heroism. Achebe has given Okonkwo the structural positon of hero and Obierika the peripheral, almost chorus-like role. However, for many readers, the reasonable Obierika may be the more heroic. Such considerations may also be extended to Sophocles' *Antigone,* in which Antigone and her more flexible and malleable sister, Ismene, provide parallels to Okonkwo and Obierika.

Works such as Buchi Emecheta's *The Joys of Motherhood* and Alice Walker's *The Color Purple* also provide rich possibilities for comparison, especially in the context of Professor Sarr's comments on gender issues. Emecheta's heroine, Nnu Ego, endures disaster after disaster as she tries, despite the unreliability of her inept husband, to live up to her culture's standards for a good wife and mother. Because she too lives in a culture which is in transition, the feminine roles which she learned in her rural village do not work very well in modern Lagos. Believing she should produce as many children as possible and take full responsibility for raising them, she obediently allows her ne'er-do-well husband to take on a second wife he cannot afford, and she patiently endures the condescension of this woman. She sacrifices to give her chidren a Westernized education, only to find that they do not contribute to her welfare or to that of the younger children. She endures all of this until toward the end of the book, old, sick, and alone, she wonders bitterly about "the joys of motherhood." Like Obierika in *Things Fall Apart,* she provides in her endurance an alternate response to that of Okonkwo to cultural change and personal trauma. She is, in fact, a perfect example of the kind of heroine described by Obi Okonkwo in *No Longer At Ease:* "I remember an old man in my village, a Christian convert, who suffered one calamity after another. He said life was like a bowl of wormwood which one sips a little at a time world without end. He understood the nature of tragedy" (43–44). Other examples can be found in both Achebe's recent book *The Anthills of the Savannah* and in William Faulkner's *The Sound and the Fury* in which strong female characters provide models of endurance in the face of masculine disintegration and death. In Achebe's book about political struggle in a modern African state, only the female characters survive to provide a source of strength and endurance, and in Faulkner's work the black servant Dilsey, who "endures" the forces of racism and sexism, is herself a stabilizing force for troubled people of both races.

Many have noted that the masculine domination of women parallels the effects of European colonialism on the non-Western cultures. This point is borne out in both *The Joys of Motherhood* and *Things Fall Apart.* Teaching the contrasting models of heroism in these works would serve to underscore such important gender issues. Latin American works which depict such parallels between colonialsm and the subjugation of women include testimonials such as *I, Rigoberta Menchu: An Indian Woman in Guatemala,* edited by Elisabeth Burgos-Debray, and *Let Me Speak! Testimony of Domitila, A Woman of the Bolivian Mines,* as well as Mario Vargas Llosa's book, *The Green House.*

A reading of *The Color Purple* in the context of these works would add an African American perspective. Walker's heroine, Celie, is a prototype of the male-dominated, colonized figure, who struggles against incredible odds to overcome poverty, ignorance, and physical and mental abuse in order to assert an identity which is counter to that accorded her by the men who presume to control her life. This work, which in many ways parallels the epistolary novels of the eighteenth century, gives us a view of experience which is ultimately comic, not tragic. Celie's good fortune in regaining material wealth and her lost relatives is a confirmation, in good fairy tale style, of her newly acquired inner wealth of identity and self-worth. This work might be profitably read in conjunction with Achebe's novel, as it deals in a contrasting manner with cultural conflicts, colonialism, missionary efforts, and gender roles.

Though some might object to the happy-ever-after fairy tale resolution of Walker's work, many readers, particularly young people, respond positively to literature which provides a sense of hope and faith in the possibilities of life. Hispanic writers whose works show cultural conflict and change, leading to hope and optimism, include Luisa Valenzuela and Rolando Hinojosa (*Becky and Her Friends*).

Many traditional folktales and myths as well as modern-day science fiction and fantasy may provide this hope which often seems lacking in modern literature. Works such as Salman Rushdie's *Haroun and the Sea of Stories* and Michael Ende's *The Neverending Story* challenge readers of all ages to rediscover the wonder and mystery of life, and many readers welcome this release from bleak realism. To counterbalance the stark endings of *Things Fall Apart* and *The Joys of Motherhood,* one might want to suggest science fiction or fantasy such as Ursula Le Guin's *The Left Hand of Darkness* or Ann McCaffrey's *Dragonsong* and *Dragonquest.* These works, also about cultural conflict and change, provide a hopeful resolution to the protagonists' problems. According to Ursula Le Guin, such works, "whether [they use] the ancient archetypes of myth and legend or the younger ones of science and technology... [tell us] about human life as it is lived, and as it might be lived, and as it ought to be lived" (Le Guin 1982, 47–48). Such works give us hope that we can deal with rapid cultural and technological changes while preserving our essential humanity. Science fiction is sometimes considered a literary subgenre, but teaching science fiction and fantasy in conjunction with more traditional genres can give a better understanding of the issues and techniques in both. On the value of science fiction, Doris Lessing writes:

> What a phenomenon it has been—science fiction, space fiction, exploding out of nowhere, unexpectedly of course, as always happens when the human mind is being forced to expand.... These... have mapped our world, or worlds, for us, have told us what is going on and in ways no one else has done, have described our nasty present long ago, when it was still the future." (Lessing 1981, x)

Lessing goes on to say that works of science fiction and fantasy "have played the indispensable and . . . thankless role of the despised illegitimate son who can afford to tell truths the respectable siblings either do not dare, or more likely, do not notice because of their respectability." As with other noncanonical works, these can provide important insights about more traditional literature, including sacred literatures of the world, which as Lessing points out, are often explored in science fiction and fantasy (Lessing 1981, x). Lessing suggests reading works such as *Gilgamesh,* and *Popul Vuh,* in relationship to science fiction and fantasy with mythical or religious content. Salman Rushdie's *The Satanic Verses* might provide interesting parallels as well.

Some of Lessing's own works with elements of science fiction and fantasy such as *Shikasta* and *Memoirs of a Survivor* provide important insights into the problems of individuals confronting social and cultural problems similar in many ways to those of her more realistic works. Lessing's works of fantasy and science fiction provide interesting countertexts to realistic works such as her story, "To Room 19," which depicts the tragedy of a woman in an unhappy marriage who chooses to die rather than try to redefine herself and her life. In contrast, in *The Golden Notebook* Lessing's heroine goes within herself to achieve the self-knowledge and radical personal development which is aborted in "To Room 19" by the heroine's death. The mystical triumph of the characters at the end of *Memoirs of a Survivor* also provides an alternative, and more hopeful, vision. Of special interest also is her *Children of Violence* series which begins with a highly realistic account in *Martha Quest* of the heroine's early days in Rhodesia and ends in the experimental and visionary work, *The Four-Gated City.*

Such works from science fiction and fantasy might be taught in conjunction with other stylistic experimentations which break the usual boundaries of realism and expand our definitions of genre. Among these are Latin American works of magical realism such as Borges's "The Circular Ruins" or Márquez's *One Hundred Years of Solitude.* Other Latin works with elements of science fiction or fantasy include Carlos Fuentes's "Aura" and stories by Julio Cortazar such as "Axolotl," "The Night Face Up," and his "House Taken Over."

Toni Morrison's *Beloved,* Alice Walker's *The Temple of My Familiar,* and Salman Rushdie's *Midnight's Children* all blend realism and fantasy in order to explore the individual's relationship to society, culture, and national identity. Juxtaposition of such works with works which are more traditional in style and form can also provide important insights.

As these various approaches suggest, the process of reading texts which, for one reason or another, are outside the traditional Western literary canon, in conjunction with more traditional works offers endless possibilities. By breaking through the boundaries imposed by literary fashion, respectability and familiarity, we may even contribute to the expansion of human understanding which Doris Lessing suggests is essential if we are to cope with the multiple forces which threaten the race and the planet. Alice Walker and Robert Penn Warren, as cited in the introductory essays of this text, suggest that literature can help us to understand ourselves and others, that writers can in some sense save lives. If this process is to work, however, we cannot be like the Commissioner at the end of Achebe's *Things Fall Apart,* who complains about the Ibo people's constant talking. The Commissioner thinks, "One of the most infuriating habits of these people was their love of superfluous words" (189). He plans to write his own version of Ibo history in which Okonkwo and his people will merit perhaps a chapter, or perhaps just a paragraph. Unlike the Commissioner, we must be willing to hear the voices of many different people, telling their own stories, knowing that in the process our own worlds will be enlarged and our own stories will be irrevocably changed. Only then can we remove the "mind-forg'd manacles" (Blake, "London," Line 8) which prevent our achieving the "larger perspective" (*Gardens,* 1983, 5) which Alice Walker considers essential to our survival. It is in this belief that all of the essays in this text have been written.

References

Achebe, Chinua. *Anthills of the Savanna.* New York: Doubleday, 1988.

———. *No Longer at Ease.* New York: Astor-Honor, 1961.

———. *Things Fall Apart.* New York: Heinemann, 1987.

Adoff, Arnold. ed. *Celebrations.* Chicago: Follett, 1977.

———. ed. *I Am the Darker Brother: An Anthology of Modern Poems by Negro Americans.* New York: Macmillan, 1968.

Allende, Isabel. *The House of Spirits.* Translated by Magda Bogin. New York: Alfred Knopf, 1985.

———. *Of Love and Shadows.* Translated by Margaret S. Peden. New York: Knopf, 1987.

Arguedas, Jose D. *Yawar Fiesta.* Translated by Frances H. Barraclough. Austin: University of Texas Press, 1985.

Arnold, Matthew. "Stanzas from the Grande Chartreuse." In *Victorian and Later English Poets.* Edited by James Stephens, Edwin L. Beck, and Royall H. Snow. 559–62. New York: American Book Company, 1949.

Baldwin, James. *Go Tell It On the Mountain.* New York: Dell, 1985.

"The Ballad of Gregorio Cortez." Edited by Americo Paredes. In *With A Pistol in His Hand.* Austin: University of Texas Press, 1958.

Beowulf. Translated by Michael Alexander. New York: Penguin, 1973.

Blake, William. *Songs of Innocence and Experience.* London: Oxford University Press, 1977.

Borges, Jorge Luis. "Emma Zunz" and "The Circular Ruins" in *Labyrinths. Selected Short Stories and Other Writings.* Edited by Donald A. Yates and James E. Irby. New York: Random House, 1984.

———. "The Other Death" in *The Aleph and Other Stories.* Translated by Norman Thomas di Giovanni. New York: Bantam Books, 1971.

Cervantes, Lorna Dee. "Refugee Ship." In *The Third Woman: Minority Women Writers of the United States.* Edited by Dexter Fisher. Boston: Houghton Mifflin, 1980.

———. "Uncle's First Rabbit" and "Visions of Mexico." In *Contemporary Chicano Poetry: A Critical Approach to an Emerging Literature* by Marta Ester Sanchez. Berkeley: University of California Press, 1985.

Cervantes, Miguel. *Don Quixote.* Translation and introduction by Samuel Putnam. New York: Random, 1978.

Chekhov, Anton. *The Cherry Orchard.* Translated by Michael Frayn. New York: Heinemann, 1978.

Cisneros, Sandra. *The House on Mango Street.* Houston: Arte Publico, 1989.

Conrad, Joseph. *Heart of Darkness.* Edited by Paul O'Prey. New York: Penguin, 1984.

———. *Lord Jim.* Edited by Morton D. Zabel. New York: Houghton Mifflin, 1958.

Cortazar, Julio. "Axolotl," "The Night Face Up," and "House Taken Over." In *Blow-up and Other Stories.* Translated by Paul Blackburn. New York: Collier Books, 1968.

De Burgos, Julia. *Poemas en veinte surcos.* Rio Piedras, Puerto Rico: Ediciones Huracban, 1982.

de la Parra, Teresa. *Ifigenia.* Zig Zag, OR: Zig Zag, 1937.

Dostoevsky, Fyodor. *Crime and Punishment.* Translated by Constance Garnett. New York: Random, 1978.

Eliot, T.S. *The Four Quartets.* New York: Harcourt, Brace, Jovanovich, 1968.

———. *The Wasteland and Other Poems.* New York: Harcourt Brace Jovanovich, 1955.

Ellison, Ralph. *Invisible Man.* New York: Random, 1989.

Emecheta, Buchi. *The Joys of Motherhood.* New York: Braziller, 1979.

Ende, Michael. *The Neverending Story.* New York: Penguin, 1984.

Esteves, Sandra Maria. *Tropical Rains. A Bilingual Downpour, poems.* African Caribbean Poetry Theater, 1984.

———. *Bluestown Mockingbird Mambo.* Houston: Arte Publico Press, 1990.

Faulkner, William. *Absalom, Absalom!* Edited by Noel Polk. New York: Random House, 1987.

———. *The Bear.* In *Three Famous Short Novels.* New York: Random House, 1958.

———. "A Rose for Emily." In *Collected Stories.* New York: Random House, 1977.

———. *The Sound and the Fury.* Edited by Noel Polk. New York: Random House, 1954.

Flaubert, Gustave. *Madame Bovary.* Translated by Lowell Bair. New York: Bantam, 1987.

Fuentes, Carlos. "Aura." Translated by Lysander Kemp. In *Latin American Writing Today.* New York: Farrar, Straus and Giroux, 1965.

———. *Change of Skin.* New York: Farrar, Straus and Giroux, 1968.

———. *The Death of Artemio Cruz.* Translated by Sam Hileman. New York: Farrar, Straus and Giroux, 1964.

Fugard, Athol. *"Master Harold" and the Boys.* New York: Penguin, 1984.

Gallegos, Romulo. *Doña Barbara.* Translated by Robert Malloy. New York: Jonathan Cape, 1931.

Gilgamesh: A Verse Narrative. Edited by Herbert Mason. New York: New American Library, 1972.

Hardy, Thomas. *The Works of Thomas Hardy in Prose and Verse.* New York: Johnson Reprint Corporation, n.d.

Hinojosa, Rolando. *Becky and Her Friends.* Houston: Arte Publico, 1989.

———. *Korean Love Songs from Klail City Death Trip.* Berkeley, CA: Editorial Justa Publications, 1980.

———. *Rites and Witnesses.* Houston: Arte Publico, 1982.

———. *The Valley.* Ypsilanti, MI: Bilingual Press, 1983.

Ibsen, Henrik. *Hedda Gabler and A Doll's House.* Translated by Christopher Hampton. Winchester, MA: Faber and Faber, 1990.

I, Rigoberta Menchu, An Indian Woman in Guatemala. Edited by Elisabeth Burgos-Debray. Translated by Ann Wright. New York: Verso, 1984.

Kherdian, David, ed. *Settling America.* New York: Macmillan, 1974.

Koran Interpreted. Translated by A. J. Arberry. New York: Macmillan, 1986.

Kundera, Milan. *The Unbearable Lightness of Being.* Translated by Michael Heim. New York: Harper Row, 1984.

Laguma, Alex. *A Walk in the Night and Other Stories.* Chicago: Northwestern University, 1967.

Le Guin, Ursula. *The Left Hand of Darkness.* New York: Ace, 1983.

———. "National Book Award Acceptance Speech." In *The Language of the Night: Essays on Fantasy and Science Fiction.* 47–48. New York: Berkley Publishing Corporation, 1982.

Lessing, Doris. *Children of Violence* series. *Martha Quest.* New York: M. Joseph, 1952.

———. *A Proper Marriage.* New York: M. Joseph, 1954.

———. *A Ripple from the Storm.* New York: M. Joseph, 1958.

———. *Landlocked.* New York: Simon and Schuster, 1966.

———. *The Four-Gated City.* New York: Knopf, 1969.

————. *The Golden Notebook.* New York: Bantam, 1981.

————. *Memoirs of a Survivor.* Edited by Anne Freedgood. New York: Random House, 1988.

————. "Some Remarks." In *Shikasta.* ix–xi. New York: Random House, Vintage Books. 1981.

————. "To Room 19." In *The Norton Anthology of World Masterpieces,* Volume II, 5th ed. Edited by Maynard Mack et al. 2026–57. New York: Norton, 1985.

Let Me Speak! Testimony of Domitilia, A Woman of the Bolivian Mines. Edited by Moema Vizzer. New York: Monthly Review Press, 1979.

Llosa, Mario Vargas. *The Green House.* Translated by Gregory Rabassa. New York: Alfred Knopf, 1985.

————. *The War of the End of the World.* Translated by Helen R. Lane. New York: Avon Books, 1984.

Lorca, Federico Garcia. "The House of Bernarda Alba." In *Three Tragedies.* Translated by Richard L. O'Connell and James Graham-Lujan. New York: New Directions, 1956.

McCaffrey, Ann. *Dragonquest.* New York: Ballantine, 1986.

————. *Dragonsong.* New York: Bantam, 1986.

Mahfouz, Naguib. *Midaq Alley.* Translated by Trevor Le Gassick. Washington, D.C.: Three Continents, 1989.

Mann, Thomas. *Joseph and his Brothers.* New York: Knopf, 1948.

Márquez, Gabriel García. *The Autumn of the Patriarch.* New York: Avon, 1977.

————. *No One Writes to the Colonel and Other Stories.* Translated by J. S. Bernstein. New York: Harper & Row, 1979.

————. *One Hundred Years of Solitude.* Translated by Gregory Rabassa. New York: Harper & Row, 1970.

Mishima, Yukio. *Spring Snow.* (Book One of *The Sea of Fertility.*) Translated by Michael Gallagher. New York: Knopf, 1972.

————. *The Temple of Dawn.* (Book Two of *The Sea of Fertility.*) Translated by E. Dale Saunders and Cecilia Segawa Seigle. New York: Knopf, 1973.

————. *The Decay of the Angel.* (Book Three of *The Sea of Fertility.*) Translated by Edward Seidensticker. New York: Knopf, 1972.

Morrison, Toni. *Beloved.* New York: Knopf, 1987.

————. *Jazz.* New York: Knopf, 1992.

————. *Song of Solomon.* New York: Knopf, 1977.

————. *Sula.* New York: Knopf, 1973.

Munif, Abdelrahmen. *Cities of Salt.* Translated by Peter Theroux. New York: Random, 1989.

New English Bible with the Apocrypha. Edited by Samuel Sandmel. Oxford Study Edition. New York: Oxford University Press, 1976.

O'Connor, Flannery. *The Complete Stories.* Edited by Robert Fitzgerald. New York: Farrar, Straus and Giroux, 1971.

Popol Vuh: The Definitive Edition of the Mayan Book of the Dawn of Life and the Glories of Gods and Kings. Edited by Dennis Tedlock. New York: Simon and Schuster, 1986.

Ribeiro, Joao Ubaldo. *An Invincible Memory.* New York: Harper and Row, 1989.

Rivera, Etnairis. *Lirica Colberica.* Guajana, 1977.

Rushdie, Salman. *Haroun and the Sea of Stories.* London: Granta Books, 1990.

———. *Midnight's Children.* New York: Avon, 1982.

———. *The Satanic Verses.* New York: Viking Penguin, 1989.

Sanchez, Luis Rafael. *Macho Comacho's Beat.* Translated by Gregory Rabassa. New York: Pantheon Books, 1980.

Shakespeare, William. *Othello.* Edited by Kenneth Muir. New York: Penguin, 1981.

Sophocles. *Antigone.* Translated by Richard E. Braun. London: Oxford University Press, 1989.

Solorzano, Carlos. *Doña Beatriz: La Sin Ventura.* Colleccion Teatro Mexicano, 1954.

Tanizaki, Junichiro. *The Makioka Sisters.* Translated by Edward G. Seidensticker. New York: Putnam, 1981.

———. *Some Prefer Nettles.* Translated by Edward G. Seidensticker. New York: Putnam Publishing Group, 1981.

Tolstoy, Leo. *The Death of Ivan Ilych.* Translated by Louise and Aylmer Maude. In *The Norton Anthology of World Masterpieces, Vol. 2,* 6th ed. Edited by Maynard Mack et al. 1205–49. New York: Norton, 1992.

Valenzuela, Luisa. *The Lizard's Tail.* Translated by Gregory Rabassa. New York: Farrar, Straus and Giroux, 1983.

———. *Open Door.* Translated by Hortense Carpentier et al. Berkeley, CA: North Point Press, 1988.

Villanueva, Alma. *Life Span.* Edited by James Cody. San Antonio, TX: Place Herons, 1984.

Walker, Alice. *The Color Purple.* New York: Harcourt Brace Jovanovich, 1982.

———. *In Search of Our Mothers' Gardens, Womanist Prose.* New York: Harcourt Brace Jovanovich, 1983.

———. *The Temple of My Familiar.* New York: Harcourt Brace Jovanovich, 1989.

Warren, Robert Penn. "Why Do We Read Fiction?" In *An Approach to Literature.* 553–58. New York: Meredith Publishing Company, 1964.

Welty, Eudora. *Collected Stories of Eudora Welty.* New York: Harcourt Brace Jovanovich, 1982.

Yeats, Williams Butler. *Selected Poems and Three Plays.* Edited by M.L. Rosenthal. New York: Macmillan, 1987.

Related Film

Kurosawa, Akira. *Ikiru.* 1952. Film. Black and White. 134 minutes.

Appendix
Audiovisual Resources

(Prepared in consultation with Charlotte Blackmon, University of Montevallo)

In courses which incorporate non-Western, nontraditional texts into traditional literature programs, audiovisual resources may play an important role in helping to establish cultural contexts, in providing information about individual writers and their works, and in providing access to film and video adaptations of individual literary works. In our research, we have also discovered many audiovisual programs to enhance the teaching of literature related to the five thematic sections of this book. Some of the programs which we have found especially useful are included in the following bibliography. Through thematic and topical listings, we suggest possibilities for such clustering, but teachers will no doubt want to devise their own ways of clustering related audiovisual resources from different cultures and time frames.

In this appendix, the audiovisual programs are grouped under the following headings:

I. Cultural Contexts: Cultural Overviews, Mythology and Religion, and the Arts.

II. Thematic Groupings Covered by this Book: Private Worlds; The Hero's Quest; The Individual, the Family, and Society; Intertextuality and Cultural Identity; Approaches to Chinua Achebe's *Things Fall Apart*.

III. Programs on Individual Authors.

The programs are in video format unless otherwise specified. In cases where the production company of an educational film is unavailable, a distributor is given.

Cultural Overviews

Legacy: the Origins of Civilization. Ambrose Video Publishing, 1991. This series of 60-minute films includes background on the history and cultures of Iraq, China, India, Egypt, Central America, and Africa.

From Mesopotamia to Iraq. Landmark Films, 1991. 26 min. Examines the land of Mesopotamia (setting for *Gilgamesh*).

Islam. WETA-TV in cooperation with Smithsonian World. n.d. 58 min. Provides information on history and beliefs of Islam, with emphasis on its identity and place in the modern world.

The World of Islam. Films for the Humanities and Sciences, 1983. 30 min. each. Series on Islamic culture, including programs on *The Islamic City* and *Islamic Knowledge* and *Islamic Art.*

Iran. Pyramid Films and Video, 1972. 18 min. Filmmaker Claude Lelouch interweaves elements of ancient Persian culture with that of modern-day Iran.

The Isfahan of Shah'abbas. Fogg Art Museum, Harvard University. n.d. 28 min. Focuses on arts and architecture of seventeenth-century capital of Persia.

The Greeks. Films for the Humanities, 1980. 52 min. each. Based on the scholarship of Sir Kenneth Dover, series on Mycenaean and classical Greek civilization. Titles include *The Classical Age, Heroes and Men,* and *The Greek Beginnings.*

It Started with the Greeks. Films for the Humanities and Sciences, 1985. 52 min. Focuses on the role of rationalism and questioning in Western culture.

Heritage: Civilization and the Jews. WNET Television, 1984. Nine 60-min. programs covering 3,000 years of Jewish history.

The Heart of the Dragon. Time-Life Video, 1988. 12-part series (55 min. each) on Chinese art and culture includes topics such as social life and customs.

The Global Village and *Rajiv's India.* Richard Keefe for the Nova series, 1985. 58 min. each. Programs in this series focus on India's history and culture, examining India's political leadership, the tension between traditions and modernization, and the effects of India's multicultural heritage.

The Africans: A Triple Heritage. WETA-TV and BBC-TV, 1986. Series of 60-min. films examining Africa's triple heritage of Islam, the West, and traditional Africa.

Latin-American History and Culture. Films for the Humanities, n. d. Includes programs of various lengths on Latin American literature, history, and culture.

The Japanese. Japan Society, 1978. 57 min. each. Series of films on Japanese life and culture, includes *Full Moon Lunch, Blind Swordsman,* and *Farm Song.*

Daimyo. Public Media, Inc., 1988. 30 min. Director and narrator John Nathan, considers the martial and civilian arts of the medieval Japanese warriors who served the ruling shogun.

Native Land: Nomads of the Dawn. Cinema Guild, 1986. 58 min. Gives Native American cultural history from ancient paleolithic nomads to the Aztecs and Incas of Middle and South America. Examines dancers, myths, art objects, and ancient ruins of these cultures.

More Than Bows and Arrows. Camera One Productions, 1978. 55 min. Examines Native American contributions in such areas as medicine, drugs, architecture, urban planning, and environmental strategies.

The Primal Mind. Cinema Guild, 1984. 58 min. Presents contrasting Native American and European beliefs about life and evolution, juxtaposing views of nature, time, space, art, architecture, and dance.

Civilizations of Ancient America. 1972. 22 min. From Origins of Man series, directed by Howard Campbell, focuses on meso-American cultures of the Olmec and Maya and also on Inca and Aztec cultures.

Mythology and Religion

The Power of Myth. Apostrophe S. Productions, 1988. Six 60-minute programs in which Bill Moyers and Joseph Campbell discuss the nature of myths from many cultures.

Shinto: Nature, Gods and Man in Japan. Japan Society, 1977. 48 min. Gives history of Shinto from early times to the present day, showing how myths of the gods and creation reveal Japanese beliefs about human relationships to nature.

Buddha in the Land of the Kami. Films for the Humanities and Sciences, n. d. 53 min. Begins with the creation myth and explains the kami concept underlying Japan's cultural identity and world view.

Ma: Space/Time in the Garden of Ryoanji. American Federation of the Arts, 1989. 16 min. Presents images of the sixteenth-century Zen garden interspersed with passages from a poetic text by Japanese architect, with music by composer, Kosugi.

Manifestations of Shiva. Philadelphia Museum of Art; Asia Society, 1985. 58 min. Examines the many ways in which the people of India worship the Hindu god Shiva.

A Common Destiny. Mystic Fire Video, 1992. Two 30-minute videos. Directed by Gayil Nalls, the films include the following: *Walking in Both Worlds* with Jewel Praying Wolf James bringing to the present the message of his ancestor, Chief Seattle, and *The Hopi Prophesy*, with eighty-year-old Thomas Banyaca, spokesman for the Hopi high religious leaders, interpreting the message of the petroglyph on Second Mesa.

The Arts

Visual Arts

World Folk Art: A Multicultural Approach. Crystal Productions, 1991. 100 min. Six programs trace common themes in folk art in different times and cultures, using resources from the Collection of the Museum of International Folk Art.

Light of the Gods. Seven League Productions in association with the National Gallery of Art, 1987. 28 min. Provides background to Greek art and its influence on Western civilization; with passages from Homer, Herodotus, Sophocles, and Sappho.

Passing Seasons: The Japanese Galleries at the Metropolitan Museum of Art. Metropolitan Museum of Art, 1990. 11 min. Scenes from the Japanese galleries of the Metropolitan Museum, using the four seasons to exemplify principles of Japanese art and aesthetics. Also includes passages from Japanese literature, ranging from *The Pillow Book of Sei Shonagon* to Tanizaki, as well as traditional koto and shakuhachi music.

Garden of Fantasy: The Imagination of Houn Ohara. Iwanami Productions, Inc., and the American Federation of Arts, 1986. 31 min. Examines the work of Houn Ohara, contemporary master of ikebana, the art of Japanese flower arranging, showing his playful innovations, including his use of influences from African masks.

Behind the Mask. BBC-TV, 1975. 52 min. Focuses on the sculpture of the Dogon people of Mali as it relates to their culture. Notes the influence of African culture on Picasso, Braque, and other European artists.

My Hands are the Tools of My Soul. Swannsway Productions, Ltd., 1975. 50 min. Portrays the Native American cultural landscape in which the arts—masks, carvings, pottery, sandpainting, songs, and dances are an integral part of the life; includes Native American poetry and music.

Art and Revolution in Mexico. Films for the Humanities and Sciences, 1984. 60 min. Describes the relationship between art and revolution in Mexico.

Two Centuries of Black American Art. Pyramid Film and Video, 1976. 26 min. Surveys the range of black American art, tracing the early African influences, the wide variety of art produced during the slave era to the cosmopolitan backgrounds, and important works of contemporary black artists.

Theatre Arts

Kabuki: The Classic Theatre of Japan. Koga Productions in cooperation with Shochiku Company Limited, n. d. 30 min. Shows Kabuki actors at work. (Available from the Ministry of Foreign Affairs of Japan.)

Noh Drama. Koga Production in Cooperation with Shochiku Company Limited. n.d. 30 min. Introduces Noh drama and includes scenes from several Noh plays. (Available from The Ministry of Foreign Affairs of Japan.)

Noh Drama. Kogima, 1968. 43 min. Enactment of a drama about a fisherman and an angel.

Traditional Bunruku Theater. NHK Films, 1976. 29 min. Demonstration of the classic puppet drama of Japan.

India: Haunting Passage. Modern Talking Picture Service, 1965. 60 min. In this film from the *World Theatre Series* Rajatham puppets enact the epic *The Ramayana;* also includes a film fable by Satyajit Ray and performances by members of Children's Little Theatre Unit of Calcutta.

Oedipus Rex. 1956. 90 min. Tyrone Guthrie's production, performed with masks; translation by William Butler Yeats.

Toqu Na and Cheko: Change and Continuity in the Art of Mali. National Museum of African Art/Smithsonian Institute, 1989. 28 min. Examines two art forms from contemporary Mali: the Dogon sculptural art of men's meeting houses, toqu na, and the Bamama's colorful Cheko performances which include puppets.

Woza Albert. BBC-TV, 1981. 55 min. Mime performers enact a drama in which Christ returns to modern South Africa where he is executed, resurrected from the dead, and awakens the dead martyrs killed for their opposition to apartheid.

Voices of Serafina. New Yorker Films, 1988. Director Nigel Noble presents a part documentary and part Broadway show about high schoolers who develop a play about Nelson Mandela.

Music

Repercussion: A Celebration of African-American Music. Uncommon Video, 1984. A seven-part series on the roots of African American music. Includes *Born Musicians,* which focuses on professional music of West Africa, particularly Mandinka music of Gambia; *On the Battlefield,* which shows integration of African musical sensibility into American gospel music; and *Africa Comeback: The Popular Music of West Africa,* which explores the influence of African popular music from Ghana and Niger.

Juju Music: King Sunny Ade. Rhapsody Films, 1988. 51 min. King Sunny Ade and Eheneger Obey perform the urban tribal music of Nigeria, known as juju which blends lively traditional songs and instruments with Western musical instruments.

Kodo: Heartbeat Drummers of Japan. Rhapsody Films, 1983. 57 min. Kodo, which means "heartbeat" in Japanese, is a group of young musicians who perform traditional and contemporary drumming; the film illustrates the importance of drumming in Japanese rituals and festivals.

Gregorian Chant. Sounds True. Cassette/CD. Chants from the medieval Catholic liturgy are sung by the Deller Consort.

Gregorian Chant from Aquitane. Sounds True. Cassette/CD. Schola Hungarica's original music from the eleventh century at a monastery in Southwestern France. Sung in Latin by the Hungarian Scholar Choir.

Missa Luba: African Mass. Sounds True. Cassette/CD. 48 min. African mass, handed down from one generation to the next, performed by the Muungano National Choir of Kenya, accompanied by gourds and drums, with lyrics in Kenyan dialects.

African Masses of the Cameroon. Sounds True. CD. 48 min. Harmonies of native tribes in a blend of Catholicism and traditional rituals characteristic of Cameroon masses.

Drums of Passion: The Invocation. Sounds True. Cassette/CD. A selection of six prayers chanted by Babatunde Olatunji with drums to *Orisas*—spirits of the dead who have become a means of communicating with God.

Vox De Nube. Sounds True. Cassette. From Glenstal Abbey, Limerick, Ireland, liturgical chants based on Latin plain chant and the writings of twelfth-century mystic Hildegard of Bingen.

Sounds of Indian America: Plains and Southwest. Sounds True. Cassette/CD. Sacred tribal music recorded live at 48th Annual Gallup Ceremonial event. Includes chants and songs from many tribes including Hopi, Ute, Zuni, Pueblo, Navaho, Apache, and more.

Discovering the Music of Africa and *Discovering the Music of the Middle East.* Phoenix, 1967. 22 min. each. Series on musical history of various cultures.

Private Worlds

Quilts in Women's Lives. Ferraro Films, 1980. Seven quilt makers from various backgrounds including a Californian Mennonite, a black woman from Mississippi, and a Bulgarian immigrant discuss their art and its meaning in their lives.

Hearts and Hands. Ferraro Films, 1987. 63 min. Includes excerpts from diaries and letters, photographs and many examples of quilts to create portraits of the lives of nineteenth-century pioneers.

And Women Wove It in a Basket: The Way it was Today. Marlene Farrum and Bushra Azzouz, 1989. 70 min. Director Azzouz Bushra gives an oral history of Native American basket weaver, Nettie J. Kuneki, member of Klikital tribe who lives with her tribe along the Columbia River in Oregon; includes images of daily life and narration of Klikitat tales and legends.

Seni's Children. Milestone Film and Video, 1990. 55 min. from series, Magicians of the Earth. Focuses on the creative process and marketing of Senegalese clay sculptor Seni Camara, filmed in her village of Bigwona.

The Learning Tree. 1969. 107 min. Adaptation of Gordon Park's autobiographical novel set in Kansas in the 1920s. Writer-director-producer Parks recreates his teen years in a small town where a young black learns about life.

Portrait of An Artist as a Young Man. 1977. 93 min. An adaptation of Joyce's autobiographical novel.

Dreams. Directed by Akira Kurosawa. 1990. 119 min. A series of eight dream sequences depicting rites of passage from childhood to old age.

Wild Strawberries. 1957. 90 min. Ingmar Bergman's film in which an elderly doctor reviews his life through memory and dream.

Diary of Anne Frank. Twentieth Century-Fox, 1959. 170 min. An account of Jewish refugees in Amsterdam during the Second World War.

Black Rain; Kuroi Ame. Imamura Production, Hayashibara Group and Tohukushinsha Film, 1989. An adaptation of Ibuse's novel about the survivors of the bombing of Hiroshima, based largely on letters and diaries.

Rhapsody in August. 1992. 98 min. Akira Kurosawa's film about four Japanese children who learn of the bombing of Nagasaki forty-seven years after the event through the recollections of their grandmother.

Autobiography of Miss Jane Pittman. 1974. 106 min. Film about a 110-year-old former slave recalling her life from the Civil War through the civil rights movement, based on Ernest Gaines's novel.

Frederick Douglass: An American Life. Britannica Films, 1972. 9 min. Depicts life and achievements of Frederick Douglass.

The Hero's Quest

The Mahabharata. The Parabola Film Library, 1990–91. A six-hour, three-tape adaptation of the 2,000-year-old Sanskrit epic poem, which integrates religion, philosophy, poetry, mythology, drama, and allegory to tell the Indian story of man's rise and fall.

Rikyu. Capitol Entertainment, 1989. 135 min. Tells the story of sixteenth-century Japanese warrior Hideyoshi and the tea master Rikyu, exploring the Japanese culture's conflict between art and power, and the custom of suicide and honor.

World of the Heike Monogatari. Japan Foundation. 24 min. Recounts the last years of reign of Kiyomori in the twelfth century.

Akira. 1988. 124 min. Director Otomo Katsuhiro's animated science-fiction feature based on a Japanese comic-book novel, depicting the importance of the comic book in Japanese popular culture.

The Old Gringo. 1989. 110 min. Luis Puenzo's film, based on Carlos Fuentes' novel about the Mexican revolution.

Dances with Wolves. 1990. 181 min. Kevin Costner's epic film on how the West was lost for the Native American population.

The Last of the Mohicans. 1932. 214 min. The twelve-part adaptation of James Fenimore Cooper's classic novel, it provides interesting insight into the context of 1930s American culture.

Lawrence of Arabia. 1962. 216 min. David Lean's film of the epic exploits of T. E. Lawrence and the role he played in establishing an English presence in the Middle East.

Hedda. 1975. 130 min. Trevor Nunn's adaptation of Ibsen's play.

Madame Bovary. 1991. 130 min. Chabrol's French production of Flaubert's classic nineteenth-century novel.

The Long Walk Home. 1989. 95 min. Richard Pearce's retelling of the historic bus boycott in Montgomery, Alabama, in 1955 from the perspectives of a white matron and her black maid.

Daughters of the Dust. 1991. Director Julie Dash explores the lives and heritage of African American women, focusing on historical islands off the coast of South Carolina.

The Individual, The Family, and Society

Artistic Representations of Social Patterns

The Flower of the Tales: The Burgerndian Miniatures in the Royal Library of Belgium. International Film Bureau, 1975. 18 min. Illustrations from fifteenth-century manuscripts depicting everyday life of that time.

The Townspeople of Edo: A Ukiyoe Portrait. Educational Media Corporation and Japan Foundation, 1984. 20 min. Uses eighteenth- and nineteenth-century woodblock prints, intercut with scenes of modern Tokyo (Edo), to present various levels of society including subjects such as courtesans, actors, fishmongers, firemen, storekeepers and views of festivals, fireworks, and landscapes.

Families in the Context of Social Conflict and Change

The Great Wall. 1986. 103 min. Peter Wang's independent American film about a Chinese family's return to their native China where they are unprepared for the cultural clashes with their Chinese relatives.

Dim Sum. Orion Classics, 1985. 88 min. Set in San Francisco's Chinese neighborhoods, the film depicts the changing relationship between a traditional middle-aged mother and her independent daughter.

Kheturni Bayo: North Indian Women. Penn State; Sharon Woods. 1980. 18 min. Examines lives of farm women in an extended family of land-owning peasants in Grijarat, India.

Dadi's Family. PBS, 1980–81. 60 min. Examines the life of a family in India and the intricate relationships that develop in an extended family of grandchildren.

The Ballad of Narayama. Home Vision, 1983. 129 min. Based on a legendary Japanese village tradition that when a person reached seventy years of age he was taken to Mt. Narayama to die; explores family life and death in Japanese culture.

Balinese Family. Gregory Bateson and Margaret Mead. 1951. 20 min. Study of Balinese family life from series on Character Formation in Different Cultures.

The Journey. Facets Multimedia Inc., 1987. 870 min. Director Peter Watkins presents a seven-part series on nuclear war, with extended conversations with family groups from many countries. The families respond to photographic images of Hiroshima.

Seasons of a Navajo. PBS, 1985. 60 min. Profiles grandparents of an extended Navajo family of two generations; explores changing lifestyles and traditions of the Navajo people.

A Sense of Loss. Krypton International, 1972. 135 min. Ophuls's film about Northern Ireland probes the living roots of hatred in family folklore, in schools, on the streets, revealing the human terms of Ireland's civil warfare.

Individuals in the Context of Social Conflict and Change

Mandabi; The Money Order. Comptori Francais du Film and Films Domirev Production, 1968. 90 min. An adaptation of Sembene Ousmane's novel, satirizing the persistence of French imperialist attitudes and bureaucratic corruption in post-colonial Senegal.

Xala; The Curse: Impotence. Films Domirev/Societe Nationale Cinematographique, 1974. 123 min. Based on Sembene's comic novel satirizing the self-absorption and mercenary values of the rising African middle class.

El (This Strange Passion). 1952. 88 min. From Bunuel's "Mexican period," this symbolic story of a wealthy Mexican's paranoid obsession with his young wife's infidelity reflects Bunuel's personal mythology.

Woman in the Dunes. 1964. 123 min. Director Hiroshi Teshigahara's film symbolizing modern Japan; about a woman doomed by villagers to incessantly shovel sand to protect the village and an unwary Japanese tourist who is trapped into helping her.

The Exterminating Angel. 1962. 95 min. Spanish filmmaker Bunuel explores the comic and disturbing realities beneath the social facade of a group of dinner guests; believed to symbolize modern man.

The Makioka Sisters. Toho Company Limited, 1983. Adaptation of novel by Junichiro Tanizaki about four sisters from a merchant family in Osaka.

Snow Country. 1967. 144 min. Director Shira Toyada's adaptation of Kawabata's novel about a middle-aged man who leaves the city to seek love with a young woman in Japan's northern mountainous regions.

Hellfire: A Journey from Hiroshima. Makuri Films, 1986. 59 min. Features the life and work of Japanese artists, Iri and Toshi Maruki, a husband and wife who have collaborated on a series of portable murals, depicting their impressions of Hiroshima immediately after the bombing.

Hiroshima Mon Amour. 1960. 51 min. Depicts the romance of a French actress and a Japanese architect; the film juxtaposes newsreel footage of the bombing of Hiroshima and its aftermath with the couple's walk through the reconstructed city.

The Unbearable Lightness of Being. 1988. 156 min. Director Philip Kaufman's adaptation of Milan Kundera's love story set in context of social and political conflict in Czechoslovakia.

At Play in the Fields of the Lord. 1991. 186 min. Hector Babneco's adaptation of Peter Mathiessen's novel. Filmed on location in the rain forest of Brazil, describes the impact on American missionaries and a Cheyenne American mercenary of threats to the survival of an Indian tribe.

Master Harold and the Boys. 1984. 88 min. Adaptation of Athol Fugard's autobiographical play about coming of age in the context of South Africa's racial division.

A Passage to India. 1984. 163 min. Director David Lean's adaptation of Forster's novel.

Changing Roles of Women in Family and Society

Women in Change: Series Women of the World. PBS, 1989. 60 min. Reviews the evolution of women's rights in many cultures.

Black Women Writers. Films for the Humanities and Sciences, 1989. 30 min. Maya Angelou, Angela Davis, Ntozake Shange, Alice Walker, and Michelle Wallace discuss black women writers, their works, experiences, and reactions of readers.

The Black Woman. NET, 1970. 51 min. Poet Nikki Giovanni, singers Lena Horne and Roberta Flack, Bibi Amira Baraka (wife of Leroi Jones), and other black women discuss the roles black women play in society today, their relationships to black men, white society, and to the black liberation struggle.

Songs are Free. PBS, 1991. 60 min. Bill Moyers's interview with Bernice Johnson Reagon, lead singer of the group Sweet Honey in the Rock. They discuss the origins of the African American music the group sings and the power of communal singing as a means for women to deal with their experiences.

Wabun Wind: The Feminine. Bear Tribe Entertainment. Facets Multimedia. Native American Wabun Wind of the Bear Tribe advocates revaluing the feminine in order to reestablish balance in a society conditioned to disregard emotions.

Intertextuality and Cultural Identity

Colonialism: Exploration and Discovery

Triumph of the West: 7 New Worlds. Films Incorporated, 1985. 53 min. Considers how Europe shaped the Americas with emphasis on the Spanish and Portuguese in Central and South America and the Protestant Northern Europeans in North America.

The Age of Discovery. Films for the Humanities, 1957. 16 min. Documentary, examining the historical context of Columbus's voyages.

The Sword and the Cross. 58 min. Explores the history of the conquistadors and their effects on indigenous populations.

In Search of Columbus. PBS. 58 min. Follows the path of Columbus's final voyages and examines impact on different nations and cultures five hundred years after his voyages.

The Paths of Colonialism. Films for Humanities, n. d. 14 min. Examines the growing British Empire, including the Far East and South Africa, as well as the French in North Africa, in support of the Mother Country's search for raw materials and markets.

Surviving Columbus. PBS, 1990. 30 min. Presents the New Mexico Pueblo people's view of their first encounter with the explorer

Coronado and his search for non-existent gold—told exclusively through the voices and visions of the Pueblo Indians.

The Indian and his Homeland: American Images, 1590–1876. Finlay Holiday Film Corporation, 1984. 25 min. Examines the art of explorer artists such as Catlin, Bodmer, Audubon, and Catesby, providing a three-hundred-year survey of the impact of European civilization on the lives and cultures of the American Indians and on native wildlife.

Catlin and the Indians. Smithsonian Series. NBC/McGraw Hill Films, 1967. 25 min. Paintings from the Smithsonian's Catlin collection and text from Catlin's journals depict ways of life of Plains Indians.

The Dutch in South Africa. Films for the Humanities and Sciences, n. d. 50 min. The program follows the establishment of the Dutch settlement in South Africa, including beginnings of apartheid— and traces these influences on to contemporary power relations between blacks and whites.

Trading in Africans: Dutch Outposts in West Africa. Films for the Humanities and Sciences, n. d. 50 min. This program looks at the European view of Africans in the mid-seventeenth century, at the nature of the slave trade, and at the life of some of the African tribes.

The Quest for National and Cultural Identity in a Colonial Context

Global Links. PBS, 1987. Six 30-minute programs take a comprehensive look at the quest for social and economic progress in those nations that account for seventy percent of the world's population.

Kenyatta. Black Man's Land Series, 1973. 28 min. Profile of Kenyatta "Black Moses," Kenyan statesman who played a dominant role in the development of African nationalism.

Africa: Living in Two Worlds. Encyclopedia Britannica Educational Corporation, 1970. 16 min. Contrasts the differences between Africa's centuries-old tribal communities and its newly developed nations.

Mau Mau. Anthony Howarth and David Koff, 1973. 27 min. From Black Man's Land Series, a history of the Mau Mau movement in Kenya.

Africa Astir. Gertrude Purple Gorham Agency, 1961. 24 min. Studies some of the little-known peoples of western Africa, emphasizing the effects of European influence on fast-disappearing cultures.

Kenya Boran. American University Field Staff, 1974. 32 min. each. Two-part series shows changes in lifestyle brought to a rural herding area by growth of a nearby town and completion of a new road.

The Essence of Being Japanese. Series: Japan Past and Present. Films for the Humanities and Sciences, n. d. 45 min. Examines the events of the twentieth century in relation to Japanese traditions and rituals.

Japan, Tradition and Modernity. M.O.A. Foundation in association with Nikkei Visual Images and Art and Technical Consultants, 1985. 30 min. Introduces aspects of traditional Japanese culture: cherry blossom festivals, Noh theatre, architecture, gardens, picture scrolls, culinary arts, and Ibeham, showing how these traditions are reflected in contemporary Japanese life.

Hiroshima: The Legacy. Films for the Humanities and Sciences, n. d. 30 min. Visits the Hiroshima Peace Museum which houses the relics of the first atomic bomb, scientific data, and photographs of survivors.

Roots; Raisces. Manuel Barbachano, 1955. 75 min. Depicts pain, hardship, and pride of native Indian life in Mexico.

The River. 1950. 99 min. Renoir's feature film about India and British colonialism.

Cry, the Beloved Country. 1951. 111 min. Director Zoltan Korda's adaptations of Alan Paton's novel about the poverty and abuses of apartheid in South Africa.

Song of Exile. Kino International, 1989. 110 min. Director Ann Hui presents the story of a young Chinese girl from Hong Kong, a recent graduate of a British university, and her turbulent return home to Hong Kong.

A Storm of Strangers: Jung Sai, Chinese American. Films Incorporated, 1977. 29 min. Directed by Freida Lee Mock and Terry Sanders; presents the quest of a young Chinese American journalist to seek out her ethnic origins in a journey through western U.S.

The Spirit of Crazy Horse. PBS, 1990. 60 min. Correspondent Milo Yellow Hair recounts the story of the massacre at Wounded Knee Creek and discusses the contemporary American Indian movement.

Winds of Change: A Matter of Promises. WHA-TV for Wisconsin Public Television, 1990. 60 min. each. In two-part series, N. Scott

Momaday explores the struggle of Native Americans in today's society to preserve their traditions; profiles the Onondaga, Navaho, and Lummi nations.

Roots of Resistance. A Story of the Underground Railroad. PBS, 1989. 60 min. Focusing on the reunion of descendents of slaves at Somerset House, the program examines the institution of slavery through the narratives of escaped slaves such as Harriet Tubman and Frederick Douglass.

The Freedom Station. PBS, 1988. 30 min. Drama set in 1850 in a root cellar in a safe house along Tubman's Underground Railroad in which a young escaped slave girl meets a farm girl from an abolitionist family.

The Story of English: 5, Black on White. PBS, 1986. 60 min. Probes the origins of African-American English on Africa's west coast through its transformations in the rural South and urban North to its presence today in the street culture of rappers and breakers.

Diversity in Related Texts and Themes

Notes for an African Orestes. Mystic Fire Video, 1970. 75 min. Italian director Pasolini's own diary of his preparations to film a modern-day version of Aeschylus' *Oresteia* in Africa.

Gospel at Colonus. WNET/Thirteen in association with Bioscope, Inc., 1985. 90 min. Tells the story of Oedipus as a gospel music program.

Praise. DLW Productions, 1982. 60 min. From Nadine Gordimer's Stories from African series. Adaptation of her contemporary version of the Pygmalion story in which an Englishwoman and a priest try to remake the life of a poor black child living in the streets of Johannesburg.

Educating Rita. 1983. 110 min. Director Lewis Gilbert's adaptation of Willie Russell's play, based on Shaw's *Pygmalion.*

Don Quixote. 1973. 107 min. Ballet version of Cervantes's novel.

Man of La Mancha. 1972. 130 min. The film version of the popular stage play.

Ran. Herald Ace and Greenwich Film Productions, 1985. 165 min. Akira Kurosawa's adaptation of Shakespeare's *King Lear.*

Throne of Blood. 1957. 105 min. Akira Kurosawa's adaptation of *Macbeth.*

A Midsummer Night's Sex Comedy. 1982. 88 min. Woody Allen's film is loosely adapted from Shakespeare's *A Midsummer Night's Dream.*

Tempest. 1982. 140 min. Set in Greece, Paul Mazursky's film is loosely adapted from Shakespeare's *The Tempest.*

Approaches to Chinua Achebe's *Things Fall Apart*

Chinua Achebe: World of Ideas. PBS, 1988. 28 min. Bill Moyers discusses the impact of colonialism on Nigerian culture with Chinua Achebe, Nigerian writer and then president of his village town council.

Chinua Achebe with Nuruddin Farah: Writers in Conversation. Institute of Contemporary Arts Video, n. d. 55 min. Achebe discusses the evolution of his art, questions related to choice of language, and the interplay of oral and written traditions in his work.

Nigerian Art: Kindred Spirits. WETA-TV and Smithsonian Institute, 1990. 60 min. A look at contemporary Nigerian artists whose work is rooted in traditional Nigerian art and society.

Art of the Dogon. Metropolitan Museum of Art TV, 1988. 24 min. Documents the art of the Dogon people in Mali, who possess one of the richest art traditions in Africa.

The Tribal Eye: Kingdom of Bronze. University of Illinois Film Center, 1976. 52 min. Examines the ethnocentric response of the European art world to a group of Nigerian bronzes brought to London in 1987.

The Glories of Ancient Benin [Nigeria]. Films for the Humanities and Sciences, n. d. 15 min. Examines the relics of ancient Benin in the museum and palace of Perto-Novo, including highly symbolic carvings and rich embroideries.

Something New Out of Africa. Maryknoll Media, n. d. Catholic priests from Nigeria come to southern Louisiana and Texas to work among African Americans. The priests and their parishioners describe how this mix of cultures affects their lives and their Catholic faith. Filmed in Nigeria and U.S.

The Dancing Church: Video Impressions of the Church in Africa. Fr. Thomas Kane, CSP, n. d. The worship, dance, and music making of Catholic churches in Africa.

Baobob: Portrait of a Tree. Joan and Alan Root. 1973. 53 min. Depicts the complex interdependence of life in and around a baobob tree.

Individual Authors

On Being a White African with Nadine Gordimer. PBS, 1990. 30 min. With Bill Moyers, Nadine Gordimer discusses growing up under apartheid, the causes of the tensions and violence in the black townships, and her views on the future of South Africa.

A Writer's Work with Toni Morrison, Parts I & II. PBS, 1989–90. 60 min. In part I, Morrison and Bill Moyers discuss her own life and work. In part II, they discuss the African American presence in American literature.

Angelou, Maya. *Creativity.* PBS, 1982. 60 min. Bill Moyers and Maya Angelou visit her home town, where they make note of the ways that memory and experience are transformed into art.

The Originals: Alice Walker. Films Incorporated, 1988. 30 min. Alice Walker discusses a variety of topics that have influenced her work and her life, including family violence and the position of black women in U.S. society.

Maxine Hong Kingston Parts I & II. PBS, 1989–90. 60 min. Bill Moyers and Kingston discuss her view of America and discuss the writer's power to change our views of the past.

Conquering America with Bharati Mukherjee. PBS/WIMM, 1990. 30 min. Mukherjee discusses the role of Asian immigrants in redefining America in a manner comparable to the original American pioneers.

Fighter for Freedom: The Frederick Douglass Story. National Audio-visual Center, 1987. 19 min. Historic photos and docudramas chronicle the life of Frederick Douglass as orator, emancipator, and statesman.

Wole Soyinka: Writers in Conversation. Institute of Contemporary Arts Video, n. d. 55 min. Soyinka discusses creative traditions and their origins in a particular cultural context.

The Power of the Word. Public Television, Inc., and David Grubin Productions, 1989. 360 min. This six-part series, hosted by Bill Moyers, celebrates such contemporary poets as Sharon Olds, William Stafford, Octavio Paz, Galway Kinnell, James Autry, Quincy Troupe, Li-Young Lee, Gerald Stern, Stanley Kunitz, W. S. Merwin, Robert Bly, and Lucille Clifton. Of special interest is *Ancestral Voices,* profiling poets such as Japanese American Garrett Kaoru Hongo and Native Americans Joy Harjo and Mary Tall Mountain.

Langston Hughes: The Dream Keeper. New York Center for Visual History, Inc., 1988. 58 min. An introduction to Hughes's life and work, looking back to Hughes's African roots as a component in his literary achievements.

Mishima: A Life in Four Chapters. 1985. 121 min. Examines the relation between Mishima's life and work.

The Strange Case of Yukio Mishima. Hearst/ABC/NBC, 1987. 55 min. Reviews Mishima's life and work, including the influences and events which led to his ritual suicide.

Voices of Latin America. PBS, 1987. 60 min. The cultural identity of Latin America is explored through its writers and literature; with dramatizations and interviews to profile G. de la Vega, El Inca, Elena Poniatowska, S.J.I. de la Cruz, Jose Marti, and J. L. Borges.

Allione, Constanzo. *Fried Shoes, Cooked Diamonds.* Facets Multimedia, 1978. 55 min. Documents the reunion of Beat poets William Burroughs, Timothy Leary, Diane Di Prima, Meredith Monk, Miguel Pinero, Chogyam Trungpa Rinpode, Amiri Baraka, and others.

Latin-American Literature Series. Films for the Humanities, n. d. Includes individual programs on writers such as Borges, Márquez, Paz, Cortazar, Asturias, and Carpentier.

Jorge Luis Borges: Borges and I. RM Arts/BBC. 76 min. Includes personal interview with Borges interspersed with sequences from his work.

Carlos Fuentes: World of Ideas. PBS, 1988. 28 min. Bill Moyers discusses current Latin American economics and politics with Carlos Fuentes.

Crossing Borders: The Journey of Carlos Fuentes. Films for the Humanities and Sciences, n. d. 58 min. A portrait of Mexico's foremost writer, covering his career in Latin America and the U.S.

The Broken Cord with Louise Erdrich and Michael Dorris: World of Ideas. PBS, 1989–90. Two 30 min. films in which husband and wife, Erdrich and Dorris, discuss the values and difficulties of modern Native Americans with Bill Moyers.

AUTHOR INDEX

Abdullah, Omanii, 242, 252
Abrahams, Peter, 55, 79
Achebe, Chinua, 12, 39, 44, 109, 118, 124, 125, 128, 172, 174, 266, 276, 283, 295–368
Adams, Henry, 276, 285
Addison, Joseph, 20, 239
Adler, Mortimer, 6, 250
Adoff, Arnold, 358, 364
Aeschylus, 171, 174, 271
Agard, Walter R., 16
Ahlawat, Usha, 193, 265, 266
Aidoo, Ama Ata, 121, 128, 171, 174, 267
Alazraki, Benito, 132
Albee, Edward, 171, 174
Alberson, Hazel, 16, 30, 31–32, 44
Ali, Agha Shahid, 21
Allen, Bonnie, 241, 242, 252
Allende, Isabel, 80, 84, 124, 128, 359, 364
Altusser, 27
Alurista, 234, 235
Alvarez, Julia, 43, 44
Alvarez de Toledo, Isabel, 82, 84
Amadi, Elechi, 122, 128, 171, 175, 348, 355
Anand, Nulk Raj, 193, 207, 265
Anderer, Paul, 109
Anderson, Sherwood, 169, 175
Angelou, Maya, 31, 34, 36, 37, 42, 43, 44–45, 82, 84, 124, 128
Anouilh, Jean, 271, 285
Anzaldua, Gloria, 237
Arden, John, 281, 287
Arguedas, Jose Maria, 357, 364
Aristophanes, 31, 242
Aristotle, 4, 20, 183–185, 265, 267
Armah, Ayi Kwei, 109, 172, 175, 354, 355
Arnold, Matthew, 27, 358, 364
Arrabal, Fernando, 267
Arroyo, Tomas, 218, 224, 228, 234
Ashcroft, Bill, 285
Atkinson, Brooks, 241
Atwood, Margaret, 38, 83, 84, 269, 274, 285

Augustine, 55, 113, 276, 285
Austen, Jane, 114, 121, 128, 265
Avgikos, Jan, 244, 252
Avildsen, John G., 127, 132
Ayling, Ronald, 51, 77, 79, 83, 139, 274, 277, 278
Azuela, Mariano, 229, 237

Bâ, Mariama, 65, 67–69, 70, 72, 73, 75, 77, 82, 84, 124, 128
Babur, 277, 285
Baca, Jimmy Santiago de, 21
Bakhtin, Mikhail, 27, 304, 309
Balderston, Daniel, 229, 238
Baldwin, James, 251, 279, 358, 365
Bambara, Toni Cade, 173, 175
Baraka, Amiri/LeRoi Jones, 254–262, 263, 270
Barrett, Gerald, 235
Barthold, Bonnie J., 299, 309
Batterberg, Michael and Ariene, 330
Beaty, Jerome, 21
Beauvoir, Simone de, 27
Becker, Ernest, 344, 346
Beckett, Samuel, 188, 266, 267, 270, 285
Behan, Brendan, 277, 285
Behn, Aphra, 268, 285
Belli, Giaconda, 79, 84
Bellow, Saul, 171, 175
Bennett, William, 16
Benston, Kimberly, 255, 256, 262
Beresford, Bruce, 122, 132, 292
Bergman, Ingmar, 127, 132
Berkove, Lawrence, 235
Bettelheim, Bruno, 135, 150
Bierce, Ambrose, 218–219, 221–222, 226–227, 234–235, 264
Bigsby, C. W. E., 254, 262
Bisoondath, Neil, 22
Blackman, Charlotte, 369
Blake, William, 20, 34–35, 45, 89, 98, 150, 246, 364, 365
Block, Haskell, 8–9, 17
Bloom, Allan, 16, 17
Bloom, Harold, 255, 269, 285
Boethius, 105

SUBJECT INDEX

396

Editors

Sandra Lott has directed the restructuring of the sophomore literature courses at the University of Montevallo. She recently conducted a summer seminar for high school teachers on incorporating nontraditional literature into secondary curricula. She has written on thematic parallels in works by women of Asian American, African American, and Caucasian American backgrounds.

Maureen S. G. Hawkins has taught at Loyola University and the University of Montevallo and was (1992–1993) visiting professor of literature and politics at the University of California, Irvine. She now teaches at the University of Lethbridge in Alberta. She has written on Anglo-Irish, African, African American, and Japanese literature and film. She has taught in Canada and West Africa.

Norman McMillan teaches at the University of Montevallo. He has written on intertextual relations between Dostoevsky and Flannery O'Connor, and he serves on the editorial board of *Thema*.

Contributors

Usha Ahlawat is completing her doctorate in English at St. Mary's College at the University of London and writing her dissertation on expatriate Indian authors' views of India.

Paul Anderer is the chair of the Department of East Asian Language and Literature at Columbia University. He has an essay in *Approaches to the Asian Classics.*

Ronald Ayling is professor of English at the University of Alberta. The literary executor of Sean O'Casey, he has published widely on O'Casey. He has taught in South Africa, where he became interested in connections between African and Irish literature.

Phanuel Egejuru, whose university education has been in both Africa and the United States, is currently teaching at Loyola University in New Orleans. She has published two books on African literature and, most recently, a novel, *The Seed Yams Have Been Eaten.*

Elizabeth Espadas teaches Spanish, Spanish American, and Hispanic literature of the United States at Wesley College, and writes on contemporary Hispanic literatures.

Milton Foley is professor of English at the University of Montevallo with a special interest in connections between Eastern and Western literatures.

Dorothy Grimes is chair of the English Department at the University of Montevallo. She specializes in linguistics and is currently interested in feminist poetics.

Bruce Henricksen is professor of English at Loyola University in New Orleans. He is the author of *Nomadic Voices: Conrad and the Subject of Narrative* (University of Illinois Press, 1992). He has written a series of reviews on multicultural novels for the New Orleans *Times-Picayune.*

J. Paul Hunter is the Chester D. Tripp Professor of English at the University of Chicago and has published widely in eighteenth-century British literature. In 1989 he co-edited *New Worlds of Literature,* an anthology of modern works in English by persons from diverse cultures.

Steven Latham teaches English at Montevallo High School. He recently participated in a summer seminar studying nontraditional texts.

Sarah Lawall is professor of comparative literature at the University of Massachusetts at Amherst and has conducted an NEH Institute for college teachers entitled *The Theory and Teaching of World Literature.* She is one of the editors of *The Norton Anthology of World Masterpieces,* which has recently been revised to include more Third World literature.

Neal Lester is a professor of African American literature and modern drama at the University of Alabama and the author of *Ntozake Shange: A Critical Study of the Plays,* forthcoming from Garland Publishing.

Mary McCay teaches at Loyola University in New Orleans. Currently she is writing a book on Rachel Carson.

Andrew Parkin is a Canadian drama critic and poet, and has published widely on Irish writing. He has recently become the professor of English at the Chinese University of Hong Kong and is a Fellow of Shaw College. For fourteen years he was editor of the *Canadian Journal of Irish Studies* and is the author of several books on drama.

Liam O. Purdon teaches English at Doane College and has published articles on Spenser's *Faerie Queene* and short verse English romances, as well as works on the *Pearl*-Poet. He is currently engaged in a longer study of chivalric ideals and the concept of youth in Middle English literature.

Ndiawar Sarr is director of the Unité d'Enseignement et de Recherches de Lettres et Sciences Humaines at the Université de Saint-Louis in Senegal. He has taught at Tuskegee University and Mount Holyoke in this country.

Sidney Vance teaches at the University of Montevallo and is a specialist in medieval literature. He has conducted summer seminars for high school teachers of literature.

Julian Wasserman, professor of English at Loyola University in New Orleans, is editor of collections of essays on Chaucer, Edward Albee, and the *Pearl*-Poet, as well as co-author of book-length studies on Gottfried von Strassburg and Thomas Hardy. He is co-editor of *Sign, Sentence, Discourse* and associate editor of *Exemplaria, A Journal of Theory in Medieval and Renaissance Studies.*

Contributors to the bibliographic essays are **Cynthia Gravlee, Maureen Hawkins, Elaine Hughes, John Lott, Sandra Lott, Sarah Palmer,** and **Elizabeth Rodgers** of the University of Montevallo. **Rita Sparks** of Wenonah High School in Birmingham, Alabama, served as a consultant on "Approaches to Achebe." **Charlotte Blackmon** of the University of Montevallo served as consultant for the bibliographical section on audiovisual resources. **Elizabeth Espadas** of Wesley College served as consultant on Hispanic literature for several of the essays.

PN 70 G57 1993

Global perspectives on
teaching literature :

PN 70 G57 1993

Global perspectives on
teaching literature :